PUNISHMENT IN AMERICA

PUNISHMENT IN AMERICA

Social Control and the Ironies of Imprisonment

Michael Welch

Sage Publications, Inc.
International Educational and Professional Publisher
Thousand Oaks ▪ Loncon ▪ New Delhi

Copyright © 1999 by Sage Publications, Inc.

All rights reserved. No part of this book may be reproduced or utilized in any form or by any means, electronic or mechanical, including photocopying, recording, or by any information storage and retrieval system, without permission in writing from the publisher.

Cover photo courtesy of the Illinois Department of Corrections.

For information:

Sage Publications, Inc.
2455 Teller Road
Thousand Oaks, California 91320
E-mail: order@sagepub.com

Sage Publications Ltd.
6 Bonhill Street
London EC2A 4PU
United Kingdom

Sage Publications India Pvt. Ltd.
M-32 Market
Greater Kailash I
New Delhi 110 048 India

Printed in the United States of America

Library of Congress Cataloging-in-Publication Data

Welch, Michael, Ph.D.
  Punishment in America: Social control and the ironies of imprisonment / by Michael Welch.
     p. cm.
  Includes bibliographical references.
  ISBN 0-7619-1083-2 (cloth: alk. paper)
  ISBN 0-7619-1084-0 (pbk.: alk. paper)
  1. Punishment—United States. 2. Imprisonment—United States.
3. Prisons—United States. 4. Social control—United States.
5. Criminal justice, Administration of—United States. I. Title.
  HV9471.W4595   1999
  364.6′0973—dc21   99-6164

This book is printed on acid-free paper.

99 00 01 02 03 04 10 9 8 7 6 5 4 3 2 1

Acquiring Editor:	Kassie Gavrilis
Production Editor:	Denise Santoyo
Editorial Assistant:	Nevair Kabakian
Designer/Typesetter:	Janelle LeMaster
Cover Designer:	Candice Harman

To my sisters and brothers:
Margaret, Patrice, Kevin, Joe, and Greg

Contents

Foreword by Todd R. Clear — ix

Preface — xiii

Introduction — xv

1. Discovery of the Penitentiary and Emergence of Social Control — 1

2. Critical Criminology, Social Justice, and an Alternative View of Incarceration — 15

3. The Contours of Race, Social Class, and Punishment: Exploring Institutional Biases in Corrections — 35

4. The War on Drugs and Correctional Warehousing: Alternative Strategies for the Drug Crisis — 51

5. Regulating the Reproduction and Morality of Women: The Social Control of Body and Soul — 69

6. Jail Overcrowding: Social Sanitation and the
   Warehousing of the Urban Underclass　89

7. A Critical Interpretation of Correctional Boot Camps
   as Normalizing Institutions: Discipline, Punishment,
   and the Military Model　107

8. The Brutal Truth: The Reproduction of Prison Violence
   and the Ironies of Social Control　129

9. The Machinery of Death: Capital Punishment and the
   Ironies of Social Control　159

10. The Poverty of Interest in Human Rights Violations
    in U.S. Prisons　187

11. Prisoners With HIV/AIDS: Discrimination, Fringe
    Punishments, and the Production of Suffering　217

12. The Immigration Crisis: Detention as an Emerging
    Mechanism of Social Control　253

13. The Corrections Industry: Economic Forces and
    the Prison Enterprise　271

Author Index　305

Subject Index　317

About the Author　319

Foreword

When it comes to the problem of imprisonment in the United States, there are indeed a host of ironies worth our contemplation. For instance:

- A nation whose self-image boasts a proud claim as the founder and defender of human freedom operates a penal system that denies freedom to a greater proportion of its citizens than almost any other nation.
- Our incarceration rate seems to have little to do with our crime rate: prison populations continue to grow, despite five consecutive years of falling crime; indeed, since 1975, we have had 10 years of declining crime rates and then 13 years of increasing crime rates—but prison populations have gone up every year regardless.
- Everyone would agree that among our most pressing social problems are disparities among the races in wealth, access to opportunity, and quality of life; yet the prison system, which locks up 7% of African American males, and will be home to almost one third of all black males sometime during their lifetimes, must surely be seen as making a major contribution to those very disparities.

When it comes to penal policy, we have a problem in language. Our penal policy seems made up of soundbites and social metaphors. We find ourselves drawn to confident-sounding phrases, such as "a thug in jail can't shoot your sister," or "don't do the crime if you can't do the time." And we seem ever to be building laws that resonate with other spheres of social activity, for instance sports ("three strikes you're out") and war (as in, "war on drugs"). This problem in the capacity of our language interferes with our ability to develop sound crime policy, since once we become enamored of the metaphor, we lose track of the meaning.

Sensible talk about crime policy requires more reflection than a soundbite and more depth than a metaphor. If we are to ever become wise in crime policy we must be willing to think about it, and to think critically about our most cherished assumptions. Let me provide an example of what I mean.

A great deal has been made recently of "truth in sentencing." The idea behind this simple phrase is that when a sentence is announced by the judge in court, the offender ought to serve it—or at least in today's version of the "truth" serve at least 85% of it—and that such "truth" will be an improvement in justice. The idea is undeniably appealing; who can argue against "the truth?" But if we look behind the soundbite, we find much that might trouble us. The most obvious question would be: Who can say that any sentence imposed by a judge is the correct sentence? Take the situation, for example, of two offenders standing before two judges, each convicted of the sale of an illegal drug. One gets a sentence of 10 years, the other a sentence of 2 years. Under "truth in sentencing," the first will serve 120 months, the second more than 20 months. Which sentence is "true," in any meaningful sense of the word "true?" If we require that justice be true, how can such disparate sentences be just? How, then, can they be "true?"

In fact, when we think about such a sentence, what "truth" is it trying to communicate? The amount of time a person will eventually serve is such a limited and insignificant portion of the "truth" at the time of the sentence, it is as though we all want to participate in a fiction and call it, the "truth," when it is only a part of the story. A judge, required to tell the *whole* truth at the time of a sentence, might need to say something like this:

> "For the crime of drug selling, I sentence you to 10 years in prison. I am doing so even though we know that this sentence will not prevent any more drugs from being sold, and that it will probably even result in someone not now involved in the drug trade being recruited to take your place while you are locked up. I impose this sentence knowing that the main reason you have been caught and convicted

is that we have concentrated our police presence in the community where you live, and that had you lived where I live, your drug use and sales would most probably have gone undetected. I impose this sentence knowing that it will cost taxpayers over a quarter of a million dollars to carry it out, money we desperately need for the schools and health care in the area where you live, but instead it will go into the pockets of corrections officers and prison builders who live miles away from here and have no interest in the quality of life in your neighborhood. I impose this sentence knowing that it will most likely make you a worse citizen, not a better one, leaving you embittered toward the law and damaged by your years spent behind bars. You think you have trouble making it now? Wait until after you have served a decade of your life wasting in a prison cell. And I impose this sentence knowing that it will make your children, your cousins, and your nephews have even less respect for the law, since they will come to see you as having been singled out for this special punishment, largely due to the color of your skin and the amount of money in your pocket. I impose this sentence knowing that its only purpose is to respond to an angry public and a few rhetorically excited politicians, even though I know that this sentence will not calm either of them down in the slightest. This is the truth of my sentence."

Now, wouldn't *that* be a "truth in sentencing!"

Of course, we never hear such a sentence imposed. In that sense, regardless of the "truth in sentencing" movement that has recently swept the nation, every sentence coming under this policy contains deep and profound untruths—the lies of silence, omission, and misrepresentation. The fact that a judge who imposes a sentence is not required to say any of the above is a social manipulation, the fact that it gets called "truth" is an insult to our intelligence.

The book you hold in your hands is about these much more subtle, more profound truths in our penal policy. These truths are described as "ironies." The dictionary defines an "irony" as "the use of language with one meaning for a privileged audience and another for those addressed or concerned." Today's penal apparatus is a litany of ironies, speaking the harsh tones of crime control and public safety to those who never come close to its manifestations, and shrieking the even harsher messages of repression and arbitrary power to those grasped in its tentacles. It is simply not possible to develop an informed view of modern penal activity without cultivating an ear attuned to both messages.

Michael Welch's book is an invitation to think. It is an invitation to grow intellectually and critically, as a consumer of crime policy and an observer of the American scene. Written by a scholar who has dedicated his work to uncovering the hidden ironies of formal crime policy, this is a collection of essays of depth and significance. Those who read it will be challenged, and those who engage with the challenges contained within these pages will have their views of the realities of penal policy changed: deepened, and made more honest, more complete. More true.

—TODD R. CLEAR
March, 1999
Tallahassee, Florida

Preface

As the title suggests, this book explores the phenomenon of punishment in America. In doing so, it draws heavily on the critical perspective on criminology, thereby placing special emphasis on social control and the ironies of imprisonment. This volume combines some of my previously published works with several original chapters on punishment, corrections, and social control. However, to ensure that these contributions flow from one chapter to the next, I carefully edited them in ways that establish a clear sense of continuity; in fact, I revised several introductions and conclusions with this concern in mind. Taken together, these 13 chapters cover a great deal of territory. While attending to key historical, conceptual, and theoretical cornerstones of the critical tradition, this volume examines significant problems facing society and the criminal justice system: violence, human rights violations, drugs, HIV/AIDS, racism, classism, sexism, and profits generated from an expanding correctional apparatus. Overall, the purpose of this book is to confront these social problems by revealing their root causes—especially social, political, and economic inequality.

Throughout this volume, my intellectual debts are quite evident. Still, there are many research assistants and colleagues whom I would like to acknowledge. Several Rutgers University students in the Administration of Justice Program in New Brunswick were instrumental in retrieving literature and assembling data: Meredith Roberts, Patricia Cavuoto, Richard Linderman, Eric Price, Karen Kabara, and Joseph Fredua-Agyman (a.k.a. Haas). I would also like to thank my colleagues at Rutgers University for their support of my work: Dean Mary E. Davidson, Lennox Hinds, Al Roberts, and Carol Fine at the New Brunswick campus and Freda Adler and Gerhard O. W. Mueller at the Newark campus. Likewise, I appreciate the assistance of my personal copy editor Marie Mark and the library staff at Rutgers University.

This volume also benefited from several meticulous and insightful reviews from Professors James Robertson at Minnesota State University, Michael Lynch at University of South Florida, and Barbara Owen at California State University, Fresno.

At Sage Publications, I wish to acknowledge Terry Hendrix, Kassie Gavrilis, Catherine Rossbach, Denise Santoyo, Julie Ellis, and Elisabeth Magnus. Thanks also to the other publishing companies who permitted me to reprint some the chapters included in this anthology.

Finally, I want to express enormous gratitude to Todd R. Clear, Associate Dean, School of Criminology and Criminal Justice, Florida State University (and guitarist in the famously obscure rock band the Retroliners) for writing the foreword to this book.

—MICHAEL WELCH
Hoboken, New Jersey

Introduction

Recently, New York Governor George E. Pataki delivered a toughly worded speech on crime and defended the punitive policies he believes are necessary to confront lawlessness. In many ways, his rhetoric mirrored that of other political campaigns for law and order. However, Pataki also took direct aim at scholars who take a deeper look at society's crime problem and ridiculed the notion that lawlessness stems from adverse societal conditions. In particular, he insisted that "the root causes of crime are the criminals who engage in it" and proclaimed, "In no uncertain terms—we, as servants of the people, are not charged with carrying out a sociological study. We are charged with maintaining public order and saving lives" (Nagourney, 1998, p. B-4). For people who do not share this conservative view of crime, Pataki's address reeks of anti-intellectualism. Indeed, the political and public forums on crime are so rife with anti-intellectualism that it is difficult for scholars to persuade policy makers and citizens to look beyond simplistic formulations of crime.

This book, like other works in the critical tradition, approaches crime and punishment as symptoms of other social problems, including political and economic inequality, and therefore advocates social change. Still, critics who question the overall justness and legitimacy of American society often are marginalized by political and economic elites who are threatened by intellectual discourse. It has been said that if you feed the poor, you will be called a saint but that if you ask why they are poor, you will be called a communist. Inequality not only is intricately structured in our society but is undergirded by (false) ideologies: for example, the belief that all citizens can live the so-called American dream. In treating inequality and punishment as interrelated entities, this book remains focused on the concept of social control and the ironies it produces—especially in the realm of imprisonment. In doing so, it features critical examinations of incarceration by taking into account historical, political, and economic forces—in the end, contributing to a broader sociology of punishment. From the standpoint of radicalism, this collection of essays attacks the prevailing hegemony of the social order and its dominant apparatus of coercive social control, namely the criminal justice and correctional systems.

Beginning in Chapter 1, we explore the discovery of the asylum, a profoundly important legacy that persists today. In his study of early institutionalization, David J. Rothman (1971) found that the emerging almshouses, insane asylums, and prisons were formal responses to growing social problems such as poverty, mental illness, and crime. Contributing to penological history, Rothman documented significant shifts in the conceptualization of crime and punishment that created the appearance that imprisonment was a legitimate, progressive, and humane form of crime control. Other scholars, however, insist that the establishment of corrections has had less to do with crime control and more to do with social control, prompting a larger debate between mainstream and critical criminologists over the true functions of incarceration. In this volume, the conceptual framework derives from leftist sociology and critical criminology. Here, *social control* refers to a form of societal management manifesting in the promotion and enforcement of conformity—even for people who face adversity, inequality, and repression (i.e., minorities, women, and the impoverished). An introductory overview of the discovery of the penitentiary sets the stage for this book by situating punishment in the historical context of social control.

Given that critical criminology remains the theoretical cornerstone of this volume, Chapter 2 delineates the radical framework as it pertains to the structures of social control. Incarceration, as a coercive measure of social control, is analyzed critically along with the dominant paradigm of criminal justice. The chapter also delves into the dialectical features of capitalism and proposes that economic inequities be resolved in ways that promote social justice. Chapters 3, 4, and 5 deconstruct elements of discrimination in the criminal justice system by race, class, and gender. To illustrate the nuances of

Introduction

racism, classism, and sexism, we examine the war on drugs, the escalating reliance on correctional warehousing, and other measures of coercive social control. While attending to the mutually reinforcing effects of racism and classism, we look at the convergence of technology and morality in creating unique forms of repression against women. In Chapter 6, the use of jails is presented as a distinct type of social control reserved predominately for the urban (minority) underclass; as we shall see, detention often incorporates a process known as social sanitation. Chapter 7 analyzes the general popularity of correctional boot camps and reveals similar biases of race and class evident in disciplinary technologies and normalizing institutions. Contradictions inherent in the political economy and their impact on social control and punishment also are described.

Institutional violence is the focus of Chapter 8. Here the sociological model of Gary T. Marx (1981) is applied to corrections in an effort to reveal the ironies of social control, most notably the tendency of authorities to contribute to rule breaking. The brutal truth is that violence behind bars is reproduced by interdependent behaviors between keepers and the kept. Typically, these dynamics are manifested in escalation, nonenforcement, and covert facilitation. Likewise, Marx's theory of irony serves as the conceptual architecture for Chapter 9 on capital punishment. The death penalty not only fails to deter homicide but paradoxically promotes it. Moreover, capital punishment extends a deadly net of social control laced with racial and socioeconomic biases; as a result, juveniles and the mentally handicapped as well as innocent people become trapped in the machinery of death.

In Chapter 10, the lack of interest in human rights violations in U.S. prisons is surveyed. While unveiling historical and contemporary abuses of power, we offer a theoretical explanation of how the state effectively conceals these harms. Human rights atrocities are "out of sight, out of mind," not only because prisons are closed institutions but also because such crimes against humanity—unlike street crimes—have yet to be conceptualized for the public. Lessons learned from social constructionism allow us to realize how public consciousness and awareness of human rights violations are suppressed and manipulated by the state, with the cooperation of the media (see also Welch, Fenwick, & Roberts, 1997, 1998). The types of abuse and neglect of prisoners with HIV/AIDS are enumerated in Chapter 11. Linking Steven Spitzer's (1975) theory of the production of deviance in capitalist society to the war on drugs, we turn our concern to another irony of social control. Rather than being treated, HIV-infected addicts are merely warehoused in prisons, where they are subject to various fringe punishments that intensify their suffering. The processes of stigma and discrimination against prisoners with HIV/AIDS are fueled by a popular cultural metaphor conveyed through a tale of morality that insinuates that their illnesses symbolize divine punishment for having indulged in illegal drugs (or homosexuality).

Another form of coercive social control, detention, recently has become a preferred mechanism of the state to deter illegal immigration (Chapter 12). This punitive strategy shows the appeal of the corrections model—and the new penology—in spheres outside the orbit of traditional criminal justice. The Immigration and Naturalization Service (INS) continues to expand its use of detention for undocumented immigrants and asylum seekers. This type of incarceration has prompted critics to question the overall fairness and utility of such a costly policy. Human rights abuses against detainees in INS detention centers are common; moreover, given that the vast majority of detainees are impoverished people of color, allegations of classism and racism abound.

Finally, it is fitting that we conclude this criticism of punishment in America with an in-depth analysis of an emerging irony of social control: that is, the corrections industry. Upon dispelling the myth that a greater use of imprisonment deters street crime, we provide evidence that the prison population is being driven up by economic and market forces. The corrections enterprise is a phenomenon created dialectically by several interlocking machinations of the political economy. Under the conditions of postindustrial capitalism, there are fewer legitimate financial opportunities for members of the lower classes; therefore, as some of them stray into illegitimate enterprises (e.g., drug trafficking), they risk being apprehended by agents of social control. Once incarcerated, prisoners' value in the commercial market soars as they are commodified into raw materials for the corrections industry. Privatization also contributes to the acceleration of prison construction because it operates on free-market principles that generate a high-volume, high-dividend system of punishment. Whereas the economic-punishment nexus is good news for financial players in the corrections enterprise, it is bad news for those snared in its net of coercive social control. As we shall elaborate further, punishment for profit imperils communities, society, and American democracy.

In sum, this book views punishment in America through the critical perspectives of intellectualism and radicalism, thereby illuminating key aspects of social control and the ironies they produce. It is argued that the state's increased reliance on punishment marks an even greater commitment to coercive social control. Higher rates of incarceration, complemented by a growing roster of penalties (e.g., "three strikes" legislation, mandatory minimum sentences, the abolition of parole and prison amenities), represent a degree of retribution rarely found in comparable democracies. There is disturbing evidence that political leaders, rather than simply treating lawbreakers firmly but fairly, are becoming increasingly intolerant and vindictive. In a sense, the state appears to have crossed the line from "getting tough" to "getting rough" by encouraging institutions and authorities to bully individuals lacking the power to defend themselves adequately against an ambitious and overzealous criminal justice system. Those most vulnerable to this prevailing spirit of meanness are the impoverished and people of color. Regrettably, the state seems to have transformed the criminal justice system from a shield designed to protect all citizens to a sword used to intimidate and control the lower classes. These unfortunate trends in American punishment suggest chilling prospects for social and economic justice.

References

Marx, G. T. (1981). Ironies of social control: Authorities as contributors to deviance through escalation, nonenforcement, and covert facilitation. *Social Problems, 28,* 221-233.

Nagourney, A. (1998, January 24). Pataki says root of crime is criminals, not society. *New York Times,* p. B-4.

Rothman, D. J. (1971). *Discovery of the asylum: Social order and disorder in the new republic.* Boston: Little, Brown.

Spitzer, S. (1975). Toward a Marxian theory of deviance. *Social Problems, 22,* 641-651.

Welch, M., Fenwick, M., & Roberts, M. (1997). Primary definitions of crime and moral panic: A content analysis of experts' quotes in feature newspaper articles of crime. *Journal of Research in Crime and Delinquency, 34,* 474-494.

Welch, M., Fenwick, M., & Roberts, M. (1998). State managers, intellectuals, and the media: A content analysis of ideology in experts' quotes in featured newspaper articles on crime. *Justice Quarterly, 15,* 101-123.

CHAPTER 1

Discovery of the Penitentiary and Emergence of Social Control

The *Discovery of the Asylum: Social Order and Disorder in the New Republic*, by David J. Rothman (1971), is widely regarded as a classic in American penology. In addition to enriching the study of prisons, this historical treatise enlarges our understanding of other normalizing institutions, such as asylums for the insane and workhouses for the impoverished. Although Rothman's book is not usually categorized as a work of critical penology, it contributes to that perspective by offering a historical revision of the emergence of institutionalization and challenging notions of American corrections that are accepted often uncritically. As we embark on a comprehensive and in-depth analysis of punishment in America, an overview of Rothman's work is presented to show how conceptualizations of imprisonment have changed over time. *The Discovery of the Asylum* also serves as an

---

AUTHOR'S NOTE: A version of this chapter appeared in *Social Pathology: A Journal of Reviews*, 2(1), 1996, 32-41. Reproduced with permission, Harrow & Heston Publishers.

excellent transition to truly critical arguments about incarceration and the emergence of social control.

In his groundbreaking book, Rothman explored the rationale for the construction of prisons, insane asylums, and reformatories in the United States between 1820 and 1830. Pointing to the role of the Jacksonian vision in reconceptualizing the social order, he discussed not only the immediate impact of the rise of institutionalization but also its lasting legacy—namely, the uncritical acceptance of wide-scale incarceration that persists today. Due to its continued influence on the literature, *The Discovery of the Asylum* was reprinted in 1990. In the revised edition, Rothman (1990) provided a new introduction but left the book in its original form, saying, "Since the book has earned a life of its own, I have refrained from making any changes in the text" (p. xii). Indeed, many penologists agree that *The Discovery of the Asylum* has earned a life of its own in that it has become standard scholarly reading for more than 25 years. This is not to suggest that Rothman offers the last word on the history of institutionalization; in fact, his contribution is only one of several historical interpretations. (Later in this chapter, we shall review other equally plausible theories of the emergence of the penitentiary.)

To its credit, *The Discovery of the Asylum* has added substantially to a discourse on the history of American corrections. Rothman noted that before 1970 there were only a handful of studies in this area; by the 1990s, hundreds of articles and books were being devoted to the social history of institutionalization. Perhaps more than at any other point in time, recent scholars have pursued their fascination with institutions and the persons confined to them. More importantly, intellectuals are attending to the significance of the larger social forces shaping institutionalization. Rather than restricting their scope exclusively to prisoners, researchers are exploring the historical, political, economic, cultural, religious, and technological forces contributing to this phenomenon (see Welch, 1996). The merits of Rothman's analysis of insane asylums and almshouses notwithstanding, the scope of this chapter will remain primarily on the penological segment of *The Discovery of the Asylum*. Overall, the historical approach supports our theme of punishment in America and the emergence of social control.

Punishment in Colonial America

Rothman's book shows us that there are distinct advantages in taking a sociohistorical view of American corrections. It simultaneously traces the emergence of a new republic and the rapid development of its penal practices.

The sequence of events begins with colonial America and continues through the Jacksonian period. In addition to expanding and enlightening our understanding of the emergence of institutionalization in America, *The Discovery of the Asylum* helps us reexamine the sustained popularity and function of punishment prevalent today.

During the colonial period, notions of crime and punishment differed fundamentally from those of the Jacksonian period. Contrasting these two time frames makes it apparent that the discovery of the penitentiary resulted from changes in ideas about crime and punishment as well as in perceptions of social disorder. These changes interacted with other changes occurring in society, especially political and economic developments in the new republic. Rothman (1971) contended that in colonial America, unlike the Jacksonian era, crime was *not* defined as a critical social problem. "They [the colonists] devoted very little energy to devising and enacting programs to reform offenders and had no expectations of eradicating crime. Nor did they systematically attempt to isolate the deviant or the dependent" (p. 3).

The colonists' perspective on crime contrasted sharply with that of the Jacksonians—who, like their modern-day counterparts, exerted enormous time and effort toward reducing crime. Unlike contemporary theories of crime that place an emphasis on the structural flaws on society, colonists did not associate crime with the structure of their community. Although colonists punished lawbreakers, they did not endeavor to eliminate crime; rather, they accepted crime as a part of society. Their disinclination to "blame society" or cite a "societal breakdown" can be explained by their belief that crime was a form of sin. The religious perspective on crime did not lead to a humane treatment of offenders; on the contrary, the use of harsh corporal and capital punishments persisted as a typical response to crime. Colonists' "Christian sense of crime as sin, their belief that men were born to corruption, lowered their expectations and made deviant behavior a predictable and inevitable component of society" (Rothman, 1971 p. 17). Colonists embraced a simplistic understanding of lawlessness and regarded errors by parents as the primary cause of crime (e.g., the failure to give one's children adequate social and religious training).

The Emergence of Institutionalization During the Jacksonian Era

The direction of American punishment took a new and sudden turn during the presidency of Andrew Jackson (in the 1820s and 1830s). During the Jacksonian era, notions of crime, poverty, and insanity were drastically reconceptualized as *critical* social problems. In response to a sense of growing social disorder, penitentiaries, insane asylums, and almshouses were constructed as monolithic institutions designed for criminals, the mentally ill, and the impoverished. Within a larger social context, the emergence of *institutionalization* occurred shortly after the American Revolution, during which time the United States was struggling with its newborn nationhood—a period marked by anxieties over social disorder and economic instability. Rapid societal changes such as a booming population, leading to dense urban centers, and geographic mobility were coupled with revised ideas about crime, poverty, and mental illness. Traditional forms of social control were believed to be inadequate in a complex society threatened by imminent social disorder; mechanisms of social control were extensively revised, resulting in the discovery of institutionalization. In contrast to colonial Americans, who used institutions only as a last resort, the Jacksonians put forth an ambitious project to combat social problems whereby prisons became places of *first* resort (Rothman, 1971). Clearly, this innovative—albeit regressive—direction in punishment has had a lasting effect on contemporary corrections (also see Hirsch, 1992; Staples, 1990; Welch, 1996).

The changes in corrections also were driven by emerging political forces in the Jacksonian era. A greater sense of civic pride among members of the new republic created a sense of responsibility for solving crime and other social problems (i.e., poverty and insanity). Because urbanization and migration had eroded the tight-knit communities that had previously engaged in crime control, banishment and corporal punishment became viewed as parochial and obsolete. Returning to the principles of William Penn, early Americans began to realize that crime—ironically—was perpetuated by the imposition of harsh penalties. Repressive British laws were rejected, and humane criminal codes were tailored specifically for the new republic.

Decades after significant legal reform, government officials realized that crime was not being controlled solely by the establishment of more rational and humane criminal codes. Moreover, a growing fear that crime eventually would endanger the social order prompted Americans during the 1820s to look further into the causes of crime.

> Citizens found cause for deep despair and yet incredible optimism. The safety and security of their social order seemed to them in far greater danger than their fathers', yet they hoped to eradicate crime from the new world. The old structure was crumbling, but perhaps they could draw the blueprints for building a far better one. (Rothman, 1971, p. 62)

To this end, the sources of lawbreaking became more relevant to an understanding of crime than the structure of the legal codes. Jacksonians sensed that crime was symptomatic of a failing social order, and two aspects of social life were scrutinized closely: the family and the community. Because the corrupting forces were believed then to exist within society, measures to deal with the criminal had to be thoughtfully reconceptualized. A movement to reduce the corrupting influences in the community earned some popular support (e.g., shutting down taverns and houses of prostitution), but these measures by themselves proved insufficient to control lawlessness.

> Another alternative then became not only feasible but essential: to construct a special setting for the deviant. Remove him from the family and community and place him in an artificially created and therefore corruption-free environment. Here he could learn all the vital lessons that others had ignored, while protected from the temptations of vice. A model and small-scale society could solve the immediate problem and point the way to broader reform. (Rothman, 1971, p. 71)

Significant developments in criminological theory occurred during the Jacksonian period: namely, an emerging environmental theory proposing that crime was rooted in adverse societal conditions. Rather than protecting society from the offender, the original rationale for imprisonment was to insulate the lawbreaker from the corrupting temptations inherent in society.

The Pennsylvania and Auburn Systems of Prison Discipline

Jacksonians formulated simultaneously theories of crime and corresponding interventions, and two notable correctional innovations during that period were the Pennsylvania and Auburn models of prison discipline. A significant cornerstone of these disciplinary systems was the enforcement of silence. This practice partly stemmed from an emerging criminological theory concerned with environmental factors shaping lawlessness; it was postulated that silence prevented criminal contamination. The enforcement of silence also was a remnant from the religious notion of spiritual reform and moral correction. Indeed, the Pennsylvania and Auburn systems regimented religious protocol; thus, the experience of imprisonment was intended to incorporate the purifying practices of penitence and monastic isolation. The term *penitentiary* derives from the Latin word meaning "penitence" and also has the same root as the words *punishment, pain,* and *revenge* (Norris, 1985). The invention of the penitentiary during the Jacksonian era, with its emphasis on architecture, internal arrangement, and daily routine, reflected the American vision of what a well-ordered society should be.

Another feature of the penitentiary during that era was the development of work programs. At Auburn, a congregate work regimen was introduced whereby prisoners worked side by side while observing silence, and due to the impressive rates of productivity, the Auburn model was replicated in other prisons. Soon the American penitentiary became an invention that fascinated government leaders and intellectuals around the world. American and European visitors, most notably Alexis de Tocqueville and Gustave Auguste de Beaumont, traveled to Auburn to witness this remarkable correctional experiment (de Beaumont & Tocqueville, 1833). In contrast to the earlier colonists, whose style of incarceration was essentially small scale and makeshift, Jacksonians boasted a grand utopian vision aimed at eradicating social problems. The penitentiary was hailed as an ingenious American innovation (Rothman, 1971; also see Klein, 1920). According to the Reverend Louis Dwight, secretary of the Boston Prison Discipline Society:

> At Auburn, we have a more beautiful example still, of what may be done by proper discipline, in a Prison well constructed.... The whole establishment from the gate to the sewer, is a specimen of neatness. The unremitted industry, the entire subordination and subdued feeling of the convicts, has probably no parallel among an equal number of criminals. In their solitary cells they spend the night, with no other book than the Bible, and at sunrise they proceed in military order, under the eye of the turnkeys, in solid columns, with the lock march, to their workshops; then, in the same order, at the hour of breakfast, to the common hall, where they partake of their wholesome and frugal meal in silence.
>
> At the close of the day, a little before sunset, the work is all laid aside at once, and the convicts return in military order to the solitary cells; where they partake of the frugal meal, which they are permitted to take from the kitchen, where it is furnished for them, as they returned from the shops. After supper they can, if they choose, read the scriptures undisturbed, and then reflect in silence on the errors of their lives. (Dwight, 1826, pp. 36-37; also see Hall, 1829; Powers, 1826)

Although advocates of the Pennsylvania and Auburn systems often debated which of the disciplinary systems was superior, the lasting Jacksonian contribution to corrections was evident in its uncritical acceptance. During that era, few questioned institutional incarceration as a primary strategy for crime control (Rothman, 1971).

Rothman's Critique of Social Control

In his introduction to the second edition of *The Discovery of the Asylum* (1990), Rothman reflected on his work by situating it within the growing literature on the social history of institutions. Although his treatise has substantially contributed to the discourse on historical penology, Rothman had become dismayed by some of the broader interpretations of his work. In particular, he disagreed ardently with scholars who classified *The Discovery of the Asylum* under the emerging rubric of the *social control* school of history. In his revised introduction, Rothman devoted several passages to this issue in an attempt to separate his work from the social control thesis. Rothman (1990) contended that the social control school of history is poorly defined and clumsy. More to the point, "The social control label is an ill-suited one, obfuscating more than it clarifies and oversimplifying a complex historical analysis" (p. xxxvi). Rothman pointed out that the concept of social control has many and various connotations. In the 1920s and 1930s, American sociologists used the term to denote instillation of the subjective and qualitative values of society. Sociologists George Herbert Mead and E. A. Ross described it as the instilling of shared values through primary and secondary socialization. In Meadian sociology, the agents of social control were not the police or other agencies of the state apparatus, but rather families, schools, and community churches. Therefore, social control was indistinguishable from socialization. At that juncture of American sociology, symbolic interactionists still were operating within a functionalist framework; hence, the concept of social control was influenced by conservative and so-called "benevolent" views of the social order.

During the post-World War II period, the notion of social control shifted to the political left, and in the process its meaning was reversed. Frances Fox Piven and Richard Cloward (especially in their book *Regulating the Poor,* 1971), as well as conflict theorists and neo-Marxist scholars, equated social control with the reproduction of a class-based society. It was postulated that the ruling class coopted the state for the purpose of imposing mechanisms of social control that were manifested in various forms of oppression, regulation, and coercion, however subtle. In the end, the criminal justice system and the welfare state would become powerful institutions in maintaining control over the lower classes. According to Rothman (1990), "It was with this negative connotation, not with its Progressive roots, that social control came to the attention of historians" (p. xxxvii). Eventually, social control—though still not clearly defined—was used by some historians to formulate unorthodox questions about corrections and the meaning of "reform." As a concept, social control invited stimulating inquiries into the history of institutionalization: "It encouraged a group of historians to stop taking claims of benevolence at face value and start investigating the purposes, benign or not so benign, that a purported reform might fulfill" (Rothman, 1990, p. xxxvii).

Rothman (1990) acknowledged that the social control perspective has served as a useful corrective to the prevailing notion of "reform." But he concluded that revisionist historians have failed to establish a persuasive interpretation of social control in the context of institutionalization. To him, it is not clear whether social control is invoked as a *statement of fact* ("This organization is charged to maintain social order") or introduced as a *proposition* ("This is an organization that attempts to buttress the social order by coercing or deceiving the lower classes") (p. xxxvii).

Summarizing his criticisms of the social control thesis, Rothman (1990) maintained that "the term in present usage neither advances knowledge nor clarifies subtle differences. The strong case that can be made for banning the word 'reform' from historians' vocabulary applies with equal force to 'social control' " (pp. xxxvii-xxxviii). Does this mean that Rothman opposed use of the term *social control* by historians, perhaps suggesting that social control might be a subject more suitable for sociologists? Was he recommending that social control be defined with greater conceptual clarity? These questions are difficult to answer. In any event, Rothman's objections to the term *social control* may have had less to do with its alleged lack of precision and more to do with how it applied to his work. Certainly, it is unfair to directly impose the social control thesis on *The Discovery of the Asylum* because social control, however defined, falls outside the immediate scope of Rothman's investigation. From a leftist perspective, Rothman avoided examining the features of the political economy that make social control comprehensible. Critics insist that Rothman neglected crucial developments such as unemployment and the emergence of monolithic industrial and financial regimes in early America (Adamson, 1984; Durham, 1989). As we shall discuss in the next chapter, these aspects of capitalism contribute to the reproduction of the underclass, which is subjected to a form of social control administered by the criminal justice apparatus. As noted in the introduction to this volume, our use of the term *social control* derives from leftist sociology and critical criminology. From these perspectives, *social control* refers to a form of societal management manifesting in the promotion and enforcement of conformity—even for people who face adversity, inequality, and repression (i.e., minorities, women, and the impoverished).

Critical Interpretations of the History of Corrections

It needs to be emphasized that there are several competing interpretations of the history of American corrections. Although Rothman's work stands as a singular contribution in the discourse of historical penology, *The Discovery of the Asylum* represents only one of several perspectives within the literature. Alexis Durham (1989) sorted the various strains of penology into four major explanatory perspectives in an effort to organize these divergent schools of thought. Whereas considerable overlap exists among the interpretations of Rothman (1971), Foucault (1979), Ignatieff (1978), and the economic determinist position, each of these historical analyses reaches a different conclusion about the emergence of corrections. The following summaries offer brief overviews and criticisms of these perspectives. Together, they remind us that historical penology has not only enriched the study of corrections but also improved critical criminology. Similarly, these contributions have refined our understanding of social control (see Ross, 1998; Welch, 1998).

ROTHMAN: SOCIAL DISORDER AND PENAL DISCIPLINE

To reiterate, Rothman found that Jacksonians reconceptualized crime, poverty, and insanity as critical social problems. As symptoms of growing social disorder, these social ills threatened the stability of the new republic; thus, institutionalization emerged as a primary strategy to regain social order. As noted previously, Rothman's analysis has been criticized for neglecting crucial economic factors, including unemployment and the rise of industrial and financial enterprises during the Jacksonian era on crime (Adamson, 1984; Durham, 1989).

FOUCAULT: THE EXTENSION OF STATE POWER

Michel Foucault's (1979) theory of the birth of the prison during the French monarchy focuses on the sovereign power of the state and its struggle with its citizenry. At that time, the king exercised corporal punishment to reinforce state power over citizens and to maintain social order. As public spectacles of punishment grew increasingly brutal, the masses began to question the legitimacy of the king's power. Eventually, lawbreakers gained sympathy from fellow citizens, who also began viewing themselves as victims of tyranny and repression. According to Foucault, the prison was born as an effort to remove punishment from public view and to undermine sympathy for offenders. By moving punishment out of the public eye, imprisonment became mystified; hence, citizens were left to imagine the horrors taking place behind prison walls. Unlike corporal punishment, which was directed at the body, imprisonment was aimed more at the mind, and in the end, prisoners were transformed from subjects to objects. Foucault proposed that the principal goal of the penitentiary was not to punish less but to punish better.

Foucault's work has drawn considerable criticism. Historians Rothman (1990) and Adamson (1984) pointed out several empirical inadequacies evident in Foucault's analysis, including his unsystematic and anecdotal examination of history (also see Megill, 1979; Stone, 1983). In a parallel vein, sociologists are dismayed by his nonsociological use of the concept of power (Dreyfus & Rabinow, 1983; Giddens, 1982; Hoy, 1979). Foucault's perspective was similar to Rothman's in that they both identified the perceived threat of internal disorder and its relation to the development of punishment (Durham, 1989). Among Foucault's contributions to the history of corrections is his insight on political forces shaping the scheme of penality (see Garland, 1990).

IGNATIEFF: INDUSTRIALIZATION AND SOCIAL DISORDER

A theme found in the work of Michael Ignatieff (1978) as well as that of Foucault and Rothman, is the notion that penal reform resulted from humanitarian social movements. Taking into account declining social solidarity and growing social disorder during the Industrial Revolution, Ignatieff studied the adverse effects of industrialization: unemployment, vagrancy, crime, public disturbances, and urban riots. The penitentiary therefore played a key role in the transformation of class relations between workers and industrialists by introducing a unique style of isolation, punishment, and correction for members of the lower classes.

ECONOMIC DETERMINISM AND THE ORIGINS OF THE PRISON

In his attempt to classify neatly the explanatory perspectives, Durham (1989) described the following penologists as *economic determinists*:

Adamson (1984), Melossi and Pavarini (1981), and Rusche and Kirchheimer (1939/1968). At the risk of oversimplifying the contributions of these penologists, it should be understood that they all place economic cycles at the center of their investigations, arguing that patterns of punishment remain consistent with particular economic cycles. For example, during economic cycles in which labor is abundantly available, convicted criminals are more likely to be imprisoned than during periods when labor is scarce. These penologists trace the historical development of the prison and its many interventions (i.e., retribution, reform, forced labor) to specific economic conditions (also see Garland, 1990; Hirsch, 1992; Staples, 1990).

Though acknowledging the diversity of these theoretical perspectives, Adamson (1984) reminded us that "no single theory accounts for the complex historical process whereby imprisonment has become the dominant form of punishment in western societies" (p. 435). Although each interpretative framework cannot escape its own limitations, these explanatory perspectives contribute to a critical understanding of the historical development of corrections.

Conclusion

Returning to Rothman, *The Discovery of the Asylum* generally is appreciated beyond a like-minded circle of historians. Even scholars who quibble over various aspects of his treatise are indebted to Rothman for bringing historical analyses to the surface of penology. Among those benefiting particularly from his work are critical criminologists; indeed, Rothman has reinforced their argument that history shapes significantly the character and content of criminal justice apparatus. As we shall see in the next chapter, the critical perspective values the historical approach because it deepens our understanding of lawlessness and punishment. Although not all revisionist historians are considered part of the critical perspective, it is the historical aim of critical criminology that distinguishes it from mainstream views of crime. Among notable contributions of critical criminology is its emphasis on historical developments that undergird prevailing structures of crime and criminal justice. Liberal and conservative criminologies, by contrast, are woefully ahistorical and fail to situate current social problems adequately in their proper historical context. As a result, the mechanisms and functions of social control—which reproduce inequality—are obscured by ahistorical conceptualizations.

Through Rothman and other penological historians, we have learned a crucial lesson concerning the rise of the penitentiary, namely the uncritical acceptance of institutionalization as the prevailing response to crime, a view that unfortunately persists today. *The Discovery of the Asylum* "is thus a fascinating reflection of our past and mirror on our troubled present and future" (Rothman, 1990, back cover). As we continue our exploration of punishment in America, it is important that we remain mindful of the role of history in shaping contemporary responses to crime and other social problems. As John F. Kennedy so aptly stated of modern efforts to remedy social ills, he that "Today's problems are the result of yesterday's solutions."

References

Adamson, C. (1984). Toward a Marxian theory of penology: Captive criminal populations as economic threats and resources. *Social Problems, 31,* 435-458.

de Beaumont, G., & de Tocqueville, A. (1833). *On the penitentiary system in the United States, and its application to France.* Philadelphia: Carey, Lea, & Blanchard.

Dreyfus, H. L., & Rabinow, P. (1983). *Michel Foucault: Beyond structuralism and hermeneutics.* Chicago: University of Chicago Press.

Durham, A. M. (1989). Newgate of Connecticut: Origins and early days of an early American prison. *Justice Quarterly, 6,* 89-116.

Dwight, L. (1826). *First annual report.* Boston: Boston Prison Discipline Society.

Foucault, M. (1979). *Discipline and punish: The birth of the prison.* New York: Vintage.

Garland, D. (1990). *Punishment and modern society: A study in social theory.* Oxford, UK: Clarendon.

Giddens, A. (1982). *Profiles and critiques in social theory.* Berkeley: University of California Press.

Hall, B. (1829). *Travels in North America: The years 1927-1828.* Edinburgh, Scotland.

Hirsch, A. J. (1992). *The rise of the penitentiary: Prisons and punishment in early America.* New Haven, CT: Yale University Press.

Hoy, D. C. (1979). Taking history seriously: Foucault, Gadamer, Habermas. *Union Seminary Quarterly Review, 34*(2), 85-95.

Ignatieff, M. (1978). *A just measure of pain: The penitentiary in the Industrial Revolution—1750-1850.* New York: Columbia University Press.

Klein, P. (1920). *Prison methods in New York State.* New York: Columbia University Press.

Megill, A. (1979). Foucault, structuralism, and the ends of history. *Journal of Modern History, 51,* 451-503.

Melossi, D., & Pavarini, M. (1981). *The prison and the factory: Origins of the penitentiary system.* Totowa, NJ: Barnes & Noble.

Norris, R. L. (1985). *Prison reformers and penitential publicists in France, England, and the United States, 1774-1847.* Unpublished dissertation, American University, Washington, DC.

Piven, F. F., & Cloward, R. A. (1971). *Regulating the poor: The functions of public welfare.* New York: Vintage.

Powers, G. (1826). *A brief account of the construction, management and discipline of the New York State Prison at Auburn.* Auburn, NY: Henry Hall.

Ross, J. I. (1998). *Cutting the edge: Current perspectives in radical/critical criminology and criminal justice.* Westport, CT: Praeger.

Rothman, D. J. (1971). *The discovery of the asylum: Social order and disorder in the new republic.* Boston: Little, Brown.

Rothman, D. J. (1990). *The discovery of the asylum: Social order and disorder in the new republic* (2nd ed.). Boston: Little, Brown.

Rusche, G., & Kirchheimer, O. (1968). *Punishment and social structure.* New York: Russell & Russell. (Original work published 1939)

Staples, W. G. (1990). *Castles of our consciousness: Social control and the American state, 1800-1985.* New Brunswick, NJ: Rutgers University Press.

Stone, L. (1983, March 31). An exchange with Michel Foucault. *New York Review of Books,* pp. 42-44.

Welch, M. (1996). *Corrections: A critical approach.* New York: McGraw-Hill.

Welch, M. (1998). Critical criminology, social control, and an alternative view of corrections. In J. I. Ross (Ed.), *Cutting the edge: Current perspectives in radical/critical criminology and criminal justice* (pp. 107-121). Westport, CT: Praeger.

CHAPTER 2

Critical Criminology, Social Justice, and an Alternative View of Incarceration

For decades, the conservative view of crime has dominated criminal justice policy and practice. While relying on "law and order" rhetoric, conservatives have made significant changes in the way government allocates funding: most notably, the transfer of financial resources from social services to criminal justice. Critics of the conservative model of crime control question seriously the prudence of gutting social services (which typically have crime control potential) while accelerating prison construction and other "tough on crime" initiatives. Adding to the criticism of the conservative perspective are critical criminologists who look more deeply at the role of capitalism: Greater investment in criminal justice is consistent with a political economy devoted to increasing capital for the wealthy while subjecting the lower classes to coercive measures of social control. Directing uncommon attention to struc-

AUTHOR'S NOTE: Reprinted from *Critical Criminology: An International Journal,* 7(2), 1996, 43-50. Reproduced with permission.

tural inequality, critical criminologists are more interested in promoting social justice than criminal justice. The purpose of this chapter is to demonstrate how the criminal justice apparatus is linked to the structural components of capitalism, which together reinforce inequality and repressive mechanism of social control. As we shall see, critical criminology provides a valuable theoretical perspective for interpreting incarceration, particularly its emergence as a form of local industry. In maintaining a sustained interest in the political economy as it shapes criminal justice and social control, this chapter examines further the relationship between unemployment and imprisonment. Finally, it considers the prospects of forging an alliance among critical and liberal criminologists and discusses recent developments in critical criminology.

The Emergence of Critical Criminology

Critical criminology, a form of radicalism, has its origin in the traditional social thought of Karl Marx. Among the central themes of his work, Marx addressed capitalism and its complex social relations among classes (i.e., the workers and the capitalists who hire the workers), which, in turn, determine social conditions. Due to the social arrangement of capitalism, the great proportion of the profits is absorbed by the capitalists, who, as a result of this wealth, enjoy luxurious lifestyles while workers are forced to live less comfortably and with less financial security. In fact, even after devoting years to their job, most workers just barely survive financially. Due to these economic conditions, a class struggle emerges, prompting the privileged class to control the unprivileged classes in an effort to protect the interest and profits of the wealthy.

Among the mechanisms of social control used by those in power is the criminal justice system. Historically, the criminal justice system has been used by the ruling class to suppress the activities of the workers, especially unionism. The criminal justice system also is in charge of controlling those who have been economically marginalized—that is, unemployed. The relationship between crime and unemployment is discussed in an upcoming section, along with how the criminal justice system functions to manage the underclass.

Though Marx's analysis of capitalist society encompassed various social aspects (economic and political power, alienation, social change, etc.), surprisingly, he wrote very little about crime. Consequently, critical criminologists have had to formulate their own theories of crime by borrowing from Marx's framework and linking crime to the political economy.

The first formal application of Marxist social thought to crime was the work of Willem Bonger, a Dutch criminologist, who published his *Criminality and Economic Conditions* in 1916. Bonger asserted that the capitalist economic system creates a culture that promotes unbridled individualism and materialism, encouraging all persons to become self-centered, selfish, and greedy. It is widely understood that most crimes are self-serving. Bonger argued that capitalists enjoyed legal opportunities to increase their wealth that often included exploiting workers by paying them wages so low that workers had to struggle to make ends meet.

According to Bonger, the greed of the powerful is reinforced by the capitalist system. At the same time, the greed of the working classes is discouraged and subject to formal penalties; consequently, the criminal justice system emerged as a social institution that criminalizes the greed of the poor while ignoring the greed of the wealthy. Also, the poor who engage in crime rely on methods that are easily detectable, such as theft of property. The methods of white-collar and corporate criminals, however, are often better concealed and difficult to detect (embezzlement, fraud, price fixing, insider trading, etc.). It should be emphasized that Bonger, along with most contemporary critical criminologists, did not romanticize the crimes of the poor. He asserted that crimes committed by members of these classes are as despicable and predatory as those of the upper classes. Bonger suggested that crime is rooted in inequality, thus contributing to antisocial acts among the poor as well as the rich. To reduce social inequality and crime, Bonger proposed socialist reforms—ideally, transforming society in ways that reduce inequality, classism, predatory individualism, and economic disparities. He advocated for a society that would promote a general concern for fellow citizens and believed that such a society would have less crime.

Though Bonger's critical approach to crime remained popular among European criminologists during the early part of the century, it did not take the stage in American criminology until the turbulent 1960s, a time when the United States was marked by enormous social unrest. Demonstrators protested such social problems as the lack of civil rights for minorities, the Vietnam war, and economic injustice. Dissent was directed at the government as well as the establishment that had the lion's share of the nation's wealth and power. At last, the time for critical interpretations of crime and criminal justice had arrived.

Contemporary Critical Criminology

Since the 1960s, critical criminology has been characterized by diverse and sometimes competing points of view. Under the larger umbrella of critical criminology, there are various radical interpretations of crime—conflict, Marxist, materialist, dialectical, feminist, postmodern, and socialist (Schwartz & Friedrichs, 1994). "Contrary to some views, critical criminology is not a utopian perspective but an invitation to struggle; it is a call to recast definitions of social offense more broadly than traditional criminologists, who rarely challenge unnecessary forms of social domination" (Thomas & O'Maolchatha, 1989, p. 148; see also Danner, Michalowski, & Lynch, 1994). Critical criminology is not so much a theory as a theoretical perspective based on social critique. According to Thomas and O'Maolchatha (1989),

> Social critique, by definition, is radical. Derived from the Greek *Krites* ("judge"), the Latin term *criticus* implies an evaluative judgment of meaning and method in search, policy and human activity. (Critical thinking implies *freedom* by recognizing that social existence, including our knowledge of this existence, was not simply imposed on us by powerful and mysterious forces. This recognition leads to the possibility of transcending our immediate social or ideational conditions. The act of critique implies that we can change our subjective interpretations and our objective conditions by thinking about and then acting on the world. (p. 147)

For the purposes of drawing a clearer picture of critical criminology, we will not dwell on the distinctions between these overlapping rubrics. Rather, it is useful to introduce some of the shared assumptions defining critical criminology as a framework that "challenges the hegemony of traditional 'classical' and 'positive' criminologies" (Bohm, 1982, p. 565).

Although critical criminologists debate the finer points of theory in greater detail, there is some consensus on the following assumptions that serve as the foundation of this perspective:

1. Conflict, domination, and repression are characteristic elements of a capitalist society.
2. The majority of crime in capitalist societies is a result of the inherent contradictions of capitalist social organization.

3. Laws and the criminal justice system generally protect the interests of the powerful to the disadvantage of the powerless.
4. Criminal justice makes sense only in the larger context of social justice. (Maguire, 1988, p. 134)

Because the first assumption (which acknowledges the conflicting spheres of society) has already been addressed, we now turn to the inherent *contradictions* of the capitalist society. First, the objective of capitalism is to generate profit, and for the most part, it accomplishes the task quite well. The contradiction here is that capitalism also generates poverty—thereby supporting the basic notion that it takes a lot of poor people to make one person rich. In other words, the capitalist system is not designed to distribute the wealth fairly among all people, even though workers directly contribute to the proliferation of profits (Glyn, 1990). In fact, in a capitalist society, wealth is highly concentrated among the few, who, as a result of their immense wealth, wield enormous political power. As a result, the economy and the nation's wealth become polarized, meaning that the rich get richer, and the poor *as well as* the middle class become poorer.

A second contradiction of the capitalist system is that unemployment is as necessary as employment itself. Obviously, the employment of workers is required to manufacture goods and provide services. At the same time, however, unemployment also is required to keep wages to a minimum. Economic stability is based on a certain level of unemployment (Glyn, 1990). If all citizens were to have jobs, then probably everyone (perhaps collectively) would demand a raise in wages; moreover, workers would probably threaten to strike to ensure an increase in wages.

Today, unemployment remains a serious social problem. Simply put, there are more people seeking employment than there are jobs. In Marxist terminology, the unemployed are referred to as the *surplus labor pool* (also known as the surplus population or the reserve army of workers). It should be noted, however, that the existence of the surplus labor pool is functional insofar as the unemployed symbolize the consequences of not complying with their employers. Consider a worker employed in a fast food restaurant and earning minimum wage. The worker soon becomes acutely aware of how difficult it is to survive while working at minimum wage. That is, if one works at minimum wage (set at $4.25 an hour) and works 40 hours per week, 52 weeks a year (no vacation), one earns $8,840 per year (before taxes). Compare these earnings to the federal poverty levels that are formulated by income and

TABLE 2.1   Weighted Average Poverty Threshold, 1990

Family Size	Annual Income in $
One	6,652
Two	8,509
Three	10,419
Four	13,359
Five	15,792
Six	17,839
Seven	20,241
Eight	22,582
Nine or more	26,848

SOURCE: U.S. Department of Commerce (1995, p. 481, Table 746).

number of people living in a household. The 1990 U.S. Census Bureau figures are reported in Table 2.1.

In light of this predicament, the worker approaches the boss requesting an increase in wages and, not surprisingly, is denied such a raise. Furthermore, the boss reminds the worker that his or her job could be easily filled by one of the many local residents who would gratefully embrace it—even at minimum wage. The worker is left with the option of continuing to work there at minimum wage or quitting and joining the ranks of the unemployed. In this case, not only does the existence of the surplus labor pool keep wages down, but the risk of unemployment is used as a viable *threat* to keep workers compliant and willing to work even at low wages. (We shall return the issue of unemployment, crime, and imprisonment later in this chapter.)

The third contradiction in a capitalist society is the tendency to treat products and services as commodities that are used for means of exchange (to generate profit) instead of using these products and services for their original purpose. "Capitalist production is guided by profit, not social need, or to put it more abstractly, by exchange value rather than use value" (Glyn, 1990, p. 108). For example, investors purchase property and housing, not for the sole purpose of providing shelter for those who need it, but to profit from their investment. The contradiction here is that houses and apartments remain vacant until prospective tenants are willing to fulfill the investor's profit expectation—that is, to pay the landlord a certain amount of rent. In America today, there exists a popular myth that there is a housing shortage, when in reality there is a shortage of *affordable* housing. Convincing arguments can also be made in terms of the lack of accessible health care, adequate education, and so forth. Again, the crux of the issue is that, in a capitalist society, even the most basic goods and services are *commodified* (Glyn, 1990).

Implications for Social Reforms and Criminal Justice

Critical criminology is sometimes viewed by its detractors as a set of theoretical propositions that are too vague and abstract for practical uses such as policy formulation. However, such sweeping generalizations are simply not justified. Critical criminologists adamantly defend their proposals for criminal justice policy.

A survey of prominent critical criminologists by Maguire (1988) addressed the recurring argument in critical criminology that any social change short of transforming capitalism to socialism may be simply a "band-aid" proposal. This "all or nothing" approach to social change hampers critical criminologists, preventing them from suggesting meaningful policy recommendations (see Bohm, 1982; Greenberg, 1981; Lynch & Groves, 1989b). The political reality is that it is unlikely that the United States will be transformed into a socialist state anytime soon, even though most mainstream Americans favor many socialist programs, such as a national health care program, unemployment benefits, and financial aid for college students. Critical criminologists advocate various forms of social change, and their policy recommendations reflect their genuine concern to make meaningful reforms, even if this means proposing short-term solutions.

It is important, however, to acknowledge that proposals of critical criminologists are rarely considered by government and policy makers. Thinkers from the critical perspective are not invited to discuss their ideas in the same forum with liberals and conservatives because their views are regarded as outside of mainstream political and economic thought (Maguire, 1988). Despite being politically marginalized, critical criminologists offer numerous practical recommendations for social and correctional policies. Regarding social values and social structures, Robert Bohm (see Maguire, 1988, p. 138) suggested that fundamental changes be made to offset the cultural emphasis on competitive individualism, narrow self-interest, and exploitation. These attitudinal changes will almost certainly have to include a national shift of consciousness toward social justice. Social justice is a fundamental theme in critical criminology, referring to the protection of basic human rights—the right to full employment, housing, food, education, and health care (Quinney, 1980; Young, 1983).

Revitalizing a sense of community is another theme in critical criminology, especially in light of the belief that the crisis of capitalism is both material and spiritual (see Quinney, 1980). Moreover, a sense of community has direct implications for crime control policies (see Michalowski, 1985). Investing in communities by way of affordable housing, jobs, and schools is a proactive measure against crime. Unfortunately, since the 1960s, and even more since the 1980s, the federal government has abandoned its efforts to support cities, communities, and neighborhoods (Currie, 1985).

Regarding criminal justice policy, critical criminologists address the individualistic and class biases of the system. At the heart of the critical perspective is the assertion that the criminal justice system functions to control crime committed by lower-income people (especially property crimes, such as theft). In fact, in the eyes of the criminal justice system, it is the lower classes for whom "correction" or "rehabilitation" is designed—implying that lower-income offenders are "defective" in some way. When members of the higher-income classes are convicted of theft (in the form of fraud or embezzlement), they may face imprisonment, but rarely is a prison term intended to "correct" such offenders; typically, such offenders are sentenced out of a sense of retribution, not rehabilitation (Maguire, 1988).

A class bias in the criminal justice system overlaps with the individualistic bias. Because correctional strategies target exclusively the lower-income individual and not groups (such as organizations or corporations that engage in illegal business practices), they ignore conditions that contribute to crime. As Bohm stated, "Regarding corrections, radicals are less interested in correcting individuals directly, whether corporate criminals or muggers, than correcting the structures and institutions that produce the behavior of individuals" (quoted in Maguire, 1988, p. 143).

Like their liberal counterparts, critical criminologists are inaccurately portrayed as being soft on crime. Yet it is important to emphasize that critical criminologists hold very strong views against crime as well as all forms of violence, whether these acts are committed by individuals or the government (as in the case of the death penalty). Although the current state of corrections is characterized by widespread misuse of prison space and resources, many critical criminologists support proposals for strong criminal justice and correctional systems. There is little justification for expanding the use of corrections, but prisons *are* needed to incarcerate violent offenders, especially those posing imminent risks to the community.

Paul Takagi adamantly supported this point:

While I intellectually understand and comprehend the offender that engages in gratuitous violence, I think given our current state of knowledge, I see no alternative but to impose a long prison sentence. Not the 50 to 100 years that is sometimes imposed on these cases, but perhaps until age 30 or 35 or whatever the age is when they begin to slow down. (Quoted in Maguire, 1988, p. 144)

David Friedrichs (see Maguire, 1988, pp. 144-145) concurred with this position and suggested that imprisonment be extended to violent corporate offenders as well. Numerous corporate offenders continue to kill and injure employees and consumers through hazardous working conditions and unsafe products. Friedrichs (1996) suggested that corporations identify in advance which executives are responsible and liable for company decisions, especially those decisions that lead to deaths and injuries. Typically, key decision makers in corporations hide behind an organizational mask to avoid prosecution. The proposals offered by Takagi (cited in Maguire, 1988) and Friedrichs (1996) further blur the distinctions among conservative, liberal, and critical perspectives. In advocating lengthy sentences for violent offenders, Takagi clearly supported a form of incapacitation. Moreover, Friedrichs appears to have endorsed a type of deterrence in dealing with violent corporate offenders.

Although critical criminologists offer numerous short-term proposals for corrections, their primary objective is to promote social justice. For critical criminologists,

> The etiology of crime has to do with social structural arrangements and institutional opportunities and constraints. Work, education, health care and the distribution of wealth and income are social justice foci that, according to radicals, have an influence on criminal behavior. (Maguire, 1988)

Critical proposals are likely to remain stunted until government's leadership and mainstream citizens change the course of dealing with the economy, crime, and corrections. Nevertheless, critical criminology has had considerable impact on mainstream criminology, including both liberals and conservatives. Economic and political factors that used to be generally associated with the critical perspective have emerged as important elements of mainstream criminology.

The Incarceration Industry as Big Business

Corrections has quickly become appreciated for its economic benefits and opportunities for big business, private industry, and government. Indeed, local, state, and federal governments continue to allocate more funds to corrections. Whereas critical criminologists call for a prison construction moratorium, many county governments fight to have state prisons placed in their communities. County policy makers identify prisons as a source of jobs for approximately 400 local residents (at starting salaries of about $25,000 a year). In Weed, California, supporters of the proposal to build a prison in their town have held prison rallies and barbecues as a way to raise money to hire a public relations expert who would argue their case to state officials. "A sign in a bakery window reads, 'A Depressed Economy Needs Corrections' " ("Residents," 1994, p. 28). This phenomenon of supporting prisons is in sharp contrast to the "not in my back yard" sentiment that has faded along with better economic times.

In economically depressed counties, such as in upstate New York, where the timber industry has declined, political leaders battle against competing counties to be selected as the site of the next state prison. The town supervisor of Chesterfield, New York, Roger E. Poland, pointed out, "A business comes in and a year or two it can't support itself and—it's gone." A prison, in contrast, "is something you know is going to be here for a long time" (quoted in "Who Wants New Prisons?" 1989, pp. B1-B2). Poland, however, understands that a prison will simply not be handed to his community, and he is painfully aware of the competition from other counties experiencing similar economic hardship. In Chesterfield, where the unemployment rate stood at 15% (in 1989), 269 residents signed the petition favoring a prison, whereas only 19 cast votes against it ("Who Wants New Prisons?" 1989, pp. B1-B2). The residents of these counties generally favor such proposals because a prison is viewed as "clean industry," unlike a nuclear plant or other industries that pollute the environment. According to James Dawson, supervisor of Brasher, New York, "Prisons are environmentally sound. They have no smokestacks, no noise, no pollution. It's like a college campus with a fence around it" ("Who Wants New Prisons?" 1989, pp. B1-B2).

Many other state governments have stimulated a similar form of competition among their counties in which the economic "prize" is having a prison built near their community. In Illinois, such a competition was promoted as a "sweepstakes." Governor James Thompson was quoted as saying that "every once in a while a tiny town in a small county ought to win one," and the mayor of one of the selected towns called the prison a "godsend" (Egler, 1986, p. 2; see Maguire, 1988, p. 148). More than a century ago, when Washington State was still a territory, the government "gave the citizens of this city [Walla Walla] a choice between a new college and a prison. They chose the prison because they didn't like the kind of people attracted to a college" ("States' Prisons," 1990, p. A1).

Whereas critical criminologists have argued that the enormous expenditures on corrections are wasted because such spending has had little effect on the crime problem, politicians favor the expansion of the prison systems. Nowadays, it is understood that the incarceration industry provides the community with badly needed jobs. According to Alvin J. Bronstein, executive director of the Prison Project of the American Civil Liberties Union, "There is a correctional-industrial complex" (Holmes, 1994, p. E3).

Unemployment and Imprisonment

Because economic forces remain the central focus of the critical perspective, it is important to delineate the relationship between unemployment and imprisonment. As mentioned, one of the contradictions of capitalism is that a certain level of unemployment remains a necessary condition of the economic structure. Moreover, one of the effects of unemployment is the *marginalization* of unemployed persons in society. In this sense, marginalization is the process by which legitimate means to survive are eliminated, leading to dependence on state assistance and other forms of welfare. Not only is such dependency is degrading, but the unemployed also face humiliation and hostility from those who are employed and paying taxes.

In light of these social conditions, some critical criminologists assert that the function of corrections in society is to manage, regulate, and control those who are socially marginalized (Irwin, 1985; Welch, 1994). Historically, corrections has been intimately related to economic forces: For example, prisoners were used as forced labor, and in some institutions inmates were given job training. As the labor market became saturated (i.e., the number of persons willing to work greatly outnumbered available jobs), the economic role of the prison became obsolete. Consequently, prisons have become associated with the crime control strategy of deterrence and with controlling lower-income people who are most adversely affected by economic downturns (Barak, 1982; Rusche, 1982; Rusche & Kirchheimer, 1939/1968).

As noted earlier, capitalism contributes to poverty because employment is not extended to all persons seeking it. Michael Lynch (1988) concluded that imprisonment is then used to offset the problems endemic to capitalist production—problems that generate a large mass of unemployed persons who have to be controlled by the state. According to Lynch and Groves (1989a), there is nothing radical or Marxist about studying imprisonment as it relates to unemployment. However, unlike conservatives and liberals, critical criminologists view unemployment as part of the normal operations of capitalism.

As capitalism ages, technological advancements render certain forms of labor obsolete. As higher profits are sought in production, labor-saving technology is employed that frees individuals from the workforce, thus swelling the size of the surplus population. Under these circumstances, economic growth creates unemployment, and unemployment increases both crime and imprisonment (Lynch & Groves, 1989a, p. 121; also see Aronowitz & DiFazio, 1994).

In a classic study of unemployment and imprisonment rates, Greenberg (1977) found a strong association between increases in prison admissions and rises in unemployment, reporting that "judges are less willing to grant probation to offenders when they are unemployed" (p. 650). Greenberg's conclusions, however, have been the target of ongoing criticism. Zimring and Hawkins (1991) stated: "There is some relationship between levels of unemployment and movements in the rate of imprisonment but nowhere near the powerful association noted in Greenberg's 1977 study" (p. 133). It should be mentioned that Zimring and Hawkins (1991) conceded that unemployment remains an important variable in further examinations between macroeconomic performance and imprisonment. However, their (1991) discussion of this issue omitted a crucial consideration: that is, the relationship between unemployment and imprisonment within lower-income groups. Zimring and Hawkins revealed that between 1984 and 1988, unemployment rates fell dramatically while imprisonment rates jumped.

Contributing to the debate surrounding unemployment and punishment, Chiricos and Bales (1991) found "a significant, strong, and independent impact of unemployment on pretrial and postsentencing incarceration" (p. 701). They also emphasized the importance of addressing the role of race as it relates to unemployment and punishment. They found that the "greatest likelihood of incarceration is for unemployed black defendants, especially those who are young males or charged with violent or public order crimes" (p. 701). Perhaps even more surprising, when compared to *employed whites* convicted of drug crimes, *employed blacks* were 5.9 times more likely to be incarcerated (also see Welch, 1996a, 1996b).

Missing in Zimring and Hawkins's (1991) discussion is a more open recognition of the effect of Reagan administration policies in the 1980s on imprisonment. Although the national unemployment rate was relatively low, lower-income groups were still swimming against the economic tide. Using unemployment as a general economic indicator is likely to conceal the adverse effects on the economically less privileged. During the Reagan years, rich and upper-middle-class Americans enjoyed considerable prosperity. The richest fifth of the population increased its share of the national income from 41.6% to 44%, whereas the median income of the blue-collar wage earners declined (Phillips, 1990). Unemployment among lower-income people (who are disproportionately racial minorities) remained high. To examine these relationships more carefully, it is crucial to isolate the effect of unemployment on people of lower socioeconomic status.

In an earlier assessment, Jankovic (1982) revealed that among lower-income people, unemployment was a more reliable predictor of incarceration than actual crimes rates (also see Box & Hale, 1982; Yeager, 1979). This means that for this group of people, crime rates could actually decrease while prison populations increased as long as unemployment was also on the rise. This finding supports the proposition, advanced by some critical criminologists, that the correctional system is used to exert social control over the lower-income population.

It is also important to examine the relationship between unemployment and the likelihood of serving a prison sentence upon conviction. Unemployed offenders, especially if they are African American, are much more likely to serve a prison sentence than offenders who are employed at the time of their offense and sentencing. Clearly, in the case of imprisonment, there is a pattern of discrimination against the unemployed that is even more apparent for racial minorities (see Chiricos & Bales, 1991).

An Alliance between Critical and Liberal Criminologists

Over the years, there has been considerable discussion about an alliance between critical and liberal criminologists. It stands to reason that because critical and liberal criminologists agree on many issues, they should form an alliance that would offset the dominance of the conservative agenda. Still, some critical criminologists are understandably uncomfortable with participating in short-term social reforms that do not ultimately lead to significant social change, specially if such reforms take a "band-aid" approach. Nevertheless, many critical criminologists enthusiastically favor joining forces with liberals (and vice versa) in attempts to fight forms of oppression that result from extremely conservative policies. Lynch and Groves (1989b) addressed this issue from a critical perspective: "Thus, the problem radicals face is to promote meaningful social changes here and now while rallying support for their future reform efforts" (pp. 3-4).

Despite their misgivings, critical criminologists have traditionally participated in short-term social reform. For example, some of the fundamental reforms that have been proposed by critical as well as liberal criminologists include raising bail funds for indigent defendants (Greenberg, 1981; Platt, 1982), aiding political prisoners, and abolishing the death penalty (Reiman, 1995). The alliance goes beyond specific policy issues toward advancing social theory. For some critical criminologists, having theoretical and practical alignments with liberalism is certainly beneficial.

> First, this broadens the appeal of radical theory—as it appears to mainstream the radical perspective—and makes it more acceptable to liberal policy officials. Additionally, it debunks the stereotypical view of radicals as having an unswerving commitment to revolution and nothing less than revolution. (Lynch & Groves, 1989b, p. 4)

Tony Platt (1985) recommended that critical criminologists join progressive liberals to combat the rise of the conservative right wing and its agenda for a "law and order" society. He noted that this movement is taking place not just in the United States but in England and Australia as well. Due to the rise of the new right and its dominance over criminal justice policy, prison populations are booming, and there is a renewed fervor over the death penalty, various "get tough" laws, and the "deregulation" of the FBI and the CIA. Among other critics, Bertram Gross (1982) conceded that the new right has succeeded in dominating current criminal justice policies because the left (radicals and progressive liberals) has failed to offer convincing programs designed to deal with crime. In sum, the importance of such alliances ought to be emphasized, particularly when they can lead to positive social change that might not otherwise occur. Frank Cullen and John Wozniak (1982) reminded us that "radicals should not forget where valuable allies in the struggle against repression might reside" (e.g., in the liberal and/or religious community) (p. 31).

Criticisms of Critical Criminology

As might be expected, conservative and some liberal criminologists have maintained a steady attack on the critical perspective. For instance, it has been noted that critical criminology has generated few quantitative studies (Sparks, 1980). Whereas there was some truth to this charge in the past, it should be pointed out that today more critical examinations of crime and corrections are implementing quantitative methods. In particular, as noted above, critical criminologists have vastly contributed to the body of research on unemployment and incarceration rates.

Charges have been also leveled at the critical claim that laws are made to protect the powerful to the exclusion of the powerless. Carl Klockars (1979) aptly pointed out that many laws against violence (such as homicide, rape, assault, and armed robbery) protect those who are *most* likely to be victimized—minorities and members of the lower-income population. Other critics have denied that there exists a class bias in the criminal justice system and the distribution of punishment and remain skeptical of the overall socialist agenda proposed by radicals (Akers, 1979; Klockars, 1979). Jackson Toby (1979) accused critical criminology of not qualifying as a social science because it has emerged as a form of "sentimental moralism" emanating from deeply ingrained radical ideology instead of testable theoretical propositions (also see Bernard, 1981; Turk, 1979).

Critical criminology is also subject to self-criticism, ranging from methods to interpretation and subject matter (see Thomas & O'Maolchatha, 1989). Interestingly, critical criminologists have been criticized by Marxist scholars who accuse them of taking liberties with traditional Marxist thought. This criticism is particularly accurate considering that Marx wrote very little about crime (Ainlay, 1975; Hirst, 1975). Whereas this problem persisted in early versions of critical criminology, today more attention is directed to improving the application of Marxist concepts (see Garland, 1990; Wilkins, 1991).

Critics commonly ask, "If critical criminology is such a valuable perspective, why are there fewer critical than mainstream studies on crime and corrections?" Several reasons are cited for the relatively few studies by critical criminologists. First, it is important to acknowledge that critical criminology is an *emerging* paradigm, meaning that it is still undergoing considerable development. By comparison, conservative and liberal criminology have been in the mainstream for much of this century. Moreover, there are simply more mainstream criminologists than critical criminologists. Nevertheless, like any emerging paradigm, critical criminology will have to correct its limitations, thereby expanding the number of critical investigations of crime and corrections. Some professional and academic developments suggest that critical criminology is becoming more recognized in the field of criminology. Recently, the largest body of criminologists, the American Society of Criminology, established its Division on Critical Criminology. (Its newsletter is entitled *The Critical Criminologist.*) Such a development is important because it adds legitimacy to critical criminology.

Another reason why there are still relatively few works in critical criminology is its unconventional approach to research. Critical criminology has long criticized positivist methods. Therefore, instead of generating empirical studies, critical criminologists have turned to historical and theoretical analyses of crime. Because criminological research is currently dominated by "number crunching," critical criminology's emphasis on theoretical synthesis appears out of the mainstream and scientifically "soft."

Recently, however, a new generation of critical criminologists is attempting to combine theoretical advances with quantitative research, especially in the area of unemployment, crime, and incarceration. To succeed, however, they require adequate funding and must turn to governmental and nongovernmental agencies for financial support. But due to critical criminology's radical assertions, the probability of securing funding from government (and nongovernmental agencies) is slim. This is especially true during an era that is politically conservative. Even mainstream criminologists are being denied funding by the National Institute of Justice (the largest funding institute for criminological research) because their research does not support the policy agenda of the U.S. Department of Justice.

In his recent book *Harm in American Penology,* Todd Clear (1994) documented several incidents in which mainline criminologists had their funding terminated by the National Institute of Justice because their findings failed to support existing criminal justice policies. For instance, Joan Petersilia of the Rand Corporation (a criminal justice think tank) conducted research in which her findings supported the claims of selective incapacitation. Naturally, the National Institute of Justice was thrilled by her findings because they endorsed the U.S. Department of Justice position. In fact, the Department of Justice provided additional funds to reproduce and publicize Petersilia's (1985) report. However, when Petersilia (1986) reanalyzed the data, she reached a different conclusion about selective incapacitation that questioned its effectiveness.

> Faced with a different set of findings that refuted the punishment-and-control agenda, in that the findings suggested that the incapacitation effect of imprisonment may be washed out, over time, by its criminogenic effects, the Department [of Justice] refused to support further dissemination. (Clear, 1994, p. 94)

The lesson here is that even mainstream criminologists struggle to secure research funding, and when they raise questions about current criminal justice policies, they undoubtedly risk losing financial support. So when critical criminologists advocate a wholesale criticism of governmental criminal justice policies (especially by challenging the policy of additional prison construction), their chances for government funding are remote.

Despite their criticisms, many mainstream criminologists acknowledge the contributions of critical criminologists, particularly their insights on law and legal institutions. The field of criminology also has greatly benefited from the historical method embraced by critical criminologists (Sparks, 1980; Sykes, 1974). Unlike liberals and conservatives, whose approach to crime and punishment they consider ahistorical, critical criminologists place enormous emphasis on the evolution of corrections. As noted in Chapter 1, contemporary correctional research has greatly benefited from the historical and economic works of researchers such as Rusche and Kirchheimer (1939/1968), Ignatieff (1978), Adamson (1984), and Foucault (1979). Such contributions are unique to the critical perspective in that they emphasize the importance of economic conditions in determining patterns of crime and punishment. Overall, critical criminologists place corrections in a much larger social context than traditional criminologists do.

Finally, critical criminologists urge us to ask why corrections has *not* succeeded in meeting the goals of punishment and rehabilitation. To those who propose that we have to "get tougher," it is clear that we have been "tough" for several decades and that that does not seem to work either. Perhaps we should consider alternative approaches to crime and corrections.

Conclusion

Critical criminology is devoted to the study of social problems and economic issues that are either ignored or inadequately addressed by traditional criminologists. Likewise, an emerging trend in critical inquiry is bringing culture into the forefront of criminological theory, especially the prevailing emphasis on materialism and predatory individualism (see Groves & Sampson, 1986; Schwartz & Friedrichs, 1994). "From an ideological standpoint, America is a materialist and individualistic society, and these orientations significantly increase the likelihood of crimes by both the powerful and the powerless" (Michalowski, 1985, pp. 409-410).

In this chapter, considerable light has been shed on the practical implications of critical criminology, particularly in response to the ongoing complaint that radicals do not offer meaningful contributions to policy. In defense of the critical perspective, Lynch and Groves (1989b) contended that "critics who neglect the practical aspect of Marxism have misinterpreted this perspective and its very preconceptions about social order, human life and the interaction of the two" (p. 2). The critical framework is indeed practical because its theory is rooted in direct, human activity, most notably as it relates to social change. It stands to reason that long-range changes in the current patterns of crime and punishment cannot occur until significant social changes take place.

In the early 1970s, the conservative revolution defeated existing liberal policies, and over time the conservatives established hegemony. As flawed as the conservative perspective is, it is important to acknowledge that today it remains the dominant approach to crime and corrections. Indeed, the rising prison population and expanded construction of prisons show that the conservative approach, though expensive, remains exceedingly popular. Critics of the conservative perspective insist that crime should be understood in the context of social and economic policies—especially as they affect lower-income individuals, families, and communities (see Clear, 1994; Currie, 1985).

References

Adamson, C. (1984). Toward a Marxian theory of penology: Captive criminal populations as economic threats and resources. *Social Problems, 31*, 435-458.
Ainlay, J. (1975). Book review: The new criminology and critical criminology. *Telos, 26*, 213-225.
Akers, R. (1979). Theory and ideology in Marxist criminology. *Criminology, 16*, 527-544.
Aronowitz, S., & DiFazio, W. (1994). *The jobless future: Sci-tech and the dogma of work.* Minneapolis: University of Minnesota Press.
Barak, G. L. (1982). Punishment and corrections. *Crime and Social Justice, 18*, 108-117.
Bernard, T. (1981). The distinction between conflict and radical criminology. *Journal of Criminal Law and Criminology, 72*, 362-379.
Bohm, R. (1982). Radical criminology: An explication. *Criminology, 19*, 565-589.
Bonger, W. A. (1916). *Criminology and economic conditions.* Boston: Little, Brown.
Box, S., & Hale, C. (1982). Economic crisis and the rising prisoner population in England and Wales. *Crime and Social Justice, 18*, 33-44.
Chiricos, T. G., & Bales, W. D. (1991). Unemployment and punishment: An empirical assessment. *Criminology, 29*, 701-724.
Clear, T. T. (1994). *Harm in American penology: Offenders, victims, and their communities.* Albany: State University of New York Press.

Cullen, F., & Wozniak, J. (1982, Winter). Fighting the appeal of repression. *Crime and Social Justice, 18,* 23-32.
Currie, E. (1985). *Confronting crime: An American challenge.* New York: Pantheon.
Danner, M., Michalowski, R., & Lynch, M. (1994). What does "critical" mean? *Critical Criminologist, 6*(2), 2.
Egler, D. (1986, June 5). Canton, Mt. Sterling win prison prize. *Chicago Tribune,* p. 2.
Foucault, M.. (1979). *Discipline and punish: The birth of the prison.* New York: Vintage.
Friedrichs, D. (1996). *Trusted criminals.* Belmont, CA: Wadsworth.
Garland, D. (1990). *Punishment in modern society: A study in social theory.* Chicago: University of Chicago Press.
Glyn, A. (1990). Contradictions of capitalism. In J. Eatwell, M. Milgate, & P. Newman (Eds.), *The new Pelgrave: Marxian economics* (pp. 104-109). New York: Norton.
Greenberg, D. F. (1977). The dynamics of oscillatory punishment process. *Journal of Criminal Law and Criminology, 68,* 643-651.
Greenberg, D. F. (1981). *Crime and capitalism.* Palo Alto, CA: Mayfield.
Gross, B. (1982). Some anticrime proposals for progressives. *Crime and Social Justice, 18,* 45-56.
Groves, B., & Sampson, R. (1986, Spring). Critical theory and criminology. *Social Problems, 33,* S58-S80.
Hirst, P. Q. (1975). Radical deviancy theory and Marxism: A reply to Taylor and Walton. In I. Taylor, P. Walton, & J. Young (Eds.), *Critical criminology* (pp. 233-237). Boston: Routledge & Kegan Paul.
Holmes, S. A. (1994, November 6). The boom in jails is locking up lots of loot. *New York Times,* p. E3.
Ignatieff, M.. (1978). *A just measure of pain: The penitentiary in the industrial revolution—1750-1850.* New York: Columbia University Press.
Irwin, J. (1985). *The jail: Managing the underclass in American society.* Berkeley: University of California Press.
Jankovic, I. (1982). Labor market and imprisonment. In A. Platt & P. Takagi (Eds.), *Punishment and penal discipline* (pp. 105-112). San Francisco: Crime and Justice Associates.
Klockars, C. B. (1979). The contemporary crisis of Marxist criminology. *Criminology, 16,* 477-515.
Lynch, M. J. (1988). The poverty of historical analysis in criminology. *Social Justice, 15,* 173-185.
Lynch, M. J., & Groves, W. B. (1989a). *A primer in radical criminology* (2nd ed.). New York: Harrow & Heston.
Lynch, M. J., & Groves, W. B. (1989b, March). *Radical criminology, radical policy?* Paper presented at the annual meeting of the Criminal Justice Sciences, Washington, DC.
Maguire, B. (1988). The applied dimension of radical criminology: A survey of prominent radical criminologists. *Sociological Spectrum, 8,* 133-151.
Michalowski, R. J. (1985). *Order, law, and crime: An introduction to criminology.* New York: Random House.
Petersilia, J. (1985). *Probation and felony offenders.* Washington, DC: National Institute of Justice.
Petersilia, J. (1986). *Prison versus probation in California: Implications for crime and offender recidivism.* Santa Monica, CA: Rand Corporation.
Phillips, K. (1990). *Politics of the rich and poor.* New York: Random House.
Platt, T. (1982). Crime and punishment in the United States: Immediate and long-term reforms from a Marxist perspective. *Crime and Social Justice, 18,* 38-45.
Platt, T. (1985). Criminology in the 1980s: Progressive alternatives to "law and order." *Crime and Social Justice, 21/22,* 191-199.
Quinney, R. (1980). *Class, state, and crime.* New York: Longman.
Reiman, J. (1995). *The rich get richer and the poor get prison: Ideology, class, and criminal justice* (4th ed.). Boston: Allyn & Bacon.

Residents of dying California town see future in a prison. (1994, May 8). *New York Times*, p. 8.
Rusche, G. (1982). Labor market and penal sanctions: Thoughts on the sociology of criminal justice. In T. Platt & P. Takagi (Ed.), *Punishment and penal discipline* (pp. 10-16). San Francisco: Crime and Social Justice Associates.
Rusche, G., & Kirchheimer, O. (1968). *Punishment and social structures*. New York: Russell & Russell. (Original work published 1939)
Schwartz, M. D., & Friedrichs, D. O. (1994). Postmodern thought and criminological discontent: New metaphors for understanding violence. *Criminology, 32*, 221-246.
Sparks, R. F. (1980). A critique of Marxist criminology. In N. Morris & M. Tonry (Eds.), *Crime and justice: An annual review of research* (pp. 116-128). Chicago: University of Chicago Press.
State's prisons continue to bulge, overwhelming efforts at reform. (1990, May 20). *New York Times*, pp. A1, A2.
Sykes, G. M. (1974). The rise of critical criminology. *Journal of Criminal Law and Criminology, 65*, 206-213.
Thomas, J., & O'Maolchatha, A. (1989). Reassessing the critical metaphor: An optimistic revisionist view. *Justice Quarterly, 6*, 143-172.
Toby, J. (1979). The new criminology is the old sentimentality. *Criminology, 16*, 516-526.
Turk, A. (1979). Analyzing official deviance: For nonpartisan conflict analysis in criminology. *Criminology, 16*, 459-476.
U.S. Department of Commerce. (1995). *Statistical abstracts of the United States*. Washington, DC: Government Printing Office.
Welch, M. (1994). Jail overcrowding: Social sanitation and the warehousing of the urban underclass. In A. R. Roberts (Ed.), *Critical issues in crime and justice* (pp. 251-276). Thousand Oaks, CA: Sage.
Welch, M. (1996a). *Corrections: A critical approach*. New York: McGraw-Hill.
Welch, M. (1996b). Race and social class in the examination of punishment. In M. Lynch & E. B. Patterson (Eds.), *Justice with prejudice: Race and criminal justice in America* (pp. 156-169). New York: Harrow & Heston.
Who wants new prisons? In New York, all of upstate. (1989, June 9). *New York Times*, pp. B-1, B-2.
Wilkins, L. T. (1991). *Punishment, crime and market forces*. Brookfield, VT: Dartmouth.
Yeager, M. (1979). Unemployment and imprisonment. *Journal of Criminal Law and Criminology, 70*, 586-588.
Young, T. R. (1983). *Social justice vs. criminal justice: An agenda for critical criminology* (Transforming Sociology Series Special Packet 352). Longmont, CO: Red Feather Institute.
Zimring, F. E., & Hawkins, G. (1991). *The scale of imprisonment*. Chicago: University of Chicago Press.

CHAPTER 3

The Contours of Race, Social Class, and Punishment

Exploring Institutional Biases in Corrections

For years, research has been devoted to studying the effects of race and social class on the criminal justice process. Still, various conceptual limitations continue to confound this area of inquiry. For instance, there is a tendency to focus attention exclusively on either race or social class, thus neglecting the interaction between these two factors. Together, race and social class determine the form and degree of punishment that lawbreakers receive. Rather than treating race and social class as independent and unidimensional constructs, studies need to take into account the ways that they overlap.

As noted in Chapter 2, minorities are more likely than whites to be unemployed, to have low levels of educational attainment, to reside in sub-

---

AUTHOR'S NOTE: An earlier version of this chapter appeared in *Punishment With Prejudice* (1996), edited by Michael J. Lynch and E. Britt Patterson (New York: Harrow & Heston Publishers). Reproduced with permission, Harrow & Heston Publishers. Michael Lynch and Marie Mark are gratefully acknowledged for their comments on this work.

standard housing, and to receive poor-quality health care. It has been argued that racial discrimination serves as a powerful mechanism of social control by limiting the mobility of low-income minorities; indeed, being locked into a lower socioeconomic status further marginalizes people of color. Similar accusations of racism and classism have been leveled at the criminal justice system (see Lynch & Patterson, 1996; Lynch & Stretesky, 1998). As we shall see in this chapter, minorities who enter the criminal justice system often are affected adversely by institutional biases predicated on race, ethnicity, and socioeconomic status. At the arrest stage of the criminal justice process, discrimination against blacks and Hispanics is typically cued by visible identifiers that mark—stigmatize—minorities as different from whites. Once arrested, many people of color are unable to afford bail or hire private attorneys due to their low socioeconomic status; the further low-income minorities proceed through the correctional apparatus, the greater their hardship becomes. Altogether, these biases illustrate the intersection of race and social class, manifesting as a form of double discrimination.

Given their commitment to equality and social justice, critical criminologists have enormous interest in issues of race and social class—as well as gender (see Chapter 5). The purpose of this chapter is to examine critically racism and classism as mutually determining forces. Exploring the contours of race and social class at each stage of the criminal justice process reveals salient and subtle prejudices, thereby shedding additional light on repressive measures of social control aimed at impoverished people of color.

The Macro and Micro Levels of Racism and Classism

Racism and classism exist at the macro and micro levels of the social order. Macrosociologically speaking, society is predicated on structural and historical forces commonly manifested in political and economic enterprises. Biases in race and social class can be found in the political economy, which relies on low-cost workers to accumulate capital and produce profits for financial elites. As explained in Chapter 2, cheap labor is recruited from the lower classes, which are composed disproportionately of racial and ethnic minorities. This economic structure reproduces social injustice because not all workers from the lower classes are absorbed into the labor market, so that the lower class becomes stratified into the working poor, the unemployed, and those straddling these categories (e.g., migrant and seasonal workers, as well as those employed periodically). Due to racial discrimination, however, lower-class minorities are more often negatively affected by economic downturns than their white counterparts. The structural effects of racism and classism generated at the macro level of the social order also pattern biases at the micro level. Individual acts of racial discrimination stem from prejudice toward racial minorities, who, "historically, have been viewed by whites as inferior, controllable, and usable" (Mann, 1993, p. 250).

Given the close relationship between racism and classism, it is important to consider some of their various permutations, which can be understood chronologically. Simply put, people are born into both a racial/ethnic group and a social class. Whereas wealthy whites benefit from this elitist stratification, lower-income minorities often are subjected to numerous forms of discrimination, including being denied comparable education, housing, and health care. Over time, these social deficiencies restrict upward mobility and access to legitimate financial opportunities, and this restriction, in turn, leaves many minorities vulnerable to illicit economic activity. Consider the following scenario: An undereducated, unemployed black male residing in the ghetto resorts to peddling drugs as a means of economic survival (or as a means to escape or modify adverse social conditions). When arrested and later convicted, it is likely that he will be incarcerated rather than sentenced to probation due to both his socioeconomic status and his race. In advancing our understanding of punishment in America, it is imperative to integrate conceptually the effects of racism and classism because they exist as mutually determining forces at the macro and micro levels of the social order.

Racism and Classism in the Criminal Justice Process

As we examine closely the effects of racism and classism on punishment, our attention turns to various stages of the criminal justice process: arrest, detention, sentencing, incarceration, and parole. In proceeding through each of these phases, we will bring to light the racial and socioeconomic biases affecting minorities. Similarly, institutional obstacles facing women of color and minority juveniles also will be addressed.

POLICE SWEEPS, ARRESTS, AND HASSLING

Critical discussions of racial discrimination and arrest often include the controversial law enforcement practice of conducting sweeps in search of suspects. Opponents of sweeps argue that dragnets are undertaken with more enthusiasm when the suspect has been identified as black, especially when the victim is white. A case in point is the well-publicized 1989 Boston case involving a young white couple. On their way home from a childbirth class, Charles Stuart murdered his pregnant wife and gave himself a superficial gunshot wound, then falsely reported that a young black man was the assailant. Boston police quickly launched an exhaustive manhunt in search of the alleged suspect and targeted a black community, where they made several illegal searches and false arrests. Eventually, it became known that Stuart himself was responsible for the killing of his wife, and later he committed suicide. The fact remains the police carried out an ambitious dragnet with little descriptive information other than that the suspect was assumed to be a young black male. Black civil rights leaders insisted that the sweep was racially motivated, and they correctly pointed out that comparable manhunts are rarely undertaken in white neighborhoods (Welch, 1996).

With this in mind, consider the 1992 incident at the State University of New York at Oneonta, where a college official was demoted for illegally providing police with a roster of black students for the purpose of facilitating a dragnet. The list was used to guide a police manhunt following an assault on a 77-year-old white woman who claimed that she had been attacked by a young black man. Other than the suspect's race (and possibly a cut on his hand), no additional information (i.e., height, weight, complexion, or hair style) had been reported. With a directory of 125 black students, the police conducted a search in the college dormitories and private housing; in all, 80 black men were questioned, but no arrests were made. One of the interrogated students responded angrily, "It is very discouraging to live in an environment where you can be harassed like that. You don't see them questioning every white man every time somebody commits a crime" (Mulvaney, 1991, p. 12). Subsequently, the university's president apologized to students and released a statement calling the incident a "breach of trust and a violation of the privacy of our students." The president also characterized the investigation as "an affront to individual dignity and human rights" ("College Official," 1992, p. B6).

Similar cases have involved well-known professional athletes falsely arrested by police because they fit a criminal profile. For example, Joe Morgan, the retired Golden Glove second baseman of the Cincinnati Reds, was arrested in an airport after he was suspected of being a drug dealer. The Morgan case illustrates the reliance on profiles in which persons are questioned or arrested because they resemble a general description of criminal type; such profiles place a heavy emphasis on race, in particular blacks. In a separate incident involving a well-known African American athlete, Dee Brown, point guard of the Boston Celtics, and his fiancee were held for questioning in a bank located in a predominately white section of Boston because the security guard believed that the black couple fit the description of bank robbers (Welch, 1996). It should be noted that the Stuart, Oneonta, Morgan, and Brown cases drew considerable media attention, but most cases of racially motivated false arrest are not publicized.

Although anecdotal evidence raises public awareness of racism, it is important to rely on research that determines systematically how discrimination against minorities affects patterns of arrest. Hepburn's (1978) often-cited study found that nonwhites were more likely than whites to be arrested under circumstances that would not constitute sufficient grounds for prosecution. Currently, researchers are looking beyond arrests to explore another controversial issue in law enforcement, namely the hassling of minorities by police. Browning, Cullen, Cao, Kopache, and Stevenson (1994) examined the "lived experiences" of minorities who reported being hassled by police without cause. Their analysis revealed a significant association between being African American and having experiences of being hassled by law enforcement officers, thereby suggesting that police surveillance is racially discriminatory. Hassling is a manifestation of institutional racism, one of those "established laws, customs and practices which systematically reflect and produce racial inequalities in American society . . . whether or not the individuals maintaining those practices have racist intentions" (Jones, 1972, p. 131; also see Cao, Frank, & Cullen 1996; Frank, Brandl, Cullen, & Stichman, 1996). It should be emphasized that patterns of racial discrimination in the form of police sweeps, arrests, and hassling commonly transcend social class: Middle-income blacks (and Hispanics), much like their lower-income counterparts, are subject to such tactics of law enforcement due to their race.

Whereas arrest and hassling (and even detention) do not meet the technical definition of a legal penalty, there is considerable support for the notion of "process as punishment." Many scholars remind us that being arrested, hassled, or detained is indeed a form of punishment even if charges are ultimately dismissed (Feeley, 1979; Irwin, 1985; Welch, 1994). Similarly, law enforcement campaigns that target the low-income residents of urban communities have been characterized as a form of social sanitation: a process by which police remove disreputable persons (e.g., street prostitutes, drug peddlers, addicts, the homeless) from specific urban zones. The objective of social sanitation is to create the illusion that certain sections of a city are reputable and not cluttered with society's underclass (Irwin, 1985; Welch, 1994; see Chapters 4 and 6 of this book).

To summarize, it is crucial to take into consideration the influence of social class and race at each phase of the criminal justice process. At the initial stage, arrests are often based on a person's resemblance to the physical description of a suspect (or criminal profile). Generally, that description is as vague as the person's race; hence, at the arrest phase of the criminal justice process, racism can become more evident than classism. However, as suspects proceed into the next stage of the criminal justice system—the courts—their socio-economic status together with race may influence the determination of guilt and the sentencing of punishment. Compared to their low-income counterparts, middle-income minorities have more of the resources that are necessary to defend effectively themselves in court, such as the funds to hire a private attorney. But low-income minorities have little choice other than to rely on court-appointed lawyers, who typically are inundated with heavy caseloads and as a result devote less time and attention to their defendants' cases. Whereas race still remains an important variable at the judicial phase, social class membership generally determines the quality of legal defense.

BAIL AND DETENTION

As mentioned previously, police sweeps that are considered racially motivated often cross socioeconomic lines insofar as middle- and low-income minorities are vulnerable to arrest campaigns. Much like the process of choosing or being assigned counsel, detention typically is shaped socioeconomically more than racially—still, minorities are disproportionately poor. Simply because suspects are black or Hispanic does not mean necessarily that they will be detained in jail; rather, suspects are more likely to be detained when the bail is higher than their financial means. The Correctional Association of New York (1991) reported that at the Rikers Island Jail Complex, two-thirds of the pretrial detainees (a population that is 95% black and Hispanic) remain in jail because they are too poor to meet their bail, even though many times their bail is set as low as $250 to $500.

Many jurisdictions have specific guidelines that determine bail decisions, and it has been widely speculated that discrimination exists in the form of bail being set in excess of these limits. However, Patterson and Lynch (1991) showed more precisely how discrimination occurs by taking into account differences in race and gender. Their data indicate that racial/gender differences among suspects do not influence decisions to set bail in *excess* of guideline limits. However, white females are significantly more likely than others to receive bail amounts *below* schedule guidelines. Further, nonwhite suspects are less likely than whites to receive bail below schedule amounts (pp. 50-51).

What can be learned from the Patterson and Lynch study is that discrimination does not always emerge in the form of harsher treatment of minorities; rather, it may manifest as favoritism for whites. As we will elaborate in Chapter 6, the trend in detention shows that jails increasingly hold more minorities than whites. According to the Bureau of Justice Statistics (1998), in 1996, 6 out of 10 jail inmates were racial or ethnic minorities; 41% were black and 18% were Hispanic. Again, it is important not to interpret jail population data solely on grounds of race but also to consider elements of low socioeconomic status: high unemployment and low income, as well as poor educational background. Socioeconomically, one in three jail inmates was unemployed at the time of his or her arrest. Jail inmates also reported low incomes: Almost half indicated earning less than $600 per month (in the month before their arrest). Similarly, 46% of the jail inmates had not completed high school. Contributing to the growing influx of minorities into detention (and into prison) is the war on drugs, which targets low-income people of color: 22% of jail inmates were held on drug charges, and 64% of all jail prisoners reported being regular drug users (Bureau of Justice Statistics, 1998; see Chapters 4, 6, and 11 of this book).

SENTENCING

Scholars continue to debate the assertion that minorities also are discriminated against during the sentencing phase of the criminal justice process. Further obscuring the issue is that researchers rely on different methods and data and thus produce competing interpretations. In his study on sentencing, Walsh (1991) contended that whites were significantly more likely to be incarcerated than blacks after adjusting for crime seriousness and prior record. Moreover, Walsh concluded that no significant racial effect existed on sentence length but that significantly harsher probation terms were imposed on whites than on blacks. Similar investigations suggest that racial discrimination has declined over the past decades and that race is no longer a strong predictor of sentencing patterns (Hagan, 1974; Klein, Petersilia, & Turner, 1990; Wilbanks, 1987).

Conversely, other researchers conclude that race is a reliable predictor in the sentencing of capital crimes and rape (Humphrey and Fogerty, 1987).

Relatedly, studies have found that racial discrimination within sentencing is more pronounced in urbanized counties and in those with relatively large minority populations (Bridges, Crutchfield, & Simpson, 1987; Myers & Talarico, 1986). Many scholars maintain that discrimination does indeed exist in sentencing but in forms difficult to detect and measure (Klepper, Nagin, & Tierney, 1983; Zatz, 1987).

In another attempt to specify the relationship between race and sentencing, Spohn and Cederblom (1991) set out to test the "liberation hypothesis" (Kalven & Zeisel, 1966), which proposes that racial discrimination in sentencing is restricted only in less serious cases. Their findings provide support for the liberation hypothesis, at least with respect to the decision to incarcerate or not. They suggest that judges confronted with defendants convicted of murder, robbery, or rape have relatively little latitude in deciding whether to sentence the defendant to prison. In less serious cases, on the other hand, the appropriate sentence is not necessarily obvious; consequently, judges are liberated from the constraints imposed by the law, by other members of the courtroom work group, and by public opinion and are free to take into account extralegal considerations such as race (Spohn & Cederblom, 1991, p. 323). Spohn and Cederblom (1991), in their study on sentencing at the municipal level (in Detroit), further suggested that unemployment may have influenced judges' decisions in these cases: "Given the high unemployment rate among blacks in Detroit, for example, judges might see black offenders as less employable than white offenders, and thus as more likely than whites to recidivate" (p. 324). Here again, social class and unemployment are variables that are not always controlled in studies of sentencing that compare racial groups.

A report prepared for the New York State's Division of Criminal Justice Services found that minorities were more likely than whites to be sentenced to prison terms after being convicted of identical crimes (Nelson, 1991, 1992). Blacks charged with robbery and having two prior arrests were more likely to receive a prison sentence than whites with a similar record charged with the same offense; whites also were more likely than blacks to be punished by fines. In New York State, minorities (blacks and Hispanics) represent less than one-fourth of the state's general population, but they make up 80% of the prison population. Missing from this report are considerations of socioeconomic status in determining sentences. Still, other statewide studies have found similar patterns of discrimination against minorities in sentencing: In particular, Steffensmeier, Ulmer, and Kramer (1998) concluded that in Pennsylvania young black males are sentenced more harshly than any other group (also see Farnworth, Teske, & Thurman, 1991; Kramer & Steffensmeier, 1993).

As we shall explore in greater detail in Chapter 9, death penalty sentencing also raises concerns of racial biases. Experts point out that the key to identifying patterns of discrimination goes beyond the race of the offender because the race of the victim is just as important. Paternoster's (1983) study revealed that blacks who kill whites have over a 4.5% greater chance of facing the death penalty than blacks who kill blacks. When the race of the victim is ignored, the likelihood of blacks and whites receiving a death sentence is almost equal (also see General Accounting Office, 1992). Whereas issues of race are well documented in the research literature, little attention has been devoted to the effects of social class (of both the victim and the criminal) on sentencing to capital punishment.

INCARCERATION

In his book *Search and Destroy: African American Males in the Criminal Justice System* (1996), Jerome Miller documented the ever-rising black population in American prisons: In 1930, the rate of incarceration for black people was 3 times that of whites; in 1950, the rate increased to 4; in 1960, the rate climbed to 5; and in 1970, the rate surpassed 6. More recently in 1989, the rate of incarceration for blacks reached 7 times that of whites, and in 1996, the rate has jumped to 8. Similarly, in 1990, the Sentencing Project found that almost one in four (23%) black men in the age group 20 to 29 years was either in prison, in jail, on probation, or on parole on any given day; furthermore, this black correctional population was greater than the total number of black men of all ages enrolled in college (Mauer, 1990). Astonishingly, that figure increased to one in three in 1995 (Mauer & Huling, 1995). It has been said rather bluntly that "not only has the prison system gotten bigger, but it also has gotten blacker" (Christianson, 1991, pp. 62-63; also see Blumstein, 1993; Tonry 1994, 1995; Walker, Spohn, & DeLone, 1996).

To reiterate, the war on drugs has had enormous detrimental effects on the African American community, and even though we shall discuss this controversy fully in the next chapter, it is worth noting the following statistics: Blacks represent 12% of the U.S. population, 13% of drug users, 35% of arrests for drug possession, 55% of convictions for drug possession, and 74% of prison sentences for drug possession (Mauer 1996, p. 12; also see Duster, 1997; Lusane, 1994; Welch, 1996; Welch, Bryan, & Wolff, 1999; Welch, Wolff, & Bryan, 1998).

Whereas sociologists have suggested that prisons are microcosms of society at large, Leo Carroll (1990) insisted that correctional institutions represent only society's worst aspect—the slum: "Over half of the residents of the contemporary prison are drawn from racial and ethnic minority groups, and most were residents of ghettos prior to their incarceration" (p. 511). This depiction of the American prison is particularly accurate when we consider elements of racism along with classism in shaping discrimination against the unemployed. As noted in the previous chapter, judicial decisions to incarcerate lawbreakers rather than sentencing them to probation are strongly influenced by offenders' employment status (see Chapter 2; Chiricos & Bales, 1991; Greenberg, 1977; Zimring & Hawkins 1991). Likewise, Jankovic (1982) found that unemployment was a better predictor of incarceration than crime rates (also see Chapter 13 of this book; Box & Hale, 1982; Yeager, 1979). This finding supports the proposition that imprisonment functions not as *crime* control but rather as *social* control aimed at the lower classes and minorities.

PAROLE

Much like the research on sentencing, studies examining racial discrimination in parole decisions yield conflicting results. The National Minority Council (1982) found that black prisoners serve longer prison terms than whites and concluded that this disparity was evidence of racial discrimination. Similarly, Petersilia (1983) concluded that "race made a difference" (p. 49) when parole decisions of whites were compared to minorities:

> In Texas, all other things being equal, blacks and Hispanics consistently served longer sentences than whites for the same crimes. In California, minority inmates also served longer sentences, but that was largely determined by the length of the sentence imposed. Michigan manifested an interesting reversal. Although blacks received longer court-imposed sentences than whites, they wound up serving about the same time. In Michigan, then, parole decisions seemed to "favor" blacks—that is, blacks evidently served less time of their original sentences than whites did. (pp. 49-50)

On the other side of the debate, Wilbanks (1987) was not convinced that Petersilia's findings actually meant that discrimination against minorities always existed in parole decisions, particularly because Petersilia revealed that in Michigan parole decisions favored blacks. Wilbanks did not necessarily deny that racism had existed throughout much of American criminal justice history. However, he contended that nowadays "most states now use objective guidelines" and that "it may be that whatever racial disparity did exist against blacks at one time no longer exists" (p. 138). It is also quite possible that forms of racism have become increasingly subtle and therefore difficult to detect. Consistent with the other literature on discrimination in criminal justice, research on parole also overlooks the importance of social class in shaping institutional biases.

Minority Women and Juveniles

As is the case in society at large, women of color entering the criminal justice system must contend with the adverse effects of racism and sexism simultaneously. Moreover, because minority women are more likely than their white counterparts to live in poverty, they must also carry the burden of classism.

> Class-oppressed men, whether they are white or black, have privileges afforded to them as men in a sexist society. Similarly, class-oppressed whites, whether they are men or women, have privileges afforded to them as whites in a racist society.... Those who are poor, black, and female have all the forces of classism, racism, and sexism bearing down on them. (Mantsios, quoted in Simpson, 1991, p. 115)

Minority women have not enjoyed to an equal extent the advances in women's rights, but their plight is not often discussed publicly. Even mainstream feminists have neglected problems affecting women of color; thus, the women's movement has been criticized for supporting a predominately white, middle-class, suburban agenda (see Simpson, 1989). In an effort to expand the rights of *all* women, progressive feminists have set out to explore the complex interplay of gender, race, and class oppression (see Collins, 1986; Davis, 1989; Mann, 1989; Simpson, 1989). As we shall explore in Chapter 5, the criminal justice apparatus has increasingly targeted impoverished women of color, especially in the war on drugs.

Research on minorities in juvenile justice has consistently confirmed widespread beliefs that whites are treated more leniently than minorities. Earlier studies found that black and Hispanic youthful offenders were more likely than whites to be committed to state institutions, regardless of their offense (Chiricos, Jackson, & Waldo, 1972; Jankovic, 1982). This form of racial discrimination is considered typical throughout the criminal justice system. Even when additional variables are controlled for, race has emerged as a powerful predictor of arrest, incarceration, and release among minority youths (Dannefer & Schutt, 1982; Peterson & Friday, 1975; Reed, 1984). More recent investigations similarly find that compared to their white counterparts, black youthful offenders are more often recommended for formal processing, referred to court, adjudicated delinquent, and given harsh depositions (Tollet & Close, 1991; also see Bishop & Frazier, 1988; Office of Juvenile Justice and Delinquency Prevention, 1990; Rosenbaum, 1988). In 1993, the percentage of youths in reform schools who were black had risen to 63%, a 7% increase from 1987 and nearly a 17% increase from 1977 (Miller, 1996).

Conclusion

The purpose of this chapter was to examine the relationship between race and social class at each stage of passage through the criminal justice system: arrest, detention, criminal defense, sentencing, incarceration, and parole. It is suggested that the interaction between race and social class may not be as great at the front end of the process as at the middle and back end of the system. Arrests (including police sweeps and hassling) are driven by surface variables such as race, regardless of social class: Middle-income blacks may be as likely as their lower-income counterparts to be suspected of criminal activity (or targeted by police for hassling). At the stage of adjudication, however, middle-income minorities typically possess the resources needed to deflect some of the institutional biases.

Still, most minorities who enter the criminal justice system and proceed further into the court and correctional phases are hamstrung by their low socioeconomic status; indeed, their socioeconomic status interacts significantly with their race, leaving them vulnerable to a double form of discrimination. Low-income people of color are simply less equipped to defend themselves against an ambitious and well-funded criminal justice system—a system that is also characterized by racism and classism.

Further research on the institutional biases in criminal justice is needed, and conceptually classism and racism ought to be understood as mutually determining forces. It is recommended that future studies on criminal justice and corrections contextualize social class and race together (see Hacker, 1992; Johnson & Leighton, 1995; Welch, Wolff, & Bryan, 1998; Wilson, 1987). Consistent with critical criminology's commitment to promoting equality and social justice, racial and economic issues will be addressed throughout this volume. The next chapter confronts dimensions of racism and classism in the war on drugs.

References

Bishop, D. M., & Frazier, C. (1988). The influence of race in juvenile justice processing. *Journal of Research in Crime Delinquency, 25,* 242-263.

Blumstein, A. (1993). Racial disproportionality of U.S. prison populations revisited. *University of Colorado Law Review, 64,* 743-760.

Box, S., & Hale, C. (1982). Economic crisis and the rising prisoner population in England and Wales. *Crime and Social Justice, 17,* 20-35.

Bridges, G. S., Crutchfield, R. D., & Simpson, E. E. (1987). Crime, social structure and criminal punishment: White and nonwhite rates of imprisonment. *Social Problems, 34,* 345-362.

Browning, S. L., Cullen, F. T., Cao, L., Kopache, R., & Stevenson, T. J. (1994). Race and getting hassled by the police: A research note. *Police Studies, 17,* 1-11.

Bureau of Justice Statistics, U.S. Department of Justice. (1998). *Profile of jail inmates, 1996.* Washington, DC: Government Printing Office.

Cao, L., Frank, J., & Cullen, F. T. (1996). Race, community context and confidence in the police. *American Journal of Police, 15,* 3-22.

Carroll, L. (1990). Race, ethnicity, and the social order of the prison. In D. Kelly (Ed.), *Criminal behavior* (2nd ed., pp. 510-527). New York: St. Martin's.

Chiricos, T. G., & Bales, W. D. (1991). Unemployment and punishment: An empirical assessment. *Criminology, 29,* 701-724.

Chiricos, T. G., Jackson, P., & Waldo, S. (1972). Inequality in the imposition of a criminal label. *Social Problems, 19,* 533-572.

Christianson, S. (1991). Our black prisons. In K. C. Hass & G. P. Alpert (Eds.), *The dilemmas of corrections: Contemporary readings* (2nd ed.). Prospect Heights, IL: Waveland.

College official who released list of black students is demoted. (1992, September 18). *New York Times,* p. B2.

Collins, P. H. (1986). Learning from the outsider within: The sociological significance of black feminist thought. *Social Problems, 33,* 514-532.

Correctional Association of New York. (1991, September 15). Letter to CANY members. Unpublished document, New York City office.

Dannefer, D., & Schutt, R. K. (1982). Race and juvenile justice processing in court and police agencies. *American Journal of Sociology, 87,* 1113-1132.

Davis, A. (1989). *Women, culture and politics.* New York: Random House.

Duster, T. (1997). Pattern, purpose, and race in the drug war. In C. Reinarman & H. Levine (Eds.), *Crack in America* (pp. 260-287). Berkeley: University of California Press.

Farnworth, M., Teske, R. H. C., & Thurman, G. (1991). Ethnic, racial, and minority disparity in felony court processing. In M. J. Lynch & E. B. Patterson (Eds.), *Race and criminal justice* (pp. 54-70). New York: Harrow & Heston.

Feeley, M. (1979). *The process is the punishment: Handling cases in a lower criminal court.* New York: Russell Sage Foundation.

Frank, J., Brandl, S., Francis T., Cullen, F. T., & Stichman, A. (1996). Reassessing the impact of race on citizens' attitudes toward the police: A research note. *Justice Quarterly, 13,* 321-334.

General Accounting Office. (1992). *Death penalty sentencing indicates pattern of racial disparities.* Washington, DC: Government Printing Office.

Greenberg, D. F. (1977). The dynamics of oscillatory punishment process. *Journal of Criminal Law and Criminology, 68,* 643-651.

Hacker, A. (1992). *Two nations: Black and white, separate, hostile, unequal.* New York: Ballantine.
Hagan, J. (1974). Extra-legal attributes and criminal sentencing: An assessment of a sociological viewpoint. *Law and Society Review, 8,* 357-383.
Hepburn, J. (1978). Race and the decision to arrest: An analysis of warrants issued. *Journal of Research in Crime and Delinquency, 15,* 54-73.
Humphrey, J. A., & Fogerty, T. J. (1987). Race and plea bargained outcome: A research note. *Social Forces, 66,* 176-182.
Irwin, J. (1985). *The jail: Managing the underclass in American society.* Berkeley: University of California Press.
Jankovic, I. (1982). Labor market and imprisonment. In A. Platt & P. Takagi (Eds.), *Punishment and penal discipline* (pp. 93-104). San Francisco: Crime and Justice Associates.
Johnson, R., & Leighton, P. (1995). Black genocide? Preliminary thoughts on the plight of America's poor black men. *Journal of African American Men, 1*(2), 3-21.
Jones, M. B. (1972). *Prejudice and racism.* Reading, MA: Addison-Wesley.
Kalven, H., Jr., & Zeisel, H. (1966). *The American jury.* Boston: Little, Brown.
Klein, S., Petersilia, J., & Turner, S. (1990). Race and imprisonment decisions in California. *Science, 247,* 812-912.
Klepper, D., Nagin, D., & Tierney, L. (1983). Discrimination in the criminal justice system: A critical appraisal of the literature. In A. Blumstein, J. Cohen, S. E. Martin, & M. H. Tonry (Eds.), *Research on sentencing: A search for reform* (Vol. 2, pp. 55-128). Washington, DC: National Academy Press.
Kramer, J., & Steffensmeier, D. (1993). Race and imprisonment decisions. *Sociological Quarterly, 34,* 357-376.
Lusane, C. (1994). *Pipe dream blues: Racism and the war on drugs.* Boston: South End.
Lynch, M., & Patterson, E. B. (1996). *Punishment with prejudice.* New York: Harrow & Heston.
Lynch, M., & Stretesky, P. (1998). Uniting class, race and criticism through the study of environmental justice. *Critical Criminologist, 9,* 1-6.
Mann, C. R. (1989). Minority and female: A criminal justice double bind. *Social Justice, 16*(4), 95-114.
Mann, C. R. (1993). *Unequal justice: A question of color.* Bloomington: Indiana University Press.
Mauer, M. (1990). *Young black men and the criminal justice system: A growing national problem.* Washington, DC: Sentencing Project.
Mauer, M. (1996). The drug war's unequal justice. *Drug Policy Letter, 28,* 11-13.
Mauer, M., & Huling, T. (1995). *Young black Americans and the criminal justice system: Five years later.* Washington, DC: Sentencing Project.
Miller, J. (1996). *Search and destroy: African American males in the criminal justice system.* New York: Cambridge University Press.
Mulvaney, J. (1991, September 12). Dragnet for blacks at college assailed. *Newsday,* p. 12.
Myers, M. A., & Talarico, S. M. (1986). The social context of racial discrimination in sentencing. *Social Problems, 33,* 263-251.
National Minority Advisory Council on Criminal Justice. (1982). *The inequality of justice: A report on crime and the admission of justice.* Washington, DC: Government Printing Office.
Nelson, J. F. (1991). Disparity in the incarceration of minorities in New York State. In M. J. Lynch & E. B. Patterson (Eds.), *Race and criminal justice* (pp. 145-160). New York: Harrow & Heston.
Nelson, J. F. (1992). Hidden disparities in case processing: New York State, 1985-1986. *Journal of Criminal Justice, 20,* 181-200.
Office of Juvenile Justice and Delinquency Prevention, U.S. Department of Justice. (1990). *Growth in minority detentions attributed to drug law violators.* Washington, DC: Government Printing Office.

Paternoster, R. (1983). Race of the victim and location of crime: The decision to seek the death penalty in South Carolina. *Journal of Criminal Law and Criminology, 74,* 754-785.

Patterson, E. B., & Lynch, M. J. (1991). Bias in the formalized bail procedures. In M. J. Lynch & E. B. Patterson (Eds.), *Race and criminal justice* (pp. 36-53). New York: Harrow & Heston.

Petersilia, J. (1983). *Racial disparities in the criminal justice system.* Santa Monica, CA: Rand Corporation.

Peterson, D., & Friday, P. (1975). Early release from incarceration: Race as a factor in the use of shock probation. *Journal of Criminal Law and Criminology, 66,* 79-87.

Reed, W. L. (1984). *Racial differentials in juvenile court decision making: Final report.* Washington, DC: U.S. Department of Justice, National Institute for Juvenile Justice and Delinquency Prevention.

Rosenbaum, J. L. (1988). Age, race, and female offending. *Journal of Contemporary Criminal Justice, 4,* 125-138.

Simpson, S. S. (1989). Feminist theory, crime, and justice. *Criminology, 27,* 607-631.

Simpson, S. S. (1991). Caste, class, and violent crime: Explaining differences in female offending. *Criminology, 29,* 115-135.

Spohn, C., & Cederblom, J. (1991). Race and disparities in sentencing: A test of the liberation hypothesis. *Justice Quarterly, 8,* 283-304.

Steffensmeier, D., Ulmer, J., & Kramer, J. (1998). The interaction of race, gender, and age in criminal sentencing: The punishment cost of being young, black, and male. *Criminology, 36,* 763-798.

Tollet, T., & Close, B. R. (1991). The over-representation of blacks in Florida's juvenile justice system. In M. J. Lynch & E. B. Patterson (Eds.), *Race and criminal justice* (pp. 86-99). New York: Harrow & Heston.

Tonry, M. (1994). Racial politics, racial disparities, and the war on crime. *Crime and Delinquency, 40,* 475-494.

Tonry, M. (1995). *Malign neglect: Race, crime, and punishment in America.* New York: Oxford University Press.

Walker, S., Spohn, C., & DeLone, M. (1996). *The color of justice: Race, ethnicity, and crime in America.* Belmont, CA: Wadsworth.

Walsh, A. (1991). Race and discretionary sentencing: An analysis of "obvious" and "non-obvious" cases. *International Journal of Offender Therapy and Comparative Criminology, 35,* 7-20.

Welch, M. (1994). Jail overcrowding: Social sanitation and the warehousing of the urban underclass. In A. Roberts (Ed.), *Critical issues in crime and justice* (pp. 251-276). Newbury Park, CA: Sage.

Welch, M. (1996). *Corrections: A critical approach.* New York: McGraw-Hill.

Welch, M., Bryan, N., & Wolff, R. (1999). Just war theory and drug control policy: Militarization, morality, and the war on drugs. *Contemporary Justice Review.*

Welch, M., Wolff, R., & Bryan, N. (1998). Decontextualizing the war on drugs: A content analysis of NIJ publications and their neglect of race and class. *Justice Quarterly, 15,* 601-624.

Wilbanks, W. (1987). *The myth of a racist criminal justice system.* Monterey, CA: Brooks/Cole.

Wilson, W. J. (1987). *The truly disadvantaged: The inner city, the underclass, and public policy.* Chicago: University of Chicago Press.

Yeager, M. (1979). Unemployment and imprisonment. *Journal of Criminal Law and Criminology, 70,* 586-588.

Zatz, M. S. (1987). The changing forms of racial/ethnic biases in sentencing. *Journal of Research in Crime and Delinquency, 24,* 69-92.

Zimring, F. E., & Hawkins, G. (1991). *The scale of imprisonment.* Chicago: University of Chicago Press.

CHAPTER

The War on Drugs and Correctional Warehousing

Alternative Strategies for the Drug Crisis

Corrections not only occupies the back end of the criminal justice system but is situated so far back that its problems remain conveniently concealed. Among the most pressing problems affecting corrections is overcrowding—a condition that is aggravated by activities at the front end of the criminal justice (i.e., arrests by law enforcement) as well as by decisions at the middle stage (i.e., sentencing by the courts). The war on drugs continues to funnel increasingly more offenders (and recidivists) into the criminal justice system, and many of these lawbreakers reach their final destination inside correctional facilities. It seems that the escalating war on drugs, particularly as it affects corrections, bears out the words of John F. Kennedy that "today's problems are the results of yesterday's solutions."

AUTHOR'S NOTE: This chapter was adapted from an article in the *Journal of Offender Rehabilitation*, 25(1/2), 1997, 43-60. Reprinted with permission. ©1997 by The Haworth Press, Inc. All rights reserved.

In this chapter, the war on drugs and its impact on corrections are explored in depth. Three schools of thought on drug control policy, those of the public health generalists, the legalists, and the cost-benefit specialists, are delineated. Four potential elements of drug control strategy (i.e., supply reduction, treatment, prevention/education, and decriminalization) also are scrutinized. In critically appraising the war on drugs, considerable discussion is devoted to issues of race, class, and the need to reach beyond criminal justice strategies, especially incarceration, in reducing the harms of drug consumption.

Booming Correctional Population

The nation's prison population has recently soared beyond the 1 million mark, and as a result of the war on drugs, the percentage of state prisoners serving a drug sentence more than *tripled* from 1980 to 1993 (6% to 22%). By 1996, that figure reached 23%. Similarly, the percentage of federal prisoners serving a drug sentence more than *doubled* from 25% in 1980 to 60% in 1993 and climbed to 72% in 1996 (Bureau of Justice Statistics, 1998b). The costs of the ongoing imprisonment binge, driven mostly by the war on drugs, are exorbitant—generating a $21 billion-per-year prison industry (Smolowe, 1994). Costs per cell range anywhere from $25,000 per year (in a minimum-security facility) to $74,000 per year (in a maximum-security penitentiary) (Smolowe, 1994; see Forer, 1994; Irwin & Austin, 1994).

It is important to look critically at the prevailing approach to reducing illegal drug consumption in American society. Illegal drug use remains largely conceptualized in terms of a *criminal justice* framework rather than a *public health* framework. Although political leaders often give lip service to treatment programs, the bulk of expenditures in the war on drugs is devoted to law enforcement; in fact, 70% of federal antidrug funding is allocated to law enforcement and only 30% to treatment and prevention (Office of the National Drug Control Strategy, 1996). Especially within corrections, administrators cite major gaps in the funding for substance abuse treatment programs.

Current antidrug policies are criticized not only for the questionable strategy of deploying vast amounts of criminal justice resources to reduce the consumption of illegal drugs but also for unfairly targeting minorities. Indeed, the war on drugs is aimed disproportionately at young African American and Hispanic males residing in low-income neighborhoods (Mauer & Huling, 1995). The war on drugs also is structured around class biases insofar as most drug offenders who ultimately serve prison sentences are members of the lower classes, including the underclass (Irwin & Austin, 1994; Klofas, 1993; Lusane, 1994; Walker, 1994; Welch, 1996a, 1996b; Welch, Bryan, & Wolff, 1999; Welch, Wolff, & Bryan, 1998). Race and class issues are further examined in an upcoming section on the war on drugs and the underclass.

Variant Approaches to Drug Control Policy

Due to the emergence of competing perspectives on the war on drugs, the complexity of the debate over drug control continues to spiral. Paradoxically, however, perspectives on drug control policy do not always conform to traditional ideologies in criminal justice: That is, conservatives and liberals sometimes disagree with their otherwise like-minded peers. Contrary to conventional wisdom, some conservatives (e.g., journalist William F. Buckley, Jr., Nobel economist Milton Friedman, and Former Secretary of State George Schultz) support legalization and/or decriminalization, whereas many liberals continue to endorse the prevailing criminalization approach to drugs along with additional prison construction. In sorting out the diversity of opinion concerning drug control, Zimring and Hawkins (1991) described three schools of thought on drug control policy: public health generalism, legalism, and cost-benefit specificism.

Public health generalists promote the notion that the consumption of psychoactive substances (including alcohol) leads to such problems as greater health treatment costs, time off from work, family problems, and shortened life spans. This perspective focuses on the harmfulness of substances rather than on their legality and views substance abuse as a disease or illness. *Legalism,* on the other hand, focuses not on the personal harm inflicted on the individual but on the social harm inflicted on society. According to this view, the consumption of legally prohibited substances should be sanctioned because such illegal behaviors strain normative boundaries and erode societal cohesion. In terms of *cost-benefit specifism,* "The formulation of drug policy involves balancing both the costs of abuse and the likelihood of reducing them by legal prohibition against the manifold costs of enforcing prohibitive laws" (Zimring & Hawkins, 1991, p. 109).

Four potential elements of drug control strategy (supply reduction, treatment, prevention/education, and decriminalization) make up the larger debate on the war on drugs; accordingly, these competing schools of thought offer perspectives on each of these issues (Zimring & Hawkins, 1991).

SUPPLY REDUCTION

The legalistic perspective, which is endorsed strongly by federal officials in *National Drug Control Strategy* (Office of the National Drug Control Policy, 1996), proposes continued expenditures in law enforcement and interdiction to reduce the supply of illegal drugs on the assumption that the consumption of illegal drugs will decline. Public health generalists disagree with efforts to limit the supply of illegal drugs because nonprohibited drugs (including alcohol) are just as harmful. Unlike public health generalists, cost-benefit specifists do not believe that all substances are equally harmful. Indeed, they contend that cocaine (especially crack), for example, is more harmful than alcohol. (Critics of this perspective, however, argue that because alcohol abuse is more widespread than cocaine abuse, it constitutes a greater social problem.) Accordingly, cost-benefit specifists support efforts to limit those drugs perceived as being more harmful (such as cocaine).

Attempts to reduce the supply of illegal drugs must also be addressed in the context of market forces. Simply put, prices attached to illegal drugs are contingent upon demand and scarcity. Therefore, reducing the supply merely drives up the price of the drug, making trafficking more attractive to those willing to take the risk. According to Wilkins (1994), "The cost [of illegal drugs] is a reflection of the risk, not the type or quality of the product. Thus, we might say that, for the most part, drug pushers are not selling drugs; rather, like insurance companies, they are trading in risk" (p. 151). In light of market forces, Wilkins insisted that if there was no risk in peddling illegal drugs, prices would drop to levels that might fail to attract even legitimate industry.

TREATMENT

Treatment in the context of the criminal justice system troubles some experts because they believe that punishment is at odds with effective rehabilitation and that coercion impedes lasting prosocial changes. Despite this problem, legalists (including proponents of the *National Drug Control Strategy*) endorse treatment programs and recommend that participants be forced or intimidated into treatment. Moreover, upon completion of these programs, participants should be similarly coerced into abstinence by threats of criminal sanctions if they suffer a drug relapse.

Cost-benefit specifists approve of treatment as long as high-risk, active users are enrolled in such programs. From their point of view, treatment will have a greater impact if those who are involved in other crimes (and needle sharing) are targeted. Under such conditions, treatment programs will be getting "more bang for the buck."

PREVENTION AND EDUCATION

Although all of these schools of thought endorses substance abuse prevention campaigns, they differ with regard to the content of preventative/educational messages. Legalists support antidrug propaganda and oppose the dissemination of factual informative messages. "The legalist drug message to children is that illegal drugs are a bad thing and that drug takers are bad people" (Zimring & Hawkins, 1991, p. 122). Popular antidrug slogans, such as Nancy Reagan's imperative "Just Say No!" and "Dope Is for Dopes," come out of this framework.

Critics of antidrug "drugspeak" and symbolic politics, however, describe how language games construct social worlds that do not reflect objective reality (Edelman, 1988; Gordon, 1994a; Zimmer, 1992). "Language games that construct and categorize social problems are called into service for the support of marginal solutions already chosen by elites, reinforcing ideologies and policy trends, and shoring up authority" (Gordon, 1994a, p. 30). Gordon (1994a) argued that antidrug slogans such as "Just Say No" are banal statements that both arouse anxiety and assuage it. Moreover, "drugspeak" as an antidrug semantic serves to legitimate law enforcement as the primary solution to America's drug crisis (Gordon, 1994a, 1994b; Zimmer, 1992). In sum, "Drugspeak provides meaning to social and cultural conservatives and a defense against the small but growing elite movement of drug policy dissidents" (Gordon, 1994a, p. 36; also see Brownstein, 1991; del Olmo, 1991; Herman, 1991; Johns, 1991).

Public health generalists believe that revealing pure information about drugs, including the desirable effects (such as euphoria or the "high") as well as the undesirable effects (withdrawals, physiological damage, etc.), is the most effective way to curb drug use in the long run. They argue that persons who are well educated about legal and illegal drugs are more likely to avoid substance abuse than those who have been subjected to inaccurate or incomplete information concerning drugs. According to Chambliss (1995),

> Decriminalization would also facilitate the accurate dissemination of knowledge about the drugs. Everyone knows the difference between the effects of beer, wine, and whiskey. Possessing this knowledge enables all of us to rationally choose which to drink under what circumstances. Law enforcement propaganda that

lumps all illegal drugs together as equally dangerous makes sensible policies and rational personal decisions impossible. It reinforces the belief on part of potential users that everything they hear about drugs is a big lie. (p. 116)

Similarly, cost-benefit specifists believe that preventative/educational messages can help draw distinctions between extremely harmful drugs (i.e., crack cocaine and injectable heroin, with particular cautions against needle sharing) and less harmful drugs (i.e., marijuana). Expectedly, legalists fear that such messages may appear to condone substance abuse and fall short of chastising those "bad persons" who have used drugs. "From the legalist perspective, this undermines the gospel of absolute abstention from illicit drugs and tends to demoralize the faithful never-users who are the most important target audience of the legalist appeal" (Zimring & Hawkins, 1991, p. 113).

DECRIMINALIZATION

Public health generalists favor decriminalization because it reconceptualizes substance abuse as a public health issue rather than a criminal justice problem. Moreover, it permits us to discuss more openly the harm caused by legal drugs (i.e., alcohol and prescription medication). Because it is likely that differentiation will be made between extremely harmful drugs and less harmful drugs, cost-benefit specifists endorse the decriminalization of less harmful drugs and the continued prohibition of more harmful drugs.

The Netherlands, for instance, continues to demonstrate the utility of alternatives to criminalizing illegal drugs. The Dutch government has decriminalized the use and sale of marijuana and decriminalized (de facto) the possession and sale of small amounts of other drugs, but it heavily regulates marijuana and hashish despite their decriminalization and restricts their use to licensed coffee shops that enforce age eligibility. Moreover, the function of the Dutch police has been redefined to include serving as conduits between drug addicts and treatment services; consequently, there are fewer arrests, trials, and convictions for drug violations. More significantly, evaluation studies of the Dutch policy report that decriminalization has not led to any increase in the use of drugs. In fact, reported drug use among those aged 12 to 17 years (especially secondary school students) is higher in the United States than in the Netherlands. Furthermore, since decriminalization was introduced in the Netherlands, there has been a reduction in the amount of crime associated with drug use and trafficking (Chambliss, 1995; Grapendaal, Leuw, & Nelen, 1992; Vliet, 1990; Wijngaart, 1990).

In the United States, the perspective of the legalists, as spelled out in their manifesto, the *National Drug Control Strategy,* staunchly opposes the reconceptualization of the drug crisis. Rather, legalists promote, with uncritical acceptance, the notion that illegal drugs should remain prohibited. Zimring and Hawkins (1991) captured the vehemence of legalists' rhetoric when they wrote that "proposals to decriminalize are characterized as 'stupid,' 'irrational,' and their purveyors are portrayed as 'naive,' with the same sinister undertones to the adjective that used to be aimed at those who were accused of communist sympathies" (p. 113).

The decriminalization proposal usually draws emotional attacks that attempt to distort the facts at hand. For example, legalists deliberately undermine the dispassionate notions of decriminalization by equating it with "legalization." This ploy often works because the word *legalization* conjures up images of a drug "free-for-all." According to the *National Drug Control Strategy* (Office of the National Drug Control Policy, 1996), the decriminalization of any drug "would be an unqualified national disaster" (p. 7). Moreover, unwavering supporters of the war on drugs take the metaphor of "war" seriously and view decriminalization as admitting defeat or as surrendering to the enemy. Critics, however, point to how crime and drug issues are exploited for political purposes. According to Chambliss (1995), "Politically, crime generally and drugs in particular have been used as a weapon by conservative politicians (Democrat and Republicans) to gain political advantage and strengthen the oppressive apparatus of the state" (p. 113).

Distinguishing between legalization and decriminalization is crucial to our understanding of drug control. The legalization of drugs parallels the regulation of drugs that are currently legal, such as alcohol and tranquilizers. Decriminalization is considered less drastic, insofar as some drug violations (i.e., marijuana possession) would not be subjected to existing punitive sanctions but rather would be considered offenses similar to traffic violations. Consequently, the violator would be given a summons and expected to appear in court and pay a fine. Although advocates of legalization and supporters of decriminalization do not agree on all aspects of drug control policy, they do agree on three basic assumptions:

1. Under legalization, drug use and abuse would not rise beyond current rates.
2. Some illegal drugs are not as harmful as widely believed; indeed, some are less harmful than some legal drugs.

3. The criminalization of drugs produces more problems than benefits (Nadelmann, 1989, 1991).

These assumptions deserve brief clarification. Supporters of legalization/decriminalization assert that simply because a substance is legally available does not mean that those who have not used drugs would begin to do so. Most persons are aware of the health hazards of various substances (alcohol, cigarettes, amphetamines, etc.); accordingly, many choose not to consume these substances. "The image the legalizers have of the so-called average man and woman is that they are reasonable, rational, temperate, measured, and genteel. Large numbers of people are not going to do that which seriously endangers their lives" (Goode, 1993, p. 359). Second, evidence indicates that illegal drugs such as marijuana are less harmful than is widely believed. In fact, because marijuana is not a physically addictive substance, it is less harmful than both alcohol and tobacco, substances known to produce physical addiction in some users.

Finally, the continued criminalization of drugs can be characterized as counterproductive insofar as it contributes to street crime owing to the profit motive. Legalization/decriminalization proposes to eliminate the profit motive from the drug trade, thereby reducing the violence common among drug dealers. Instead of being excessively allocated to the forces of the war on drugs (i.e., law enforcement, courts, corrections), tax dollars could be spent on education, housing, health care, and so forth. (For additional reading on drugs in society, see Goode, 1993, and Musto, 1988; for in-depth analysis of the war on drugs, see Inciardi, 1986, 1992, and Currie, 1993.)

The War on Drugs and the Underclass

It is important to acknowledge the significance of the economic trends that contribute to the growing underclass in the United States, especially economic trends that have led to the erosion of manufacturing jobs that once served as a reliable sources of employment for the urban working class (see Aronowitz & DiFazio, 1994). By definition, members of the underclass are those who have few meaningful economic opportunities and resources available to them for financial survival (Wilson, 1987). Currently, minorities in the inner cities constitute the fastest growing segment of the underclass.

Obviously, not all members of the underclass consume drugs, but for some residents of low-income neighborhoods, drug use is driven by the desire to escape harsh living conditions, including feelings of alienation that stem from a sense of not having a future, as well as feelings of hopelessness and defeat. According to Rosenbaum (1989), "The drug abuse of the underclass is a *symptom* of a much deeper problem faced by tens of millions of individuals with blocked opportunities and severely limited life options" (p. 18).

For many inner-city drug peddlers, selling drugs is an attempt to modify their bleak existence. Earning cash through drug dealing enables peddlers to purchase status-enhancing commodities (e.g., trendy clothes, jewelry, and luxury and sports cars, to name just a few) as well as to buy drugs for their own consumption (see Spitzer, 1975). Indeed, many drug peddlers are viewed by some experts as merely exercising one of just a few economic options available to them; moreover, their willingness to engage in risky drug dealing typically stems from their own perception that they have little or nothing to lose. By contrast, persons with meaningful jobs, intact families, and other social ties are less likely to engage in risky conduct (i.e., drug trafficking) than those who have less stake in society.

With scant recognition of the root causes of drug use in the inner city, local, state, and federal authorities have accelerated the war on drugs in low-income neighborhoods (see Chambliss, 1994, 1995). Contrary to "drugspeak" rhetoric, the war on drugs is waged less against the so-called "kingpins" than against low-level drug violators, who are typically minority and poor and have few resources to defend themselves legally against ambitious law enforcement campaigns. Walker, Spohn, and DeLone (1996) reminded us that drug enforcement campaigns contribute to the disproportionate numbers of African Americans in corrections because police target minority communities, where drug dealing is more visible and it is easier to make arrests (also see Lynch & Patterson, 1996; Tonry, 1995).

Although the war on drugs has not reduced the supply or consumption of illegal drugs, it is "successful" insofar as it boasts an increase in arrests and convictions, thereby fueling the correctional-industrial complex (see Christie, 1993). "Success" in the war on drugs also contributes to a booming minority population within corrections (see Klofas, 1993; Lusane, 1994). As noted in the previous chapter, the number of African American men in corrections has grown dramatically since 1990, when one in four men in their 20s were incarcerated or under some form of correctional supervision (Mauer, 1990); in 1995, that ratio was adjusted to *one in three* (Mauer & Huling, 1995).

In 1996, the rate among black males was 3,098 prisoners per 100,000 residents, compared to 1,278 among Hispanic males and 370 among white males (all age groups included). For those aged 25 to 29 years, 8.3% of black males were in prison in 1996, compared to 2.6% of Hispanic males and about

0.8% of white males. Overall, drug offenders accounted for 30% of the growth among blacks, 23% among Hispanics, and 16% among whites (Bureau of Justice Statistics, 1998b).

Critical criminologists deplore the institutional biases of the American criminal justice system, which assigns disparate penalties for similar drug offenses. One of the most blatant institutional biases in American criminal justice is the discrepancy between penalties for crack versus powdered cocaine. Such an institutional bias indeed draws greater attention to egregious forms of racism and classism in American criminal justice (Welch, 1998). In October 1995, prisoner disturbances erupted in five federal correctional facilities. Some observers believe that the uprisings were in reaction to the congressional vote favoring the imposition of harsher punishments for possession of crack cocaine than for powdered cocaine. Such legislation has a disproportionate impact on impoverished African American offenders, especially compared to their white, middle-class counterparts. This is particularly true because crack is more prevalent among inner-city African American drug users, whereas powdered cocaine is more prevalent in the middle-class suburbs and its users are more evenly divided racially (see Jones, 1995; Smothers, 1995).

Many experts conclude that the pharmacological differences between crack and powdered cocaine are negligible. Nevertheless, legislators who support tougher sanctions for crack argue that the nature of the crack traffic invites greater violence and gang activity. However, critics disagree, insisting that the policy is unfair, impractical, and perhaps in the end profoundly racist. Laura Murphy of the American Civil Liberties Union asked, "How can you go to an inner-city family and tell them their son is given 20 years, while someone in the suburbs who's using powdered cocaine can get off with 90 days probation?" (Jones, 1995, p. A-1). According to the Bureau of Justice Statistics (1995), the average federal sentence in 1994 for trafficking crack was 133 months in prison, whereas the trafficking of powdered cocaine drew an average of 94 months.

Ironically, Congress legislated against the recommendations of the U.S. Sentencing Commission, which proposed that violations of crack and powdered cocaine be subject to *equal* penalties. Under current federal law, a conviction of possession or distribution of 5 grams of crack cocaine would draw a mandatory 5-year sentence with no parole. By contrast, someone would have to possess or distribute 500 grams of the more expensive powdered cocaine to get the same sentence, thereby establishing a 100-to-1 ratio. Currently, 14,000 of the 90,000 federal prisoners are serving sentences under these laws for crack cocaine offenses (U.S. Sentencing Commission, 1995).

Paul Martin, deputy staff director for the U.S. Sentencing Commission, points out that crack is the only drug that carries a mandatory prison term for possession, whether or not the intent is to distribute. By contrast, possession of heroin or powdered cocaine without intent to sell is a misdemeanor carrying a maximum of 1 year in jail (Jones, 1995).

The Bureau of Justice Statistics (1995) reported that although half of crack users are white, the sale and use of the substance (a cheaper form of cocaine) is often concentrated in impoverished inner-city neighborhoods where minorities are overrepresented. Moreover, the bureau also found that in 1994, 90% of those convicted of federal crack offenses were African American and 3.5% were white. By contrast, 25.9% of those convicted on federal powdered cocaine violations were white, 29.7% were African American, and 42.8% were Hispanic.

According to Scott Wallace of the National Legal Aid and Defender Association, "Part of what amazes a lot of us is that Congress and the President are rejecting the recommendation of a body that was set up precisely to remove politics and snap judgments from the sentencing process so there isn't discrimination" (Smothers, 1995, p. A-18). In light of the crack controversy, perhaps one can concede critical criminology's assertion that the American criminal justice system sets out to incarcerate lower-class offenders with greater fanfare than middle- (and upper-) class offenders.

Substance Abuse Treatment in Corrections

Substance abuse histories are prevalent among a large proportion of inmates. The Bureau of Justice Statistics (1998a) reported that among jail inmates, 55% had used drugs in the month before the offense and 36% used drugs at the time of the offense. Moreover, 6 in 10 convicted jail inmates reported being under the influence of drugs or alcohol at the time of their offense. Similarly, in 30% of violent crime victimizations, victims reported that they believed their assailants were under the influence of drugs or alcohol (Bureau of Justice Statistics, 1995).

In light of the immediate need for substance abuse intervention, questions persist about how the problem is actually being tackled in corrections. Prisons may offer many types of drug intervention or treatment: detoxification, counseling, education and or awareness programs, urine surveillance, and treatment in special residential units within the facilities (Bureau of Justice Statistics, 1995). Although political leaders often allude to the importance of substance abuse treatment, overall most programs are insufficiently funded. Without adequate funding for substance abuse treatment, it is unlikely that intervention will translate into promoting prosocial and law-abiding lives on the part of its participants. This is especially true for drug offenders who return to inner-city neighborhoods where poverty, chronic unemployment, and violence as well as drugs await them.

Substance abuse treatment for drug violators continues to retain the moral support of most citizens; however, financial support on the part of the government is lacking. Inadequate funding for substance abuse treatment programs in both corrections and the community is compounded by government cutbacks in social programs. The contradiction apparent here is that substance abuse programs are not only cheaper than idle incarceration but also cost-effective. From almost every possible angle, making substance abuse treatment readily accessible for persons in and outside of the criminal justice system makes good sense (see Welch, 1995).

Several noteworthy programs claim significant success in treating drug-addicted offenders, including the Stayin' Out Program (New York), the Lantana Program (Florida), and the Cornerstone Program (Oregon). Similar substance abuse programs are incorporated into unique correctional programs, such as the military-style correctional boot camps (known as shock incarceration or high-impact programs) in New York State and New York City.

In correctional facilities, substance abuse treatment programs are known by different titles, and the content and focus of each program are often determined by the host institution. Despite their differences, however, many treatment programs resemble one another by addressing the various dimensions of substance abuse. For example, the Federal Correctional Institution (FCI) at Fort Worth, Texas, is regarded as one of the most heavily programmed institutions in the federal prison system. At the Ft. Worth FCI, the Chemical Abuse Program (CAP) was designed to meet the individual needs of inmates who have been identified as having problems with drugs or alcohol or both (Welch, Ford, & Mabli, 1988). In fact, this determination is often made before sentencing when the judge reviews the offender's pre-sentence investigation (PSI) report: The PSI report identifies problem areas that, ideally, should be addressed while serving a prison sentence.

One objective of the FCI Ft. Worth CAP program is to determine the severity of the inmate's chemical abuse history, thereby placing the inmate at the appropriate treatment level. The structure of the program includes such treatment modalities as drug education, health and wellness, nutrition, chemical abuse and its implications for the family, values and decisions, Rational

Behavior Therapy, stress management, Alcoholics Anonymous, and Narcotics Anonymous (Welch et al., 1988).

In 1987, the U.S. Department of Justice's Bureau of Justice Assistance funded the development of three model demonstration jail substance abuse treatment programs. One of these programs is the Hillsborough County Sheriff's Office Substance Abuse Treatment Program in Tampa, Florida. In their evaluation of the Hillsborough program, Peters, Kearns, Murrin, Dolente, and May (1993) found that over a 1-year period following release from custody, inmates participating in the 6-week jail treatment program "remained significantly longer in the community until rearrest, experienced fewer arrests, and served less jail time in comparison to a group of untreated inmates" (p. 2). The assessment team also revealed that program participants exhibited coping skills in responding to high-risk situations that might have led to a drug relapse. In light of the program's success, the assessment team also emphasized the importance of aftercare. Indeed, "Specialized efforts are required to insure that these individuals continue in treatment, seek and maintain employment, and are involved in other activities such as vocational training and support groups" (p. 33).

In addition to the need for aftercare following institutional substance abuse treatment, experts remind us of the importance of formulating evaluation techniques that can improve our understanding of the treatment process. For instance, Scarpitti, Inciardi, and Pottieger (1993) insisted that our knowledge about substance abuse treatment ought to go beyond whether particular forms of intervention succeed or fail; in fact, it is just as important to discover *why* and *how* such programs succeed or fail. By taking into account various process factors of substance abuse treatment (e.g., the political, economic, and social environment of the program; the people and institutions involved in establishing the program; the clinical staff of the program), evaluators can more accurately appraise the scope and impact of the intervention. In sum, "An evaluation allows us to know why and how a program is working, how it fits into and is influenced by the social, political and economic contexts within which it operates, and how it may be replicated to operate with equal or greater success elsewhere" (p. 79).

It ought to be emphasized that most treatment programs extend beyond the use of illegal drugs to include treatment for alcohol abuse as well. Not only does alcohol abuse overlap with other forms of drug use, but its link to violent crime is well documented: The Johnson Foundation (1993) reported that alcohol use is involved in two-thirds of homicides and serious assaults (also see Gentry, 1995). Similarly, the Bureau of Justice Statistics (1998b) reported that more than 40% of jail inmates committed their offense under the influence of alcohol. (For more discussion on alcohol and drug rehabilitation in the criminal justice system, see Pallone, 1993.)

Conclusion

Perhaps now more than ever, the nation has become a criminal justice-oriented society insofar as government and citizens alike expect the police, the courts, and corrections to solve many of society's persistent problems. Indeed, the list of expectations imposed on the criminal justice system continues to expand, ranging from duties directly related to law enforcement, such as protecting citizens from violence, to those less related to law enforcement, such as removing society's outcasts (e.g., streetwalking prostitutes and the homeless) from so-called respectable sections of our cities (Welch, 1994). It is in this social context that the criminal justice system is expected to solve America's drug crisis.

Whereas it is reasonable to rely on police to guard citizens against the violence associated with drugs, critics question whether nonviolent drug addicts should be processed into the criminal justice system. Because nonviolent drug violations (i.e., possession) are victimless crimes, it is suggested that the criminal justice system refer these lawbreakers to social, not criminal justice, agencies. Medicalizing drug addiction makes treatment, not punishment, the goal of intervention. However, the dominant model of drug control is still based on punishment, and in some progressive jurisdictions, punishment is accompanied by a mild commitment to treatment (Lesieur & Welch, 1991, 1995).

Still, America's drug crisis will not be contained by reliance solely on treatment either. Wide-scale substance abuse essentially is a symptom of deeper social problems. Therefore, any attempt to deal with America's drug crisis without addressing social and racial inequality leading to poverty, unemployment (underemployment), substandard education, and inaccessible health care is doomed to fail. For more than 40 years, researchers have confirmed that endemic drug abuse is strongly associated with mass deprivation, economic marginality, and cultural and community breakdown (Clear, 1994; Currie, 1993). According to Currie (1993), the quality of life for many Americans continues to spiral down. Just as significant, this decline has occurred without a sense that life will get better. As life for many members of society's lower classes become bleaker and more stressful, the rewards of consuming and selling drugs become more tempting. For treatment to maintain long-term effectiveness, it has to be coupled with realistic possibilities for an alternative way of life. For drug intervention to achieve lasting effectiveness, work programs leading to viable employment must be linked to substance abuse treatment (see Welch, 1995; Welch et al., 1999).

References

Aronowitz, S., & DiFazio, W. (1994). *The jobless future: Sci-tech and the dogma of work.* Minneapolis: University of Minnesota Press.
Brownstein, H. (1991). The media and the construction of random drug violence. *Social Justice, 18,* 85-103.
Bureau of Justice Statistics. (1995). *Drugs and crime facts, 1994.* Washington, DC: U.S. Department of Justice.
Bureau of Justice Statistics. (1998a). *Prisoners in 1997.* Washington, DC: U.S. Department of Justice.
Bureau of Justice Statistics. (1998b). *Profile of jail inmates. 1996.* Washington, DC: U.S. Department of Justice.
Chambliss, W. J. (1994). Policing the ghetto underclass: The politics of law and law enforcement. *Social Problems, 41,* 177-194.
Chambliss, W. J. (1995). Another lost war: The costs and consequences of drug prohibition. *Social Justice, 22*(2), 101-124.
Christie, N. (1993). *Crime control as industry.* Oslo: University-flag.
Clear, T. R. (1994). *Harm in American penology: Offenders, victims, and their communities.* Albany: State University of New York Press.
Currie, E. (1993). *Reckoning: Drugs, the cities, and the American future.* New York: Hill & Wang.
del Olmo, R. (1991). The hidden face of drugs. *Social Justice, 18*(4), 10-48.
Edelman, M. (1988). *Constructing the political spectacle.* Chicago: University of Chicago Press.
Forer, L. G. (1994). *A rage to punish: The unintended consequences of mandatory sentencing.* New York: Norton.
Gentry, C. (1995). Crime control through drug control. In J. Sheley (Ed.), *Criminology: A contemporary handbook* (pp. 477-493). Belmont, CA: Wadsworth.
Goode, E. (1993). *Drugs in American society* (4th ed.). New York: McGraw-Hill.
Gordon, D. (1994a). Drugspeak and the Clinton administration: A lost opportunity for drug policy reform. *Social Justice, 21*(3), 30-36.
Gordon, D. (1994b). *The return of the dangerous classes: Drug prohibition and policy politics.* New York: Norton.
Grapendaal, M., Leuw, E., & Nelen, H. (1992). Drugs and crime in an accommodating social context: The situation in Amsterdam. *Contemporary Drug Problems, 19,* 303-326.
Herman, E. S. (1991). Drug "wars": Appearance and reality. *Social Justice, 18*(4), 76-84.
Inciardi, J. A. (1986). *The war on drugs.* Palo Alto, CA: Mayfield.
Inciardi, J. A. (1992). *The war on drugs II.* Mountain View, CA: Mayfield.
Irwin, J., & Austin, J. (1994). *It's about time: America's imprisonment binge.* Belmont, CA: Wadsworth.
Johns, C. (1991). The war on drugs: Why the administration continues to pursue a policy of criminalization and enforcement, *Social Justice, 18,* 147-165,

Johnson Foundation. (1993). *Substance abuse: The nation's no. 1 health problem.* Princeton, NJ: Author.
Jones, C. (1995, October 28). Crack and punishment: Is race the issue? *New York Times,* pp. A-1, A-10.
Klofas, J. M. (1993). Drugs and justice: The impact of drugs on criminal justice in a metropolitan community. *Crime and Delinquency, 39,* 204-224.
Lesieur, H., & Welch, M. (1991). Public disorder and social control. In J. Sheley (Ed.), *Criminology: A contemporary handbook* (pp. 175-198). Belmont, CA: Wadsworth.
Lesieur, H., & Welch, M. (1995). Vice crimes: Individual choices and social controls. In J. Sheley (Ed.), *Criminology: A contemporary handbook* (2nd ed., pp. 200-247). Belmont, CA: Wadsworth.
Lusane, C. (1994). *Pipe dream blues: Racism and the war on drugs.* Boston: South End.
Lynch, M., & Patterson, E. B. (Eds.). (1996). *Justice with prejudice: Race and criminal justice in America.* New York: Harrow & Heston.
Mauer, M. (1990). *Young black men and the criminal justice system.* Washington, DC: Sentencing Project.
Mauer, M., & Huling, T. (1995). *Young black Americans and the criminal justice system: Five years later.* Washington, DC: Sentencing Project.
Musto, D. F. (1988). *The American disease: Origins of narcotic control* (2nd ed.). New York: Oxford University Press.
Nadelmann, E. (1989, September 1). Drug prohibition in the United States: Costs, consequences, and alternatives. *Science, 245,* 939-947.
Nadelmann, E. (1991). The case for legalization. In J. Inciardi (Ed.), *The drug legalization debate* (pp. 17-43). Newbury Park, CA: Sage.
Office of the National Drug Control Policy. (1996). *National drug control strategy,* Washington, DC: Government Printing Office.
Pallone, N. (Ed.). (1993). Alcohol and drug rehabilitation [Special issue]. *Journal of Offender Rehabilitation,* 19(3/4).
Peters, R. H., Kearns, W. D., Murrin, M. R., Dolente, A. S., & May, R. L., II. (1993). Examining the effectiveness of in-jail substance abuse treatment. *Journal of Offender Rehabilitation, 19*(3/4), 1-40.
Rosenbaum, M. (1989). *Just say what? An alternative view on solving America's drug problem.* San Francisco: National Council on Crime and Delinquency.
Scarpitti, F. R., Inciardi, J. A., & Pottieger, A. E. (1993). Process evaluation techniques for corrections-based drug treatment programs. *Journal of Offender Rehabilitation, 19*(3/4), 71-80.
Smolowe, J. (1994, February 7). And throw away the key. *Time,* pp. 55-59.
Smothers, R. (1995, October 24). Wave of prison uprisings provoke debate on crack, *New York Times,* p. A-18.
Spitzer, S. (1975). Toward a Marxian theory of deviance. *Social Problems, 22,* 638-651.
Tonry, M. (1995). *Benign neglect.* New York: Oxford University Press.
U.S. Sentencing Commission. (1995). *Report on penalties for crack and powdered cocaine.* Washington, DC: Author.
Vliet, H. (1990). Separation of drug markets and the normalization of drug problems in the Netherlands: An example for other countries? *Journal of Drug Issues, 20,* 436-471.
Walker, S. (1994). *Sense and nonsense about crime and drugs: A policy guide* (3rd ed.). Belmont, CA: Wadsworth.
Walker, S., Spohn, C., & DeLone, M. (1996). *The color of justice: Race, ethnicity, and crime in America.* Belmont, CA: Wadsworth.

Welch, M. (1994). Jail overcrowding: Social sanitation and the warehousing of the urban underclass. In A. Roberts (Ed.), *Critical issues in crime and justice* (pp. 251-276). Newbury Park, CA: Sage.

Welch, M. (1995). Rehabilitation: Holding its ground in corrections. *Federal Probation: A Journal of Correctional Philosophy and Practice, 59*(4), 3-8.

Welch, M. (1996a). *Corrections: A critical approach.* New York: McGraw-Hill.

Welch, M. (1996b). Race and social class in the examination of punishment. In M. Lynch & E. Patterson (Eds.), *Justice with prejudice: Race and criminal justice in America* (pp. 156-169). New York: Harrow & Heston.

Welch, M. (1998). Critical criminology, social control, and an alternative view of corrections. In J. Ross (Ed.), *Cutting the edge: Current perspectives in radical critical criminology and criminal justice* (pp. 107-121). Westport, CT: Praeger.

Welch, M, Bryan, N., & Wolff, R. (1999). Just war theory and drug control policy: Militarization, mortality, and the war on drugs. *Contemporary Justice Review, 2*(1), 49-76.

Welch, M., Ford, T. E., & Mabli, J. (1988, August). *Inmates' attitudes toward substance abuse and the limitations of programs and their evaluation.* Paper presented at the annual meeting of the Society for the Study of Social Problems, Atlanta.

Welch, M., Wolff, R., & Bryan, N. (1998). Decontextualizing the war on drugs: A context analysis of NIJ publications and their neglect of race and class. *Justice Quarterly, 15,* 601-624.

Wijngaart, G. (1990). The Dutch approach: Normalization of drug problems. *Journal of Drug Issues, 20,* 667-678.

Wilkins, L. T. (1994). Don't alter your mind—It's the world that's out of joint. *Social Justice, 21*(3), 148-153.

Wilson, W. J. (1987). *The truly disadvantaged.* Chicago: University of Chicago Press.

Zimmer, L. (1992, October). *The anti-drug semantic.* Paper presented at the Drug Policy Foundation Conference, Washington, DC.

Zimring, F. E., & Hawkins, G. (1991). What kind of drug war? *Social Justice, 18*(4), 104-121.

CHAPTER 5

Regulating the Reproduction and Morality of Women

The Social Control of Body and Soul

The American correctional system remains a male-dominated enterprise, partly because men constitute nearly 94% of the inmate population, but more importantly because men occupy the positions of power that determine the course of punishment in society. Men, particularly white middle- and upper-class men, dominate government, the judiciary, and the legal profession, as well as criminal justice administration and personnel. Therefore, from every conceivable angle, the policies and strategies of corrections emerge from male-dominated perspectives about crime and punishment.

This chapter explores punitive strategies designed to regulate the reproduction and morality of women. In doing so, it examines political, economic,

---

AUTHOR'S NOTE: Adapted with permission from *Women and Criminal Justice*, 9(1), 1997. ©1997 by The Haworth Press, Inc. All rights reserved. I gratefully acknowledge Marie Mark, Laura Colatrella, Jeanne Flavin, and Cynthia B. Dailard (National Women's Law Center) as well as the ACLU Reproductive Freedom Project for their assistance. I also appreciate the constructive comments offered by the anonymous reviewers.

religious/moral, and especially technological forces in the context of gendered social control. Beginning with a historical view of the punishment of female lawbreakers, it offers a critique of traditional theories of female criminality, especially in light of renewed interest in positivistic biological notions of female crime. Similarly, various applications of androcentric positivism are discussed, particularly those addressing the effects of premenstrual syndrome (PMS) and fetal (drug) abuse. In addition to explaining how these technological developments contribute to repressive mechanisms of gendered social control, the chapter directs attention to the controversy over Norplant as a form of coercive contraception.

A Historical Note on "Correcting" Wayward Women

A prominent theme in the history of women and punishment is the persistent emphasis on regulating female morality (see Faith, 1993). Compared to their male counterparts, women engaging in deviant or criminal behavior are viewed as more depraved and morally corrupt. This biased perception has historically generated more extensive forms of social control for women than for men. Fidelity, obedience, and other aspects of conventional morality were closely monitored by earlier European as well as colonial societies. For example, women accused of adultery, as well as those critical of men (or spreading gossip), were subjected to various punishments specifically designed for women, such as the brank and the ducking stool.

Similarly, men could be punished for not properly disciplining their wives. Husbands of disobedient women, for instance, were publicly humiliated by the "cuckold's court"—a degradation ceremony that forced men to ride backward on a donkey (Burford & Schulman, 1992; Dobash, Dobash, & Gutteridge, 1986). This spectacle was intended to embarrass the husband, thereby reinforcing the traditional belief that the social order required men to discipline and control women.

In the early 1800s, women prisoners became the concern of key European reformers, most notably Elizabeth Fry. As noted in *Observations on the Siting, Superintendence and Government of Female Prisoners* (1825), Fry advocated the improvement of institutional conditions as well as the development of programs based on promoting discipline, work, training, religion, and routine. Fry's approach to corrections emphasized femininity by teaching women prisoners manners and etiquette in efforts to transform them into traditional "ladies." Fry recommended women warders instead of male guards because, among other things, they served as role models for "true womanhood" (cited in Freedman, 1974). In America, similar reforms of female prisons began in the 1820s through the 1870s. Houses of refuge were established for wayward women, providing religious instruction, education, and discipline. In addition, wayward women were immersed in domestic chores to instill a greater sense of femininity, humility, and obedience (Barnes & Teeters, 1946; Freedman, 1981).

A Critique of Traditional Female Criminology

Men not only have dictated the practice of punishment throughout history but have dominated criminology, creating a masculine view of crime. Indeed, "Theoretical criminology was constructed by men, about men" (Leonard, 1982, p. xi). As a form of male-dominated science, criminology has been criticized for being patriarchal because it casts women as submissive to men. In criticizing traditional criminology, feminists argue that prevailing theories of crime are androcentric (male centered). Among the problems with patriarchal and androcentric criminology is its failure to comprehend adequately women in crime.

In the late 19th century, criminological theory set out to distinguish male criminality from its female counterpart. Initial attempts to explain the differences between male and female criminality were rooted in positivism. Positivist criminology is based on the pioneering work of Cesare Lombroso (1835-1909), who emulated the natural sciences in an effort to elevate the academic status of criminology. As an emerging form of empirical criminology, positivist criminology set out to pinpoint the source of crime in personal characteristics (such as biological and psychological defects, including low intelligence and insanity) as well as adverse social conditions (such as poverty). Interestingly, however, under positivism a biological orientation continued to dominate research in female criminality long after its demise in the study of male criminality (see Lombroso & Ferrero, 1894/1920; Pollak, 1950). Moreover, in extreme forms, traditional theories reflected misogynist views of women in that female lawbreakers were depicted as more defective and immoral than male lawbreakers (see Faith, 1993; Welch, 1996).

Although biological determinism was viewed as state-of-the-art science in the late 19th and early 20th century, its portrayal of women continued to be drawn from late medieval times:

> The message was that all women were by nature susceptible to deviancy, and it was up to men to domesticate women and to keep them under control and in service. None of the early criminologists gave women credit for rational human agency; that is, they viewed women as victims of the normal-pathologized female body. (Faith, 1993, p. 44)

Even when women were depicted in a sympathetic light (e.g., as "victims" instead of representations of evil), they were still condescendingly viewed as biologically determined to be betrayed by their own bodies. Such patronizing portrayals of women conveniently justified the patriarchy. Thus, it seems that as modern science "advances," it does not entirely abandon medieval images of women.

Until recently, criminologists tended to adhere to one of two theoretical models of female criminality. The first theory was social determinism, which advocated sterilization and lengthy periods of confinement for female offenders so they would not breed future criminals. The second theory pointed to the influence that "bad" men have on "weak" women. That is, female criminals were essentially viewed as victims of manipulative men and consequently as unable to take control over their own lives. Accordingly, treatment specialists advocated improving moral and social habits that would enable women to attract "good" men (Freedman, 1981). Regardless of the differences between these competing theories, both were based on sexist stereotypes, depicting women in condescending and patronizing terms.

PMS and the Return of Androcentric Positivism

Karlene Faith (1993) reminds us that the earliest "theories" of female crime were transmitted through biblical authorities, including St. Paul and St. Augustine. Yet religious interpretations of female crime and misconduct also were channeled through biological perspectives that equated the female body with sin, particularly in the realm of sexuality. Moreover, during the emergence of institutional Christianity, clerics often borrowed from earlier pagan notions of women by insinuating that the female body was cursed. However, whereas the earliest versions of biological theories of female behavior were contextualized in religious and moral terms, modern theories of biological determinism tend to be compelled more by secular forces—namely, "neutral" science and "benevolent" politics. Regardless, the result is the same: Women are marginalized by being reduced to "their unruly bodies and irrational emotions" (Faith, 1993, p. 45; also see Kendall, 1992, p. 139).

At the turn of the century, well-established researchers continued to view female crime according to biological perspectives, especially in reference to menstruation. Havelock Ellis was one such figure; he proclaimed in 1904 that "whenever a woman has committed any offence against the law, it is essential that the relation of the act to her monthly cycle should be ascertained as a matter of routine" (quoted in Zedner, 1991, p. 87).

More recently, a renewed interest in positivistic female biology emerged in the 1980s. Crime specialists, borrowing from the psychiatric community, formulated contemporary theories of female criminality based on premenstrual syndrome (PMS). In fact, the American Psychiatric Association (APA) contributed to a recent wave of biological determinism by including PMS, under the name of *late luteal phase dysphoric disorder,* in the APA's *Diagnostic and Statistical Manual of Mental Disorders* in 1987. Here, the APA, as a "neutral" scientific authority, catalogued PMS along with other mental disorders and diseases (see Kendall, 1992).

Interpreting PMS in a broader social context, Faith (1993) pointed out the importance of law and the scientific (especially medical) establishment in forming contemporary notions of PMS.

> Independently and in collusion, the discourses of law and medicine are grounded in sex/gender power relations, and within a political economy in which women are subordinate. . . . Medicine provides the scientific framework within which female subordination is ideologically justified and law supplies the mechanism. (Faith, 1993, p. 45)

Similarly, Stoppard (1992) highlighted the ideological dimensions of PMS in that sexist beliefs about women and their bodies masquerade as scientific knowledge.

Criminological PMS theories, as a form of androcentric positivism, rest on the assumption that women are prone to "acting out" violently and engaging in bizarre behavior during critical stages of their menstrual cycle. Although the debate over the relationship between PMS and crime continues, Rittenhouse (1991) offered reasons why biological theories about female criminality have become popular once again.

Cultural context and dramatic events, according to Rittenhouse, promote the introduction of PMS as a plausible theory of crime. The prevailing cultural context promotes sexist beliefs that women are prone to losing control over their behavior as a result of PMS. This belief was formally advanced by the dramatic events of British trials in which two women charged with manslaughter blamed PMS in their defense. In the early 1980s, the British "courts reduced to manslaughter the sentences of two women charged with murder on the grounds that severe PMS reduced their capacity to control their behavior" (Rittenhouse, 1991, p. 413). The defendants in these cases were given medical diversion on the grounds that their violent acts were brought on by premenstrual tension, thereby contributing to "diminished responsibility" (see *R. v. Craddock,* 1981; *R. v. English,* 1981). Interestingly, in Canada, the PMS defense is listed in the insanity provision of the *Criminal Code* (CC § 16(2), R.S.C. 1985) (Osborne, 1989). Thus, in essence, gynecological "disorders" have the potential to offer compelling legal defenses (i.e., diminished capacity) because PMS is considered to be a form of insanity.

In this vein, we should not overlook the etymology of *hysteria*, "a psychiatric condition variously characterized by emotional excitability, excessive anxiety, and sensory and motor disturbances" (*Webster's New Twentieth Century Dictionary,* 1983, p. 898). The term *hysteria* derives from the Greek *hystera*, meaning the uterus or womb and is synonymous with uncontrollable fits of laughing or crying. More significantly, the term *hysterical* is traced to the Greek *hysterikos,* "suffering in the uterus: because women seemed to be hysterical more than men, hysteria was attributed by the ancients to disturbances of the uterus" (*Webster's,* 1983, p. 898). As recently as 1970, Goldenson wrote in *The Encyclopedia of Human Behavior*:

> Most hysterical personalities are women. Studies indicate that they have usually been overprotected and spoiled in childhood, and their dramatic behavior is more or less consciously adopted to attract attention or get their way. When faced with frustration, they are likely to throw a temper tantrum or put on a violent scene. And when others ignore or outdo them, they regain the center stage by having a fainting spell or making a scene in some other way.
>
> Many of these women are provocative and exhibitionistic with men, but their purpose is to make a conquest rather than to establish a deeper (or even sexual) relationship with them. (Goldenson, 1970, p. 588)

As a medical, psychiatric, and legal construct, PMS strips women of their dignity and individual responsibility. Faith (1993) reported a British Columbia case in which the provincial supreme court denied a woman custody of her child because the court ruled that PMS diminished her effectiveness as a parent

(*Babcock v. Babcock,* 1986). In the United States, a judge acquitted a dentist accused of rape and sodomy after the defendant held that "the plaintiff had reported the incident during a period of premenstrual irrationality" (Kendall, 1992, p. 132).

Similarly, in several Canadian cases, women have been acquitted or sentenced to compulsory treatment for assault and shoplifting because the defendants claimed that PMS compelled them to commit crime (Kendall, 1992). Many experts, however, dispute the validity of the PMS theory of crime, questioning, among other things, methodological procedures such as unreliable self-reports (Morris, 1987). Yet it is just as important to take into consideration the cultural context that facilitates such *scientistic*—as opposed to scientific—reasoning. Undoubtedly, there is still strong social resistance against women seeking equality, and one of the primary means of opposing the upward mobility of women is to question their competency. Hence, the belief that women experience diminished responsibility while suffering from PMS serves to marginalize women. Certainly, pleading the PMS defense serves a woman's immediate interests, "but it is dubious whether becoming captive of the medical and psychiatric professions is less punitive than criminal incarceration" (Faith, 1993, p. 47). Technological forces, indeed, have made compulsory treatment (especially in the form of involuntary commitment and forced medication) a more insidious form of social control than conventional penalties administered by the courts (see Lesieur & Welch, 1995; Welch, 1996).

In sum, PMS, as a form of androcentric positivism, medicalizes female crime by securing nonmedical societal conditions that women experience, particularly adverse conditions perpetuated by sexism, discrimination, and inequality (Faith, 1993; Kendall, 1992; Stoppard, 1992). The question remains why so much attention is focused on the relatively few violent incidents committed by women when the vast majority of violence is committed by men. In effect, PMS theories of female crime are functional because they conveniently divert attention from two pressing social issues: inequality and violence committed by men.

The Criminalization of Fetal (Drug) Abuse

One of the several functions of the "war on drugs" is to portray illegal drug users as immoral or evil. Indeed, perhaps the most unpopular and sensational targets of the "war on drugs" are pregnant women who use illegal drugs.

Pregnant addicts are depicted as "bad" or "unfit" mothers willing to endanger their child's health in pursuit of a self-indulgent high. Harming innocent children, especially through the use of illegal drugs, arouses intense public anger. Moreover, from a logistical stance, pregnant addicts serve as prime targets for the criminalization of drugs because they constitute "a group that is easy to identify, dislike, and control" (Gustavsson, 1991).

The emergence of fetal (drug) abuse began in the late 1980s when stories of babies born to crack-addicted mothers reported that they had significantly lower birth weights, had smaller heads, suffered seizures, and exhibited more behavioral aberrations than babies born to drug-free women. Without waiting for additional research to validate the claims that crack was *solely* responsible for these complications, the mass media generated countless stories about crack babies. These messages were employed by political leaders to bolster the "war on drugs"—in fact, government officials frequently cited crack babies and fetal (drug) abuse as further justification to accelerate antidrug efforts (see Inciardi, Lockwood, & Pottieger, 1993).

Interestingly, however, statements made by government officials, newspaper editors, and other influential figures concerning crack babies were more than exaggerated; they were simply false. While serving as federal drug "czar," William Bennett declared that each year (in the late 1980s) more than 375,000 crack babies were born in the United States. However, a careful examination of that figure suggests that crack babies would have accounted for 1 out of 10 of all births. Not only was Bennett's claim patently false, but reputable newspaper columnists Jack Anderson and *New York Times* editor A. M. Rosenthal did their readers a disservice by uncritically publishing the falsehood (Gieringer, 1990; Goode, 1993).

Had government officials and other interested parties waited for further studies to ascertain the precise impact that crack has on pregnancy, they would have learned that previous research lacked crucial methodological safeguards, most importantly controls. As Goode (1993) pointed out, many of these women also drank alcohol, and those who drank heavily were at high risk to give birth to infants suffering from fetal alcohol syndrome and fetal alcohol effects. Significantly, the nutrition of these women was poor, and many of them smoked cigarettes (a carcinogen also linked to low birth weight). Further, these women had received virtually no prenatal care, and many had also contracted sexually transmitted diseases. As Goode (1993) noted, "Factors that vary with cocaine use are known to determine poorer infant outcomes; mothers who smoke crack and use powdered cocaine are more likely to engage in *other* behaviors that correlate with poor infant health" (p. 56). Therefore, it is difficult to determine exactly what effect crack has on the fetus when evidence of other toxins (alcohol, nicotine, etc.) and risky behaviors are also present.

This is *not* to suggest that crack does not adversely affect the health of the mother and infant. However, to sound the alarm of crack babies without mentioning the influence of other contributing factors is socially irresponsible and politically manipulative. "Even from the beginning, some experts challenged the veracity of the crack-baby syndrome. But it was not until the early 1990s that enough medical evidence was assembled to indicate that the syndrome is, in all likelihood, mythical in nature" (Goode, 1993, p. 56; see also Coles, 1991; Day, Richardson, & McGauhey, 1992; Neuspiel, Hamel, Berg, Greene, & Campbell, 1991; Richardson, 1992; Richardson & Day, 1991). Although the early hype surrounding the emergence of crack babies was headline news, later research findings disputing the alleged syndrome have not been as well publicized.

Regardless of the most recent developments in research on crack babies, support for the arrest and prosecution of pregnant women who use illegal drugs continues. Indeed, advocates of the criminalization strategy justify their position by relentlessly making reference to crack babies and other infants born to drug-addicted mothers. Attorney Paul Logli (1990) endorsed legal intervention to protect "defenseless babies" from the alleged health hazards created by their drug-addicted mothers. Logli insisted that "local prosecutors have a legitimate role in responding to the increasing problem of drug abusing pregnant women and their drug-affected children" (p. 23; also see Alexander, 1989).

Critics charge that these criminal prosecutions symbolize an intersection between the militaristic "war on drugs" and the militant prolife movement that campaigns to restrict the reproductive freedom of women. In fact, Farr (1995) cited *Roe v. Wade* (1973) as an unwitting factor in the push to criminalize fetal (drug) abuse. Although *Roe* acknowledged a woman's right to (reproductive) privacy, the U.S. Supreme Court did not grant the fetus personhood (see Smith & Dabiri, 1991). In reaction to *Roe*,

> The antiabortion movement strengthened its commitment to secure legal recognition of and thus protection for the fetus. In the late 1970s, fetal rights got a boost from the fledgling 'war on drugs.' Exposed to addictive and toxic substances through pregnant women's use of them, the fetus came to be seen as an innocent victim of the drug problem. (Farr, 1995, p. 237)

In addition to the legal (i.e., *mens rea*) and constitutional (i.e., right to privacy and equal protection) concerns raised in efforts to criminalize fetal (drug) abuse (see Farr, 1995; *Johnson v. Florida,* 1992; Pollock-Byrne & Merlo, 1991; Roberts, 1991; Schroedel & Peretz, 1994), efforts to criminalize fetal (drug) abuse are discriminatory because they concentrate primarily on impoverished (often minority) teenagers who do not have the legal resources to defend themselves (Mariner, Glantz, & Annas, 1990, pp. 39-40).

Opponents of the criminalization movement also argue that such coercive and punitive measures simply do not work and that they emerge in the absence of adequate prenatal care and accessible substance abuse treatment. In fact, clinics often refuse to admit pregnant drug abusers because administrators fear becoming liable for birth defects and subsequently sued in civil court. In New York City, for instance, more than half of all drug treatment programs refuse to treat any pregnant woman, and two-thirds refuse to accept pregnant women on Medicaid. Further, 90% of the facilities in New York City denied treatment to pregnant crack users who were on Medicaid (Chavkin, 1990, p. 485). "This means that pregnant substance abusers have only two choices if they decide to have the baby: to remain on drugs or to go through withdrawal. Either one can result in serious harm to the fetus" (Schroedel & Peretz, 1994, p. 341). Taken together, attempts to criminalize fetal (drug) abuse are self-defeating because they drive pregnant women away from sources of assistance, including prenatal care and substance abuse treatment (Maher, 1990; Mariner et al., 1990; Pollock-Byrne & Merlo, 1991). Due to the coercive nature of the criminalization strategy (which is firmly grounded in deterrence theory), pregnant addicts fear losing custody of their babies if they seek drug treatment.

Critics of the criminalization strategy do *not* morally defend the ingestion of toxins (legal or illegal) that might complicate pregnancy. However, "injecting the criminal law can only deepen the tragedy. . . . Drug use during pregnancy is a real problem that can only be compounded by treating it as a crime" (Mariner et al., 1991, p. 293; also see Humphries, 1993; Merlo, 1993; Reed, 1993; Sagatun, 1993). In sum, it is argued that taking a public health approach to substance abuse is more humane and cost-effective than subjecting pregnant addicts to a host of criminal (and civil) sanctions that are punitive, ineffective, and discriminatory (Pollock-Byrne & Merlo, 1991).

Critics also take aim at how the issue of fetal abuse is framed, especially in the context of patriarchal (unconscious) belief systems. According to Schroedel and Peretz (1994), fetal abuse is understood *solely* in terms of maternal behaviors while the effects of paternal behaviors that can also cause or contribute to fetal harm are ignored. The definition of fetal abuse is driven by a generalized system of beliefs about natural gender roles in society and the "separate spheres" of responsibility. In a patriarchal culture, childbearing and rearing are viewed as female responsibilities and providing for the family as a male responsibility. Hence, fetal abuse is blamed on women because in a patriarchal culture, that is how the responsibility or division of labor is assigned.

In contrast to the prevailing image of maternal fetal abuse, Schroedel and Peretz (1994) identified two sources of *male* fetal abuse that are commonly overlooked by the legal and scientific (medical) communities as well as by the media—institutions that together create an image of fetal abuse as caused by female behaviors. They contended that male fetal abuse encompasses substance abuse and domestic violence. The scope of substance abuse by men includes alcohol, tobacco, and drug (legal and illegal) consumption as well as exposure to industrial chemicals. These toxins are cited as having adverse effects on the morphology of sperm, which might complicate pregnancy (John, Savitz, & Sandler, 1991; Office of Technology Assessment, 1985; Robinson, 1988; also see Pollock-Byrne & Merlo, 1991). Admittedly, this area of research is underdeveloped; however, it also remains underfunded, particularly because the prevailing definition of fetal abuse is understood as harm caused by maternal, not paternal, behavior.

Whereas more research is needed to ascertain the effects of substance abuse and male fetal abuse, much is already known about the impact of battering on pregnancy. Research by Campbell, Poland, Waller, and Ager (1992) demonstrated that pregnant battered women are subjected to more severe and frequent beatings than other battered women; moreover, the pregnancy itself is often cited as a reason for such violence. Anger toward or jealousy of the baby contributes to this type of violence, and usually the batterer is aware of the harm inflicted on the fetus. The Washtenaw County Sheriff's Department recorded the following battering incident of a pregnant wife: "Victim is six months pregnant at this time. Victim stated that accused kept telling victim, 'Bitch, you are going to lose that baby,' and the accused would beat the victim in the stomach again" (Eisenberg & Micklow, 1979, p. 139). Other corroborating evidence of deliberate fetal abuse is found in the bodily location of battering: Pregnant women commonly suffer blows to the abdominal region, whereas nonpregnant women are typically subjected to blows to the face and breasts (Berenson, Stiglich, Wilkinson, & Anderson, 1991, p. 1493; Hilberman, 1980, p. 1340; Hilberman & Munson, 1977-78, p. 462).

Schroedel and Peretz (1994) enumerated four ways that battering can cause adverse birth outcomes:

First, there is a strong association between battering and inadequate prenatal care. Battered women are quite often prevented by their partners from receiving medical care while pregnant (Helton, 1987, p. 5; Campbell et al., 1992, p. 225). Second, there is strong anecdotal evidence and some empirical research indicating that the rates of miscarriage and stillbirths among battered women may be up to two times greater than among nonbattered pregnant women (Hillard, 1985, p. 189; McFarlane, 1989, p. 70; Helton et al., 1987, p. 1338; Helton and Snodgrass, 1987, p. 143). Third, one large study showed a significant correlation between low-birthweight babies and battering during pregnancy. A baby's birthweight is a major determinant in the child's survival, growth, and development (Bullock and McFarlane, 1989, pp. 1153-55). Finally, there are indications that battering can cause physical injuries to the fetus. (pp. 345-346)

Despite compelling evidence of male fetal abuse, the issue is framed as a problem *solely* attributable to maternal behavior. In a Wyoming case, a pregnant woman was treated in an emergency room for injuries sustained in a battering by her husband. Yet *she*, not her husband, was arrested because she also had been drinking (Pollitt, 1990, p. 416). Similarly, in a California case, a child was born with severe brain damage and died shortly after birth. Physicians cited sexual intercourse in the latter stages of the pregnancy as the principal cause of the birth defect. However, the woman was also beaten by her husband, and the baby's injuries were probably sustained from that battering. Nevertheless, the cause of the birth defect was attributed to the mother, even though the husband *also* violated the physician's prohibition against engaging in sexual intercourse with his wife (Berrien, 1990, pp. 244-246; Johnsen, 1989, pp. 208-210; McNulty, 1990, p. 33; Pollitt, 1990, p. 416).

The enduring power of cultural biases continue to shape how fetal abuse is perceived by members of society, including its experts, namely lawyers, medical professionals, and journalists. Yet defining fetal abuse as a maternal issue is not the result of a conspiracy on the part of society's experts; rather, "There is simply a predisposition to view the world through analytical lenses that replicate and reinforce the existing gender biases" (Schroedel & Peretz, 1994, p. 355).

Norplant: Coercive Contraception in Sentencing and Welfare

The misuse of Norplant is another example of how technological forces shape the regulation of reproduction and morality of women. Upon its approval by the Food and Drug Administration in 1991, Norplant, a form of contraception, was recognized as a device that could enhance reproductive freedom. In fact, by the end of 1992, more than 500,000 American women were using Norplant, costing $350 per kit and $500 for surgical insertion ("Birth Control Implant," 1992). (Incidentally, Norplant, like other forms of conception, is covered by Medicaid in all 50 states.)

Norplant consists of six matchstick-size silicone capsules that are surgically inserted in a woman's upper arm, releasing progestin over 5 years. Although there are side effects (menstrual changes, headaches, and acne, just to name a few), physicians report an annual pregnancy rate of less than 1% over a 5-year span (ACLU Reproductive Freedom Project, 1994b). However, several suits have been filed against Wyeth-Ayerst (which markets Norplant) for failure to warn women of the complications in removing Norplant (Alan Guttmacher Institute, 1994; Cockburn, 1994).

Although Norplant has a liberating potential, it also can be administered in ways that impinge on the reproductive autonomy of women.

> The unique characteristic of Norplant is that it removes virtually all control over contraception from the woman. In fact, it is this lack of control that makes Norplant an attractive coercive device. . . . Norplant is a contraceptive that is susceptible to coercive use because it does not depend on the cooperation of the woman. (Albiston, 1994, p. 11)

The most pronounced misuses of Norplant have been committed by judges who mandate Norplant in sentencing of women convicted of child abuse or drug use during pregnancy (Albiston, 1994; Arthur, 1992). In 1991, less than a month after Norplant was approved by the FDA, in Tulare County, California, Superior Judge Howard Broadman ordered Darlene Johnson (convicted of child abuse) to use Norplant as a condition of probation. Ms. Johnson's attorney, Charles Rothman, said that she agreed to the order "only because she was afraid that if she refused she would go to jail for four years" (Lewin, 1991a, p. A-1). On the basis of the judge's remarks in court, Mr. Rothman concluded that Ms. Johnson's status as a welfare recipient also played a role in the sentencing of Norplant (see Rosenblum, 1992). Similar coercive applications of Norplant by judges have surfaced in Texas, Florida, Illinois, California, and Nebraska (see Alan Guttmacher Institute, 1994).

Legal experts report that there has never been a ruling by a federal appellate court clarifying the limits of forced contraception (ACLU Reproductive Freedom Project, 1994b). Yet civil libertarians insist that the 1973 *Roe v. Wade* decision extends to general rights of reproduction. Although the Johnson case is the first to involve Norplant, several judges have resorted to forced contraception as a condition of probation (ACLU Reproductive Freedom Project, 1994b; Alan Guttmacher Institute, 1994). In light of these cases, medical ethicists fear that other judges might use Norplant as a sanction against women deemed unfit mothers.

Norplant also has been proposed by legislators as a condition of (or financial incentive for) receiving welfare benefits. Representative David Duke introduced legislation in Louisiana to compensate women on welfare with $100 a year, provided they use Norplant (Mertus & Heller, 1992). In Ohio, a bill was introduced in 1994—and is still pending—that proposed to pay $1,000 to women (and men) on Aid to Families with Dependent Children (AFDC) who agree to be sterilized and to raise their welfare benefit to 150% above the base level. Women who chose Norplant (or DepoProvera) would receive a $500 bonus and a 5% increase in their welfare payments every 6 months until the payments reached 150% (ACLU Reproductive Freedom Project, 1994a). Similar bills and policy initiatives are pending in Maryland, South Carolina, Tennessee, and Washington. In 1993, Norplant-related bills failed in several states: Arizona, Colorado, Florida, Maryland, and North Carolina (ACLU Reproductive Freedom Project, 1994a; Alan Guttmacher Institute, 1994; Coale, 1992; also see "Birth Control Implant," 1992).

Although judges (and legislators) claim that they offer these women a "choice" between using Norplant and incarceration (or being awarded welfare benefits), critics insist that these women are coerced into using Norplant (see Bartrum, 1992; Persels, 1992).

> Offering a "choice" between prison and forced contraception is unconstitutional. Such a choice violates the fundamental constitutional right to reproductive autonomy and bodily integrity by interfering with the intimate decision of whether and when to bear a child and by imposing an intrusive medical procedure on individuals who are not in a position to reject it. (ACLU Reproductive Freedom Project, 1994b, p. 1)

Furthermore, incentive plans proposed by legislators are just as coercive because low-income women face dire financial emergencies that pressure them to use Norplant in exchange for welfare benefits. In response to a 1991 Kansas state bill that proposed to pay $500 to any mother on welfare who uses Norplant, Julie Mertus (of the ACLU) stated, "We would be delighted if this were part of a package to improve reproductive health care for women, and there were no monetary incentives, but it's a bribe that pushes women into one choice instead of creating more choices" (Lewin, 1991b, p. 14). Civil libertarians argue that incentive plans violate the constitutional right to reproductive and bodily autonomy. In sum, "Allowing judges and legislators to control the reproduction of some women would legitimize the role of government as an overseer of women's childbearing capacity in general" (ACLU Reproductive Freedom Project, 1994b, p. 2).

The abuse of Norplant by legislators perpetuates the notion that poverty can be controlled or "cured" by technological or medical intervention. The assumption underlying the coercive application of Norplant is that women receiving welfare benefits (pejoratively referred to as "welfare queens") are irresponsible and bear children indiscriminately in order to remain on welfare indefinitely. Yet "the average number of children in a family on welfare is 1.9 (a figure no larger than that for the general population), and in 1990 the median period for receipt of Aid to Families with Dependent Children was 23 months" (ACLU Reproductive Freedom Project, 1994b, p. 2).

According to those who oppose the coercive use of Norplant, proper solutions to drug abuse and problems endemic to poverty reside in substance abuse treatment and social services. Norplant prevents pregnancies but does not reduce drug abuse or prevent mothers (or fathers) from abusing their children. Further, the coercive use of Norplant in sentencing and welfare is aimed disproportionately at low-income women of color. Indeed, the social meaning of Norplant is that it reinforces racist stereotypes while neglecting the broader implications of poverty.

> Although the application of Norplant as a condition of probation seems impartial, poor women of color are most likely to receive the condition because institutional biases make them most likely to be prosecuted for child abuse and drug use during pregnancy. Furthermore, the seemingly impartial application of Norplant as a condition of probation hides how this policy derives from and reinforces stereotypes of poor women of color. The Norplant policy resonates with racist and sexist stereotypes such as the welfare queen, the "evil" woman, and the inadequate mother. (Albiston, 1994, p. 12)

These coercive policies and tactics are reminiscent of the eugenics movement. Earlier in this century, the eugenics movement set out to limit population growth among "undesirable" groups of women by coercively sterilizing impoverished, non-English-speaking women, particularly women of color, as well as mentally retarded women (ACLU Reproductive Freedom Project, 1994b; Blank, 1993; Mertus & Heller, 1992). Following the FDA approval of Norplant (1991), the *Philadelphia Inquirer* issued an editorial entitled "Poverty and Norplant: Can Contraception Reduce the Underclass?" which suggested that poverty among African Americans in inner cities could be reduced by widespread use of Norplant. The editorial was denounced as racist, and the newspaper later issued an apology (cited in Lewin, 1991b).

Some medical ethicists as well as the American Medical Association condemn the coercive use of Norplant in both sentencing and welfare. Similarly, the epidemiologist who developed Norplant, Sheldon Segal, is dismayed that Norplant has been used punitively. Segal explained,

> I just don't believe in restricting human rights, especially reproductive rights.... And I'm also bothered because this is a prescription drug with certain side effects and there are certain groups of women for whom it may not be appropriate. How does the judge know if the woman is diabetic, or has some other contraindication to the drug? That's not his business. (quoted in Lewin, 1991a, p. A-20)

Conclusion

In this chapter, emerging measures of social control of women were examined in light of the political, economic, religious/moral, and technological forces that shape punishment. In particular, the focus was on "correctional" initiatives patterned by cultural imperatives, especially those upholding traditional views of female morality as well as those regulating female reproduction. Here it was argued that androcentric positivism serves as a basis to "correct" female immorality (e.g., sexual promiscuity) and to regulate the reproduction of women deemed unfit for motherhood.

Androcentric positivism draws heavily on technological advances, and backed by a supposedly "neutral" science, these *appear* legitimate in the realm of criminal sentencing and welfare policy. Among the supporters of "neutral" science are social agents (e.g., civic, political, and religious leaders) who extend moral justifications in endorsing certain forms of social control, namely coercive contraception and sterilization. Critics, however, remind us that even though technology offers the potential to enhance reproductive freedom, as is the case with Norplant, it also carries the threat of oppression, coercion, and more intrusive measures of social control (Lesieur & Welch, 1995; Maher, 1990; Smart, 1989). In fact, "Science in the form of new reproductive technologies has, in effect, made the criminalization of 'crack pregnancies' possible" (Maher, 1990, p. 120).

In this discourse on gendered social control, biases in race and class as patterned by larger political, economic, and moral forces are also taken into consideration. For instance, low-income women, many of whom are women of color, are more likely than their white, middle-class counterparts to face coercive contraception and other punitive measures by the criminal justice system. According to Maher (1990), "The rewards and punishments distributed because of women's reproductive choices are differentially allocated by race and class criteria" (p. 121). Similarly, proposals to deal with female immorality stem from stereotypes and social myths of women of color: "One stereotype of women of color, particularly black women, is sexual promiscuity. Historically, black women have been viewed as sexual savages, the embodiment of female evil and sexual lust, jezebels and sexual temptresses" (Albiston, 1994, p. 16). Indeed, racist and sexist stereotypes (e.g., promiscuity and personal irresponsibility) of women of color have traditionally fueled the policing of morality and the repression of fertility.

References

Alan Guttmacher Institute. (1994, June). *Norplant opportunities and perils for low-income women* (Special Report No. 3). New York: Author.

Albiston, C. (1994). The social meaning of the Norplant condition: Constitutional conditions of race, class, and gender. *Berkeley Women's Law Journal, 11,* 9-57.

Alexander, R. (1989). Drug addicted, pregnant women: Punishment or treatment? *Criminal Justice Policy Review, 3,* 423-435.

American Civil Liberties Union Reproductive Freedom Project. (1994a). *1993-94 Norplant legislative activity.* New York: Author.

American Civil Liberties Union Reproductive Freedom Project. (1994b). *Norplant: A new contraceptive with the potential for abuse.* New York: Author.

American Psychiatric Association. (1987). *Diagnostic and statistical manual of mental disorders* (3rd ed., Rev.). Washington, DC: Author.

Arthur, S. L. (1992). The Norplant prescription: Birth control, woman control, or crime control? *UCLA Law Review, 40,* 19-20.

Babcock v. Babcock, December 5, 1986, New Westminster E0010084 B.C.S.C.

Barnes, H. E., & Teeters, N. K. (1946). *New horizons in criminology.* New York: Prentice Hall.

Bartrum, T. E. (1992). Birth control as a condition of probation: A new weapon in the war against child abuse. *Kentucky Law Review, 80,* 1037-1050.

Berenson, A. B., Stiglich, N. J., Wilkinson, G. S., & Anderson, G. D. (1991). Drug abuse and other risk factors for physical abuse in pregnancy among white non-Hispanic, black, and Hispanic women. *American Journal of Obstetrics and Gynecology, 164,* 1491-1499.

Berrien, J. (1990). Pregnancy and drug use: The dangerous and unequal use of punitive measures. *Yale Journal of Law and Feminism, 2,* 239-250.

Birth-control implant gains among poor under Medicaid. (1992, December 17). *New York Times,* pp. A-1, B-21.

Blank, R. H. (1993). *Fertility control: New techniques, new policy issues.* New York: Greenwood.

Burford, E. J., & Schulman, S. (1992). *Of bridles and burnings: The punishment of women.* New York: St. Martin's.

Campbell, J. C., Poland, M. L., Waller, J. B., & Ager, J. (1992). Correlates of battering during pregnancy. *Research in Nursing and Health, 15,* 219-226.

Chavkin, W. (1990). Drug addiction and pregnancy: Policy crossroads. *American Journal of Public Health, 80,* 483-487.

Coale, D. S. (1992). Norplant bonuses and the unconstitutional conditions doctrine. *Texas Law Review, 71*, 189.
Cockburn, A. (1994, July 25). Norplant and the social cleansers, Part II. *Nation*, pp. 116-117.
Coles, C. D. (1991, May). *Substance abuse in pregnancy: The infant's risk: How great?* Paper presented at the annual meeting of the American Psychiatric Association, New Orleans.
Day, N. L., Richardson, G. A., & McGauhey, P. J. (1992). The effects of prenatal exposure to marijuana, cocaine, heroin, and methadone. In H. L. Needleman (Ed.), *Prenatal exposure to pollutants and development of infants* (pp. 184-212). Baltimore: Johns Hopkins University Press.
Dobash, R. E., Dobash, R., & Gutteridge, S. (1986). *The imprisonment of women*. New York: Basil Blackwell.
Eisenberg, S. E., & Micklow, P. L. (1979). The assaulted wife: "Catch 22" Revisited. *Women's Rights Law Reporter, 3*, 138-161.
Faith, K. (1993). *Unruly women: The politics of confinement and resistance*. Vancouver: Press Gang.
Farr, K. A. (1995). Fetal abuse and the criminalization of behavior during pregnancy. *Crime and Delinquency, 41*, 235-245.
Freedman, E. (1981). Their sister's keepers: Women's prison reforms in America, 1830-1930. Ann Arbor: University of Michigan Press.
Freedman, E. (1974). Their sister's keepers: A historical perspective of female correctional institutions in the U.S. *Feminist Studies, 2*, 77-95.
Gieringer, D. (1990, March-April). How many crack babies? *Drug Policy Letter, 11*, 4-6.
Goldenson, R. M. (1970). *The encyclopedia of human behavior, psychology, psychiatry and mental health*. Garden City, NY: Doubleday.
Goode, E. (1993). *Drugs in American society* (4th ed.). New York: McGraw-Hill.
Gustavsson, N. S. (1991). Pregnant chemically dependent women: The new criminals. *Affilia, 6*, 61-73.
Hilberman, E. (1980). Overview: The "wife-beater" reconsidered. *American Journal of Psychiatry, 137*, 1336-1347.
Hilberman, E., & Munson, K. (1977-78). Sixty battered women. *Victimology, 2*, 460-470.
Humphries, D. (1993). Mothers and children, drugs and crack: Reactions to maternal drug dependency. In R. Muraskin & T. Alleman (Eds.), *It's a crime: Women and justice* (pp. 130-145). Englewood Cliffs, NJ: Regents/Prentice Hall.
Inciardi, J. A., Lockwood, D., & Pottieger, A. E. (1993). *Women and crack-cocaine*. New York: Macmillan.
John, E., Savitz, D., & Sandler, D. (1991). Prenatal exposure to parents' smoking and childhood cancer. *American Journal of Epidemiology, 133*, 123-132.
Johnsen, D. E. (1989). The creation of fetal rights: Conflicts with women's constitutional rights to liberty, privacy, and equal protection. *Yale Law Journal, 95*, 599-625.
Johnson v. Florida, WL 171-213 (1992).
Kendall, K. (1992). Sexual difference and the law: Premenstrual syndrome as legal defense. In D. H. Currie & V. Raoul (Eds.), *Anatomy of gender: Women's struggle for the body*. Ottawa, Canada: Carleton University Press.
Leonard, E. (1982). *Women, crime and society*. New York: Longman.
Lesieur, H., & Welch, M. (1995). Vice crimes: Individual choices and social controls. In J. F. Sheley (Ed.), *Criminology: A contemporary handbook* (2nd ed., pp. 200-247). Belmont, CA: Wadsworth.
Lewin, T. (1991a, February 22). Implanted birth control device renews debate over forced contraception. *New York Times*, p. A-20.
Lewin, T. (1991b, February 9). A plan to pay welfare mothers for birth control. *New York Times*, p. 14.

Logli, P. A. (1990). Drugs in the womb: The newest battlefield in the war on drugs. *Criminal Justice Ethics, 9*(1), 23-28.

Lombroso, C., & Ferrero, W. (1920). *The female offender.* New York: Appleton. (Original work published 1894)

Maher, L. (1990). Criminalizing pregnancy: The downside of a kinder, gentler notion? *Social Justice, 17*(3), 111-135.

Mariner, W. K., Glantz, L. H., & Annas, G. J. (1991). Pregnancy, drugs, and the perils of prosecution. *Criminal Justice Ethics, 9*(1), 30-40.

McNulty, M. (1990). Pregnancy police: Implications of criminalizing fetal abuse. *Youth Law News, 11,* 33-37.

Merlo, A. V. (1993). Pregnant substance abusers: The new female offender. In R. Muraskin & T. Alleman (Eds.), *It's a crime: Women and justice* (pp. 146-158). Englewood Cliffs, NJ: Regents/Prentice Hall.

Mertus, J., & Heller, S. (1992). Norplant meets the new eugenicists: The impermissibility of coerced contraception. *St. Louis University Public Law Review, 11,* 395, 362.

Morris, A. (1987). *Women, crime and criminal justice.* New York: Blackwell.

Neuspiel, D. R., Hamel, S. C., Berg, E. H., Greene, J., & Campbell, D. (1991). Maternal cocaine use and infant behavior. *Neurotoxicology and Teratology, 13,* 229-233.

Office of Technology Assessment. (1985). *Reproductive health hazards in the workplace.* Washington, DC: Government Printing Office.

Osborne, J. A. (1989). Premenstrual syndrome: Women, law and medicine. *Canadian Journal of Family Law, 8,* 165-184.

Persels, J. (1992). The Norplant condition: Protecting the unborn or violating fundamental rights? *Journal of Legal Medicine, 13,* 237, 258.

Pollak, O. (1950). *The criminality of women.* Philadelphia: University of Pennsylvania Press.

Pollitt, K. (1990, March). Fetal rights: A new assault on feminism. *Nation,* pp. 409-418.

Pollock-Byrne, J. M., & Merlo, A. V. (1991). Against compulsory treatment: No "Quick fix" for pregnant substance abusers. *Criminal Justice Policy Review, 5,* 79-99.

Poverty and Norplant: Can contraception reduce the underclass? (1990, December 12). *Philadelphia Inquirer,* p. A-18.

R. v. Craddock, 1 C.L. 49 (1981).

R. v. English, November 10, 1981, Norwich Crown Court.

Reed, S. O. (1993). The criminalization of pregnancy: Drugs, alcohol, and AIDS. In R. Muraskin & T. Alleman (Eds.), *It's a crime: Women and justice* (pp. 93-117). Englewood Cliffs, NJ: Regents/Prentice Hall.

Richardson, G. A. (1992). *Prenatal cocaine exposure.* Unpublished paper, Western Psychiatric Institute and Clinic, Pittsburgh, PA.

Richardson, G. A., & Day, N. L. (1991). Maternal and neonatal effects of moderate cocaine use during pregnancy. *Neurotoxicology and Teratology, 13,* 455-460.

Rittenhouse, A. (1991). The emergence of premenstrual syndrome as a social problem. *Social Problems, 38,* 412-425.

Roberts, D. E. (1991). Punishing drug addicts who have babies: Women of color, equality, and the right of privacy. *Harvard Law Review, 104,* 1419-1482.

Roe v. Wade, 410 U.S. 113,93 S.Ct. 705, 35 L.Ed.2d. 147 (1973).

Robinson, R. (1988). High proof paternity. *Health, 20,* 20.

Rosenblum, E. R. (1992). The irony of Norplant. *Texas Journal of Women and the Law, 4,* 275.

Sagatun, I. J. (1993). Babies born with drug addiction: Background and legal responses. In R. Muraskin & T. Alleman (Eds.), *It's a crime: Women and justice* (pp. 118-129). Englewood Cliffs, NJ: Regents/Prentice Hall.

Schroedel, J. R., & Peretz, P. (1994). A gender analysis of policy formation: The case of fetal abuse. *Journal of Health Politics, Policy and Law, 19,* 335-360.

Smart, C. (1989). *Feminism and the power of law.* New York: Routledge.
Smith, G. B., & Dabiri, G. M. (1991). Prenatal drug exposure: The constitutional implications of three governmental approaches. *Constitutional Law Journal, 2,* 53-126.
Stoppard, J. (1992). A suitable case for treatment? Premenstrual syndrome and the medicalization of women's bodies. In D. H. Currie & V. Raoul (Eds.), *Anatomy of gender: Women's struggle for the body.* Ottawa, Canada: Carleton University Press.
Webster's new twentieth century dictionary (2nd ed.). (1983). New York: Simon & Schuster.
Welch, M. (1996). *Corrections: A critical approach.* New York: McGraw-Hill.
Zedner, L. (1991). *Women, crime and custody in Victorian England.* Oxford, UK: Clarendon.

CHAPTER

6

Jail Overcrowding

Social Sanitation and the Warehousing of the Urban Underclass

Applying the critical perspective to jails is not a difficult task because the practice and process of detention is shaped enormously by race and social class. Thus, a critical analysis of jails not only raises more questions about basic fairness in American criminal justice but also sheds light on mechanisms of social control. In this chapter, we explore a distinct form of social control called social sanitation, a process by which police remove lawbreakers (e.g., drug addicts) from the street who are considered offensive but not dangerous. The jail facilitates this measure of social control by serving as a warehouse reserved mostly for the urban underclass. In addition to these conceptual considerations, current information about jails, inmates, overcrowding, and the experience of detention is presented in full detail. We begin this examination with a description of what it is like to be warehoused in a overcrowded jail.

AUTHOR'S NOTE: Reprinted from *Critical Issues in Crime and Justice*. (1994). Albert Roberts (editor) Thousand Oaks, CA: Sage.

On Being Warehoused in an Overcrowded Jail

Immediately after being arrested and booked on drug charges or any similar offense, most white, middle-class people are detained only as long as it takes for a family member to arrive with the cash needed to secure their release. In cases such as these, bail may be set at $1,000: high enough to ensure their court appearance but certainly not high enough to prevent their release from jail. But for unemployed people from the lower classes facing similar charges, the same $1,000 bail may readily prevent their release. Therefore, they will remain in jail until their court appearance, a wait that may last weeks or even months.

During this wait, they will experience the horrific aspects of pretrial detention, which are exacerbated by jail overcrowding. For instance, every day for the next number of weeks or months, they will wait in line to use the telephone for nearly 1 hour before they can call their family and their court-appointed lawyer, whom they will not actually meet until moments before they appear before the judge. In fact, because most pretrial detainees have such difficulty calling their family and reaching their attorney, they eventually realize that waiting in line for the telephone is a waste of time.

Due to overcrowded jail conditions, pretrial detainees may have to sleep on the floor for several days or weeks before a bed becomes available. However, the actuality of being able to sleep should not be taken for granted. Loud voices of other inmates can be heard at all hours of the day and night. Thoughts of release become an obsession, especially when it is painfully clear that being held in jail means being denied even the most basic elements of outside living.

Pretrial detention also means eating cold institutional food, wearing dirty clothes reeking of body odor, and having to shower and go to the bathroom without privacy. In overcrowded jails, the plumbing cannot keep pace with the demands placed on the toilets; hence, the clogged toilets and flooding create an unbearable stench. These nauseating odors are worsened by the summer heat, which generates a permanent stench of urine that permeates the living units. As detainees develop a heightened sense of vigilance, the insufferable conditions eventually fade into the background. Detainees maintain close surveillance over the other inmates to ward off any potential threats of physical and sexual assault.

Understandably, pretrial detention in an overcrowded jail is a punishing experience. And this form of punishment raises two serious issues. First, being forced to undergo this punishment *before* trial violates the "innocent until proven guilty" principle of criminal justice. Second, this form of pretrial punishment is often reserved for people who cannot financially secure their release by meeting the bail. In other words, even at the early stages of determining one's guilt or innocence, the criminal justice system treats suspects differently on the basis of their social class. Upper- and middle-class suspects are more likely to spend time in the community while awaiting trial, whereas those who are poor face months of detention in an overcrowded jail.

An Overview of Jails

While campaigning for mayor, candidate Ronald S. Lauder expressed his antagonism toward street crime following a visit to Rikers Island, the largest penal colony in the world, located off the banks of New York City. Lauder was outraged at what he saw at Rikers Island: Inmates were allowed to watch television and had access to recreational facilities. Lauder proclaimed that he would remove televisions and close the recreational facilities, which he believed helped criminals strengthen their bodies for their return to the streets. Regarding jails, Lauder quipped, "It says that, hey, it is not so bad. If it were up to me, I would have them breaking stones to pebbles" (Barbanel, 1989, p. B1).

Although Lauder's condemnation of the jail system may have earned him some votes from those equally fed up with street crime, it is clear that Lauder did not know the fundamental differences between jails and prisons. He failed to realize that Rikers Island is a jail complex in which 65% of the population are pretrial detainees. Moreover, according to the Correctional Association of New York (1989), most of these pretrial detainees are held there because they are too poor to meet their bail, which is sometimes as low as $250 to $500.

Corrections officials at Rikers Island responded to Lauder's misinformed remarks by pointing out that exercise and television are essential to managing the inmate population by easing tensions and relieving stress. Furthermore, the policy at Rikers Island that grants inmates 1 hour of recreation per day is consistent with the minimum standards of incarceration that are also observed by federal penitentiaries (Barbanel, 1989).

Even though we might expect politicians to be aware of the basic differences between jails and prisons, Lauder's level of confusion is common among many persons who are uneducated about the various components of the criminal justice system. In brief, although jails and prisons differ in numerous ways, the distinction has traditionally been drawn along the lines of the legal status of their inmates. For example, whereas prisons house convicted felons (those serving sentences for 1 year or more), jails hold pretrial detainees, convicted misdemeanants (those serving sentences of less than 1 year), and convicted felons who are awaiting transfer to their assigned prison. Furthermore, jails are usually local and county institutions, whereas prisons are governed by state or federal authorities. Due to these basic differences, jails and prisons are destined to remain distinct institutions that face problems unique to their respective roles in the criminal justice system (Welch, 1992a).

Again, the purpose of this chapter is to promote a heightened awareness of how jails differ from prisons. As we explore the use of jails, particularly in major urban settings, we will learn that jails also serve a distinct function in society known as *social sanitation*. Moreover, we will examine jail overcrowding in light of correctional *warehousing*: the practice of incarcerating massive numbers of inmates with the sole institutional goal of securing custody. Human storage, not rehabilitation or reform, is the primary objective in warehousing, and it is society's *urban underclass* that is most likely to undergo this form of incarceration.

Jail Overcrowding

Overcrowding is considered the most pressing problem facing jails; in fact, jail overcrowding poses a more serious problem than prison overcrowding. The "war on drugs" has contributed to booming populations in both prisons and jails, and the unique role of the jail within the criminal justice system adds to the persistent problem of having to admit more inmates than there is space (see Klofas, Stojkovic, & Kalinich, 1992; Welsh, Leone, Kinkade, & Pontell, 1991).

The jail has been viewed as a "strange correctional hybrid" because it is used as a detention center for suspects, a correctional facility for misdemeanants, and a refuge to hold social misfits (Clear & Cole, 1990, p. 205). Throughout history, the poor have disproportionately occupied jails. Hence, jails live up to their reputation as being the "poorhouses of the twentieth century," the "ultimate ghettos," and "storage bins for humans," as well as social "garbage cans" used to discard society's "rabble" (Clear & Cole, 1990; Glaser, 1979; Goldfarb, 1975; Irwin, 1985; Moynahan & Steward, 1980; Welch, 1991a). Much like the persons detained there, jails are the most neglected institutions within the criminal justice system.

As of 1997, 567,079 persons were incarcerated in the nation's jails: a 28% increase from 1989 (Bureau of Justice Statistics, 1998c). Jail overcrowding not only is produced by daily processing from street arrests but also is compounded by the large number of state inmates awaiting transfer to prisons. This dynamic in corrections is known as hydraulic overcrowding. Thirty-one states reported holding 34,000 state prisoners in local jails (Bureau of Justice Statistics, 1998b; Kerle, 1998). Unlike prisons, which contain a relatively stable population in terms of admissions and releases, the jail operates more like a "people-processing station" distinguished by a constant flow of traffic with around-the-clock activity. In 1997, a total of 637,319 inmates were held in local jails. Overall, 212 of every 100,000 residents were processed through detention, a figure that was up from 163 per 100,000 in 1990 (Bureau of Justice Statistics, 1998a). Unquestionably, jails have more contact with the general population than do prisons; however, that contact is largely determined by race and social class because the majority of detainees are impoverished people of color.

Who Goes to Jail?

Unlike the board game Monopoly, one does not end up in jail by mere chance; there is a clear pattern of detention. The jail population does *not* represent a cross section of the general population; rather, its inmates are disproportionately black, Hispanic, and, most significantly, poor, uneducated, and unemployed. According to the Bureau of Justice Statistics (1998c), in 1996, 6 in 10 inmates were racial or ethnic minorities (see Table 6.1). In an attempt to help answer the question "Who goes to jail?" let us examine the following findings from the most recent survey on jail inmates (Bureau of Justice Statistics, 1998c).

- One in three inmates was not working before being arrested.
- Six in 10 jail inmates grew up living in homes without both parents.
- Over a third of jail inmates reported a physical or mental disability.
- Nearly half of all female inmates reported past physical or sexual abuse.
- Proportionately more black and Hispanic inmates than whites were in jail for drug offenses. More than one in four blacks and Hispanics compared to one in seven whites were in jail for a drug law violation.

- Regardless of race or Hispanic origin, about half of the drug offenders were in jail for drug possession.
- Fewer than half of adult jail inmates were convicted.
- Among sentenced jail inmates, half would serve less than 6 months from admission.
- The 25 largest jail jurisdictions housed more than a quarter of all jail inmates.

Characteristics of Jail Inmates

To further our understanding of who goes to jail, it is important to consider additional research findings. We have already established that jail inmates are disproportionately young (aged 18 to 34) black men from the inner city with a history of drug abuse. But from Tables 6.1 and 6.2 we can identify additional characteristics of jail inmates. For example, 46% of the jail inmates have not completed high school: 33.4% report having some high school education, and 13% have achieved an eighth-grade education or less. Another 40% are high school graduates, and 13.5% report some college.

Prearrest employment status figures in Table 6.2 shed additional light on the population characteristics of jail inmates. At the time of arrest, 49.3% of jail inmates were employed full time, 10.4% were employed part time, and 35.8% were unemployed and either looking or not looking for work. Prearrest income among those jail inmates who were free for at least 1 year prior to arrest is provided in Table 6.2. More than one-fourth (25.1%) of the jail inmates reported incomes of less than $300 per month. In addition, one in five jail inmates received government payments (e.g., Aid to Families With Dependent Children) (Bureau of Justice Statistics, 1998c).

Perhaps the most accurate interpretation of the education, employment, and income figures is that jail inmates generally represent two segments of the lower class: They are either members of the working poor or permanent members of the underclass. Moreover, if one considers their educational background, it is clear that many of them have limited means to survive economically.

As mentioned previously, and as shown in Table 6.3, a huge proportion (22%) of jail inmates were detained in 1996 for drug law violations, and more than half of those arrests involved possession (11.5%). The percentage of drug charges among jail inmates was down slightly from 1989 (23%) but up

TABLE 6.1 Selected Characteristics of Jail Inmates, by Conviction Status, 1996, 1989, and 1983

	% of Jail Inmates				
	1996				
	Total	Convicted	Unconvicted	1989	1983
Sex					
Male	89.8	89.8	90.3	90.5	92.9
Female	10.2	10.2	9.7	9.5	7.1
Race/Hispanic origin					
White non-Hispanic	37.3	39.7	32.4	38.6	46.4
Black non-Hispanic	40.8	38.9	44.7	41.7	37.5
Hispanic	18.5	18.3	19.1	17.4	14.3
Other[a]	3.5	3.2	3.8	2.3	1.8
Age					
17 or younger	2.3	1.4	4.1	1.5	1.3
18-24	28.5	27.9	30.2	32.6	40.4
25-34	37.4	38.9	34.7	42.9	38.6
35-44	23.9	24.4	22.6	16.7	12.4
45-54	6.3	6.0	6.9	4.6	4.9
55 or older	1.5	1.5	1.4	1.7	2.4
Marital status					
Married	15.7	16.0	14.4	19.0	21.0
Widowed	1.4	1.3	1.8	1.0	1.4
Divorced	15.6	16.3	14.2	15.1	15.7
Separated	8.7	8.4	9.1	8.2	7.9
Never married	58.6	58.0	60.5	56.7	54.1
Education[b]					
8th grade or less	13.1	12.7	14.2	15.6	17.7
Some high school	33.4	31.7	36.6	38.2	41.3
High school graduate	40.0	42.5	35.3	33.1	29.2
Some college or more	13.5	13.1	14.0	13.1	11.8
Military service					
Veteran	11.7	11.9	11.1	15.5	21.2
Nonveteran	88.3	88.1	88.9	84.5	78.8
U.S. citizenship					
Citizen	91.8	93.2	89.1	—	—
Noncitizen	8.2	6.8	10.9	—	—
Number of jail inmates	507,026	318,068	169,377	395,554	223,552

SOURCE: Bureau of Justice Statistics (1998c, p. 3).
NOTE: Total includes inmates with an unknown conviction or no offense. Data were missing for marital status on 0.1% of the inmates; for education, on 0.7%; for military service, on 0.1%; and for citizenship, on 0.1%.
— = not available.
a. Includes Asians, Pacific Islanders, American Indians, Alaska Natives, and other racial groups.
b. See *Methodology* for change in measurement.

TABLE 6.2 Prearrest Employment and Income for Jail Inmates, 1996

	% of Jail Inmates
Prearrest employment	100.0
Employed	64.3
Full time	49.3
Part time	10.4
Occasionally	4.6
Not employed	35.8
Looking for work	19.6
Not looking	16.2
Monthly income[a] (Free less than 1 year)	100.0
Less than $300[b]	25.1
$300-$599	20.5
$600-$999	18.7
$1,000-$1,999	22.2
$1,500 or more	13.5

SOURCE: Bureau of Justice Statistics (1998c).
a. Monthly income figures for inmates who were free for less than 1 year prior to the offense for which they were sent to jail.

dramatically since 1983 (9.3%). From Table 6.3, we also find that other jail inmates were charged with violent offenses (26.3%): assault accounted for the largest violent offense (11.6%), followed by robbery (6.5%). Murder accounted for 2.8% of the total detainee population, which was the same as in 1989 but lower than in 1983 (4.1%). The percentage of violent offenses had increased from 1989 (22.5%) but was lower than in 1983 (30.7%). Property offenses accounted for nearly 27% of the charges: Larceny/theft and burglary were the largest subcategories, 8.0% and 7.6% respectively. The percentage of property offenses was down from 1989 (30%) and 1983 (38.6%). Finally, approximately one-fourth of jail inmates were held for public order offenses, a figure that had increased since 1989 (22.8%) and 1983 (20.3%). Driving while intoxicated remained the most frequently charged public order crime (7.4%). As these data indicate, the vast majority of detainees are held for nonviolent and typically less serious offenses.

The Jail: Managing the Underclass in American Society

The aforementioned profile of jail inmates provides ample evidence indicating that jail populations are disproportionately poor, young, black, Hispanic,

TABLE 6.3 Most Serious Offense of Jail Inmates, 1996, 1989, and 1983

	% of Jail Inmates				
		1996			
Most Serious Offense	Total	Convicted	Unconvicted	1989	1983
Violent offenses	26.3	21.8	36.6	22.5	30.7
Murder[a]	2.8	1.2	6.0	2.8	4.1
Negligent manslaughter	0.4	0.3	0.5	0.5	0.6
Kidnaping	0.5	0.5	0.6	0.8	1.3
Rape	0.5	0.3	0.8	0.8	1.5
Other sexual assault	2.7	2.7	2.9	2.6	2.0
Robbery	6.5	5.6	8.8	6.7	11.2
Assault	11.6	10.0	15.4	7.2	8.6
Other violent[b]	1.3	1.2	1.5	1.1	1.3
Property offenses	26.9	28.6	25.5	30.0	38.6
Burglary	7.6	8.0	7.7	10.7	14.3
Larceny/theft	8.0	9.5	5.7	7.9	11.7
Motor vehicle theft	2.6	2.3	3.3	2.8	2.3
Arson	0.4	0.3	0.6	0.7	0.8
Fraud	4.6	4.8	4.3	4.0	5.0
Stolen property	2.1	2.4	1.9	2.4	2.5
Other property[c]	1.6	1.4	2.2	1.6	1.9
Drug offenses	22.0	23.7	20.2	23.0	9.3
Possession	11.5	12.6	10.0	9.7	4.7
Trafficking	9.2	9.5	9.2	12.0	4.0
Other drug	1.3	1.5	1.0	1.3	0.6
Public order offenses	24.3	25.5	17.4	22.8	20.6
Weapons	2.3	2.4	2.2	1.9	2.3
Obstruction of justice	4.8	3.3	4.0	2.8	2.0
Traffic violations	3.2	3.8	1.7	2.7	2.2
Driving while intoxicated[d]	7.4	9.5	3.6	8.8	7.0
Drunkenness/morals[e]	2.0	1.9	2.4	1.7	3.4
Violation of parole/probation[f]	2.6	2.7	1.7	3.0	2.3
Other public order[g]	2.0	1.8	1.8	1.8	1.6
Other offenses[h]	.5	.4	.3	1.6	.8
Number of jail inmates	496,609	315,442	166,295	380,160	219,573

SOURCE: Bureau of Justice Statistics (1998c, p. 4).
NOTE: Excludes inmates for whom offense was unknown.
a. Includes non-negligent manslaughter.
b. Includes blackmail, extortion, hit-and-run driving with bodily injury, child abuse, and criminal endangerment.
c. Includes destruction of property, vandalism, hit-and-run driving without bodily injury, trespassing, and possession of burglary tools.
d. Includes driving while intoxicated and driving under the influence of drugs or alcohol.
e. Includes drunkenness, vagrancy, disorderly conduct, unlawful assembly, morals, and commercialized vice.
f. Includes parole or probation violations, escape, AWOL, and flight to avoid prosecution.
g. Includes rioting, abandonment, nonsupport, immigration violations, invasion of privacy, liquor law violations, tax evasion, and bribery.
h. Includes juvenile offenses and other unspecified offenses.

uneducated, and unemployed persons who have drug abuse problems and reside in the lower-class neighborhoods of our nation's major cities. Given these socioeconomic characteristics, the issue of social class is simply too important to ignore. As mentioned, those in jail occupy one of two segments of the lower class: the working poor and the underclass. Whereas the jail experience adversely affects both groups, the working poor appear to be less disrupted because, at the very least, they possess some skills and the opportunity to survive economically upon their release. In contrast, the underclass, by its very definition, consists of those who have limited means to survive: They are uneducated, possess virtually no job skills, and have little or no work experience. For them, the jail experience reinforces their inability to lead a productive and economically independent life (see Gibbs, 1982; Weisheit & Klofas, 1989; Welch, 1989, 1991b, 1996; Wilson, 1987).

John Irwin greatly contributed to the discourse of the social function of jails and the underclass in his book *The Jail: Managing the Underclass in American Society* (1985). Irwin contended that jails are used in American society to manage the underclass, and in his analysis of jails he identified a specific economically subordinate social group known as the *rabble*. The rabble are socially detached (not belonging to any conventional social network), disorganized, disorderly, and viewed by the conventional middle-class world as *offensive*. Irwin claimed that most persons who occupy jails (the rabble) are detained for minor offenses and do not fit the stereotype of the dangerous and threatening criminal. Whereas one might believe that jail inmates are detained for the purpose of protecting society while they await trial, Irwin found that many jail inmates represent various types of "disreputables" such as petty hustlers, derelicts, and junkies. These "disreputables" are generally detained for nonviolent and minor offenses (e.g., drug possession) and are simply too poor to meet their bail. Moreover, by the very nature of their economic standing, the rabble are unable to adequately defend themselves legally. Therefore, from the moment of arrest, they are at the mercy of the police, the jail staff, their court-appointed attorney, and the courts.

Placing his findings in a larger social context, Irwin concluded that the jail functions as an extension of the welfare state and becomes a means by which society manages and controls the underclass. Similar arguments have been developed by other researchers, such as Piven and Cloward in *Regulating the Poor: The Functions of Public Welfare* (1971). In that work, Piven and Cloward asserted that throughout contemporary history, welfare has been used to reduce social unrest and reinforce the poor's social position in a class society.

According to Irwin (1985), criminal justice resources are likely to continue placing disproportionate emphasis on managing the underclass instead of pursuing more serious offenders. Such forms of law enforcement serve as a "political diversion" that draws attention from the apparent lack of success in dealing with serious offenders (p. 112). Although critics argue that Irwin overstated his case by "claiming that jailed persons are less involved in serious criminality than is the case," there is agreement with him "regarding the broader issues of public policy toward members of the rabble class who get caught up in lawbreaking, and in many cases, who get sent to jails" (Backstand, Gibbons, & Jones, 1992, p. 228). (Also refer to Table 6.3 for current offense data.)

In taking a closer look at the jail experience, Irwin learned that the rabble undergo a distinct form of socialization by which they are stigmatized and kept constrained within the underclass. Inspired by the work of Erving Goffman in *Asylums* (1961), Irwin outlined four stages of the jail experience: disintegration, disorientation, degradation, and preparation.

DISINTEGRATION

Unlike white, employed, middle-class persons, who are perceived as being reputable and thus are generally released on their own recognizance or are able to meet bail, disreputable persons (the rabble) are detained. Detainment is the beginning of the disintegration stage in that it tends to destroy the few social ties the rabble might have. Simply being denied convenient access to telephones makes it difficult to contact one's family, friends, and court-appointed attorney. Moreover, being detained prevents one from "taking care of business," such as calling one's employer and paying bills.

Although convenient access to telephones in jail is often rare, sometimes circumstances make this problem worse. For example, in New York City's Rikers Island jail complex, there are reports that black inmates monopolize one telephone while Hispanic inmates dominate the other, leaving white inmates (who represent only 5% of the pretrial detainee population) without regular access to telephones.

Obviously, without regular contact with family, friends, and lawyers, jail inmates undergo considerable disintegration. Upon release, inmates have the stressful task of "picking up the pieces." As Irwin (1985) noted,

> Unlike released convicts and mental patients, they [jail inmates] have received no official preparation for their release. And when they do get out, city, county,

and private agencies rarely offer them any help in coping with the problems of reentering society. In trying to pick up the pieces of their shattered lives, most of them will be working alone, with virtually no resources and many handicaps. (p. 52; see also Weisheit & Klofas, 1989)

DISORIENTATION

Among the psychological effects of being arrested and detained is a profound sense of internal disorganization and demoralization. After months of detention, released inmates understandably reenter society in a state of confusion similar to "being in a fog." This degree of disorientation is compounded by the replacement of their personal routine by the institution's. For example, they eat according to a schedule organized by the staff, and assuming they can actually sleep, that too is dictated by the institution. Eventually, their sense of independence is replaced by feelings of powerlessness, which are further compounded by the humiliation inherent in being in jail. Moreover, in jail they eat, urinate, defecate, wash, change clothes, and bathe without privacy. They are continuously subjected to stares, comments, insults, and threats.

According to Irwin (1985), "Persons who are arrested and thrown in jail experience a sudden blow that hurls them outside society. It not only unravels their social ties; it stuns them and reduces their capacity and their resolve to make the journey back into society" (p. 66). Irwin conceded that being detained once or twice does not lead to permanent social isolation, but because many inmates are rabble who are detained rather frequently, their ability to "bounce back" is strained. "The jail is not the only expelling process, of course; economic misfortune and drug abuse are others" (p. 66).

DEGRADATION

As might be expected, the jail experience also involves relentless humiliation as inmates are continuously stripped of their dignity. Inmates are met with unyielding hostility from police officers, deputies, guards, and other detainees. Under routine surveillance by the staff, they are subjected to frisks, strip searches, and body cavity examinations. Irwin (1985) provided us with a glimpse of the humiliation one feels during a "kiester search" as described by a deputy:

"Now bend over and spread your cheeks," I ordered. The kid bent over and grabbed his buttocks, pulling them apart. The plastic bag [of narcotics] inserted into his rectum had broken. The red pills had partially melted from his body heat, and his anus was a flaming scarlet color. The intestinal pressure had forced some of the pills out through his sphincter where they remained matted in his anal hair. We began to laugh with black humor at the grotesque sight. When the cops became bored with the game, the kid was ordered to dig the narcotics out of his rectum. (p. 77)

In some jails, inmates are required to wear orange jumpsuits instead of their own clothes, which might help preserve some sense of personal identity. Additional aspects of the degradation process are the loss of privacy and being forced to live in an environment where the human density is intolerable; indeed, inmates are literally *warehoused*.

While in jail, inmates also endure a barrage of insults. They are routinely called slime balls, dirt balls, pukes, scum, kronks, and, the most popular reference, assholes. Following months of detention, their outward appearances are likely to change: Because shaving is not always easy, many inmates grow beards, and their hair becomes long and straggly. Not only is this an extension of degradation, but at their court appearance, inmates are judged not solely or even primarily on the basis of crimes, but rather on the basis of their character, which is generally assessed by their physical appearance (Irwin, 1985).

PREPARATION

Irwin (1985) pointed out that a great majority of those arrested and those detained are not sentenced to serve a jail or prison term. Considering the humiliation and degradation experienced at the hands of the criminal justice system, however, all those arrested are subjected to some form of punishment, even those whose charges are dismissed. Indeed, one way to view this pattern of social disgrace is to recognize it as "process as punishment."

Whereas reputable persons are likely to "pick up the pieces" and move forward with their lives, the rabble are less likely to do so. With limited means to survive and few resources and economic opportunities at their disposal, the rabble fall victim to the self-fulfilling prophecy constructed by the criminal justice system. For many, accepting the labels of "loser" or "asshole" and dropping out of society becomes the inevitable option. Considering this, the rabble become even more defeated and more socially disintegrated or marginalized, and, as Irwin asserted, "The jail experience prepares them for an acceptance of the rabble life" (p. 84).

Social Sanitation

So why is the jail in the business of locking up poor and disreputable persons? What larger social purpose is served by warehousing the rabble, especially when it is clear that these persons are *not* dangerous and do *not* pose an imminent threat to the community? One objective is *social sanitation,* the process by which police remove socially offensive (disreputable) persons from specific urban zones, thereby creating the illusion that certain sections of a city are indeed reputable.

Every medium to large city in the nation has a so-called "good" section and a so-called "seedy" section. Among the many tasks expected of city police is to keep the "good" section free of "riffraff" or disreputable persons: those who offend the middle-class sensibilities of the conventional world, such as streetwalking prostitutes, the homeless, drug addicts, and drug peddlers. Again, it is important to emphasize that the rabble are not regarded by the police as dangerous but rather as offensive to society at large. Whereas the truly dangerous go to prison, the merely offensive are sent to jail for a temporary stay (Irwin, 1985, p. 3; also see Klofas, 1987; McCarthy, 1990; Spitzer, 1975). In this sense, social sanitation is more *social control* than *crime control* because it emphasizes sweeping the urban streets of persons deemed offensive but not necessarily dangerous.

Therefore, the jail should always be placed in the context of social sanitation. As mentioned, the role of the jail in social sanitation has historical precedents. As early as the 16th century in Europe, when feudalism was unraveling and more vagabonds, beggars, prostitutes, "gonophs" (petty thieves), and peasants were drifting into the urban centers, jails were constructed for the purposes of social sanitation (Chesney, 1972).

The Effects of Jail Overcrowding

Not only is overcrowding itself a problem, but it becomes a source of other institutional problems as well. For example, it places enormous strain on classification, sorting, housing assignments, food, medical services (especially in light of HIV/AIDS and tuberculosis), security, and various programs, such as substance abuse counseling. Overcrowding also disrupts the daily routine of the facility and places additional pressure on budgetary allowances.

But the consequences of overcrowding reach beyond institutional operations by affecting both inmates and staff. The social psychological effects of overcrowding can be traced primarily to the stress it creates, resulting in anger, hostility, violence, anxiety, and depression. Jails are by their very nature stressful environments; overcrowding merely compounds preexisting problems that result from warehousing too many persons in too little space.

More specifically, recent studies have documented the effects of overcrowding on staff in terms of increased sick call and disciplinary violation rates, as well as higher mortality rates (Werner & Keys, 1988). This places additional stress not only on the staff and inmates but also on the jail as an institution, which must respond to the requirements of health care, security, and maintaining internal order.

The degree of disruption caused by overcrowding is far greater in jails than in prisons because of a number of factors. First, because jails are designed for short-term confinement, there is little emphasis on long-range routines for inmates. Consequently, few programs and services are available that can occupy and pacify the inmates. In fact, many violent incidents can be traced directly to inmates' resorting to fistfights to relieve the boredom caused by idleness. Again, this is a feature of warehousing, whereby inmates are merely tossed into jails until their court appearances. In addition, the inmates' relatively short stay in jail makes it difficult for staff to keep sorting out the troublemakers who are responsible for aggravating the already volatile conditions. Moreover, corrections officers have the onerous task of ensuring that fistfights do not escalate to large-scale disturbances and riots (see Chapter 8).

Civil Suits and Court Orders

As noted in *Cook v. City of New York* (1984), inmates do not forfeit all of their constitutional rights when they are incarcerated, even though the facility may limit some inmate rights in order to meet reasonable institutional needs (*U.S. v. Lewis,* 1975). Yet among the numerous consequences of overcrowding are civil and class action suits filed by attorneys representing jail inmates against the jail administrators (see Champion, 1991; Embert, 1986). Figures from the latest Bureau of Justice Statistics (1997) survey show that 378 state correctional facilities (27%) were under court order to reduce population or to improve conditions of confinement.

In 1979, a landmark case known as *Bell v. Wolfish* was filed in federal court. This case challenged the double-bunking practices of the Metropolitan Correctional Center (also known as the MCC), which serves as a federal jail in

New York. The double-bunking policy was initiated when the pretrial detainee population dramatically increased, thus inducing the Federal Bureau of Prisons to assign sentenced and unsentenced inmates to single-occupancy accommodations. The class action suit alleged violations of constitutional rights (such as undue length of confinement, improper searches, and inadequate employment, recreational, and educational opportunities). The U.S. Supreme Court rejected the allegations that these conditions violated inmates' constitutional rights. More important, because nearly all pretrial detainees were released within 60 days, double bunking was not regarded as unconstitutional.

Despite the *Bell v. Wolfish* ruling, sheriffs and jail wardens remain alert because the courts are capable of holding them personally liable for damages in cases filed by inmates who allege violations of their constitutional rights. Even if the courts rule in favor of the jail administrators, the time and effort involved in litigation become a major distraction to jail management. In light of these developments, many of the large urban jails continue to face similar lawsuits and court orders.

Conclusion

In this chapter, we have examined jail overcrowding in a larger social context by drawing attention to the urban underclass and social sanitation. By exploring the various ways in which large city jails cope with overcrowding, we have learned that jail policy tends to exacerbate complex social problems such as poverty, unemployment, homelessness, substance abuse, inadequate education, and inaccessible health care, each of which directly or indirectly contributes to street crime and jail overcrowding (Welch, 1992b).

In light of the interconnection between jail policy and social forces, it is important that we expand our awareness of social problems facing our cities and demand more ambitious social policies. For example, we have noted throughout this chapter that drug arrests account for the latest surge in jail populations. As mentioned, it makes more sense to treat drug abuse as a public health problem than as a criminal justice problem. Clearly, treatment upon demand is more cost-effective and goal oriented than mere warehousing.

Other areas of social policy requiring additional development are employment and educational programs. Indeed, serious investment in such programs is actually a crime control strategy. According to Mauer (1992), "Studies of the Head Start program, for example, have shown that every $1 invested in early intervention resulted in savings of $4.75 in remedial education, welfare, and crime costs" (p. 82; see also Currie, 1985). Such educational and employment programs are particularly relevant in light of the problems facing the urban underclass. Moreover, such interventions go to the root of the problem instead of relying on warehousing as a form of social sanitation.

Finally, has Irwin (1985) has argued, social reforms must be addressed before jail reform: "No progress at all can be made on reforming the jail until we begin to reform our fundamental societal arrangements. Until we do, the police will continue to sweep the streets of the rabble and dump them in the jails" (p. 118).

References

Backstand, J. A., Gibbons, D., & Jones, J. F. (1992). Who is in jail? An examination of the rabble hypothesis. *Crime and Delinquency, 38,* 219-229.
Barbanel, J. (1989, June 15). Lauder likes TV but at Rikers Jail it's an 'outrage'. *New York Times,* p. B-1.
Bell v. Wolfish, 441 U.S. 520 (1979).
Bureau of Justice Statistics. (1997). *Census of state and federal correctional facilities, 1995.* Washington, DC: Government Printing Office.
Bureau of Justice Statistics. (1998a). *Prison and jail inmates at midyear 1997.* Washington, DC: Government Printing Office.
Bureau of Justice Statistics. (1998b). *Prisoners in 1997.* Washington, DC: Government Printing Office.
Bureau of Justice Statistics. (1998c). *Profile of jail inmates, 1996.* Washington, DC: Government Printing Office.
Champion, D. J. (1991). Jail inmate litigation in the 1990s. In J. A. Thompson & G. L. Mays (Eds.), *American jails: Public policy issues* (pp. 197-215). Chicago: Nelson-Hall.
Chesney, K. (1972). *The Victorian underworld.* New York: Schocken.
Clear, T., & Cole, G. F. (1990), *Introduction to corrections* (2nd ed.). Monterey, CA: Brooks/Cole.
Cook v. City of New York, 578 F. Supp. 179 (1984).
Correctional Association of New York, (1989). *Basic prison and jail fact sheet.* New York: Author.
Currie, E (1985). *Confronting crime: An American challenge.* New York: Pantheon.
Embert, P. S. (1986). Correctional law and jails. In D. B. Kalinich & J. Klofas (Eds.), *Sneaking inmates down the alley: Problems and prospects in jail management* (pp. 63-84). Springfield, IL: Charles C Thomas.
Gibbs, J. J. (1982). The first cut is the deepest: Psychological breakdown and survival in the detention setting. In R. Johnson & H. Toch (Eds.), *The pains of imprisonment* (pp. 97-114). Prospect Heights, IL: Waveland.
Glaser, D. (1979). Some notes on urban jails. In D. Glaser (Ed.), *Crime in the city.* New York: Harper & Row.
Goffman, E. (1961). *Asylums.* Garden City, NY: Doubleday.
Goldfarb, R. (1975). *Jails: The ultimate ghetto.* Garden City, NY: Doubleday.
Irwin, J. (1985). *The jail: Managing the underclass in American society.* Berkeley: University of California Press.
Kerle, K. (1998). *American jails.* Boston: Butterworth-Heinemann.
Klofas, J. (1987). Patterns of jail use. *Journal of Criminal Justice. 15,* 403-411.

Klofas, J., Stojkovic, S., & Kalinich, D. A. (1992). The meaning of correctional crowding: Steps toward an index of severity. *Crime and Delinquency, 38,* 171-187.

Mauer, M. (1992, February 11). "Lock em up" is not key to crime control. *New York Newsday,* pp. 44, 82.

McCarthy, B. R. (1990). A micro-level analysis of social structure and social control: Intrastate use of jail and prison confinement. *Justice Quarterly, 7,* 325-340.

Moynahan, J. M., & Stewart, E. K. (1980). *The American jail: Its growth and development.* Chicago: Nelson-Hall.

Piven, F. F., & Cloward, R. A. (1971). *Regulating the poor: The functions of public welfare.* New York: Vintage.

Spitzer, S. (1975). Toward a Marxian theory of deviance. *Social Problems, 22,* 638-651.

U.S. v. Lewis, 400 F. Supp. 1046 (1975).

Weisheit, R. A., & Klofas, J. M. (1989). The impact of jail on collateral costs and affective response. *Journal of Offender Counseling, Services and Rehabilitation, 14,* 51-66.

Welch, M. (1989). Social junk, social dynamite and the rabble: Persons with AIDS in jail. *American Journal of Criminal Justice, 14,* 135-147.

Welch, M. (1991a). The expansion of jail capacity. Makeshift jails and public policy. In J. A. Thompson & G. L. Mays (Eds.), *American jails: Public policy issues* (pp. 148-162). Chicago: Nelson-Hall.

Welch, M. (1991b). Persons with AIDS in prison: A critical and phenomenological approach to suffering. *Dialectical Anthropology, 16,* 51-61.

Welch, M. (1992a, July/August). How are jails depicted by corrections textbooks? A content analysis provides a closer look. *American Jails: The Magazine of the American Jail Association,* pp. 28-34.

Welch, M. (1992b). Social class, special populations, and other unpopular issues: Setting the jail research agenda for the 1990s. In G. L. Mays (Ed.), *Setting the jail research agenda for the 1990s* (pp. 17-23). Washington, DC: National Institute of Corrections.

Welch, M. (1996). *Corrections: A critical approach* New York: McGraw-Hill.

Welsh, W., Leone, M. C., Kinkade, P., & Pontell, H. (1991). The politics of jail overcrowding: Public attitudes and official policies. In J. A. Thompson & G. L. Mays (Eds.), *American jails: Public policy issues* (pp. 131-147). Chicago: Nelson-Hall.

Werner, R. E., & Keys, C. (1988). The effects of changes in jail population densities on crowding, sick call, and spatial behavior, *Journal of Applied Social Psychology, 18,* 852-866.

Wilson, W. J. (1987) *The truly disadvantaged: The inner city, the underclass and public policy.* Chicago: University of Chicago Press.

CHAPTER 7

A Critical Interpretation of Correctional Boot Camps as Normalizing Institutions

Discipline, Punishment, and the Military Model

> Is it surprising that prisons resemble factories, schools, barracks, hospitals, which all resemble prisons?
>
> Michel Foucault (1979, p. 228)

Contributing to a critical interpretation of the penitentiary, Michel Foucault (1979) reminded us of the utility of *penal calculus* (or penal arithmetic), a concept by which punishment is organized and quantified. Based on an inverse formula, penal calculus proposes that prison sentences can be shortened—without evoking a negative reaction by retributionists—provided that the experience of imprisonment is simultaneously harshened.

AUTHOR'S NOTE: Reprinted from the *Journal of Contemporary Criminal Justice*, *13*(2), 1997, 184-205. ©1997 Sage Publications, Inc. Adapted with permission. I gratefully acknowledge the anonymous reviewers for their constructive comments and Marie Mark for her assistance in preparing this chapter.

In this vein, Foucault insisted that the early penitentiary was designed to punish more effectively, not to punish less.

Nowadays, the logic of penal calculus remains a crucial but implicit feature of correctional boot camps. Compared to traditional prison sentences, the length of confinement in correctional boot camps is reduced considerably; however, the experience of incarceration is intensified by the imposition of the rigors of a quasi-military regimen. Advocates of retribution and deterrence support penal calculus in the form of correctional boot camps primarily because it offers an appropriate and rational form of punishment. Coupled with administrative needs, correctional boot camps "have been enthusiastically embraced because they are designed to save scarce correctional dollars by reducing time served in institutions while simultaneously providing adequate *punishment* by virtue of the quasi-military environment, strict schedule, and daily work assignments" (MacKenzie, Brame, McDowall, & Souryal, 1995, p. 327; see also Cronin, 1994, and U.S. General Accounting Office, 1993; for more elaborate discussions on the temporal quantification of punishment, see Beccaria, 1764/1981; Goffman, 1961; Meisenhelder, 1985; Sykes, 1958; Welch, 1991b, 1996).

It is difficult to overlook the motif of militarism evident in the image and content of correctional boot camps. In examining correctional boot camps as normalizing institutions, this chapter critically explores the meaning of the military influence in corrections, especially vis-à-vis other normalizing institutions and disciplinary technologies.

The Emergence of Correctional Boot Camps

During the past 10 years, correctional boot camps have emerged as one of the most publicized alternatives to incarceration. Replete with grueling images of military basic training, correctional boot camps subject young, nonviolent offenders to a relatively brief but intense form of imprisonment. This seemingly innovative approach to alternative incarceration is based on the expectation that young, nonviolent (often first-time) offenders will respond more positively to a quasi-military regimen than to traditional imprisonment (see MacKenzie, 1996).

Currently, there are more than 59 state and 10 local correctional boot camps for adults operating in 30 states (Cronin, 1994). Nationwide, more than 7,000 beds are devoted to boot camp programs where offenders spend between 90 and 180 days; potentially, more than 23,000 offenders per year could complete a boot camp regimen. The largest correctional boot camp program is in New York State, where 1,500 beds are reserved for a boot camp-style program known as shock incarceration. Many other states also offer sizable programs: Georgia, 800 beds; Oklahoma, 400 beds; Michigan, 600 beds; Texas, 400 beds; and Maryland, 440 beds (MacKenzie, 1993). In addition, eight programs have been implemented for juveniles, and 13 states and the Federal Bureau of Prisons offer shock incarceration for women (MacKenzie, 1993). It is likely that such programs will continue to proliferate; in 1993, Congress began spending hundreds of millions of dollars to open additional military-style programs for young offenders (Nossiter, 1993).

Although correctional boot camps target offenders who are highly screened volunteers, there is, surprisingly, considerable attrition: Many inmates either voluntarily withdraw from the program or are dismissed for various infractions. Indeed, the attrition rate can be quite high, reaching 50% in some programs (MacKenzie & Shaw, 1990). Inmates who do not complete the program must serve their sentences in prison or return to the court for resentencing (MacKenzie, 1993). Upon completion of the program, some boot camp graduates are placed under intensive supervision or aftercare in the community (Bourque, Han, & Hill, 1996).

The popularity of correctional boot camps is mainly fueled by images of intense punishment in the public mind (Simon, 1995); undoubtedly, these programs are promoted more by public relations campaigns than other intermediate sanctions and alternatives to prison (e.g., dispute resolution, community service, day fines, electronic monitoring, and substance abuse treatment). Yet correctional boot camps are also driven by the administrative forces of correctional systems, particularly the need to alleviate prison and jail overcrowding (MacKenzie & Piquero, 1994). Like correctional systems as a whole, correctional boot camps draw on several fundamentally different— though not mutually exclusive—correctional philosophies—not only retribution and deterrence but also, in many cases, rehabilitation. And, borrowing from the military model, correctional boot camps also attempt to instill in offenders a sense of discipline and respect for authority.

Despite their widespread popularity, correctional boot camps are subject to considerable criticism. Among the more basic concerns, critics question the utility of the military model in contemporary corrections. Morash and Rucker (1990) asked, "Why would a method that has been developed to prepare people to go into war, and as a tool to manage legal violence, be considered as having such potential in deterring or rehabilitating offenders?" (p. 206). They argued that many of the militaristic features of correctional boot camps are incompatible with the goals of rehabilitation. For instance, they suggested that correctional boot camps, like the military, promote unquestioned obedience to authority as well as aggression, both of which are incongruent with prosocial behavior (Morash & Rucker, 1990; also see Marlowe et al., 1988; Raupp, 1978).

It should be noted that the introduction of militarism into corrections is not entirely new. In 1821, John Cray developed a military-correctional plan at Auburn prison for the purpose of maintaining order in an overcrowded institution (McKelvey, 1977, p. 14). The military model was later emulated at the Elmira Reformatory during the Progressive era; however, Superintendent Zebulon Brockway later eliminated lockstep marching and compulsory silence at Elmira because he regarded them as humiliating, thereby defeating efforts to reform young offenders (Cole, 1986, p. 497). Eventually, Elmira's military-correctional regimen incorporated other aspects of reform, such as academic and vocational training, as well as measures to improve self-esteem (Smith, 1988).

Interestingly, the U.S. military officially abandoned the traditional, confrontation style of basic training because of the adverse effects that intimidation and humiliation have on recruits. In fact, a military task force cited numerous problems inherent in traditional basic training, including inconsistent philosophies, policies, and procedures; unreasonable leadership; dysfunctional stress; and the arbitrary use of authority, leading to stress and anger (Faris, 1975; Marlowe et al., 1988; Morash & Rucker, 1990; Raupp, 1978). In light of the negative aspects of the outmoded military boot camp, a crucial question persists: How could a quasi-military approach to corrections encourage prosocial behavior among offenders, especially considering that correctional boot camps have the potential to increase aggression, thereby leading to antisocial behavior?

Within the realm of correctional boot camps, Morash and Rucker (1990) explored the influence and significance of popular stereotypes of masculinity: By focusing on gender, they illuminated the unstated importance of defining masculinity in terms of aggression. Correctional boot camps, like the traditional military boot camps, cultivate exaggerated images of masculinity while derogating any qualities considered feminine, including empathy, sensitivity, and cooperation. In the traditional military, as well as correctional boot camps, drill instructors often challenge the masculinity of their recruits by resorting to sexist antagonism, including such insults as "little girl," "woman," "wife," and "girly-man" (see Eisenhart, 1975; Steihem, 1981).

In response to the criticism that correctional boot camps draw too heavily on the military model and not enough on the treatment model, many of these programs evolved into a more pronounced hybrid or eclectic model by incorporating elements of rehabilitation and education (see Clark, Aziz, & MacKenzie, 1994; Cowles, Castellano, & Gransky, 1995; McCorkle, 1995). A case in point: The New York State shock incarceration program is described in its brochure as a highly structured and regimented routine that involves extensive discipline, physical labor, exercise, and intensive drug rehabilitation. Moreover, the program claims to offer education, work ethic, and job skills. The percentages of time dedicated to each of the program's components are as follows: hard labor, 31%; alcohol and substance abuse counseling, 27%; personal time (includes meals, church, visits, homework, etc.), 12.9%; drill, 10%; academics, 9.8%; and physical training, 9.3% (New York State Department of Corrections, 1992).

Correctional Boot Camps and Recidivism

Crucial questions surround the effectiveness of correctional boot camps, particularly their impact on recidivism. In fact, MacKenzie, Shaw, and Gowdy (1993) conceded that correctional boot camps have not been successful in reducing recidivism:

> At this time, the effectiveness of IMPACT [Intensive Motivational Program of Alternative Correctional Treatment] in reducing recidivism remains questionable. Positive changes may be apparent as more community supervision data become available. Clearly, offenders need additional support or help in making the transition back into the community. Although offenders experience some positive changes when in the program, these changes are not enough to enable them to successfully overcome the difficulties they face when they return to their home environment. (pp. 6-7)

Similarly, MacKenzie et al. (1995) evaluated correctional boot camps and recidivism in eight states and concluded that "those who complete boot camp do not inevitably perform either better or worse than their comparison group counterparts" (p. 327). The National Institute of Justice (1994) also reported that the return-to-prison rates for shock incarceration graduates were not much different from rates for those who did not participate in the boot camp style program (also see Osler, 1991).

These findings are subject to competing interpretations. On one hand, it could be debated that correctional boot camps are unsuccessful because their recidivism rates are not any better than those of traditional prisons. Conversely, boot camps could be deemed successful because they yield the same rate of recidivism as traditional prison but in less time, thereby accruing fewer costs and being more cost-effective. (These findings also illuminate the limitations and costliness of traditional prison sentences, especially with respect to recidivism.)

Criticisms of Correctional Boot Camps

Correctional boot camps are criticized on several conceptual grounds. First, the uncritical acceptance of correctional boot camps as an intermediate sanction remains a significant concern. For instance, Georgia's governor, Zell Miller, fervently defended the state's correctional boot camps against questions about their long-term impact: "Nobody can tell me from some ivory tower that you take a kid, you kick him in the rear end, and it doesn't do any good. And I don't give a damn what they say, we're going to continue to do it in Georgia" (Nossiter, 1993, p. 9).

A second criticism of correctional boot camps is their assumption that young offenders can be scared into discipline, obedience, and respect for authority. There is no compelling evidence supporting the claim that intimidation leads to prosocial behavior. In light of what scholars have learned from evaluating other intimidation-style interventions, such as "Scared Straight" programs (see Buckner & Chesney-Lind, 1983; Cavender, 1981; Finckenauer, 1982; Vito & Wilson, 1985), there is little reason to believe that correctional boot camps can somehow transform balky recruits into law-abiding citizens in just 6 weeks.

A third conceptual issue is correctional boot camps' reliance on an outmoded military basic training model that promotes exaggerated images of masculinity. As noted, it has been argued that confrontation-style boot camps tend to produce aggression among its participants, thereby undermining their objective of inducing prosocial behavior (Morash & Rucker, 1990).

In sum, correctional boot camps rest on several key contradictions; perhaps most significant is their routine release of young offenders from intensive boot camp training into an economy that is unlikely to absorb them. "Even if the typical 90-day regime of training envisioned by proponents of boot camps is effective in reorienting its subjects, at best it can only produce soldiers without a company to join" (Feeley & Simon, 1992, p. 464). Considering this, boot camps represent yet another correctional strategy inherently flawed by its attempt to correct the individual while neglecting adverse social conditions (e.g., poverty, social inequality) and their relationship to crime (see Fowles & Merva, 1996; Gans, 1995; Welch, 1990, 1991a, 1996; Wilson, 1987).

Correctional Boot Camps as Normalizing Institutions

In addition to being a symbolic response to society's demand for order, control, and regulation of social conduct, prisons in general—and correctional boot camps in particular—are normalizing institutions. According to Foucault (1979), normalization is a corrective process rather than a strictly punitive one, as conformity—not retribution—is its main objective. "And since the object is to correct rather than punish, the actual sanctions used tend to involve exercises and training, measures which in themselves help bring conduct 'into line' and help make individuals more self-controlled" (Garland, 1990, p. 145). From this perspective, Foucault characterized normalization as a gentler form of social control.

In light of the many criticisms facing correctional boot camps, a key question remains: Why has the military become the normalizing institution of choice in modeling this form of correctional intervention? Foucault reminded us that the prison is merely one of several institutions that discipline the wayward. Families, churches, and schools also serve as vital socializing institutions, but when these traditional normalizing institutions fail at their task of instilling discipline, the state, via the criminal justice apparatus, assumes a legitimate role in normalization (see Habermas, 1975). In addition to numerous other sanctions, the state uses prisons to discipline the wayward. Extending beyond mere retribution, however, prisons were originally designed to transform offenders into law-abiding citizens. To facilitate transformation or conversion, prison officials employed key disciplinary technologies (Foucault, 1979).

> In several respects, the prison must be an exhaustive disciplinary apparatus: it must assume responsibility for all aspects of the individual, his physical training, his aptitude to work, his everyday conduct, his moral attitude, his state of mind; the prison, much more than the school, the workshop or the army, which always involved a certain specialization, is omnidisciplinary. (Foucault, 1979, pp. 235-236)

Various Normalizing Institutions and Disciplinary Technologies

Given the existence of various institutions that could be replicated, why does the state fashion alternatives to incarceration according to the military model? Moreover, why don't corrections officials explicitly develop normalizing programs based on other social institutions, such as the family, churches or monasteries, hospitals/clinics, schools, factories, farms, corporations, or even athletics or martial arts? Because each of these social institutions and agencies instills normalization and discipline, let us explore them as templates for intermediate sanctions vis-à-vis correctional boot camps.

THE FAMILY MODEL

First and foremost, the family, especially through primary socialization, functions as the ideal normalizing institution. Although correctional administrators have never formally adopted the family model per se, pseudofamilies in some correctional facilities offer emotional support and comfort for female inmates (Culbertson & Fortune, 1986; Fox, 1984; Hart, 1995; MacKenzie, Robinson, & Campbell, 1989; Pollock-Byrne, 1990). Similarly, prison gangs and cliques provide emotional support as well as a sense of identity for some male inmates (Jacobs, 1974; also see Welch, 1996). It should also be noted that in therapeutic correctional settings where group counseling is offered (e.g., substance abuse treatment), familial-type support often emerges among participants as a positive group dynamic (Peat & Winfree, 1992; Welch, Ford, & Mabli, 1988; Yablonsky, 1989). Unlike the violent and combative overtones of the military model, the family model has the potential to engender genuine forms of support and guidance, thereby facilitating correctional reform.

THE CHURCH AND MONASTIC MODEL

Historically, religious forces have shaped the course of punishment and the emergence of the penitentiary (Barnes & Teeters, 1946; Foucault, 1979; Newman, 1978). In fact, the term *penitentiary* derives from the word *penance*, and from its inception, incarceration was meant to be a monastic experience. Much like European penitentiaries, American prisons built during the Jacksonian period (1820s and 1830s) formally adopted the monastic model (Rothman, 1971). Religious instruction, particularly in the form of reading scripture while subjected to solitary confinement, was believed to accelerate reform (Foucault, 1979; Garland, 1990). Nowadays, religion continues to mold the prison experience of some inmates, particularly those who engage in religious activities (Dammer, 1996); however, with the exception of hiring chaplains and accommodating religious practices, the contemporary prison does not officially pattern itself after the monastery, even though religion does offer the potential to normalize and discipline inmates.

THE HOSPITAL AND CLINICAL MODEL

As rehabilitation was ushered into corrections, especially during the Progressive era (1870s) and again with the formal application of the medical model in the 1930s through the 1960s, the hospital or clinical model was officially adopted (Rothman, 1980). Replete with state-of-the-art corrective technologies and clinical staff, prisons embraced rehabilitation through classification and individualized treatment (Rothman, 1980). Though contemporary corrections has given way to a more punitive orientation, rehabilitation today continues to enjoy considerable popularity (Welch, 1995). Indeed, public opinion polls demonstrate that citizens generally support correctional rehabilitation, especially in the form of substance abuse treatment (Maguire & Pastore, 1995, pp. 165, 176, 198; also see Cullen, Cullen, & Wozniak, 1988; Welsh, Leone, Kinkade, & Pontell, 1991).

Though the clinical model offers potential to treat and normalize offenders (Gendreau, 1996a; 1996b), it is no longer a guiding model for the contemporary prison. In fact, even the Federal Bureau of Prisons—at one time the leader in innovative treatment—has officially abandoned rehabilitation in favor of a perspective known as humane control (Welch, 1996). Despite criticisms of the treatment model, however, many correctional boot camps (e.g., New York State) emphasize rehabilitation, particularly in the realm of substance abuse treatment (see Cowles et al., 1995). In fact, it has been suggested that correctional boot camps offer greater access to rehabilitation than is available in traditional prisons (Clark et al., 1994).

THE SCHOOL AND EDUCATIONAL MODEL

In conjunction with rehabilitation, the school model of reform (i.e., education and vocational training) also has been formally adopted in corrections throughout much of America's history. For example, during the Progressive era, Elmira Reformatory was established as a progressive institution that stressed education; in fact, it donned the nickname "the college on the hill" with considerable pride (Rothman, 1980). Although Superintendent Zebulon

Brockway endorsed militaristic decorum in the daily regimen at Elmira, the focus remained on reform through education (Rothman, 1980; Smith, 1988). Though some correctional institutions continue to promote education in adult and juvenile facilities, many programs remain grossly underfunded and understaffed (see Maguire & Pastore, 1995, p. 560). As previously noted, correctional boot camps offer, in addition to substance abuse treatment, educational programs within a militaristic regimen.

THE FACTORY, PLANTATION, AND CORPORATE MODELS

Throughout the history of punishment and corrections, work has remained a significant motif in disciplining offenders as well as making them more useful (see Ignatieff, 1978; Melossi & Pavarini, 1981; Rusche & Kirchheimer, 1939/1968). During the rise of the American penitentiary, prison labor was also viewed through a religious lens as a means of promoting a work ethic. In that era, Northern prisons structured inmate labor according to the factory, whereas Southern prisons emulated the plantation (Barnes & Teeters, 1946).

Although the contemporary prison and correctional boot camps both require work as part of the daily regimen (especially working the land and other chores borrowed from the plantation), few transferable job skills are actually attained—which is perhaps a fringe punishment. Today, even if correctional boot camps were devoted to developing transferable job skills for their prisoners, it would be unrealistic to expect that such skills could be acquired during a few months of imprisonment.

Yet given the social functions of employment, especially its implications for crime control (see Barlow, Barlow, & Johnson, 1996; Box & Hale, 1982; Chiricos & Bales, 1991; Chiricos & DeLone, 1992; Fowles & Merva, 1996; Greenberg, 1977; Hale, 1989; Wilkins, 1991; also see Welch, 1996, pp. 111-114), the question remains: Why don't prisons place a greater emphasis on vocational training and job placement? Arguably, the factory, plantation, or even corporate (e.g., use of computers for information-based and service-oriented tasks) models of normalization seem more immediately relevant to the correctional population than the military model. Given the importance of employment as a crime control strategy, we shall return to this issue.

THE ATHLETIC AND MARTIAL ARTS MODELS

As noted, correctional boot camps also set out to instill motivation, discipline, and physical conditioning, yet these objectives can be achieved without adhering to the military model. Athletics, for instance, remains a popular extracurricular activity in schools largely because sports cultivate motivation, discipline, and physical conditioning. It should be mentioned that athletics is a powerful normalizing institution insofar as achievers enjoy elevated status in schools (as well as society), often overshadowing achievers in other social spheres (e.g., academics and community service). In fact, athletics is such a powerful normalizing institution that male adolescents who are not successful at sports are often marginalized, labeled, and stigmatized as "losers," "geeks," "nerds," "dorks," and so on.

Athletics is also credited with teaching and rewarding teamwork, competition, and pride. Much like the military, athletic teams wear uniforms, enforce good grooming, discourage individualism (via slogans and sports mantras such as "Be a team player" and "There is no 'I' in 'We' "), follow the instructions of team "captains," and set their sights on earning victories. Interestingly, the military occasionally mimics sports by engaging in "war games."

For the sake of argument, why not use athletics as a viable model in designing intermediate sanctions? Instead of, or in addition to, correctional boot camps, perhaps corrections officials could develop a correctional program similar to football summer training camp. As a model for correctional intervention, football summer training camp is probably a better choice than baseball spring training because of its inherent rigor and emphasis on strenuous conditioning drills in the searing heat. Comedian George Carlin delves into the distinctions between football and baseball, concluding that baseball is a "sissy" sport whereas football is a "manly" sport. Baseball, for example, is played on a diamond; batters often hit fly balls; and the object of the game is to go home. By contrast, football is played on a gridiron where the quarterback (often the team captain, "field general," and hero) throws bombs over the defense and into the end zone (though from a religious point of view, the quarterback sometimes throws desperation passes known as "Hail Marys"). When a tied score must be resolved, baseball games are subject to extra innings, whereas football contests move into sudden death. In a humorous and perceptive way, Carlin's comments on football draw attention to exaggerated images of masculinity—images widely prevalent in the military as well (see Eisenhart, 1975; Morash & Rucker, 1990). Similarly, martial arts might serve as a viable model for correctional programming because karate, judo, kung fu and so on, teach discipline, motivation, and self-control. Furthermore, like the religious model, the martial arts model emphasizes spirituality. Though critics would probably disapprove of the violent aspects of martial arts, it can hardly be said that the martial arts are more violent than the military. Furthermore, spirituality and self-restraint are endorsed by martial artists, whereas the U.S. military is not known to advocate explicitly any form of spirituality.

Target Audience Versus Target Population

By its very name, correctional boot camps imply a militaristic intervention for normalizing young, nonviolent offenders. Yet many correctional boot camps are increasingly eclectic, borrowing from several other normalizing institutions—most notably, the clinic, school, and plantation. In fact, many correctional boot camps are omnidisciplinary institutions featuring substance abuse treatment, education, and strenuous plantation-style labor. Thus, given the inclusion of treatment, education, and plantation chores, why do such correctional programs call themselves boot camps, especially when there is a strong case for naming them correctional clinics, correctional schools, or even correctional plantations? Given the potential of other normalizing institutions, why does the military persist as the model of choice in naming these correctional programs?

In answering these questions, we should acknowledge the target audience to whom correctional boot camps are presented. At first glance, it would seem that correctional boot camps were developed for the benefit of the target population—young, low-income, urban (implicitly minority) offenders. Yet correctional boot camps have become tremendously popular because they are geared toward and appeal to middle-income (implicitly white) suburban citizens and their political representatives (see Simon, 1995). Indeed, correctional boot camps are image-driven sanctions that promote tough, macho, and militaristic depictions of normalization. Hence, correctional boot camps are perhaps publicized by the state to placate a public that has grown skeptical about conventional use of prisons (see Maguire & Pastore, 1995, p. 157). It should be noted that newspaper articles and televised news programs that examine correctional boot camps—whose audience is typically white, suburban, and middle income—are often accompanied by photographs or videotape footage depicting boot camps' grueling regimen.

The Job Corps as a Model for Alternatives to Incarceration

Given the importance of gainful employment in leading a law-abiding life (as already noted), perhaps correctional programs should incorporate meaningful job training. With this mind, alternatives to prison could emulate, for instance, the Job Corps. As a federal program administered by the Labor Department, the Job Corps trains young men and women in vocational trades, thereby enabling them to compete better for employment. According to Donziger (1996),

> The federal Job Corps program helps at-risk youth overcome the barriers to employment. . . . Every dollar invested in Jobs Corps returned $1.46 to society through decreased income maintenance payments, reductions in costs of incarceration, and taxes paid by former Jobs Corps students. The private sector also has a role to play through vocational training programs, summer internships for teenagers, and a variety of programs designed to bring people into the workforce. (pp. 216-217)

As mentioned, throughout much of America's correctional history, prison labor was modeled after the factory and the plantation (Barnes & Teeters, 1946; Rusche & Kirchheimer, 1939/1968). One rationale for requiring inmates to work was that prisoners were learning transferable job skills; upon closer scrutiny, however, prison labor practices were driven more by the pursuit of profit than by the benevolence of vocational training (Rothman, 1971). Nevertheless, a Job Corps model that emphasizes job training seems more appropriate than a military model that offers a boot camp experience.

As compelling as the idea is, the Job Corps (or the factory, plantation, or corporate) model is not likely to be the actualized in today's correctional system. Certainly, if training inmates with viable job skills translated into securing gainful employment (and reducing recidivism), such a program would have been established long ago. As plausible as the Job Corps model seems, one can speculate why job-oriented programs for inmates have not been ambitiously developed on a large scale.

Perhaps an obvious explanation for the dearth of job-oriented programs for prisoners is the decline in employment opportunities for the general population; indeed, there are more qualified individuals seeking employment than there are jobs (Aronowitz & DiFazio, 1994; Mishel & Bernstein, 1994; Phillips, 1990). With job-hiring freezes and wholesale corporate downsizing, securing employment is becoming increasingly difficult, even for college educated, middle-class persons. Moreover, an economic trend that greatly affects the working and lower classes is the erosion of manufacturing jobs that once provided viable employment for urban workers (Aronowitz & DiFazio, 1994; Currie, 1985; Gans, 1995; Stewart, 1996; Wilson, 1987). This economic trend is particularly relevant to a vast segment of the correctional population (most of whom are from the working and lower classes) because workforces in many traditional blue-collar jobs have been dramatically reduced. Macroeconomic trends and policies that contribute to the massive reduction of manufacturing jobs in the United States notwithstanding, the problem remains: Without the likelihood of viable employment, the Job Corps model in corrections would merely raise false expectations. Moreover, the lack of success in securing employment after incarceration would probably exacerbate alienation, frustration, and loss of hope among former prisoners (see Irwin & Austin, 1994).

Perhaps one unstated function of correctional boot camps is to serve as a substitute for a Job Corps model. Similarly, make-work devices (e.g., the treadmill, crank, and shot drill) were invented during the early 1800s when prison jobs were scarce and again in the early 1900s when prison labor was restricted by union activism (Barnes & Teeters, 1946, p. 691). Thus, prisoners, instead of being offered meaningful work, were assigned meaningless tasks that resembled labor only in form and ritual. Much like militaristic exercises (e.g., drills, marching, inspections), make-work devices were monotonous, repetitive, and degrading (Welch, 1996, p. 55).

Correctional boot camps set out to instill discipline and, just as importantly, a sense of optimism (instead of alienation) among their participants; paradoxically, however, they transform recruits to be more obedient but not necessarily more useful. Ironically, graduates of correctional boot camps participate in commencement ceremonies but are then released back into a society whose economy is not likely to absorb them. According to *The Report of the National Criminal Justice Commission,*

> When military boot camp is completed, the new soldier is at least assured of a job. In boot camps for inmates, there are usually not even services to help the offender look for a job. It is unrealistic to expect that a few weeks of rigorous physical training will prepare offenders to avoid or overcome the problems that led to their conviction. (Donziger, 1996, p. 57)

Let us not, of course, overlook another key obstacle facing ex-cons in their efforts to secure employment, namely the principle of *less eligibility.* From this perspective, lawbreakers ought not be granted services or opportunities that law-abiding citizens have difficulty attaining (e.g., employment, education, and adequate health care; Garland, 1985, 1990; Rusche & Kirchheimer, 1939/1968). Understandably, in an economy where employment is becoming increasingly scarce, policies that recommend placing ex-cons in jobs that might otherwise be occupied by law-abiding citizens promise to provoke the wrath of the public.

In the final analysis, then, it seems that correctional boot camps function as a metaphor for transformation instead of actually producing substantive improvements in prisoners' lives after they serve their prison sentences. Rather than contributing to significant changes in offenders' lives that might occur with viable employment, correctional boot camps at best offer symbolic and cosmetic changes with a militaristic flair. Though many correctional boot camps offer substance abuse treatment and remedial education, given the brief duration of the program (approximately 6 to 8 weeks), it is unrealistic to expect that any enduring changes can be achieved without extensive follow-up and substantive improvements in the graduates' life chances.

The Military as a Model and Metaphor for Ordering Criminal Justice as Well as Society

Why is the military the model and metaphor of choice in formulating intermediate sanctions? In answering this question, let us explore how the military serves as a model and metaphor for ordering both the criminal justice system and society.

In many societies, the military symbolizes strength, discipline, and public safety. Similarly, the military serves as a model of organization in criminal justice and offers a method of transforming problem populations (i.e., lawbreakers) into law-abiding citizens (Spitzer, 1975). In fact, throughout much of America's history, the criminal justice system has modeled itself after the military: For instance, law enforcement agencies and correctional institutions are typically paramilitary organizations. Like the military, paramilitary organizations conform to a rigid hierarchy: Orders emanate from top officials, traveling down the chain of command to the rank and file (Jacobs, 1977). In sum, the military model remains an integral part of criminal justice agencies partly because it serves as a means of organization but also because it maintains power relations within the criminal justice professions (Hepburn, 1985).

Similarly, the military functions as a metaphor in criminal justice. Criminal justice agencies deliberately borrow from the military in formulating messages (and propaganda) delivered to the civilian population (see Chambliss, 1995; Gordon, 1994): Consider the phrase *law and order,* the promise of police "to protect and serve," and the "wars" on crime and drugs—appropriately, directed by the attorney "general" and the drug "czar" (Welch, 1997). The use of military metaphors ought not be dismissed as trivial. Crime control messages (and propaganda) are aimed primarily at a white, suburban, and middle-income audience (Gordon, 1994; also see Edalman, 1988; Zimmer, 1992), and crime (including illegal drugs) continues to be a highly emotional issue in part because it continues to be framed in military terms by so-called law-and-order politicians seeking election and reelection (Clear, 1994; Welch, 1997).

At a higher level of abstraction, the military model and metaphor in criminal justice reflect the larger social forces that tend to order society. Arguably, the military model is used by the state as a template for shaping the order as well as the stratification of society, thereby reinforcing class divisions through coercive mechanisms. Foucault (1979) supported this notion in describing

> a military dream of society; its fundamental reference was not to the state of nature, but to meticulously subordinated cogs of a machine, not to the primal social contract, but to permanent coercions, not to fundamental rights, but to infinitely progressive forms of training, not to the general will, but to automatic docility. (p. 169)

For political leaders and citizens alike, the military offers an appealing and rational model for society, especially when society is threatened by crime and disorder (see Leighton, 1995). Accordingly, the mainstream accepts the military model and metaphor in criminal justice as well as society as a whole because together they represent a sense of order, safety, and protection.

Conclusion

Recent surveys report that many citizens have little confidence in the criminal justice system (Maguire & Pastore, 1995, pp. 145-146) and even blame the courts and prisons for the increase in crime (Maguire & Pastore, 1995, p. 157). In light of this criticism, correctional boot camps, as intermediate sanctions, seem to draw support from the mainstream, in part because the quasi-military regimen offers a renewed image of effective punishment and discipline. Despite their limited effectiveness (Feeley & Simon, 1992; Morash & Rucker, 1990; Sechrest, 1989; Simon, 1995), correctional boot camps continue to proliferate. Thus, the trend in correctional boot camps generally supports Foucault's (1979) contention that many forms of punishment and correction remain perfunctory and ceremonial long after their lack of utility has been acknowledged. The military aspect of correctional boot camps appears to have only symbolic and political value, yet it endures in large part because its symbolic and political value.

Thus, it is suggested that if prison officials want correctional boot camps to be more effective, they should emulate other normalizing institutions, namely the school and the clinic. Indeed, many correctional boot camps have already begun incorporating education and treatment into their programs. In New York State, for example, where correctional boot camps involve a great deal of substance abuse treatment, various other interventions also show promise. As in other states, a large portion (34%) of New York's 68,000 prisoners are drug offenders, yet New York courts and caseworkers do not treat all drug offenders the same. In fact, special consideration is given to the severity of their offenses as well as their addictions. Each year, the Court Employment Project (New York City) enrolls 900 young, first-time (adult felony) offenders who have been convicted of drug offenses (e.g., selling), robbery, or burglary and who are not significant drug users. These offenders are subjected to intensive supervision for 6 months, then are assigned to probation for 3 to 5 years. During that period, various forms of rehabilitation are offered: education, employment, drug counseling, and health services. The savings from diverting these felons from prison were estimated at $6 million dollars in 1995. Moreover, the recidivism rate of its graduates was 31% within the first 2 years, compared with 50% for similar felons serving traditional state prison sentences ("Successful Alternatives to Prison," 1996).

For second-felony offenders who have more severe drug problems, another program is available—Drug Treatment Alternatives to Prison (Brooklyn, NY). Because these offenders face lengthy sentences under the state's repeat-offender law, prosecutors persuade (or perhaps coerce) them to participate in residential drug treatment. Initial evaluation figures show a 19% recidivism rate among the program's first 161 graduates (the program is limited to 350 beds). The annual cost is set at $270,000 for administration and $18,000 per participant. At another drug rehabilitation center, known as Willard (NY), 600 nonviolent felons began treatment in November 1995. Following 3 months of drug treatment, inmates receive 6 months of outpatient treatment and community supervision ("Successful Alternatives to Prison," 1996).

Taken together, these rehabilitation programs offer multiple services (e.g., drug and medical treatment, education, employment guidance, aftercare, and supervision), all at a cost much lower than traditional prison (ranging from $25,000 per inmate annually for minimum security to $74,000 for maximum security; Welch, 1996). Moreover, traditional prisons do not offer these types of rehabilitation programs, or at least not with the same commitment to treatment. It should also be noted that these programs also save tax dollars by alleviating prison crowding, thus averting additional prison construction, which costs $100,000 per cell (Dao, 1994).

These treatment programs appear more sensible than expensive prisons that lack rehabilitation programs—perhaps explaining why some correctional boot camps are increasingly emulating the clinic as a normalizing institution. The actual content and objective of many correctional boot camps is omnidisciplinary, with a growing commitment to rehabilitation. Thus, it seems that correctional boot camps are given a militaristic image purely for public relations reasons. Recently, even MacKenzie et al. (1995, p. 154) cast doubt on the application of the military model as a normalizing institution by asking, "Does the military atmosphere add anything above and beyond a short-term, quality prison treatment program?"

Unfortunately, bona fide treatment programs and correctional boot camps are mere specks on the larger correctional radar screen. Drug offenders assigned to these special treatment programs represent only a minute fraction of those sentenced to prison. Unquestionably, the vast proportion of offenders sentenced to prison are shuffled off to institutions equipped only for warehousing. Although the military model is problematic, correctional boot camps are a much better alternative than traditional incarceration, especially if rehabilitation is a primary objective. However, there is a significant problem when correctional boot camps divert offenders, particularly drug abusers, from bona fide treatment programs. Further, prudent social policy ought to reach beyond the drug problem and stay committed to creating viable employment as a mechanism of crime control. In the end, achieving greater employment reduces the need for remedial normalizing institutions (see Donziger, 1996, pp. 195-219, for detailed social and economic policy recommendations).

References

Aronowitz, S., & DiFazio, W. (1994). *The jobless future: Sci-tech and the dogma of work.* Minneapolis: University of Minnesota Press.

Barlow, D. E., Barlow, M. H., & Johnson, W. W. (1996). The political economy of criminal justice policy. *Justice Quarterly, 13,* 223-241.

Barnes, H., & Teeters, N. (1946). *New horizons in criminology* (3rd ed.). New York: Prentice Hall.

Beccaria, C. (1981). *On crimes and punishments* (H. Paolucci, Trans.). Indianapolis, IN: Bobbs-Merrill. (Original work published 1764)

Bourque, B. B., Han, M., & Hill, S. M. (1996, May). A national survey of aftercare provisions for boot camp graduates. In *National Institute of Justice Research in Brief.* Washington, DC: National Institute of Justice.

Box, S., & Hale, C. (1982). Economic crisis and the rising prison population in England and Wales. *Crime and Social Justice, 17,* 20-35.

Buckner, J. C., & Chesney-Lind, M. (1983). Dramatic cures for juvenile crime: An evaluation of a prisoner-run delinquency prevention program. *Journal of Criminal Justice and Behavior, 10,* 227-247.

Cavender, G. (1981). Scared straight: Ideology and the media. *Journal of Criminal Justice, 9,* 431-439.

Chambliss, W. (1995). Another lost war: The costs and consequences of drug prohibition. *Social Justice, 22*(2), 101-124.

Chiricos, T. G., & Bales, W. D. (1991). Unemployment and punishment: An empirical assessment. *Criminology, 29,* 701-724.

Chiricos, T. G., & DeLone, M. A. (1992). Labor surplus and punishment: A review and assessment of theory and evidence. *Social Problems, 39,* 421-446.

Clark, C. L., Aziz, D. W., & MacKenzie, D. L. (1994). *Shock incarceration in New York: Focus on treatment.* Washington, DC: National Institute of Justice.

Clear, T. R. (1994). *Harm in American penology: Offenders, victims, and their communities.* Albany: State University of New York Press.

Cole, G. (1986). *The American system of criminal justice.* Monterey, CA: Brooks/Cole.

Cowles, E. L., Castellano, T. C., & Gransky, L. A. (1995, July). "Boot camp" drug treatment and aftercare interventions: An evaluation review. In *National Institute of Justice Research in Brief.* Washington, DC: National Institute of Justice.

Cronin, R. C. (1994). *Boot camps for adult and juvenile offenders: Overview and update.* Washington, DC: National Institute of Justice.

Culbertson, R. G., & Fortune, E. P. (1986). Incarcerated women: Self-concept and argot roles. *Journal of Offender Counseling, Services, and Rehabilitation, 10*(3), 25-49.

Cullen, F. T., Cullen, J. B., & Wozniak, J. F. (1988). Is rehabilitation dead? The myth of the punitive public. *Journal of Criminal Justice, 16,* 303-317.

Currie, E. (1985). *Confronting crime: An American challenge.* New York: Pantheon.

Dammer, H. R. (1996). Religion in prison. In M. McShane & F. Williams (Eds.), *Encyclopedia of American prisons* (pp. 399-403). New York: Garland.

Dao, J. (1994, April 4). Alternatives to jailing addicts: Treatment approach to drugs helps users and cuts costs. *New York Times,* p. B-3.

Donziger, S. R. (1996). *The real war on crime: The report of the National Criminal Justice Commission.* New York: Harper/Perennial.

Edalman, M. (1988). *Constructing the political spectacle.* Chicago: University of Chicago Press.

Eisenhart, R. W. (1975). You can't hack it, little girl: A discussion of the covert psychological agenda of modern combat training. *Journal of Social Issues, 31,* 13-23.

Faris, J. H. (1976). The impact of basic combat training: The role of the drill sergeant. In E. Goldman & D. R. Segal (Eds.), *The social psychology of military service* (pp. 13-24). Beverly Hills, CA: Sage.

Feeley, M. M., & Simon, J. (1992). The new penology: Notes on the emerging strategy of corrections and its implications. *Criminology, 30,* 449-474.

Finckenauer, J. O. (1982). *Scared straight! and the panacea phenomenon.* Englewood Cliffs, NJ: Prentice Hall.

Foucault, M. (1979). *Discipline and punish: The birth of the prison.* New York: Vintage.

Fowles, R., & Merva, M. (1996). Wage inequality and criminal activity: An extreme bounds analysis for the United States, 1975-1990. *Criminology, 34,* 163-182.

Fox, J. (1984). Women's prison policy, political activism, and the impact of the contemporary feminist movement: A case study. *Prison Journal, 64,* 15-36.

Gans, H. J. (1995). *The war against the poor: The underclass and antipoverty policy.* New York: Basic Books.

Garland, D. (1985). *Punishment and welfare: A history of penal strategies.* Brookfield, VT: Gower.

Garland, D. (1990). *Punishment and modern society: A study in social theory.* Oxford, UK: Oxford University Press.

Gendreau, P. (1996a). Offender rehabilitation: What we know and what needs to be done. *Criminal Justice and Behavior, 23,* 144-161.

Gendreau, P. (1996b). The principles of effective intervention with offenders. In A. Harland (Ed.), *Choosing correctional options that work* (pp. 117-130). Thousand Oaks, CA: Sage.

Goffman, E. (1961). *Asylums: Essays on the social situation of mental patients and other inmates.* Garden City: Anchor.

Gordon, D. (1994). Drugspeak and the Clinton administration: A lost opportunity for drug policy reform. *Social Justice, 21*(3), 30-36.

Greenberg, D. F. (1977). The dynamics of oscillatory punishment process. *Journal of Criminal Law and Criminology, 68,* 643-651.

Habermas, J. (1975). *Legitimation crisis.* Boston: Beacon.

Hale, C. (1989). Economy, punishment and imprisonment. *Contemporary Crisis, 13,* 327-350.

Hart, C. B. (1995). Gender differences in social support among inmates. *Women and Criminal Justice, 6*(2), 67-88.

Hepburn, J. (1985). The exercise of power in coercive organizations: A study of prison guards. *Criminology, 23*(1),145-164.

Ignatieff, M. (1978). *A just measure of pain: The penitentiary revolution.* New York: Pantheon.

Irwin, J., & Austin, J. (1994). *It's about time: America's prison binge.* Belmont, CA: Wadsworth.

Jacobs, J. B. (1974). Street gangs behind bars. *Social Problems, 21,* 395-409.

Jacobs, J. B. (1977). *Stateville: The penitentiary in mass society.* Chicago: University of Chicago Press.

Leighton, P. (1995). Industrialized social control. *Peace Review, 7,* 387-392.

MacKenzie, D. L. (1993, November). Boot camp prisons in 1993. *National Institute of Justice Journal,* pp. 21-28.

MacKenzie, D. L. (1996). Boot camps. In M. McShane & F. Williams, III (Eds.), *Encyclopedia of American prisons* (pp. 61-65). New York: Garland.

MacKenzie, D. L., Brame, R., McDowall, D., & Souryal, C. (1995). Boot camp prisons and recidivism in eight states. *Criminology, 33,* 327-357.

MacKenzie, D. L., & Piquero, A. (1994). The impact of shock incarceration programs on prison crowding. *Crime and Delinquency, 40,* 222-249.

MacKenzie, D. L., Robinson, J. W., & Campbell, C. S. (1989). Long-term incarceration of female offenders: Prison adjustment and coping. *Criminal Justice and Behavior, 16,* 223-238.

MacKenzie, D. L., & Shaw, J. W. (1990). Inmate adjustment and change during shock incarceration: The impact of correctional boot camp programs. *Justice Quarterly, 7,* 125-147.

MacKenzie, D. L., Shaw, J. W., & Gowdy, V. B. (1993, June). An evaluation of shock incarceration in Louisiana. In *National Institute of Justice Research in Brief.* Washington, DC: National Institute of Justice.

Maguire, K., & Pastore, A. L. (Eds.). (1995). *Sourcebook of criminal justice statistics 1994.* Washington, DC: U.S. Department of Justice, Bureau of Justice Statistics.

Marlowe, D. H., Martin, J. A., Schneider, R. J., Ingraham, L., Vaitkus, M. A., & Bartone, P. (1988). *A look at army training centers: The human dimensions of leadership and training.*

Washington, DC: Department of Military Psychiatry, Walter Reed Army Institute of Research.

McCorkle, R. C. (1995). Correctional boot camps and change in attitude: Is all this shouting necessary? A research note. *Justice Quarterly, 12,* 365-375.

McKelvey, B. (1977). *American prisons: A history of good intentions.* Montclair, NJ: Patterson Smith.

Meisenhelder, T. (1985). An essay on time and the phenomenology of imprisonment. *Deviant Behavior, 6,* 39-56.

Melossi, D., & Pavarini, M. (1981). *The prison and the factory: The origins of the penitentiary system.* Totawa, NJ: Barnes & Noble.

Mishel, L., & Bernstein, J. (1994). *The state of working America.* Washington, DC: Economic Policy Institute.

Morash, M., & Rucker, L. (1990). A critical look at the idea of boot camps as a correctional reform. *Crime and Delinquency, 36,* 204-222.

National Institute of Justice. (1994). *Shock incarceration in New York.* Washington, DC: U.S. Department of Justice.

New York State Department of Corrections. (1992). *The fourth annual report to the legislature on shock incarceration: Shock parole supervision in New York State.* Albany, NY: Author.

Newman, G. (1978). *The punishment response.* Philadelphia: Lippincott.

Nossiter, A. (1993, December 18). As boot camps for criminals multiply, skepticism grows. *New York Times,* pp. A-1, A-9.

Osler, M. (1991, March). Shock incarceration: An overview of existing programs. *Federal Probation, 55,* 34-42.

Peat, B. J., & Winfree, L. T. (1992). Reducing the intra-institutional effects of "prisonization": A study of a therapeutic community for drug-using inmates. *Criminal Justice and Behavior, 19,* 206-225.

Phillips, K. (1990). *Politics of the rich and poor: Wealth and the American electorate in the Reagan aftermath.* New York: Random House.

Pollock-Byrne, J. M. (1990). *Women, prison, and crime.* Pacific-Grove, CA: Brooks/Cole.

Raupp, E. R. (1978). *Toward positive leadership for initial entry training: A report by the taskforce on initial entry training leadership.* Fort Monroe, VA: U.S. Army Training and Doctrine Command.

Rothman, D. J. (1971). *The discovery of the asylum: Social order and disorder in the new republic.* Boston: Little, Brown.

Rothman, D. J. (1980). *Conscience and convenience: The asylum and its alternatives in progressive America.* Boston: Little, Brown.

Rusche, G., & Kirchheimer, O. (1968). *Punishment and social structure.* New York: Columbia University Press. (Original work published 1939)

Sechrest, D. K. (1989). Prison "boot camps" do not measure up. *Federal Probation, 53*(3), 15-20.

Simon, J. (1995). They died with their boots on: The boot camp and the limits of modern penalty. *Social Justice, 22*(2), 25-48.

Smith, B. A. (1988, March). Military training in New York's Elmira reformatory. *Federal Probation, 52,* 33-40.

Spitzer, S. (1975). Toward a Marxian theory of deviance. *Social Problems, 22,* 638-651.

Stewart, J. B. (1996). *African Americans and post-industrial labor markets.* New Brunswick, NJ: Transaction.

Steihem, J. H. (1981). *Bring me men and women: Mandated change at the U.S. Air Force Academy.* Berkeley: University of California Press.

Successful alternatives to prison. (1996, June 1). *New York Times,* p. 18.

Sykes, G. (1958). *The society of captives.* Princeton, NJ: Princeton University Press.

U.S. General Accounting Office. (1993). *Short-term prison costs reduced but long-term impact uncertain.* Washington, DC: Government Printing Office.

Vito, G. F., & Wilson, D. G. (1985). *The American juvenile justice system.* Beverly Hills, CA: Sage.

Welch, M. (1990, November). *Prison boot camps and the uncritical acceptance of the military model in corrections.* Paper presented at the annual meeting of the American Society of Criminology, Baltimore.

Welch, M. (1991a). Persons with AIDS in prison: A critical and phenomenological approach to suffering. *Dialectical Anthropology, 16*(1), 51-61.

Welch, M. (1991b, February 14). *Prison boot camps, correctional policy and social theory.* Paper presented at a symposium on correctional boot camp programs, sponsored by John Jay College of Criminal Justice, City University of New York.

Welch, M. (1995). Rehabilitation: Holding its ground in corrections. *Federal Probation, 59*(4), 3-8.

Welch, M. (1996). *Corrections: A critical approach.* New York: McGraw-Hill.

Welch, M. (1997). The war on drugs and correctional warehousing: Alternative strategies to the drug crisis. *Journal of Offender Rehabilitation, 25,* 43-60.

Welch, M., Ford, T. E., & Mabli, J. (1988, August). *Inmates' attitudes toward substance abuse and the limitations of programs on their evaluation.* Paper presented at the annual meeting of the Society for the Study of Social Problems, Atlanta, GA.

Welsh, W., Leone, M. C., Kinkade, P., & Pontell, H. (1991). The politics of jail overcrowding: Public attitudes and official policies. In J. Thompson & G. L. Mays (Eds.), *American jails: Public policy issues* (pp. 131-147). Chicago: Nelson-Hall.

Wilkins, L. T. (1991). *Punishment, crime and market forces.* Brookfield, VT: Dartmouth.

Wilson, W. J. (1987). *The truly disadvantaged: The inner city, the underclass, and public policy.* Chicago: University of Chicago Press.

Yablonsky, I. (1989). *The therapeutic community.* New York: Garden.

Zimmer, L. (1992, October). *The anti-drug semantic.* Unpublished paper presented at the Drug Policy Foundation Conference, Washington, DC.

CHAPTER 8

The Brutal Truth

The Reproduction of Prison Violence and the Ironies of Social Control

Traditional American criminology has often taken cues from broader sociological notions of social control, particularly the idea that crime stems from the absence of social control (Hirschi, 1969; Reiss, 1951). However, the presence of social control has also been credited with inadvertently contributing to crime. In a word, social control becomes *ironic* when it escalates the very behavior it intends to deter (Marx, 1981). Departing from functionalist sociology, labeling theorists in the early 1960s began to acknowledge the role that authorities play in creating crime, deviance, and various forms of rule breaking (Becker, 1963; Kitsuse, 1962; Scheff, 1966; Wilkins, 1965; also see Hawkins & Tiedeman, 1975; Lemert, 1972; Schneider, 1975). Gary Marx (1981) further developed this sociological perspective by setting out to identify and explain the ironies of social control, thus directing greater attention to critical situations that generate rule breaking. In doing so, Marx underscored Blumer's (1969) key sociological observation: Whereas some actions are motivated, others are *situated* and *structured* (see also Colvin, 1981; Ferrell, 1996; Gil, 1996; Reiman, 1998; Sullivan, 1980; Young, 1982).

By examining the contradictions of social control, Marx (1981) and likeminded symbolic interactionists offer key insights into the creation of lawlessness by authorities; still, these analyses tend to be limited primarily to such social control agents as law enforcement officers. Yet penologists also have recognized patterns of irony in corrections, noting that rule breaking, often with violent overtones, is frequently *reproduced* in prisons. Porporino (1986), for instance, pointed out that "it is ironic that the most violent individuals in society, once apprehended and convicted, are isolated within settings where violence is especially commonplace" (p. 213). In a similar vein, Lowman and MacLean (1991) insisted that "prison seems to either produce or reinforce the very behavior it is suppose to correct" (p. 130). Some have gone so far as to suggest that prison managers take a more insidiously utilitarian approach to the ironies of social control in corrections in that "violence and tension between prisoners are encouraged by prison managers as a tool to control and distract prisoners from the conditions of their confinement" (Coalition for Prisoners' Rights, Santa Fe, quoted in Welch, 1996a, p. 324; also see Fleisher, 1989; Henderson & Simon, 1994; Marongiu & Newman, 1987, 1995; Newman, 1985, 1995; Newman & Lynch, 1987; Silberman, 1995; Welch, 1995, 1996b, 1998, 1999).

Though examples of seemingly contradictory correctional practices are scattered throughout the penological literature, few attempts have been made to integrate these ironies within a coherent conceptual structure. In this chapter, we intend to apply Marx's model on the ironies of social control to the world of corrections, thereby introducing a sense of order to our understanding of the dialectical nature of incarceration and the reproduction of violence behind bars. Drawing on the three elements of Marx's framework (i.e., escalation, nonenforcement, and covert facilitation), we will elaborate on three types of violence—inmate versus inmate violence, staff versus inmate violence, and self-inflicted injuries—as they are manifested at both the individual and collective levels. Overall, this chapter sheds light on the interdependence between keepers and the kept, thus demonstrating that the prison enterprise that is supposedly designed to control violence ironically engenders it.

The Ironies of Social Control

Marx (1981) organized his approach to the ironies of social control around three types of situations that contribute to, and at times generate, rule-breaking behavior. In the first, escalation, authorities *unintentionally* encourage rule breaking by taking enforcement action. In the second situation, nonenforcement, agents of social control, by taking no enforcement action, *intentionally* permit rule infractions. In the third situation, covert facilitation, the authorities engage in hidden or deceptive enforcement action to *intentionally* encourage rule breaking. In the following sections, we shall expand upon these concepts by applying them to corrections, especially as they pertain to the maintenance of institutional violence.

ESCALATION

The ironies of escalation provoke questions about the virtues of law enforcement in general and corrections in particular. According to Marx (1981), escalation is the clearest illustration of self-defeating measures of social control. Several forms of evidence indicate that intervention can be conducive to rule breaking and violence. Escalation results in increases in the frequency and seriousness of the original violations; likewise, it creates new categories of violators (e.g., gangs, toughs, gorillas, peddlers) and victims (e.g., snitches, punks, short-eyes). It also contributes to the commitment to violence and the skill and effectiveness of violence, inciting types of rule breaking whose very definitions are tied to social control intervention (e.g., taking down the man, busting up the joint, sticking a pig). Indeed, these challenges to authority almost invariably provoke strong-armed tactics by corrections officers, who set out to punish inmates who have failed to show proper deference to prison staff, thereby perpetuating a vicious cycle of rebellion and abuse of authority (see Adams, 1998).

The interdependence of rule enforcers and rule breakers in correctional facilities is reproduced at the situational level by three key factors: lack of expertise, self-fulfilling prophecies, and sanctions that increase secondary gains for rule breaking (Marx, 1981). Lack of expertise remains a crucial problem in prisoner management because violence by guards against inmates is likely to escalate when the situation involves staff who are unprofessional, insensitive, insecure (i.e., racist and bigoted), and poorly trained in dealing with interpersonal conflicts—sometimes resulting in "oilin' the fire" (Marx, 1970; Stark, 1972). Poor institutional conditions and poor facility design also contribute to the escalation of violence.

Lack of Expertise

Consider the 1971 uprising at Attica penitentiary in New York. The chronology of events began the day before the riot, when a misunderstanding between guards and prisoners escalated into a confrontation in which an inmate assaulted an officer. Later that night, two inmates were removed from their cells and placed in administrative detention, further escalating the incident. Fellow inmates vowed revenge, and the next morning the guard who was at the center of the controversy was attacked. At that same moment, prisoners attacked officers, took hostages, and destroyed property. By 10:30 a.m., prisoners had seized control of four cell blocks, including the yards and tunnels. Soon, 1,281 inmates and over 40 hostages gathered in the D Yard. The lack of training and expertise among corrections personnel became increasingly evident: Prison officials, who did not have a riot control plan and relied on an antiquated communications system, were unable to quell the disturbance. Contributing to the magnitude of the disturbance was overcrowding: Attica contained more than 2,200 prisoners. More accurately, these inmates were simply "warehoused," for few meaningful programs of education and rehabilitation were offered, even though such programs function to reduce tension and frustration among prisoners. It should also be noted that the riot was able to spread because of a key structural flaw in the institution's security fortress: Prisoners broke through a defective weld in the gate located in the Times Square section of the prison and were thus able to take control over the entire prison (Mahan, 1994; New York State Special Commission, 1972; Useem, 1985; Useem & Kimball, 1985, 1989; Wicker, 1975; also see Oswald, 1972, and the 1991 commemorative issue of *Social Justice* devoted to the Attica riot [Weiss, 1991]).

The eventual storming of the prison by the authorities, however, did not end the violence; rather, for many inmates, it marked the beginning of a sequence of brutal acts committed by guards. Hundreds of inmates were stripped naked and beaten by correction officers, troopers, and sheriffs' deputies. The agony of the inmates and hostages was prolonged because prison officials withheld immediate medical care for those suffering from gunshot wounds and injuries stemming from the widespread reprisals. In fact, there were only 10 medical personnel, only two of whom were physicians, available to treat more than 120 seriously wounded inmates and hostages. Doctors at local hospitals who could have assisted the wounded were not dispatched by prison officials until 4 hours later. Reprisals by officers against inmates were characterized as brutal displays of humiliation. Injured prisoners, some on stretchers, were struck, prodded, or beaten with sticks, belts, bats, or other weapons. "Many more inmates were injured when guards and troopers took over the yard and set up a gauntlet in which naked inmates were

The Brutal Truth 133

beaten with clubs as they were herded back into the cellblocks" (Jackson, 1992, p. 122). Some prisoners were dragged on the ground, marked with an "X" on their backs, spat upon, burned with matches, and poked in the genitals or arms with sticks (Deutsch, Cunningham, & Fink, 1991; *Inmates of Attica v. Rockefeller*, 1971).

A class action suit, *Al-Jundi v. Mancusi* (1991), was filed on behalf the 1,200 prisoners who were killed, wounded, denied medical care, and beaten by officers. The jury found Deputy Warden Pfeil liable for violent reprisals following the riot for permitting police and guards to beat and torture inmates. Flawed prison management had not only failed to contain the violence but had ironically escalated it.

Lack of expertise also has contributed to other institutional disturbances, most notably at the New Mexico State Prison. Apparently, lessons were not learned from Attica, for a containable incident rapidly erupted into a brutal riot in which 33 inmates were killed by other prisoners. The incident began after midnight, when an officer approached two rowdy inmates who had become intoxicated by drinking prison hooch (prisoner-made alcohol). The situation escalated when an altercation ensued and prisoners overpowered the guard and his two backups. The incident would have remained isolated, but the inmates snatched the prison keys and sought entry to other sections of the prison. Meanwhile, the three officers were taken hostage, raped, and beaten into unconsciousness. As was the case in the riot at Attica, the officials at New Mexico were not prepared to deal with a large-scale riot. The institution was overcrowded and inexcusably understaffed: At the time of the riot, there were only 22 guards supervising 1,157 inmates in a prison built to hold 800. Moreover, the riot could not be prevented from spreading because other officers were unable to locate a complete set of prison keys. Compounding the problems at New Mexico was a key architectural flaw—the failure of "shatter-proof" glass installed at the control center, the prison's lifeline. By breaking the protective glass and seizing the control center, the inmates gained complete, unobstructed access to the facility and electronically opened all interior gates. The violence spread rapidly, and the degree of brutality that awaited selected inmates was beyond belief (Colvin, 1982, 1992; Mahan, 1994; Morris, 1983; Rolland, 1997; Saenz, 1986; Stone, 1982; Useem, 1985; Useem & Kimball, 1989).

Another incident of escalation facilitated by the lack of expertise and inhumane conditions of confinement occurred in Elizabeth, New Jersey, at an Immigration and Naturalization Service (INS) detention facility operated by the ESMOR corporation, a private corrections contractor. The institution had been open less than a year when officials learned of physical abuse perpetrated by staff against detainees. Subsequently, in 1995, INS Commissioner Doris Meissner ordered a review of the ESMOR facility, but before the investigation could begin, a riot broke out. The scope of the investigation was consequently expanded to include probable causes of the disturbance, adequacy of response by ESMOR and INS personnel, and emergency plans that were in effect at the time of the disturbance (INS, 1995).

The INS assessment team concluded that ESMOR guards and their mid-level supervisors had failed to exhibit proper control during the disturbance. Moreover, there was considerable evidence to support the allegations of abuse and harassment of detainees by ESMOR guards. Many incidents of abuse were serious: According to the assessment team's report, ESMOR guards were implicated in numerous acts of physical abuse and theft of detainee property. In addition, women detainees complained that they had been issued male underwear on which large question marks had been scrawled on the crotch. Other accounts of harassment included the unjustified waking of detainees in the middle of the night under the guise of security checks (INS, 1995). It was determined that ESMOR did not have sufficient personnel and resorted to inappropriate uses of overtime. The ESMOR staff was hamstrung by considerable turnover, as high as 60%. Moreover, low salaries for these guards not only contributed to turnover but exacerbated the ongoing problem of hiring poorly qualified staff who were placed on duty without the mandatory training required by INS (INS, 1995; also see Peet & Schwab, 1995).

The INS assessment team reported that ESMOR did not properly implement its emergency plan; the failure to carry out an effective emergency plan was attributed to poor personnel training, especially with regard to emergency procedures. At the onset of the disturbance, 14 ESMOR staff and one INS officer were supervising 315 detainees. The disturbance commenced at 1:15 a.m. on June 18 and was brought under control at 6:30 a.m. after a tactical entry by local law enforcement officers. It was concluded that detainees participated in the disturbance largely due to their frustration with harassment by ESMOR staff, harsh treatment of confinement, prolonged periods of detention, lack of communication about their cases, and the inefficient hearing process.

With the closing of the INS facility at Elizabeth, detainees were transferred either to other INS detention centers or to county jails in New Jersey and Pennsylvania. For many of these detainees, unfortunately, the harshness of treatment not only continued but in some cases worsened. For instance, 25 detainees (none of whom participated in the riot) were sent to the Union County Jail (NJ), where they were confronted by a group of guards who formed a gauntlet, punching and kicking them in an ordeal that lasted more than 4 hours. "The guards broke one detainee's collarbone, shoved other detainees' heads in toilets, used pliers to pull out one man's pubic hair and forced a line of men to kneel naked on the jail floor and chant, 'America is No. 1' " (Sullivan, 1995, p. A-1).

Initially, six guards were arrested and charged with the beatings of INS detainees, but prosecutors contended that at least two dozen officers participated in the beatings (Misseck, 1995; Sullivan, 1995; also see Hassel & Misseck, 1996; Welch, 1997a, 1998a). In 1998, three jailers were convicted of assault, misconduct, and conspiracy to obstruct the investigation; two of them were sentenced to 7 years in prison and a third received a 5-year sentence ("Prison Terms for Officers," 1998; Smothers, 1998).

Besides internal conditions that contribute to escalation (such as lack of expertise and poor institutional conditions), it is important to acknowledge external forces that compound these problems. The punitive stance of political leaders and the criminal justice establishment has led to an increase in prison overcrowding as more offenders (typically nonviolent) are sentenced to prison for longer periods of time. Overcrowding has been further compounded by the abolition of parole in some jurisdictions. At the federal level, such structural changes have contributed to the increase in violence evident in prisons. Thus, due to stricter sentencing and parole requirements (resulting from legislation passed by Congress in the 1980s), inmates are serving longer prison terms with little opportunity to earn "good time." Federal prisoners are currently required to serve 85% of their sentence before being eligible for parole. Traditionally, the use of parole was an important method of imposing control over inmates in that violating institutional rules would lead to a forfeiture of their "good time." But now correctional officers who have the daily chore of prisoner management enjoy fewer control devices (see Holmes, 1995). Moreover, overcrowding exacerbates prison tensions, thereby further jeopardizing the stability of the institution, where guards have the daunting task of supervising a growing number of newly admitted prisoners. This destabilization is a key source of aggression and violence (Ellis, 1984; Porporino, 1986).

Another external force contributing to escalation is a social movement devoted to making prison life harsher by eliminating amenities (e.g., weight rooms, televisions) and programs (e.g., education) and in some cases deliberately humiliating prisoners (e.g., chain gangs and striped prison uniforms) (Welch, 1997b). Attempts to harshen prison life aggravate tensions because the lack of programs reduces prosocial opportunities for inmates to alleviate stress, and the termination of programs increases prisoner frustration and boredom, which may lead to violence.

As noted previously, institutional violence is often precipitated by unjust treatment of prisoners; indeed, the riot at Attica became a metaphor for governmental oppression, racism, and injustice. More recently, the federal government, in the midst of a "tough on crime" frenzy, enacted legislation that critics characterize as unfair and racist because it assigns disparate penalties for similar drug offenses. In what many observers report were reactions to the congressional vote favoring the imposition of harsher punishments for possession of crack cocaine than for powdered cocaine, prisoner disturbances erupted in five federal correctional facilities in 1995 (Smothers, 1995). The legislation has a disproportionate impact on impoverished African American offenders (U.S. Sentencing Commission, 1995; see Chapters 3 and 4). To reiterate, correctional institutions are affected by both internal (micro-and mesosociological) and external (macrosociological) forces. Incidents of violence typically are precipitated—and escalated—by a lack of management expertise compounded by inadequate training, abysmal conditions, and poor facility design.

Self-Fulfilling Prophecies

Self-fulfilling prophecies also contribute to the escalation of deviance and violence. Marx (1981) reminded us that "the appearance of deviant behavior may stem from 'self-fulfillment' of initially erroneous beliefs by authorities about a group or an individual" (p. 234). The effects of labeling are easily detected in prison partly because convicts have already been subjected to the formal degradation ceremony of the criminal justice apparatus (Becker, 1963; Garfinkel, 1956; Goffman, 1961). Behind prison walls, correctional officers (already operating under preconceived notions of prisoners) are trained not to trust inmates under any circumstances and are told, "*Con*victs will *con* you." More to the point of escalation, the labeling of prisoners can contribute to violence when perceptions of "us versus them" are shaped by racist stereotypes. In many states, prisons (whose population is composed mostly of urban minorities) are constructed primarily in rural areas and staffed by local white residents. For example, Attica prison is located in Wyoming County, upstate New York, where "most people there work in the prison, work in service industries connected to the prison, or are related to the white rural guards who staffed the prison at the time of the rebellion" (Jackson, 1992, p. 124). At the time of the riot, the majority of Attica's prisoners were black (54%; 37% of the prisoners were white, and 8.7% were Spanish speaking), and nearly 80% of the black inmates were from urban ghettos (New York State Special Commission, 1972).

Contrary to popular belief, a group of inmates—not the staff—eventually contained the uprising. Following a period of random destruction, inmate leaders (who were not involved in the initial violence) representing the Muslims, Black Panthers, and Young Lords (groups the authorities labeled, distrusted, and routinely hassled) organized inmates and took control of the volatile situation in an effort to reach a peaceful resolution. Still, the climate surrounding the negotiation was tense and plagued with rumors that inflamed the situation. Drawing on stereotypes of violent criminals, prison officials manufactured a disinformation campaign, deliberately reporting false rumors to the media: specifically, that "hostages had died because their throats had been slit by the inmates and that several hostages had been found with their genitals stuffed in their mouths" (Jackson, 1992, p. 123). For the record, the Rochester medical examiner told reporters days after the riot that, except for Officer William Quinn, who later died of injuries sustained in the initial violence at Times Square, "All guards had been killed by police and guard bullets; none had their throats cut, and none had their genitals removed and stuffed in their mouths" (Jackson, 1992, p. 123). Despite the truth, the disinformation campaign already had shaped the prison officials' narrative, and local newspapers ran full-page articles full of false information about "slit throats" and "genitals stuffed in the guards' mouths." The momentum of the labeling process proved difficult to correct, for the belief that the riot had been "precipitated by a number of down-state violent 'niggers' never lost currency" (Jackson, 1992, p. 125).

In the end, it was the authorities who resurrected the violence by reacting with deadly force when state police ambushed the prisoners. During 15 minutes of gunfire, 39 inmates were killed, and 80 others were wounded (in all, 43 people lost their lives during the riot). One out of every 10 persons in D Yard that morning was struck by gunfire, and more than a quarter of the hostages died of bullet wounds (New York State Special Commission, 1972). "With the exception of Indian massacres in the late 19th century, the state police assault that ended the four-day prison uprising was the bloodiest one-day encounter between Americans since the Civil War" (New York State Special Commission, 1972, p. 130).

At the New Mexico state penitentiary, the effects of labeling further exacerbated hostility and distrust between staff and prisoners. But unlike the inmates of Attica, who had joined forces across race to challenge the prison regime, prisoners at New Mexico became deeply—and dangerously—divided against each other, even within ethnic groups. During a critical period leading up to the riot, officers initiated a system of snitching based on involuntary rather than voluntary informing, thereby placing prisoners in a classic "Catch 22." Officers privately told inmates that they had to snitch on fellow prisoners; if they did not cooperate, officers would falsely tell other inmates that they had informed. Either way, inmates were "screwed."

The involuntary snitch system pressured prisoners to become increasingly suspicious of their peers. Mistrust among prisoners gradually fragmented the inmate society into small cliques. In effect, the staff divided and conquered the inmate society by turning inmates against each other. During that period, inmates endeavored to develop violent reputations for the purpose of protecting themselves from snitches. Researchers have found that "prisoners who achieve notoriety as fighters are much less likely to be attacked [and snitched on] than those who appear to fear overt conflict" (Toch, 1992, p. 64; also see Robertson, 1995). As violence grew more prevalent, the administration, seemingly oblivious to their own role in escalation, decided that they were dealing with a "new breed" of inmate who could be controlled only through coercive measures. The New Mexico prison riot serves a powerful example of how labeling and self-fulfilling prophecies escalated violence by creating a new class of perpetrators (e.g., new breeds) who preyed on a new class of victims (e.g., snitches and sex offenders, especially pedophiles) with a commitment to greater and more *skillful* violence.

Small cliques of inmates sought revenge against those labeled prison outcasts, including snitches and convicted child molesters, who were known as "diddlers" or "short-eyes." To prepare themselves for skillful acts of revenge, inmates confiscated prison records identifying informers and those convicted of sex offenses, the two most despised criminal types in the prison world. Finally, inmates added to their arsenal by arming themselves with hammers, meat cleavers, and blowtorches stolen from the prison maintenance supply room. The impending rampage would exceed by far the usual forms of prison violence. For the next several hours, inmates stalked, raped, burned, decapitated, castrated, and eviscerated their victims. A reporter asked an inmate, "What was it like in there?" to which the prisoner answered, "Man, what can I tell you? It was like the Devil had his own butcher shop, and you could get any cut you wanted" (Morris, 1983, p. i). Consider the following incident involving the *skillful* torture of Jimmy Perrin, serving a life sentence for raping and murdering two little girls and their mother. Four executioners

The Brutal Truth

blowtorched his door open, dragged Perrin out of his cell, "tied him spread-eagle to the bars and cooked him slowly with the roaring flame of the acetylene torch, melting his three hundred pounds of flesh to bone" (Stone, 1982, p. 127). For 30 minutes, the executioners tortured Perrin, "first burning his genitals, then his face, moving the torch up and down his body, bringing him around with smelling salts when he drifted into the comfort of unconsciousness" (Stone, 1982, p. 127, 129; also see Akerstrom, 1986; Morris, 1983; Rolland, 1997).

Other inmates suffered similar acts of torture, shocking those who had the grim task of uncovering the human remains. Many victims were burned to death when rioters threw flammable liquids through the bars and ignited them with matches and blowtorches. Some inmates were burned so extensively that their race could not be determined when their corpses were recovered; three bodies were not conclusively identified until anthropologists reassembled the bone fragments (Morris, 1983). Dozens of inmates suspected of being informants were found slashed to death in their cells: One inmate was found with a steel rod driven completely through his skull, and another was stomped to death and had the word "RATA" carved into his abdomen. In fact, several other victims had whisker-shaped gashes on their faces, signifying the stigma of prison "rats." In one brutal snitch killing, a prisoner was beaten to death by metal pipes; his lifeless body was thrown off the two-story tier, and an accomplice planted "a shovel into the corpse, cutting off his genitalia" (Morris, 1983, p. 100). The rage continued long after their victims perished: "As an afterthought, [rioters] broke the fingers of one hand on an already burned, dismembered body. Several corpses were mutilated, then sodomized, the torsos left at grotesque angles" ("The Killing Ground," 1980; Morris, 1983, p. 105).

As we shall see in Chapter 10, the labeling process emerges in the assignment of certain inmates to supermaximum security units. In this process, officials turn to unreliable and questionable criteria to determine who is incorrigible. In fact, human rights experts contend that many prisoners are erroneously labeled incorrigible and are transferred to abysmal supermaximum security units, where they conform to a self-fulfilling prophecy by becoming aggressive and violent (Human Rights Watch, 1997; also see Hamm, Coupez, Hoze, & Weinstein, 1994). A similar process of labeling applies to prisoners unjustly placed in solitary confinement, where they too become the unstable inmates they are accused of being (Haney, 1993; refer to Chapter 10).

Secondary Gains

When sanctions create secondary gains, they serve as another source of escalation. Under such conditions, punishment does not deter deviance; ironically, it promotes deviance. "Prohibiting something can make it more attractive for those with rebellious needs or in search of excitement and 'kicks'" (Marx, 1981, p. 234; see also Ferrell, 1996; Katz, 1988; Welch & Bryan, in press). Public condemnation of deviance may arouse curiosity and generate a "forbidden fruit" effect. This phenomenon especially applies to juveniles who experience an increase in peer status when arrested, verifying the rebellious belief that "it's good to be bad." In prison, secondary gains are attached to numerous forms of rule breaking, including violence and the contraband trade.

In the realm of prisons, secondary gains engender a type of violence known as instrumental (Bowker, 1980). The rational and calculative nature of instrumental violence makes it distinguishable from expressive violence (i.e., annoyance-motivated aggression), which is motivated by the need to terminate annoyances. As a form of incentive-motivated aggression, instrumental violence facilitates the pursuit of rewards. This phenomenon is particularly evident when inmates threaten or assault other prisoners for the purpose of garnering power, enhancing status, or promoting a particular self-image within the prison society. In their quest to dominate fellow prisoners, inmates may exact violence (or threaten violence) to obtain, for example, a more desirable living situation, sexual contact, commodities (cigarettes, junk food, sneakers), contraband (drugs, weapons), and various other services (laundry tasks, paper work for legal matters) (Bowker, 1980; Ellis, Grasmick, & Gilman, 1974; Porporino & Marton, 1983; Toch, 1992; Welch, 1995, 1996a, 1999).

It should be noted that instrumental violence is not restricted to individual violence; it also is evident in collective disturbances (e.g., riots, disturbances, hostage taking, gang-banging), particularly when rebellion against the authorities produces in-group solidarity. Secondary gains are *payoffs* for those who resort to violence. As sanctions generate alternative status, rule breakers wear their punishment as a badge of honor. Given the very nature of correctional institutions, the demand for illegal goods and services (e.g., weapons, drugs, sex) is immense, and when the demand for contraband is coupled with punishment, the underground economy is shaped by the principles of a crime tariff (Packer, 1968). Efforts to ban certain commodities increase not only the *risk* but also the *gain* for peddlers. Under these conditions, the dialectical relations between rule enforcers and rule breakers undergird the underground economy. "Cost and benefit exist in an equilibrium not found in other situations. Classical deterrence theory assumes that increasing the penalty will decrease the activity. This does not hold when the rule-breaking decision flows from rational calculation and the potential gain from the deviance remains constant" (Marx, 1981, p. 235). Failed attempts to reduce the supply of illegal drugs (both inside and outside of prison) should also be understood within the context of market forces. Simply put, prices attached to illegal drugs are contingent upon demand and scarcity. Therefore, reducing the supply merely drives up the price of the drug, which makes trafficking more profitable, attracting those willing to take such risks (Wilkins, 1994).

Some officers also participate in the underground economy. Sometimes guards, in the attempt to be "nice guys," give inmates items believed to harmless, such as junk food. But on occasion, guards may import drugs for personal profit or to lure inmates into sexual favors. The most prevalent form of participation in the underground economy stems from guards "looking the other way" and not reporting such violations (a form of nonenforcement). In doing so, guards create another form of leverage that can be used as bargaining power to informally control inmates; as a result, staff directly and indirectly perpetuate the sub rosa economy (Kalinich, 1980; Kalinich & Stojkovic, 1985, 1987; McCarthy, 1995).

Secondary gains in the underground economy are patterned by the struggle for power, thereby contributing to violence in several ways. As mentioned, the tariff placed on contraband entices those interested in peddling: For instance, drugs create the need for weapons, another form of contraband. Weapons are used to protect the enterprise against competition (e.g., turf wars) and to threaten or injure those who might consider snitching to authorities. All these activities offer secondary gains to those who can rise to the top of the underground economy in the form of enhancing their peer status and power; ultimately, this hierarchy engenders further violence in those interested in challenging and conquering the elite (e.g., gang-banging).

NONENFORCEMENT

Another irony of social control is nonenforcement, in which authorities intentionally permit rule breaking by strategically taking no enforcement action. In nonenforcement, compared to escalation and covert facilitation, the contribution of authorities to deviance is more indirect. Although nonenforcement extends to a vast array of prison violations (e.g., various types of contraband), we shall maintain the thrust of this chapter by focusing on institutional violence, specifically in three forms: inmate versus inmate, staff versus inmate, and self-inflicted injuries (including suicide).

Inmate-Versus-Inmate Violence

As previously discussed, several institutional features contribute to nonenforcement, thus escalating prison and jail violence. First and foremost, violence can be attributed to lack of adequate supervision by officers. As overcrowding outpaces the hiring of additional guards, violence becomes increasingly likely, especially if the interior architecture limits supervision (Welch, 1991a, 1995, 1996a; Zupan, 1991). The proliferation of weapons in an institution results from security lapses; subsequently, when officers feel that they do not have the ability to control inmates, they engage in nonenforcement by allowing prisoners to protect themselves by any means necessary (see Abbott, 1981; Colvin, 1982; Robertson, 1995).

In more elaborate terms, nonenforcement involves an *exchange* relationship between rule enforcers and rule breakers. Certainly, nonenforcement may be offered as a reward to selected prisoners who have been granted the role of regulating fellow inmates; typically, this form of social control involves the threat and use of violence (Sykes, 1958). Classic illustrations of the exchange between authorities and selected prisoners are found in the Arkansas and Texas prison systems. Like many states, Arkansas instituted an elaborate management structure for its prisons involving the use of convict-guards, known as trusties. These elite inmates ruled the institution and were rewarded for controlling—often with the use of force—the inmate population. Trusties enjoyed better living arrangements, clothing, food, and numerous privileges: They were permitted to gamble, consume alcohol and drugs, and even live in shacks outside of the institution where they entertained girlfriends. Prison administrators found that using trusties rather than hiring additional guards reduced operating costs of the institution. Owing to the degree of nonenforcement, however, this exchange relationship between authorities and trusties bred violence among prisoners.

The Texas Department of Corrections (TDC), often referred to as "America's toughest prison," also relied on trusties, known as building tenders (BTs), to supervise and manage the inmate population. BTs were hardened convicts "deputized" by the administration as elite prisoners: "They were the inmates who really ran the asylum: the meanest characters the administration could co-opt into doing the state's bidding" (Press, 1986, p. 46). Although Texas law forbids inmates from serving in supervisory and administrative roles, corrections officials ignored this prohibition. Moreover, some BTs were supplied with weapons to bolster their control of other inmates. Often with the tacit approval of the staff, BTs armed with homemade clubs would brutally beat stubborn or aggressive inmates, a form of victimization called "counseling" or "whipping them off the tank" (Marquart & Crouch, 1985).

The BT system was elaborate, featuring its own hierarchy of high-, medium-, and low-level convict guards—a structure of social control that insidiously pitted inmates against inmates. This form of nonenforcement cultivated an atmosphere of fear and distrust among the inmate population (Marquart & Crouch, 1985). In the 1970s and 1980s, TDC was notorious for its institutional problems: enormous overcrowding (230% capacity), lengthy sentences (brought about by several mandatory sentencing laws), poor chances for parole, and excessive violence. During a 7-day stretch in 1981, 11 inmates were killed by fellow prisoners, and 70 prisoners and guards were severely injured. Although some administrators believed that BTs reduced aggression at TDC, critics argue that BTs *escalated* violence (Marquart & Crouch, 1985; Martin & Ekland-Olson, 1987).

In *Ruiz v. Estelle* (1980), federal judge William Wayne Justice declared the operations at TDC unconstitutional and abolished the BT system; his order also called for measures to reduce overcrowding and improve medical, mental health, and educational services. Though such court orders create a sense of optimism, prison reformers realize that litigation rarely leads to immediate or smooth changes in correctional institutions. In the case of TDC, years passed before any noticeable reforms occurred; meanwhile, overcrowding, physical abuse, poor services, corruption, graft, mismanagement, and especially violence persisted. In one of a series of scholarly examinations of TDC, Marquart and Crouch (1985) studied the court-ordered reforms and their impact on prisoner control and discovered that after court-ordered reforms, violence among inmates and between inmates and guards escalated to new heights (also see Martin & Ekland-Olson, 1987).

Although advocates of prison reform applaud court-ordered intervention, they concede that as traditional control structures (order based on coercion) are dismantled, violence (related to gang activity) often occurs during a period of disorganization before new control structures (order based on bureaucratic-legal initiatives) can be established (Irwin, 1980; Jacobs, 1977). This irony has become known as the "paradox of reform" (Engel & Rothman, 1983). Crouch and Marquart (1990) tested the "paradox of reform" hypothesis at TDC and found that the period of destabilization—contributing to an upswing in violence—is short term. Crouch and Marquart challenged the popular view that inmates felt safer in the "old days" (DiIulio, 1987). Given the coercive nature of inmate control, few prisoners felt safe in the "old days," especially those most threatened by BTs, namely black inmates. "Our data make it apparent that perceptions of risk and actual rates of violence in a prison do not covary; low rates of violence before reforms do not mean that prisoners felt safe" (Crouch & Marquart, 1990, p. 121). To reduce the likelihood of violence and disorder during reforms, greater intervention is needed to neutralize gang activity. Furthermore, Marquart and Crouch (1985) recommended that reforms be "phased in gradually rather than established by rigid timetables" (p. 585).

Another important type of nonenforcement leading to violence among prisoners is deliberate indifference, a legal concept advanced significantly by *Farmer v. Brennan* (1994). In 1986, Dee Farmer was sentenced to federal prison upon his conviction of credit card fraud. At the time of his incarceration, the 18-year-old Farmer was undergoing medical treatment to change his sex to female. As a preoperative transsexual, Farmer exhibited feminine traits and mannerisms, commonly wearing a T-shirt off one shoulder. Federal Bureau of Prisons officials classified Farmer as a "biological male" and designated him to the Federal Correctional Institution at Oxford, Wisconsin. For his safety, Farmer was confined to protective custody during much of his incarceration at Oxford. Upon a disciplinary infraction in 1989, Farmer was transferred to a higher-security institution within the system, the U.S. penitentiary in Terre Haute, Indiana. At Terre Haute, Farmer resumed serving his sentence in administrative segregation but was later transferred to the general population. Approximately a week later, he was raped and physically beaten in his cell after he spurned the sexual advances of another prisoner (Vaughn, 1995).

Farmer filed action against corrections officials, complaining that "placing a known transsexual with feminine traits in the general population within a male prison with a history of violent inmate-against-inmate assaults" amounts to "deliberate indifference" (Vaughn, 1995, p. 3). In his suit, Farmer contended that such action violates the Eighth Amendment's ban on cruel and unusual punishment. The U.S. District Court for the Western District of Wisconsin ruled that prison officials did *not* demonstrate deliberate indifference by failing to prevent the assault. On appeal, the U.S. Court of Appeals for the Seventh Circuit affirmed without comment. However, the U.S. Supreme Court agreed to hear the case in order to resolve a dispute among the circuits regarding the definition of *deliberate indifference* in cases of assault between inmates. In a 9-0 ruling, the High Court ruled in *Farmer* that prison officials can be found liable for failing to protect a prisoner from attacks from other inmates if administrators did not act when they knew of a "substantial risk of serious harm." Justice Souter, writing for a unanimous Court, ruled that because imprisonment deprives inmates of the means to protect themselves, prison officials cannot "let the state of nature take its course" (*Farmer v. Brennan,* 1994; Vaughn, 1995). *Farmer* offers a glimpse of how correctional staff, by taking no enforcement action, permit sexual violence in prisons and jails. In a classic study of prison rape, Lockwood (1980, 1982) found that sexual violence illustrates the need of some prisoners to dominate weaker inmates. "The primary causes of violence are subcultural values upholding men's rights to use force to gain sexual access" (Lockwood, 1982, p. 257); to take the argument a step further, staff nonenforcement reinforces these subcultural beliefs.

Although sexual attacks occasionally occur, experts insist that rape in correctional institutions is not a common event; several studies suggest that the frequency of sexual assault in correctional institutions is often exaggerated (Lockwood, 1980, 1982; Nacci, 1982; Nacci & Kane, 1984). Still, the nature of sexual assault in prisons remains poorly understood, largely because the authorities, through nonenforcement, often refuse to acknowledge the problem. Reported estimates may underrepresent the frequency of institutional rape because correctional officers may inhibit reporting by treating victims insensitively or by ignoring assaults altogether (Eigenberg, 1994, p. 145). What is far more common than homosexual rape in correctional institutions is *sexual harassment,* in which the *threat* of sexual assault emerges as a form of incentive-motivated aggression. The overarching fear—real and imagined—of sexual assault reveals the consequences of nonenforcement because it contributes to a predatory atmosphere of mistrust that can lead to violence (Bowker, 1980; Chonco, 1989; Jones & Schmid, 1989; Lockwood, 1980; Nacci, 1982; Tewksbury, 1989). According to Robertson (1995),

> Incarceration exposes male inmates to a "world of violence" where staff cannot or will not protect them from rape, assault, and other forms of victimization. To make matters worse, retreating in the face of danger is neither normative nor feasible; in prison your back is always against the wall. Most inmates have but two options: to fight in self-defense or become passive victims of a predatory subculture. (p. 339)

Because nonenforcement allows prisoners to prey on weaker victims, the vulnerable, left to their own devices, must either "fuck or fight" (Eigenberg, 1994, p. 159; Robertson, 1995). Under these conditions, nonenforcement contributes to four configurations of violence: (a) The aggressor sexually assaults his victim; (b) during the attack, the victim wards off the aggressor with violence; (c) the potential victim carries out a preemptive strike against the aggressor as a measure of self-protection; (d) the victim later retaliates against the aggressor. Ironically, nonenforcement tends to blur the line between aggressor and victim (Robertson, 1995; also see Abbott, 1981). Consider the following testimony:

> Well, the first time [a potential sexual aggressor] says something to you or looks wrong at you, have a piece of pipe or a good heavy piece of two-by-four. Don't say a damn thing to him, just get that heavy wasting material and walk right up to him and bash his face in and keep bashing him till he's down and out, and yell loud and clear for all the other cons to hear you, Mother fucker, I'm a man. I came in here a mother fucking man and I'm going out a mother fucking man. Next time I'll kill you. (Thomas, 1967, quoted in Robertson, 1995, p. 340)

Nonenforcement leading to predatory violence between inmates also is evident in the victimization of prison outcasts, most notably convicted sex offenders and prisoners with HIV/AIDS. A defining component of the prison social world is its hierarchy, prompting inmates to compare themselves to other offenders on the basis of their respective crimes. Generally, nonviolent offenders feel superior to inmates convicted of violent and sexual offenses, and convicted rapists and child molesters occupy the lowest strata in the inmate caste system. Consequently, the mistreatment of sex offenders by other inmates tends to exceed mere harassment; at times, these outcasts are assaulted, thus prompting some sex offenders to serve their sentences in isolation for their own protection. Whereas attacks on sex offenders are sometimes limited to minor injuries, other incidents have involved severe beatings and torture (e.g., James Perrin during the New Mexico state prison riot). While working as a correctional counselor in a Southern jail, I witnessed the aftermath of a brutal beating of an inmate by approximately 20 prisoners. The episode was precipitated by a jail guard who sadistically announced to a crowded tank of detainees that the inmate was being held for raping two young girls. In a ruthless act of nonenforcement, the guard smirked and vacated the area, returning to the scene an hour later to transfer the severely injured prisoner to solitary confinement. To no avail, I tried to persuade the staff to hospitalize the injured prisoner. This incident shows that authorities have the power to create situations that connote that it is "open season" on selected inmates; likewise, prisoners often take cues from staff who tacitly grant them a license to commit violence against despised convicts.

Attacks on prisoners with HIV/AIDS remind us of another element of escalation, namely the creation of new categories of victims (Marx, 1981). As prison outcasts, prisoners with HIV/AIDS are condemned and stigmatized, and due to the nature of HIV transmission, these inmates are commonly viewed as evil and morally corrupt—suggesting that their illness is deserved punishment for homosexuality or use of illegal drugs (Sontag, 1989; Welch, 1989; see Chapter 11). Inside correctional institutions, the condemnation of prisoners with HIV/AIDS can lead to their being ostracized and victimized (Potler, 1988; Welch, 1989, 1991a, 1991b). To reiterate, the victimization of prisoners with HIV/AIDS and other prison outcasts demonstrates that nonenforcement not only fosters deliberate indifference among the staff but breeds violence among prisoners as well.

Staff-Versus-Inmate Violence

By not taking enforcement action against staff who commit violence against prisoners, authorities intentionally encourage this type of rule breaking, which typically functions as a form of informal control. Several court cases have brought to light the degree to which corrections authorities have turned their backs on violence carried out by guards. As mentioned previously, in a class action suit filed against Attica's corrections administration, Deputy Warden Pfeil was found liable for violent reprisals that followed in the wake of the riot and for permitting police and guards to beat and torture inmates (*Al-Jundi v. Mancusi,* 1991). In *Hudson v. McMillian* (1992), prisoner Keith Hudson charged that beatings inflicted by officers constituted a form of cruel and unusual punishment. The High Court concurred that when officers maliciously and sadistically assault inmates, contemporary standards of decency are violated. More importantly, assaults do not have to be as severe as broken bones or concussions to be considered unconstitutional. Even assaults involving injuries as minor as a split lip or a broken dental plate, as in the Hudson case, are unconstitutional. The beating of Hudson clearly reveals the extent of nonenforcement: A supervisor watched and quipped: "Don't be having too much fun, boys" (Elvin, 1992, p. 6).

Whereas the *Hudson* and Attica cases illustrate particular incidents, we should realize that in some institutions, cruel and unusual punishments are more pervasive and systematic. At the Arkansas state penitentiary, a particularly barbaric punishment was the use of the "Tucker telephone." Until 1968, staff punished inmates by restraining them to a treatment bed in the Tucker hospital and attaching electrical wires to their big toe and penis. As an officer turned the crank of the generator (taken from an old crank-style telephone), an electrical current flooded the prisoner's body—often causing fainting and sometimes irreversible damage to the testicles. The administration routinely overlooked the brutality inflicted by guards against inmates: In addition to being punished with starvation, many inmates also were subjected to having needles rammed under their fingernails and being whipped with a leather strap 5 feet long. The scandal at the Arkansas state penitentiary also included allegations that more than 100 inmates had been murdered and buried in a neighboring pasture (*Holt v. Sarver,* 1970; Murton, 1976; Murton & Hyams, 1969).

Unofficial force, as a measure of informal control reinforced by nonenforcement, may be used against inmates by individual staff members or, even more reprehensibly, by groups of officers, known as "goon squads." In a rare examination of unofficial force, James Marquart (1986) conducted a participant observation at the Texas Department of Corrections. Marquart's primary research question was: How and why do guards use unofficial force as a routine mechanism for informal social control? His study identified varying degrees of nonenforced violence against prisoners: verbal intimidation (racial and ethnic slurs), minor incidents of physical abuse (known as "tune-ups," "attitude adjustment," or "counseling"), and severe acts of violence (known as "ass whipping"). Marquart learned that unofficial force, as a mechanism of social control, serves various sociological and organizational purposes. First, coercion maintains control and order; indeed, those who challenge authority are commonly subjected to informal punishment. Second, unofficial force maintains status and deference by instilling fear and an attitude of subordination among inmates toward the prison staff. Third, unofficial force provides an opportunity for young ambitious guards to prove themselves in order to move upward in the prison organization.

Suicide and Self-Inflicted Injuries

Although most institutional suicides are preventable, such tragedies remain the leading cause of death in jails (Cohen, 1992; Hayes, 1988; Hayes & Rowan, 1988; Kappeler, Vaughn, & del Carmen, 1991; Robertson, 1993, 1996b; Winfree & Wooldredge, 1991). Thus, suicide and self-inflicted injuries by prisoners are another form of violence stemming from nonenforcement. Such nonintervention leading to suicide and self-inflicted injuries is generally brought on by *deliberate indifference* (culpability beyond mere negligence) compounded by various sources of escalation: lack of training, lack of policies

The Brutal Truth 149

and procedures, poor institutional conditions, and poor facility design (Welch & Gunther, 1997a, 1997b).

Nonenforcement is traced commonly to the staff perception that many inmates are simply "gesturing" and not seriously contemplating suicide. Such inmates are viewed as manipulative, and their actions are viewed as attempts to attract attention from the staff. This is particularly true in cases involving self-injury and mutilation; indeed, some cases feature rather bizarre behaviors, including ingesting razor blades and lightbulbs as well as cutting oneself with sharp objects ("Case Suicide," 1992).

To illustrate the role of deliberate indifference in nonenforcement, we turn to *Natriello v. Flynn* (1993), in which the decedent reported a history of substance abuse and suicide attempts during the intake assessment. While in custody, he was placed on suicide watch for engaging in self-destructive behavior. The decedent committed suicide by hanging himself with a bed sheet by securing it to the ceiling grate: an example of how poor facility design contributes to suicide. It was concluded that the decedent had been dead for nearly 7 hours prior to being discovered. In their suit against the sheriff and his staff, the family alleged various acts of deliberate indifference, including inadequate training and inadequate supervision. Evidence showed that two officers were asleep (or at least lying down) with the lights off at the time of the suicide. The jury returned a verdict for the plaintiff (see Welch & Gunther, 1997a, 1997b).

In a case that also involves the need to intervene, the plaintiffs in *Heflin v. Stewart County, Tenn.* (1992) prevailed in presenting compelling evidence that the jailers had acted with deliberate indifference after discovering the decedent hanging in his cell. The deputy and his staff left the decedent hanging while they checked for a pulse and signs of respiration. Because the deputy did not detect a pulse or respiration, he left the decedent hanging, even though he reported that the body was warm and the feet were touching the floor. The body was not removed from the hanging position until photographs were taken—approximately 20 minutes after the hanging was discovered. The appeals court affirmed the award of damages to the plaintiffs, concluding that the deputy and his staff demonstrated unlawfulness by doing nothing to attempt to save the decedent (also see *Thomas v. Benton County, Ark.*, 1988, for a similar case involving the failure to intervene; Cohen, 1992; Robertson, 1993, 1996b; Welch & Gunther, 1997a, 1997b).

Jail suicide has increasingly become the subject of further investigation because numerous incidents suggest foul play. In particular, civil rights leaders have questioned the circumstances of "suspicious" suicides in Southern jails. In Mississippi, 43 hanging deaths were reported between 1987 and 1992. All of these deaths were classified as suicides, and civil rights leaders were concerned because 20 of the victims were black. In 1990, Scott Campbell, a 21-year-old black man who had been dating a white teen in a town known for its racial violence, was found hanging in his cell in the Neshoba County Jail. Investigators have begun to reexamine this and other suspicious cases, and critics of local criminal justice system charge that some of these deaths were in fact murders and not suicides. "At the very least, the leaders say they want to explore if the state's local jailers are causing suicides by failing to stop them—a question of neglect being raised at jails nationwide" (Mayfield, 1993, p. 2).

COVERT FACILITATION

In covert facilitation, authorities intentionally encourage rule breaking by taking *hidden* or *deceptive* enforcement action (Marx, 1981). Covert facilitation involves "setting up" or framing rule breakers, sometimes in the form "sting operations," considered by their proponents to be *lawful* entrapment. Compared to the *passive* tactics of nonenforcement, authorities become more *active* in covert facilitation by consciously enticing their target to violate a rule. Covert facilitation and nonenforcement are often reciprocally connected. For example, authorities may grant rule breakers a license to commit violence to further the objectives of covert facilitation; as we have discussed earlier, authorities have relied on BTs and snitches in ways that combine escalation, nonenforcement, and covert facilitation.

In prisons, covert facilitation has been linked to various tactics of trickery, including the infiltration of gangs and creation of opportunities in which rule breakers can more easily "get busted."[1] Covert facilitation also extends to cases in which guards target certain prisoners and plant contraband in their cells, giving them justification, however false, to transfer prisoners to solitary confinement. In maintaining our focus on institutional violence, we turn to an infamous incident at Soledad Prison, California, allegedly involving covert facilitation (Jackson, 1970). In 1969, corrections officers at Soledad Prison singled out eight white and seven black inmates to be searched for weapons. In the process, they were ordered outdoors to the exercise yard, where the already tense situation escalated into a brawl between the groups of inmates. Though controversy continues to obscure the sequence of events, it was reported by inmates that a tower guard—without warning—fired pinpoint strikes at the black prisoners. Three black inmates were fatally wounded.

The Brutal Truth

Inmates accused the guards of contributing to the death of one of the injured prisoners who lay bleeding to death but was not allowed to be moved for more than 20 minutes, thereby delaying crucial medical attention (Jackson, 1970).

Days following the shooting, a grand jury in Monterey County ruled that the guard's use of force was justifiable. The news from the court fueled the anger of prisoners at Soledad. Later that day, a white guard was beaten to death by inmates. After days of investigation, authorities charged three black inmates with murder—Fleeta Drumgo, John Clutchette, and George Jackson. Their supporters contested that they were not involved in the murder of the guard; rather, prison authorities had accused them because they were known as black militants. Following a highly controversial public campaign of support for the prisoners, charges against Drumgo, Clutchette, and Jackson were dismissed (Jackson, 1970). Oddly, in 1971, George Jackson, radical leader and author of *Soledad Brother,* was killed by guards in an alleged prison escape, an event that also remains shrouded by suspicion of covert facilitation.

In 1985, a similar incident of alleged covert facilitation occurred in a Southern jail where a prisoner was seemingly enabled to escape. While still handcuffed after being fingerprinted, the prisoner was left unattended in the processing room—arguably "set up" or enticed to escape. As the prisoner fled through the unlocked back door, he was immediately spotted by an armed officer, who shot the escapee in the back of the head. The bullet exited the escapee's cheek, and he continued to flee, running into traffic, where he was struck by a van; he managed to regain his balance only to be hit again by another vehicle. Astonishingly, he was alive and conscious. Law enforcement officers escorted him to a hospital, where he was treated for several injuries and then returned to the county jail and placed in solitary confinement. Within an hour, a trustie discovered him committing suicide. The attending guard initially refused to open the cell, but when urged by the trustie, he unlocked the cell, and the trustie removed the prisoner from a hanging position. The guard refused to perform CPR, so the trustie desperately attempted, albeit unsuccessfully, to revive the prisoner, who was pronounced dead on the floor of the jail.[2]

The creation of prison gladiator matches by authorities is another insidious instance of covert facilitation of violence. It has been reported at various prisons around the nation that correctional officers orchestrate fights between inmates for sport and wagering. In a widely publicized incident, an inmate—due to his size and strength—was repeatedly coerced by guards to engage in gladiator games at the institution. During one such brutal contest that occurred in the exercise yard, the inmate was shot—without warning—from a guard in the watchtower. The bullet lodged in his spine, permanently paralyzing him below the waist. The crippled prisoner insists that he was victimized by staff, first by being forced to fight as a gladiator and second by the marksman's bullet (Nieves, 1998). In sum, the concept of covert facilitation captures an irony of social control, exposing the various ways authorities take hidden or deceptive enforcement action that in turn encourages rule breaking. As this section points out, covert facilitation contributes to the reproduction of violence in correctional institutions.

Conclusion

Admittedly, the ironies of social control described here are ideal types, and although they are useful as analytical categories, they have limitations when used to attend to empirical evidence. Escalation, nonenforcement, and covert facilitation commonly overlap, thereby blurring their conceptual boundaries. The secretive nature of these activities also makes it difficult to gather data, especially in situations involving nonenforcement and covert facilitation. Indeed, these actions occur within closed systems—most notably prisons—where official deviance remains conveniently concealed from public, legal, and scientific scrutiny.

Another limitation of this conceptual framework is the uncertainty of correctly arranging the causal order of official actions and their perceived consequences. For instance, is it possible that violence is *escalated* by the activation of special operations response teams (SORTs) during institutional disturbances? Perhaps. But once again, the causal sequence of events is not always evident. Despite these drawbacks, this chapter sheds additional light on factors contributing to institutional violence, namely lack of expertise (e.g., lack of training, poor institutional conditions, poor facility design), self-fulfilling prophecies (e.g., labeling), and secondary gains.

The penological literature is full of vivid examples of ironies of social control; still, there are few available conceptual frameworks that systematically link and explain incidents of escalation, nonenforcement, and covert facilitation. Fittingly, Marx's (1981) model—though primarily applied to law enforcement—can serve valuable heuristic purposes for correctional research. By exploring the paradoxes of social control in corrections, we stand to learn more about the dynamics and consequences of managing prisons and jails. The implications for policy emerge as we acknowledge the increase in correctional populations compounded by glaring management deficiencies (e.g., lack of adequate supervision), all of which contribute to the escalation of institutional violence (see Clear, 1995).

The sociology of irony enables researchers to situate authorities—and their interdependent relations with rule breakers—at the crux of social control analysis, thereby illuminating the dialectics of regulating individual and collective behavior (Schneider, 1975). This framework is particularly relevant if we accept the conclusion that social control is becoming increasingly dispersed, penetrating, and intrusive, as well as more specialized and technical (Cohen, 1979; Marx, 1981; Staples, 1997). Foucault (1979) referred to this phenomenon as the modern state's "subtle calculated technology of subjection" (pp. 220-221). This does not, however, necessarily mean that measures of social control are becoming more coercive. "If Hobbes is correct that there are two basic forms controlling others, force and fraud, then it is not surprising that a decrease in the former is accompanied by an increase in the latter" (Marx, 1981, p. 239). Marx reminded sociologists that they should give more than a passing thought to deception, paradox, incongruity, trade-offs, and irony. Not only are these concepts apparent in modern life, but they also have become prominent themes in the correctional apparatus of social control.

Notes

1. Covert facilitation is also found in the controversial prison "catchall" rules that give authorities blanket authority over institutional conduct. "Catchall rules deny inmates fair warning of punishable behavior and provide prison staff with unwarranted discretion in distinguishing permissible from punishable conduct" (Robertson, 1994, p. 153). Ironically, "catchall" rules facilitate rule breaking, thereby permitting staff to penalize inmates. However, these rules (e.g., disrespect, insubordination, insolence) are "so vague and indefinite that it is difficult to differentiate between what might be permissible conduct and what might constitute a violation" (Robertson, 1994, p. 153; Robertson, 1996a).

2. While investigating this incident, I interviewed several witnesses, including the trustee who intervened.

References

Abbott, J. H. (1981). *In the belly of the beast: Letters from prison.* New York: Vintage.
Adams, R. (1998). *Abuses of punishment.* New York: St. Martin's.
Akerstrom, M. (1986). Outcasts in prison: The cases of informers and sex offenders. *Deviant Behavior, 7,* 1-12.

Al Jundi v. Mancusi, F.2d 2287 (1991).
Becker, H. S. (1963). *Outsiders: Studies in the sociology of deviance*. New York: Free Press.
Blumer, H. (1969). *Symbolic interactionism: Perspective and method*. Englewood Cliffs, NJ: Prentice Hall.
Bowker, L. (1980). *Prison victimization*. New York: Elsevier.
Case suicide of a manipulative inmate. (1992). *Jail Suicide Update, 4*(4), 6-8.
Chonco, N. (1989). Sexual assaults among male inmates: A descriptive study. *Prison Journal, 69,* 72-82.
Clear, T. R. (1995, June). *The unintended consequences of incarceration*. Paper presented at the Vera Institute of Justice, New York, NY.
Cohen, F. (1992). Liability for custodial suicide: The information base requirements. *Jail Suicide Update, 4*(2) 1-11.
Cohen, S. (1979). The punitive city: Notes on the dispersal of social control. *Contemporary Crisis, 3,* 339-363.
Colvin, M. (1981). The contradictions of control: Prisons in class society. *Insurgent Sociologist, 10*(1), 33-45.
Colvin, M. (1982). The New Mexico prison riot. *Social Problems, 29,* 449-463.
Colvin, M. (1992). *The penitentiary in crisis: From accommodation to riot in New Mexico*. Albany: State University of New York Press.
Crouch, B. M., & Marquart, J. W. (1990). Resolving the paradox of reform: Litigation, prisoner violence, and perceptions of risk. *Justice Quarterly, 7,* 103-123.
Deutsch, M., Cunningham, D., & Fink, E. (1991). Twenty years later: Attica civil rights case finally cleared for trial. *Social Justice, 18*(3), 13-25.
DiIulio, J. (1987). *Governing prisons*. New York: Free Press.
Eigenberg, H. (1994). Rape in male prisons: Examining the relationship between correctional officers' attitudes toward male rape and their willingness to respond to acts of rape. In M. Braswell, R. Montgomery, & L. Lombardo (Eds.), *Prison violence in America* (pp. 145-166). Cincinnati, OH: Anderson.
Ellis, D. (1984). Crowding and prison violence: Integration of research and theory. *Criminal Justice and Behavior, 11,* 277-308.
Ellis, D., Grasmick, H., & Gilman, B. (1974). Violence in prisons: A sociological analysis. *American Journal of Sociology, 80,* 16-34.
Elvin, J. (1992). A rare win for man behind bars. *Civil Liberties, 376,* 6.
Engel, K., & Rothman, S. (1983, Fall). Prison violence and the paradox of reform. *Public Interest, 43,* 91-105.
Farmer v. Brennan, 114 S.Ct. 1970 (1994).
Ferrell, J. (1996). *Crimes of style*. Boston: Northeastern University Press.
Fleisher, M. (1989). *Warehousing violence*. Newbury Park, CA: Sage.
Foucault, M. (1979). *Discipline and punish*. New York: Vintage.
Garfinkel, H. (1956). Conditions of successful degradation ceremonies. *American Journal of Sociology, 61,* 420-424.
Gil, D. (1996). Preventing violence in a structurally violent society: Mission impossible. *American Journal of Orthopsychiatry, 66,* 77-84.
Goffman, E. (1961). *Asylums: Essays on the social construction of mental patients and other inmates*. Garden City, NY: Doubleday.
Hamm, M. S., Coupez, T., Hoze, F. E., & Weinstein, C. (1994). The myth of humane imprisonment: A critical analysis of severe discipline in U.S. maximum security prisons, 1945-1990. In M. Braswell, R. Montgomery, & L. Lombardo (Eds.), *Prison violence in America* (pp. 167-200). Cincinnati, OH: Anderson.
Haney, C. (1993, Spring). Infamous punishment: The psychological consequences of isolation. *Journal of the National Prison Project, 410,* 1-4.

Hassel, J., & Misseck, R. E. (1996, January 31). 6 more union county officers arrested in probe of alleged abuse of detainees. *The Star Ledger,* pp. 1, 10.

Hawkins, R., & Tiedeman, G. (1975). *The creation of deviance.* Columbus, OH: C. Merrill.

Hayes, L. M. (1988). *National study of jail suicides: Seven years later.* Alexandria, VA: National Center on Institutions and Alternatives.

Hayes, L. M., & Rowan, J. R. (1988). *Training curriculum on suicide detection and prevention in jails and lockups.* Alexandria, VA: National Center on Institutions and Alternatives.

Heflin v. Stewart County, Tenn. 958 F.2d 709 (6th Cir.1992).

Henderson, J. H., & Simon, D. R. (1994). *Crimes of the criminal justice system.* Cincinnati, OH: Anderson.

Hirschi, T. (1969). *Causes of delinquency.* Berkeley: University of California Press.

Holmes, S. A. (1995, February 9). Inmate violence is on rise as federal prisons change. *New York Times,* pp. A-1, A-14.

Holt v. Sarver, 309 F. Supp. 362 (E.D. Ark 1970), affirmed, 442 F.2d 304 (8th Circuit, 1971).

Hudson v. McMillian, 60 U.S. Law Week 4151 (Feb. 25 1992).

Human Rights Watch. (1997). *Cold storage: Super-maximum security confinement in Indiana.* New York: Author.

Immigration and Naturalization Service. (1995). *Interim report, executive summary: The Elizabeth, New Jersey Contract Detention Facility operated by ESMOR Inc.* Washington, DC: Author.

Inmates of Attica v. Rockefeller, 453 F.2d 12, 18, 22 (2d Cir. 1971).

Irwin, J. (1980). *Prisons in turmoil.* Boston: Little, Brown.

Jackson, B. (1992). The Indians of Attica: A taste of white man's justice. In B. Jackson (Ed.), *Disorderly conduct* (pp. 122-128). Urbana: University of Illinois Press.

Jackson, G. (1970). *Soledad brother.* New York: Bantam.

Jacobs, J. (1977). *Stateville: The penitentiary in mass society.* Chicago: University of Chicago Press.

Jones, R., & Schmid, T. (1989). Inmates' conceptions of prison sexual assault. *Prison Journal, 69,* 53-61.

Kalinich, D. B. (1980). *Power, stability and contraband: The inmate economy.* Prospect Heights, IL: Waveland.

Kalinich, D. B., & Stojkovic, S. (1985). Contraband: The basis for legitimate power in a prison social system. *Crime and Behavior: An International Journal, 12,* 435-451.

Kalinich, D. B., & Stojkovic, S. (1987). Prison contraband systems: Implications for prison management. *Journal of Crime and Justice, 10*(1), 1-21.

Kappeler, V., Vaughn, M., & del Carmen, R. (1991). Death in detention: An analysis of police liability for negligent failure to prevent suicide. *Journal of Criminal Justice, 19,* 381-393.

Katz, J. (1988). *Seductions of crime: Moral and sensual attractions in doing evil.* New York: Basic Books.

The killing ground. (1980, February 18). *Newsweek,* pp. 66-76.

Kitsuse, J. (1962). Societal reactions to deviant behavior: Problems of theory and method. *Social Problems, 9,* 247-256.

Lemert, E. (1972). *Human deviance, social problems and social control.* Englewood Cliffs, NJ: Prentice Hall.

Lockwood, D. (1980). *Prison sexual violence.* New York: Elsevier.

Lockwood, D. (1982). The contribution of sexual harassment to stress and coping in confinement. In N. Parisi (Ed.), *Coping with imprisonment* (pp. 45-64). Beverly Hills, CA: Sage.

Lowman, J., & MacLean, B. (1991). Prisons and protests in Canada. *Social Justice, 18*(3), 130-154.

Mahan, S. (1994). "An orgy of brutality" at Attica and the "killing ground" at Sante Fe. In M. Braswell, S. Dillingham, & R. Montgomery (Eds.), *Prison violence in America* (2nd ed., pp. 253-264). Cincinnati, OH: Anderson.

Marongiu, P., & Newman, G. (1987). *Vengeance: The fight against injustice*. Totowa, NJ: Littlefield-Adams.
Marongiu, P., & Newman, G. (1995). *Vendetta*. Florence: Giuffe.
Marquart, J. W. (1986). Prison guards and the use of physical coercion as a mechanism of prisoner control. *Criminology, 24,* 347-366.
Marquart, J. W., & Crouch, B. M. (1985). Judicial reform and prisoner control: The impact of Ruiz v. Estelle on a Texas penitentiary. *Law and Society Review, 19,* 557-586.
Martin, S. J., & Ekland-Olson, S. (1987). *Texas prisons: The walls came tumbling down*. Austin: Texas Monthly Press.
Marx, G. T. (1970). Civil disorder and the agents of social control. *Journal of Social Issues, 26,* 19-57.
Marx, G. T. (1981). Ironies of social control: Authorities as contributors to deviance through escalation, nonenforcement, and covert facilitation. *Social Problems, 28,* 221-246.
Mayfield, M. (1993, March 17). Jail suicides invisible issue: Hearings today highlights the problem. *USA Today,* pp. 1-A, 2-A.
McCarthy, B. (1995). Patterns in prison corruption. In D. Close & N. Meier (Eds.), *Morality in criminal justice: An introduction to ethics*. Belmont, CA: Wadsworth.
Misseck, R. E. (1995, October 13). 6 guards held in beatings. *The Star Ledger,* pp. 1, 15.
Morris, R. (1983). *The Devil's butcher shop: The New Mexico prison uprising*. New York: Franklin Watts.
Murton, T. O. (1976). *The dilemma of prison reform*. New York: Holt, Rinehart & Winston.
Murton, T. O., & Hyams, J. (1969). *Accomplices to crime: The Arkansas prison scandal*. New York: Grove.
Nacci, P. L. (1982). *Sex and sexual aggression in federal prisons*. Unpublished manuscript, U.S. Federal Prison System, Office of Research.
Nacci, P. L., & Kane, T. R. (1984, March). Sex and sexual aggression in federal prisons: Inmate involvement and employee impact. *Federal Probation, 8,* 46-53.
Natriello v. Flynn, 837 F.Supp. 17 D. Mass. (1993), affirmed 985 F.2d 579, 26 ATLA L. Rep. 368 (Dec. 1993).
New York State Special Commission on Attica. (1972). *Attica: The official report of the New York State Commission*. New York: Bantam.
Newman, G. (1985). *The punishment process*. New York: Harrow & Heston.
Newman, G. (1995). *Just and painful: A case for corporal punishment of criminals*. New York: Harrow & Heston.
Newman, G., & Lynch, M. (1987). From feuding to terrorism: The ideology of vengeance. *Contemporary Crises, 11,* 223-247.
Nieves, E. (1998, November 7). California examines brutal, deadly prisons. *New York Times,* p. A-7.
Oswald, R. B. (1972). *Attica: My story*. New York: Doubleday.
Packer, H. (1968). *The limits of the criminal sanction*. Stanford, CA: Stanford University Press.
Peet, J., & Schwab, D. (1995, October 22). Critics praise INS for "candid" report. *The Star Ledger,* p. 8.
Porporino, F. J. (1986). Managing violent individuals in correctional settings. *Journal of Interpersonal Violence, 1,* 213-237.
Porporino, F. J., & Marton, J. P. (1983). *Strategies to reduce prison violence*. Ottawa: Correctional Service of Canada.
Potler, C. (1988). *AIDS in prison: A crisis in New York State corrections*. New York: Correctional Association of New York.
Press, A. (1986, October 6). Inside America's toughest prison. *Newsweek,* pp. 46, 61.
Prison terms for officers in beatings of immigrants. (1998, May 2). *New York Times,* p. B-6.
Reiman, J. (1998). *The rich get richer and the poor get prison*. Boston: Allyn & Bacon.

Reiss, A. (1951). Delinquency as the failure of personal and social control. *American Sociological Review, 16,* 196-207.
Robertson, J. E. (1993). Fatal custody: A reassessment of Section 1983, liability for custodial suicide. *University of Toledo Law Review, 24,* 807-830.
Robertson, J. E. (1994). "Catchall" prison rules and the courts: A study of judicial review of prison justice. *Saint Louis University Public Law Review, 24,* 153-173.
Robertson, J. E. (1995). "Fight or F. . ." and constitutional liberty: An inmate's right to self defense when targeted by aggressors. *Indiana Law Review, 29,* 339-363.
Robertson, J. E. (1996a). The decline of negative implication jurisprudence: Procedural fairness in prison discipline after *Sandin v. Conner. University of Tulsa Law Journal, 32,* 39-56.
Robertson, J. E. (1996b). Jailers' liability for custodial suicide after *Farmer v. Brennan. Jail Suicide/Mental Health Update, 6*(3), 1-5.
Rolland, M. (1997). *Descent into madness: An inmate's experience of the New Mexico State Prison riot.* Cincinnati, OH: Anderson.
Ruiz v. Estelle, 74-329. (E. D. Tex., Dec. 19, 1980).
Saenz, A. (1986). *Politics of a riot.* Washington, DC: American Correctional Association.
Scheff, T. (1966). *Being mentally ill: A sociological theory.* Chicago: Aldine.
Schneider, L. (1975). Ironic perspective and sociological thought. In L. Coser (Ed.), *The idea of social structure* (pp. 323-339). New York: Harcourt Brace Jovanovich.
Silberman, M. (1995). *A world of violence: Corrections in America.* Belmont, CA: Wadsworth.
Smothers, R. (1995, October 24). Wave of prison uprisings provoke debate on crack. *New York Times,* p. A-18.
Smothers, R. (1998, March 7). 3 prison guards guilty of abuse of immigrants. *New York Times,* pp. A-1, B-4.
Sontag, S. (1989). *AIDS and its metaphors.* New York: Farrar Straus Giroux.
Staples, W. G. (1997). *The culture of surveillance: Discipline and social control in the United States.* New York: St. Martin's.
Stark, R. (1972). *Police riots: Collective violence and law enforcement.* Belmont, CA: Wadsworth.
Stone, W. G. (1982). *The hate factory: The story of the New Mexico penitentiary riot.* Agoura, CA: Dell.
Sullivan, D. (1980). *The mask of love: Corrections in America.* Port Washington, NY: Kennikat.
Sullivan, J. (1995, October 13). 6 guards in New Jersey charged with beating jailed immigrants. *New York Times,* pp. A-1, B-5.
Sykes, G. (1958). *The society of captives: A study of a maximum security prison.* Princeton, NJ: Princeton University Press.
Tewksbury, R. (1989). Fear of sexual assault in prison inmates. *Prison Journal, 69,* 62-71.
Thomas v. Benton County, Ark., 702 F.Supp. 737 (W.D. Ark., 1988).
Toch, H. (1992). *Living in prison.* New York: Free Press.
Useem, B. (1985). Disorganization and the New Mexico prison riot. *American Sociological Review, 50,* 677-688.
Useem, B., & Kimball, P. A. (1987). A theory of prison riots. *Theory and Society, 16,* 87-122.
Useem, B., & Kimball, P. A. (1989). *States of siege: U.S. prison riots 1971-1986.* New York: Oxford University Press.
U.S. Sentencing Commission. (1995). *Cocaine and federal sentencing policy.* Washington, DC: Government Printing Office.
Vaughn, M. (1995). Civil liability against prison officials for inmate-on-inmate assault: Where are we and where have we been. *Prison Journal, 75,* 12-28.
Weiss, R. P. (Ed.). (1991). Attica: 1971-1991, a commemorative issue. *Social Justice, 18,* 3.
Welch, M. (1989). Social junk, social dynamite and the rabble: Persons with AIDS in jail. *American Journal of Criminal Justice, 14,* 135-147.

Welch, M. (1991a, March/April). A book review of *Jails: Reform and the new generation philosophy* by Linda L. Zupan. *American Jails: The Magazine of the American Jail Association,* pp. 132-135.

Welch, M. (1991b). Social class, special populations, and other unpopular issues. In G. L. Mays (Ed.), *Setting the jail research agenda for the 1990s* (pp. 17-23). Washington, DC: National Institute of Corrections, U.S. Department of Justice.

Welch, M. (1995). A sociopolitical approach to the reproduction of violence in Canadian prisons. In J. I. Ross (Ed.), *Violence in Canada: Sociopolitical perspectives* (pp. 250-283). New York: Oxford University Press.

Welch, M. (1996a). *Corrections: A critical approach.* New York: McGraw-Hill.

Welch, M.. (1996b). Prison violence in America: Past, present, and future. In R. Muraskin & A. R. Roberts (Eds.), *Visions for change: Crime and justice and the twenty-first century* (pp. 184-198). Englewood Cliffs, NJ: Prentice Hall.

Welch, M. (1997a). Questioning the utility and fairness of INS detention: Criticisms of poor institutional conditions and protracted periods of confinement for undocumented immigrants. *Journal of Contemporary Criminal Justice, 13,* 41-54.

Welch, M. (1997b). Tougher prisons? *Critical Criminologist, 8,* 7-11.

Welch, M. (1998). Problems facing Immigration and Naturalization Service (INS) Centers: Policies, procedures, and allegations of human rights violations. In T. Alleman & R. L. Gido (Eds.), *Turnstile justice: Issues in American corrections* (pp. 192-204). Englewood Cliffs, NJ: Prentice Hall.

Welch, M. (1999). The reproduction of institutional violence in U.S. prisons. In R. Muraskin & A. R. Roberts (Eds), *Visions for change: Crime and justice in the twenty-first century* (pp. 313-328). Englewood Cliffs, NJ: Prentice Hall.

Welch, M., & Bryan, J. (in press). Moral campaigns, authoritarian aesthetics, and amplification: Flag desecration in the post-*Eichman* era. *Critical Criminology: An International Journal, 9*(2).

Welch, M., & Gunther, D. (1997a). Jail suicide and crisis intervention: Lessons from litigation. *Crisis Intervention and Time-Limited Treatment, 3,* 229-244.

Welch, M., & Gunther, D. (1997b). Jail suicide under legal scrutiny: An analysis of litigation and its implications to policy. *Criminal Justice Policy Review, 8,* 75-97.

Wicker, T. (1975). *A time to die.* New York: Quandrangle.

Wilkins, L. (1965). *Social deviance.* Englewood Cliffs, NJ: Prentice Hall.

Wilkins, L. (1994). Don't alter your mind: It's the world that's out of joint. *Social Justice, 21*(3), 148-153.

Winfree, L. T., & Wooldredge, J. (1991). Exploring suicides by natural causes in America's large jails: A panel study of institutional change, 1978 and 1983. In J. A. Thompson & G. L. Mays (Eds.), *American jails: Public policy issues* (pp. 63-78). Chicago: Nelson-Hall.

Young, J. (1982). The role of the police as amplifiers of deviancy, negotiators of reality and translators of fantasy. In S. Cohen (Ed.), *Images of deviance* (pp. 27-61). New York: Penguin.

Zupan, L. (1991). *Jails: Reform and the new generation philosophy.* Cincinnati, OH: Anderson.

CHAPTER

The Machinery of Death

Capital Punishment and the Ironies of Social Control

Mechanical terms abound in criminal justice, connoting efficiency, stability, and equilibrium. Consider, for instance, the depiction of criminal justice as a *system* with law *enforcement*. Even critics rely on mechanical metaphors while describing criminal justice as a social control *apparatus* whose *mechanisms* function as *tools* of the ruling class (Lynch & Groves, 1989; Welch, 1996a, 1996b). Contributing to this lexicon, Justice Harry A. Blackmun referred to capital punishment as a *machinery* of death (also see Harlow, Matas, & Rocamora, 1995). The momentum behind executions has increased dramatically since the late 1970s due to several social forces, including political pandering to—and manipulation of—public opinion, the expansion of capital crimes, and the reduction of appeals, which hastens executions.

At year end 1996, 3,219 prisoners were under sentence of death, 5% more than at year end 1995: California holds the largest number of death row inmates (454), followed by Texas (438), Florida (373), and Pennsylvania

159

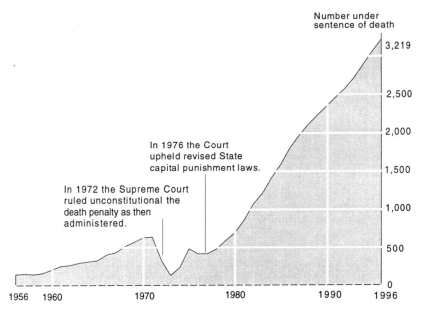

Figure 9.1. Persons Under Sentence of Death, 1995-1996
SOURCE: Snell (1997, p. 2).

(203). Since the reinstatement of the death penalty in the United States in 1976, 358 prisoners have been executed (as of year end 1996: see Figures 9.1 and 9.2). A startling two-thirds of these executions have occurred in just six states: Texas (107), Florida (38), Virginia (37), Missouri and Louisiana (23 each), and Georgia (22) (currently 38 states and the federal jurisdiction authorize the death penalty) (Snell, 1997).

The efficiency of the machinery of death has been streamlined recently in accordance with the principles of Frederick Taylor's "scientific management."[1] For example, in Arkansas, a triple execution was carried out in 1997 (the second of its kind since capital punishment was resumed). It has been said by prison officials that "such multiple executions minimize overtime costs and reduce stress on prison employees" (Kuntz, 1997, p. E-7). For capital punishment, 1997 was a benchmark year: 17 states executed 74 prisoners, the most executions in a single year since the 76 inmates executed in 1955. In 1997, Texas carried out 37 executions—the most of a single state in U.S. history (Snell, 1997).

Though not quite conforming to banker's hours, executions in Texas, under a 1995 act of legislation, have been rescheduled from midnight to the early evening—in the words of one state prison official, "to make it easier on

The Machinery of Death

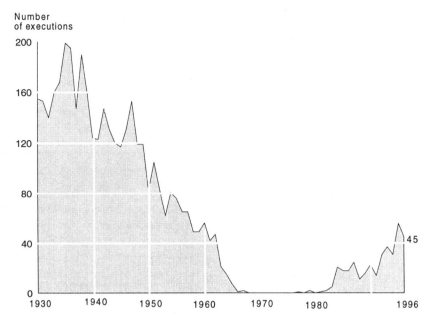

Figure 9.2. Persons Executed, 1930-1996
SOURCE: Snell (1997, p. 11).

everyone involved" (Verhovek, 1997, p. A-22). Thus, convenience has become a prominent feature of the machinery of death. "I don't know too many people who like to stay up after midnight," says R. J. Parker, assistant warden. "People have to get up and work the next day" (Verhovek, 1997, p. A-22). Some legislators, moreover, view appeals as obstacles interfering with the efficiency of the death penalty. Like other states, Texas has succeeded in reducing the appeals process, which promises to cut the stay on death row from 9 years to half that or less. Executions in Texas have become not only increasingly efficient, frequent, and routine but also virtually uneventful: Newspapers in the state's largest cities no longer send reporters to cover them (Verhovek, 1997).

Although the death penalty is portrayed by its supporters as a precise, reliable, and necessary armament of criminal justice, in reality this machinery of death has proven to be imprecise, unreliable, and reckless. Opponents criticize capital punishment for perpetuating injustice because it is fraught with errors, contradictions, and various ironies. In the previous chapter on prison violence, we examined the ironies of social control in demonstrating how authorities encourage rule breaking. Likewise in this chapter, we apply

Marx's (1981) notions of escalation, nonenforcement, and covert facilitation to capital punishment to illuminate its contradictions. In addition to exploring how the machinery of death produces counterdeterrent effects, creates new categories of violators and victims, and falsely convicts the innocent, we shall remain mindful of the significance of racism and classism in shaping the patterns of executions.

Escalation

As defined in the previous chapter, escalation implies that "by taking enforcement action, authorities unintentionally encourage rule breaking" (Marx, 1981, p. 222). In this analysis of capital punishment, murder is one type of rule breaking we shall examine; thus, it is argued that executions not only fail to deter homicide but, ironically, promote violence. To support this claim, there is an emerging body of research documenting that capital punishment may indeed have counterdeterrent effects.

BRUTALIZATION VERSUS DETERRENCE

Despite the volume of empirical studies demonstrating that there is *no* conclusive evidence linking deterrence with capital punishment, the myth persists. Walker (1994) characterized the myth of deterrence as a crime control theology, a belief that resembles a religious conviction more than an intellectual position because it rests on faith rather than on facts. But the issue is not whether the death penalty offers greater deterrence than no penalty at all—of course it does. Rather, the issue is whether the death penalty deters more than other severe penalties, such as life imprisonment without parole.

The debate over deterrence stems from a 1975 article by Isaac Ehrlich, an economist who claimed that each execution prevented seven or eight murders. In the early 1970s, the nation took a dramatic shift toward a conservative "law and order" approach to crime. Ehrlich's research was understandably celebrated by supporters of the death penalty (also see Yunker, 1976); in fact, his study was cited in *Gregg v. Georgia* (1976), in which the U.S. Supreme Court permitted states to resume executions. Ehrlich had given deterrence theory a much needed boost following Zimring and Hawkins's (1973) persuasive criticism of deterrence propositions. Despite the popularity of Ehrlich's research, its high-level statistical analysis was not free of methodological problems. Several reexaminations of Ehrlich's data *failed* to replicate what he claimed was a "deterrent effect" (Bowers & Pierce, 1975; Forst, 1983; Passell,

The Machinery of Death

1975; also see Bowers, 1984; Klein, Forst, & Filatov, 1978; Peterson & Bailey, 1991; Stack, 1987).

Proponents of deterrence theory argue that publicizing executions is a necessary component of capital punishment because it is through such publicity that the tough "law and order" message of death sentences is widely communicated. Conversely, a competing theory about publicized executions has challenged the notion of deterrence. Brutalization theory suggests that publicized executions not only fail to deter violence but, paradoxically, increase it. To appreciate fully brutalization theory, we must deconstruct the central element of deterrence theory, namely the assumption that potential killers are restrained from committing murder because they *identify* with those who have been executed. Brutalization theory suggests that *some* persons, rather than identifying with the condemned, identify with the executioner (Bowers & Pierce, 1980b). It is crucial here to return to the principal message inherent in capital punishment: Those who commit heinous crimes *deserve* to die. Supporting this perspective, advocates of the death penalty view executions as a "public service" performed by the state, ridding society of its despicable members.

According to brutalization theory, however, publicized executions create an *alternative identification process* that promotes imitation, not deterrence. Bowers and Pierce (1980b) found an increase in homicides soon after well-publicized executions, suggesting that some murderers liken their victims to the condemned. This finding was presented as evidence of a counterdeterrent effect (also see Bailey, 1983, 1998; Bowers, 1988; Cochran, Chamlin, & Seth, 1994; Decker & Kohfeld, 1990; Forst, 1983; King, 1978). It is important to emphasize that Bowers and Pierce specified that the brutalization effect has an impact on individuals who are prone to violence, not persons who are generally nonviolent; in such cases, the publicized execution reinforces the belief that lethal vengeance is justified. Executions devalue human life and "demonstrate that it is appropriate to kill those who have gravely offended us" (Bowers & Pierce, 1980b, p. 456). In the context of social control, evidence engendered by brutalization studies supports the claim that capital punishment produces an ironic and escalating effect by promoting, rather than deterring, murder.

THE CREATION OF NEW CATEGORIES AND NET WIDENING

Marx (1981) reminded us that escalation leads to the creation of new categories of violators and victims and that this in turn reproduces the ironies of social control. Accordingly, capital punishment is escalated by the creation of new categories (of violators and victims), resulting in a net-widening effect. In 1996, several states amended their death penalty statutes in ways that further contributed to escalation. Florida added as aggravating factors the commission of a capital felony by a convicted felon under sentence of imprisonment; commission of a capital felony while engaged in abuse of an elderly or disabled adult, resulting in bodily harm or permanent disability or disfigurement; commission of a capital felony against a person in a vulnerable state due to advanced age, disability, or the defendant's position of familial/custodial authority; and commission of a felony by a "criminal street gang member" (Snell, 1997).

In the same manner, several other states also expanded their death penalty statutes in 1996. Indiana, for instance, amended its penal code to include as an aggravating factor burning, mutilation, or torture of the victim while the victim was alive. Pennsylvania added to its penal code as an aggravating factor killing a woman who was in her third trimester of pregnancy when the defendant had knowledge of the victim's pregnancy. South Carolina revised its death penalty statute to include as an aggravating factor murder of a witness or potential witness committed for the purpose of impeding or deterring prosecution of any crime. Murder of emergency medical or rescue workers, paramedics, or firefighters engaged in official duty when the defendant knew or reasonably should have known the occupation of the victim was attached to the Tennessee penal code. Finally, Virginia amended the definition of capital murder to include, among enumerated kidnapping offenses, intent to defile the victim and the killing of more than one person within a 3-year period (Snell, 1997).

These new categories of violators and victims add to a wide array of existing conditions for capital punishment, including treason (Arkansas, California, Georgia), train wrecking, perjury causing execution (California), capital drug trafficking (Florida), aircraft hijacking (Georgia), aircraft piracy, capital rape (Mississippi), contract murder, and solicitation by command or threat in furtherance of a narcotics conspiracy (New Jersey). At the federal level, the death penalty has been extended to, among other things, murder related to the smuggling of aliens; destruction of aircraft, motor vehicles, or related facilities resulting in death; murder committed during a drug-related drive-by shooting; murder committed at an airport serving international civil aviation; murder of a member of Congress, an important executive official, or a Supreme Court Justice; espionage; genocide; and assassination or kidnaping resulting in the death of the president or vice president (Snell, 1997; see Table 9.1).

TABLE 9.1 Federal Laws Providing for the Death Penalty, 1996

8 U.S.C. 1342—Murder related to the smuggling of aliens.
18 U.S.C. 32-34—Destruction of aircraft, motor vehicles, or related facilities resulting in death.
1 8 U.S.C. 36—Murder committed during a drug-related drive-by shooting.
18 U.S.C. 37—Murder committed at an airport serving international civil aviation.
18 U.S.C. 115(b)(3)(by cross-reference to 18 U.S.C. 1111]—Retaliatory murder of a member of the immediate family of law enforcement officials.
18 U.S.C. 241, 242, 245, 247—Civil rights offenses resulting in death.
18 U.S.C. 351 [by cross-reference to 18 U.S.C. 1111]—Murder of a member of Congress, an important executive official, or a Supreme Court Justice.
18 U.S.C. 794—Espionage
18 U.S.C. 844(d), (f), (i)—Death resulting from offenses involving transportation of explosives, destruction of government property, or destruction of property related to foreign or interstate commerce.
18 U.S.C. 924(i)—Murder committed by the use of a firearm during a crime of violence or a drug trafficking crime.
18 U.S.C 930—Murder committed in a federal government facility.
18 U.S.C. 1091—Genocide.
18 U.S.C. 1111—First-degree murder.
18 U.S.C. 1114—Murder of a federal judge or law enforcement official.
18 U.S.C. 1116—Murder of a foreign official.
18 U.S.C. 1118—Murder by a federal prisoner.
18 U.S.C. 1119—Murder of a U.S. national in a foreign country.
18 U.S.C. 1120—Murder by an escaped federal prisoner already sentenced to life imprisonment.
18 U.S.C. 1121—Murder of a state or local law enforcement official or other person aiding in a federal investigation; murder of a state correctional officer.
18 U.S.C. 1201—Murder during a kidnaping.
18 U.S.C. 1203—Murder during a hostage taking.
18 U.S.C. 1503—Murder of a court officer or juror.
18 U.S.C. 1512—Murder with the intent of preventing testimony by a witness, victim, or informant.
18 U.S.C. 1513—Retaliatory murder of a witness, victim, or informant.
18 U.S.C. 1716—Mailing of injurious articles with intent to kill or resulting in death.
18 U.S.C. 1751 (by cross-reference to 18 U.S.C. 1111)—Assassination or kidnaping resulting in the death of the president or vice president.
18 U.S.C. 1958—Murder for hire.
18 U.S.C. 1959—Murder involved in a racketeering offense.
18 U.S.C. 1992—Willful wrecking of a train resulting in death.
18 U.S.C. 2113—Bank-robbery-related murder or kidnaping.
18 U.S.C. 2119—Murder related to a carjacking.
18 U.S.C. 2245—Murder related to rape or child molestation.
18 U.S.C. 2251—Murder related to sexual exploitation of children.
18 U.S.C. 2280—Murder committed during an offense against maritime navigation.
18 U.S.C. 2281—Murder committed during an offense against a maritime fixed platform.
18 U.S.C. 2332—Terrorist murder of a U.S. national in another country.
18 U.S.C. 2332a—Murder by the use of a weapon of mass destruction.
18 U.S.C. 2340—Murder involving torture.
18 U.S.C. 2381—Treason.
21 U.S.C. 848(e)—Murder related to a continuing criminal enterprise or related murder of a federal, state, or local law enforcement officer.
49 U.S.C. 1472-1473—Death resulting from aircraft hijacking.

SOURCE: Snell (1997, p. 4).

TABLE 9.2 Minimum Age Authorized for Capital Punishment, 1996

Age 16 or Less	Age 17	Age 18	None Specified
Alabama (16)	Georgia	California	Arizona
Arkansas (14)[a]	New Hampshire	Colorado	Idaho
Delaware (16)	North Carolina[b]	Connecticut[c]	Montana
Florida (16)	Texas	Federal system	Louisiana
Indiana (16)		Illinois	Pennsylvania
Kentucky (16)		Kansas	South Carolina
Mississippi (16)[d]		Maryland	South Dakota[e]
Missouri (16)		Nebraska	Utah
Nevada (16)		New Jersey	
Oklahoma (16)		New Mexico	
Virginia (14)[f]		New York	
Wyoming (16)		Ohio	
		Oregon	
		Tennessee	
		Washington	

SOURCE: Snell (1997, p. 5).
NOTE: Reporting by states reflects interpretations by state attorney general offices and may differ from previously reported ages.
a. See Arkansas Code Ann.9-27-318(b)(1)(Repl. 1991).
b. The age required is 17 unless the murderer was incarcerated for murder when a subsequent murder occurred; then the age may be 14.
c. See Conn. Gen. Stat. 53a-46a(g)(1).
d. The minimum age defined by statute is 13, but the effective age is 16, based on a Mississippi Supreme Court decision.
e. Juveniles may be transferred to adult court. Age can be a mitigating factor.
f. The minimum age for transfer to adult court is 14 by statute, but the effective age for a capital sentence is 16, based on interpretation of a U.S. Supreme Court decision by the state attorney general's office.

Juvenile Offenders

Increasingly, the application of the death penalty has expanded to include juveniles. Although eight states do not specify a minimum age at which the death penalty may be imposed, 14 states and the federal system require a minimum age of 18, and 16 states indicate an age of eligibility between 14 and 17 (Snell, 1996; see Table 9.2). In 1997, California Governor Pete Wilson reported that he would consider a state law allowing executions of 14-year olds, and Cruz M. Bustamante said he might support executions for "hardened criminals" as young as 13 (Verhovek, 1998b, p. A-7). Texas State Representative Jim Pitts in 1998 proposed the death penalty for 11-year-old killers. Pitts reasoned: "This is a drastic step. . . . But some of the kids are growing up today, they just aren't the 'Leave it to Beaver' kids that I grew up with" (Verhovek, 1998b, p. A-7). Reacting to the 1998 Arkansas schoolyard killings, Pitts argued that the state needs to "send a message to our kids that they can't do these kinds of crimes" (Verhovek, 1998b, p. A-7).

Mentally Handicapped Offenders

The new categories of offenders eligible for the death penalty also include the emotionally and mentally handicapped. Although in recent memory the U.S. Supreme Court has prohibited the execution of emotionally disturbed capital defendants (*Ford v. Wainwright,* 1986; Miller & Radelet, 1993; Paternoster, 1991), such restrictions have been not been uniformly enforced. In 1995, Varnall Weeks, a convicted murderer diagnosed by psychiatric experts as a paranoid schizophrenic, was executed in Alabama. Weeks was clearly disturbed: Living in a maze of delusions, he believed that "he would come back to life as a giant flying tortoise that would rule the world" (Bragg, 1995, p. 7). At one of his hearings, Weeks described himself as God, wore a domino on a band around his shaved head, and responded to the court's question with a "rambling discourse on serpents, cybernetics, albinos, Egyptians, the Bible, and reproduction.... [He also] sat in his cell naked in his own feces, mouthing senseless sounds" (Shapiro, 1995, p. A-29). Although prosecution and defense acknowledged that he suffered from paranoid schizophrenia, the courts contended that he was sane enough to be executed. The U.S. Supreme Court unanimously rejected his appeal. To date, legislators and the courts have not established a consistent or humane definition of how sane or competent a capital defendant needs to be in order to be executed.

Whereas the death penalty for mentally ill murderers is characterized by inconsistent court rulings, there are no such obstacles interfering with the execution of mentally retarded capital defendants (those scoring below 70 on a standardized intelligence test). It has been speculated that throughout history, mildly retarded offenders have been commonly executed but that their level of intelligence was never known to the courts because such tests were not conducted. Today, defendants are routinely administered intelligence tests; thus, the courts are fully aware of the defendant's level of intelligence. In 1989, the High Court ruled in *Penry v. Lynaugh* that states have the right to execute mentally retarded persons convicted of capital murder.

Critics point out that executing mentally retarded (even mildly retarded) offenders raises serious moral and ethical issues, especially because mental retardation constitutes a serious liability affecting every dimension of that person's life. "Many individuals who are sentenced to death and executed in this country have mental retardation" (Harlow et al., 1995, p. 1; Reed, 1993). Persons with mental retardation are quite susceptible to suggestion and have serious difficulty in logic, planning, and understanding consequences. With this in mind, Professor of Special Education Ruth Luckasson asked, "Can you imagine anyone easier to execute?" (quoted in Harlow et al., 1995, p. 1).

Luckasson added, "I have seen people with mental retardation sitting in their own capital trials, with their lives as stake, who had absolutely no understanding of what was going on" (quoted in Harlow et al., 1995, p. 1). In 1992, Bill Clinton, then governor of Arkansas, refused to halt the execution of Ricky Ray Rector, who had blown away part of his brain in a suicide attempt just after he had killed a police officer. At the time of his trial, Rector was so mentally retarded that "he did not understand that death was permanent" (Ridgeway, 1994, p. 23). On the day of his death, he told his lawyer that "he planned to vote for Mr. Clinton that November" (Shapiro, 1995, p. A-29) and asked the guards to "save his dessert for a snack before bedtime" (Terry, 1998, p. 22).

In 1995, Mario Marquez was executed by the state of Texas after being convicted of double murder and rape. Marquez, a grade-school dropout with an IQ of 65, was the 10th of 16 children born to a migrant farmworker. As a child, he was beaten with a horsewhip by his father and abandoned to the streets and a life of drug abuse at the age of 12. During the trial, Marquez asked his lawyer "if he [Marquez] was going to have a good job when he goes to heaven" and wanted his lawyer to tell him "if he could get a job being a gardener, or taking care of animals" (Hentoff, 1995, p. 30).

Horace Kelly, convicted of triple murder, currently sits on death row, inching his way to execution, even though a panel of three psychiatric experts has testified that he is insane and incompetent. Kelly often sits in his own waste and neglects to bathe, and guards—who have nicknamed him "Smelly Kelly"—typically wear masks to clean his cell because of the unbearable stench. It has been determined that Kelly, who mumbles incoherently, is mentally retarded and is generally confused about the nature of his involvement in the criminal justice system. He said to his lawyer that "he was going to court because the judge had to decide whether he could join the Marines.... To him death row is a vocational school and as soon as he gets his 'certification' he can go home" (Terry, 1998, p. 22). Kelly was born 3 months premature to a mother who drank alcohol throughout the pregnancy; he remained hospitalized for the first 8 weeks of his life. His father scalded him with hot water when he was 3 years old and subsequently beat him periodically throughout his childhood, including an incident in which he rammed his head into a wall (Terry, 1998).

Kelly's court-appointed attorney, Richard Mazur, reported that prison guards have been trying to coach him to answer enough questions to meet the competency threshold for execution: in effect, "training him like a pet" (Terry, 1998, p. 22). To be deemed competent for execution, a condemned prisoner must understand either that he or she is going to be put to death or the reasons for the execution. If the jury concludes that Kelly is *too* incompetent to be executed, the state will be required to transfer him to a prison mental hospital for treatment, and if his condition improves sufficiently, then he will be executed. A distressed Mazur reacted: "Treating him just so he can be killed, now that's really insane" (Terry, 1998, p. 22).

The state's practice of imposing treatment for the purpose of completing an execution—a policy opposed by the American Medical Association—remains one of the more bizarre ironies of the modern machinery of death. Indeed, merging the medical model with the punishment model has produced some outlandish effects. Consider Alvin Ford who was convicted of killing a Florida policeman and sentenced to be executed. While on death row, Ford became a paranoid schizophrenic, referring to himself as "Pope John Paul III" and believing that "135 of his friends and family were being held hostage in the prison and that he was their only salvation" (Paternoster, 1991, p. 92). In addition, Ford's delusions extended to his belief that he would not be executed because he "owned the prisons and controlled the governor of Florida through mental telepathy. . . . Over time Ford became almost completely incomprehensible, speaking only in a bizarre, codelike language" (Paternoster, 1991, pp. 92-93; also see Miller & Radelet, 1993)

In *Ford v. Wainwright* (1986), the U.S. Supreme Court blocked the execution, and Ford was removed from death row and placed in a psychiatric hospital, where he was treated with the intent of furthering his execution. Eventually, Ford was returned to death row following a ruling by a federal district judge that Ford had regained his sanity. Ford's attorneys appealed the judge's decision and were waiting for a ruling when Ford died of natural causes in 1991. In the Ford case, the medical model provided an avenue for rehabilitation that was intended not to return the offender to the community but simply to resume the workings of the machinery of death (Miller & Radelet, 1993; Paternoster, 1991).

An equally ironic case was reported by Alvin Bronstein (ACLU, National Prison Project), whose client required triple-bypass heart surgery but refused treatment. Prison officials allegedly urged the prisoner to undergo surgery so he could be alive for his execution. The prisoner subsequently died of a heart attack (Johnson, 1990, p. 49). In 1995, Robert Brecheen, a condemned Oklahoma inmate, slipped into a self-induced drug stupor. State prison officials forced him to regain consciousness by having his stomach pumped in a nearby hospital so they could—just 2 hours later—execute him with state-approved drugs. "Certainly, there's irony," quipped the director of the state's corrections department. Approving of the state's actions, the husband of Brecheen's murder victim pronounced, "It wasn't his job to take his life." But Reverend Brooks thought otherwise: "This shows the absurdity of the situation.... The idea that they're going to stabilize him and bring him back to be executed is plainly outrageous" ("Revived From Overdose," 1995, p. 6).

Finally, in a case against the use of coercive medication, Charles Singleton —convicted of murdering a female grocer—awaits a court decision that will determine whether the state of Arkansas can execute him. Singleton has been diagnosed as a paranoid schizophrenic and wishes to stop taking prescribed psychotropic medication, without which he becomes delusional and incompetent. As long as he remains medicated, he is executable. The state's tactic has prompted his attorney, Jeff Rosenzweig, to counter, "We have to convince the court that you can't involuntarily medicate to competency if that is what is making him executable" (Verhovek, 1998a, p. 4).

In sum, capital punishment generates an escalating, counterdeterrent effect because, by taking enforcement action (i.e., performing executions), authorities unintentionally encourage a type of rule breaking, namely homicide. The irony of this form of social control is supported by brutalization research. To reiterate, a particularly important analytic element of escalation is the creation of new categories of violators and victims. Such categories are the products of legislation, driven by relentless political pandering to the public on crime. Not only do these self-serving political activities widen the net of capital punishment, but they tend to snare violators—juveniles, the mentally handicapped, the emotionally disturbed—who paradoxically become vulnerable victims of an overzealous criminal justice apparatus.

Nonenforcement

By way of review, nonenforcement constitutes another irony of social control in that authorities, by taking no enforcement action, intentionally permit rule breaking (Marx, 1981). Arguably one of the more tragic examples of nonenforcement can be found in America's history of vigilante "justice," particularly lynching. Authorities deliberately encouraged these travesties of justice by refusing to impose sanctions on persons who carried them out. In addition, many of these incidents of nonenforcement were motivated by racism, in that blacks served as convenient scapegoats.

Contemporary examinations of racism and the death penalty should not neglect the history of formal (executions) and informal (lynchings) penalties imposed on black defendants and suspects. Following the Civil War, black codes were *formally* established to perpetuate the economic subordination of former slaves. Such codes employed harsher penalties for crimes committed by blacks and led to a disproportionate number of black executions. *Informally,* black men also were subject to lynching (illegal execution) by vigilante mobs. Bowers (1984) reported that in the 1890s there were more lynchings (1,540) than legal executions (1,098). Though lynchings gradually declined, nearly 2,000 illegal executions occurred in the early part of the 20th century: Between 1900 and 1909 there were 885 reported lynchings, between 1910 and 1919, 621 lynchings, and in the 1920s, 315 (Bowers, 1984; also see Brundage, 1993; Jackson, 1996; Tolnay & Beck, 1992, 1994).[2]

Nowadays, a long-standing criticism of the death penalty is that despite efforts to guard against arbitrariness (as enumerated in *Gregg v. Georgia,* 1976), it continues to be administered in ways that are racially biased. Casual observers of the death penalty controversy might assume that the death penalty is racially discriminatory because black murderers, compared to white murderers, are disproportionately sentenced to death. This assumption, however, would be too simplistic. To clarify the extent of racism evident in the death penalty, one must look at the race of the victim as well as the race of the offender. In the United States, approximately half of those murdered each year are black. However, since 1977, about 85% of capital defendants who have been executed had killed a white person, whereas only 11% had murdered a black person (Baldus, Woodworth, & Pulaski, 1990). Research continues to demonstrate that killers of whites are more likely than killers of blacks to be sentenced to death: Paternoster (1983) revealed that blacks who kill whites have a 4.5 times greater chance of facing the death penalty than blacks who kill blacks. When the race of the victim is ignored, the chances of blacks' and whites' receiving a death sentence are almost equal. Furthermore, Keil and Vito (1989) found that when controlling for seriousness of the murder (in Kentucky), "Prosecutors were more likely to seek the death penalty in cases in which blacks killed whites and . . . juries were more likely to sentence to death blacks who killed whites" (p. 511). Baldus et al. (1990) concluded that when the murder victim was white, the chance of a death penalty was roughly doubled in certain kinds of cases: in particular, those cases catalogued as "middle-ground" incidents in which the victim was killed during the commission of a felony (e.g., homicide during a robbery).[3] In a recent study on racial disparities in capital punishment, Baldus (in press) reported that in Philadelphia, black defendants in murder cases are four times more likely than other defendants to be sentenced to death, even when the circumstances of the killings are the same (see Butterfield, 1998).

Numerous studies also have found that blacks charged with murdering whites are more likely to be sentenced to death than are other combinations of race, offender, and victim (Baldus, Pulaski, & Woodworth, 1983; Baldus et al., 1990; Bowers, 1980; Bowers & Pierce, 1980a; Foley & Powell, 1982; Lewis, 1978; *McClesky v. Kemp,* 1987; Radelet & Pierce, 1985; Riedel, 1976; Zimring, Eigen, & O'Malley, 1976). A report by the General Accounting Office (1990) that was presented to the Senate and House Committees on the Judiciary further supported charges the death penalty is racially biased:

> In 82% of the studies race of the victim was found to influence the likelihood of being charged with capital murder or receiving the death penalty, i.e., those who murdered whites were more likely to be sentenced to death than those who murdered blacks. (p. 5)

The racial bias in capital punishment should be viewed as another irony of social control, especially in the realm of nonenforcement. Given that only 11% of all executions involve capital defendants convicted of killing a black person, there is the appearance that the lives of white victims are more valuable than black victims. From 1977 to 1995, 88 black men were executed for murdering whites, whereas only 2 white men have been executed for killing blacks (Eckholm, 1995). To date, Texas—the all-time leader of executions with 404 at year end 1996—has never executed *anyone* for killing a black person.

By taking less (or no) enforcement action of imposing death sentences and carrying out executions, is it possible that authorities intentionally or unintentionally encourage the murder of blacks? Even the most cynical critics would probably say this is not the case; still, we must face the disconcerting fact that more than half of all homicide victims are black. Thus, it seems that there is less criminal justice for black murder victims than those who are white. The apparent indifference concerning black victims—as a product of racism—has been found throughout American history. For instance, in his classic 1944 study, Gunnar Myrdal reported that when blacks committed crimes against each other, the penalties were less harsh than in cases where whites were harmed by blacks. Today, critics point to a similar apathy concerning black victims. In his novel *Clockers* (adapted to film by Spike Lee), Richard Price (1992) described an incident at a housing project where white policemen mark off the perimeter around a dead black man, presumably killed by a black drug peddler. In an indifferent and sarcastic tone, a cop shrugs and comments, "It's like a self-cleaning oven."

Incidentally, In Virginia in 1998, Louis Ceparano pleaded guilty to burning alive a black man, Garnett P. Johnson, and chopping off his head with an ax. Ceparano was one of two white men accused of soaking Johnson with gasoline and subjecting him to racial slurs, then setting fire to him. Ceparano was spared the death penalty and received two consecutive life terms without possibility of parole ("White Man Pleads Guilty," 1998).

Advocates who believe that the death penalty can be modified to eliminate its racial bias (van den Haag & Conrad, 1983) are likely to encounter an even greater irony. Because in most murders, the assailant and the victim are of the same race, eliminating the disparity linked to the race of the victim would be likely to result in a higher proportion of blacks sentenced to death.

> If killers of black people were executed at the rate of killers of whites, many more blacks would receive death sentences. If, on the other hand, killers of whites were executed at the same rate as killers of blacks, many whites would be spared. (Eckholm, 1995, p. B-4)

The history of black lynchings in America serves as a reminder of egregious acts of nonenforcement that authorized and perpetuated the racist practice of unlawful executions. Nowadays, incidents of nonenforcement are not as clear-cut and obvious. Admittedly, it is unlikely that authorities *intentionally* encourage lethal violence against blacks. Still, executions remain significantly patterned by the race of the victim, thereby suggesting that in the eyes of the state, white murder victims are inherently more valuable than their black counterparts. Thus, racial disparities in capital punishment contradict fundamental principles of justice in a democratic society.

Covert Facilitation

Although sentencing disparities according to the race of murder victims violate basic ideals of fairness, such contradictions are compounded when innocent people are falsely convicted, and worse, executed. False convictions in capital crimes may be the result of error, wrongdoing, or a combination of the two. Whereas the former serves as evidence of an imperfect criminal justice system, the latter reveals an insidious side of the machinery of death. The deliberate prosecution of innocent people typically emerges in the form of covert facilitation: hidden or deceptive enforcement action in which authorities intentionally encourage rule breaking (Marx, 1981). In this context, *rule breaking* refers to wrongdoing by the prosecutors and police that is encouraged by the state for the purpose of securing capital convictions, even if the suspect is innocent (e.g., framing a suspect, prosecutorial misconduct, allowing perjured testimony). Cases of false conviction shed additional light on racism and classism because people of color and the impoverished are more vulnerable to these miscarriages of justice.

Capital punishment experts have long speculated that numerous innocent persons have been convicted, and in some instances, executed; still, a general understanding of such injustices was previously based on anecdotal and unsystematic research. Then, in 1987, Hugo Bedau and Michael Radelet published a systematic study of 350 defendants believed to have been wrongly convicted in capital (or potential capital) cases between the years 1900 and 1985. It is important to note that Bedau and Radelet did not simply include any case that appeared suspect. Rather, they applied strict standards of miscarriages of justice and accepted cases only on the basis of *overwhelming* evidence that an innocent person had been falsely convicted. In an expanded volume of their work, Radelet, Bedau and Putnam released *In Spite of Innocence: Erroneous Convictions in Capital Cases* (1992), cataloguing 416 cases of falsely convicted capital defendants between 1900 and 1991. Approximately one-third of these defendants were sentenced to death, and the authors persuasively documented 23 cases in which innocent people were executed. Most of the remaining defendants, though initially trapped in the machinery of justice, fortunately escaped execution. Radelet et al. referred to them as the lucky ones. Nevertheless, they still experienced years of incarceration along with the agony of uncertainty; consequently, their lives were virtually ruined (also see Dieter, 1997; Huff, Rattner, & Sagarin, 1996).

Covert facilitation is commonly found in the most egregious cases of false convictions, and as we shall see, racism and classism also permeate many such travesties of justice. Consider Walter McMillian, who, after spending 6 years on Alabama's death row, was released in 1993. Upon further scrutiny, different prosecutors conceded that the state had withheld evidence from his lawyers and had relied on perjured testimony to falsely convict McMillian. In a case that fits the "middle-ground" category of homicide, Ronda Morrison, an 18-year-old white female clerk, was murdered by a black male during a robbery in Monroeville, Alabama—coincidentally, the home town of Harper Lee, author of *To Kill a Mockingbird* (1960), a story of race and justice in the Jim Crow South. While being interrogated in connection to another killing, Ralph Myers, an ex-con with a lengthy criminal record, accused McMillian of murdering Morrison. In an unusual move, McMillian was assigned to death row before his trial. After a one-and-a-half day trial, McMillian was convicted on the testimony of three witnesses, including that of Myers and another criminal suspect. The defense lawyer called a dozen witnesses who each testified that McMillian was at home the day of the murder, socializing with friends at a fish fry. The prosecution offered no physical evidence linking McMillian to the murder; thus, critics insist that the trial was driven by racism. It was well known that McMillian was dating a white woman and that one of his sons had married a white woman; both McMillian and his attorney believed that these interracial relationships motivated the prosecution (Dieter, 1997).

The Alabama Bureau of Investigation eventually discredited the prosecution's case against McMillian. All three witnesses recanted their testimony, and Myers also reported that he was pressured by law officers to accuse McMillian. The case emerged at a time when federal appeals for capital defendants were becoming increasingly restricted, a reminder of how flawed—and corrupt—the machinery of death can be. Bryan Stevenson, McMillian's attorney, said, "It's clear that he had nothing to do with this crime. There are other folks in prison who don't have the money or the resources or the good fortune to have folks come in and help them" (Applebome, 1993, p. B-11).

In another recent case, all charges were dropped against three black men who were incarcerated in an Illinois prison from 1978 to 1996 for a double murder they did not commit. Dennis Williams spent much of that sentence waiting on death row, as did Verneal Jimerson, a fourth black inmate whose charges were dismissed a month earlier. Their case not only underscores the flaws of the criminal justice system but sheds additional light on the controversy over the restriction of federal death penalty appeals recently affirmed by the U.S. Supreme Court. The reduction of federal appeals for capital defendants is expected to cut in half the time between conviction and execution (from approximately 8 to 4 years). Richard C. Dieter, director of the Death Penalty Information Center, warns that these restrictions mean that the length of appeals would "fall well below the average time it takes to discover new evidence of innocence. . . . This rush to get on with the death penalty by shortening the appeals process will raise the danger of executing innocent people" (Terry, 1996, p. A-14).

The case against Williams, Jimerson, and their codefendants, Willie Rainge and Kenneth Williams, stems from the murder of a white couple in suburban Chicago in 1978, but new DNA evidence, witness recantations, and a jailhouse confession led to their release. Cook County State's Attorney Jack O'Malley said his office was trying to determine how the original investigation "got derailed and why it is the wrong people were charged" (Terry, 1996, p. A-14).

To this, Dennis Williams quickly responded *racism*: "The police just picked up the first young black men they could and that was it. . . . They didn't care if we were guilty or innocent. . . . We are victims of this crime too" (Terry, 1996, p. A-14). In a strange turn of events, Jimerson had been previously released when the only witness connecting him to the crime recanted; later, in a deal to get released from prison, the witness changed her testimony again. Jimerson was then rearrested, convicted, and sentenced to die. Jimerson and his codefendants believe they were indeed *framed* by the prosecution.

Contrary to popular belief, capital cases often are not meticulously litigated. Indigent defendants assigned court-appointed attorneys stand a good chance of being consumed by the machinery of death. Consider the case of George McFarland, who, in 1992, was convicted of murdering convenience store owner Kenneth Kwan in Texas. Observers noted that the trial proceeded with "bullet-train velocity": opening statements on August 10, guilty verdict on August 12, death sentence on August 14. Altogether, the trial took no more than 16 hours total (Shapiro, 1997, p. 27). Still, what McFarland complained most about was the conduct of his court-appointed attorney, 72-year old John Benn, who spent much of the trial asleep at the defense table. McFarland is not the only capital defendant to be represented by a sleeping lawyer. In 1996, three other death row inmates petitioned the Texas Court of Appeals, insisting that they were denied effective counsel because their attorneys slept in court; all three petitions were denied.

The murder occurred during a robbery, but there was no physical evidence, and witnesses could not offer a specific description of the criminal other that than he was a black man and about 6 feet tall. Responding to a Crime Stoppers public service announcement days later, Craig Burks accused his uncle George McFarland of the crime. Prosecutors were eager to have Burks' cooperation and testimony, despite the fact that he had lengthy criminal and psychiatric histories. Not only was Burks motivated by the $900 reward, but he was also facing prison time if convicted for aggravated robbery. The deal was simple: Burks' charges would be reduced substantially, and he would collect the reward money.

At the trial, Burks could not recall the events or pinpoint the day of the murder. Nevertheless, the machinery of death continued to work. Even a second lawyer, Sanford Melamed, assigned by the court to assist Benn, would not keep McFarland from death row. Benn reported that he prepared by "reading the State's case and briefing a few points of law on evidence" and that Melamed spent "five, six, seven hours" in preparation: In tandem, they spent only two workdays in preparation and did not conduct their own investigation or attempt to locate other witnesses (Shapiro, 1997, p. 29). Although one federal appeals court in 1984 issued a decision that sleeping counsel is equivalent to no counsel at all, the Texas Court of Criminal Appeals ruled against McFarland's petition. The U.S. Supreme Court, which has never ruled on a sleeping lawyer appeal, refused to grant McFarland an expedited hearing.

To reiterate, covert facilitation in capital cases can be fueled by racism and classism, typically in the form of racially motivated cases against minorities who are also poor—the two commonly go hand in hand. A key obstacle facing many capital defendants is the lack of funds and resources necessary to defend themselves successfully against the machinery of death, which enjoys unlimited resources. The effects of classism in criminal justice are even more pronounced when indigent defendants face the death penalty; thus, the lives of many these defendants, some of whom have been framed by racially motivated prosecutions, depend on court-appointed attorneys. It is a well-established fact that court-appointed defense lawyers are overburdened by huge caseloads and are poorly paid. For example, in Kentucky, court-appointed attorneys are paid $2,500 for an entire trial; in some rural areas of Texas, they receive $800 per case; in Virginia, they are paid $13 per hour; and in Mississippi, they are paid $11.75 per hour (Bright, 1994, 1997; Ridgeway, 1994; Shapiro, 1997). Such low fee schedules adversely affect defendants. A compelling study by Coyle, Strasser, and Lavelle (1990) found that capital defendants in six states (Alabama, Florida, Georgia, Louisiana, Mississippi, and Texas, which account for 70% of all executions since 1976) are sentenced to death row after being represented by inexperienced, unskilled, or unprepared court-appointed lawyers.

Many impoverished capital defendants are subjected to a trial that is short, sharp, and shocking—or what attorney Stephen B. Bright (1994, 1997) called "slaughterhouse justice." Pointing to covert facilitation, racism, and classism, Bright commented,

> The death penalty is a product of race, poverty, and politics; it has always been imposed on minorities and the poorest people. I see poor people being used every day by little petty demagogues out in the boonies who are using these people to advance their political careers. . . . Prosecutors are seeking the death penalty in cases involving African Americans charged with crimes against white people for publicity, for political aggrandizement to advance their career, knowing full well it's not serving any law-enforcement function. (Ridgeway, 1994, p. 24)

Undoubtedly, both demagoguery and political aspirations fuel the machinery of death, especially in cases against members of minority organizations that are unpopular with the white political establishment. As we shall see in Chapter 10, during the 1960s and 1970s, the FBI and its Counter-Intelligence Program (COINTELPRO) targeted and framed hundreds of Black Panthers (e.g., Geronimo Pratt) and key members of the American Indian Movement (e.g., Leonard Peltier). Although those cases illustrate covert facilitation on a much grander scale with the intent of "neutralizing" radical organizations, today we continue to find cases of covert facilitation motivated by a prosecutor's desire to advance his or her career. This aspect of careerism has been called into question in numerous cases, most notably that of Randall Dale Adams, who was falsely convicted of killing a Dallas cop in 1976. Though he was within days of execution, Adams was released in 1988 after a documentary (Errol Morris's *The Thin Blue Line*) revealed that he was the victim of covert facilitation; prosecutors had knowingly relied on perjured testimony and suppressed evidence. In a similar case of cop killing in 1976, V. James Landano was released in 1989 after serving 13 years following his questionable conviction of murdering a Newark, New Jersey, police officer. A federal judge ruled that the prosecution had engaged in egregious misconduct by "systematically" withholding evidence that could have proved him not guilty. Attorney Neil Mullen presented evidence that the prosecutors had coerced witnesses to identify Landano. The defense reported that it had never been informed of an eyewitness who reviewed police photographs and said that Landano was not the assailant. The prosecution also suppressed evidence that two of the state's witnesses had been convicted of armed robberies. County prosecutors, however, proceeded toward retrying Landano. According to Landano's attorney, "The prosecutor's office was trying to pressure Mr. Landano into accepting a plea bargain, which would bar him from suing the prosecutor's office and the investigators who he says framed him" (Sullivan, 1995, p. B-5). In 1998, Landano was retried for murder and found not guilty (Petrick, 1998).

Although the term *presumed innocence* rings of democratic notions of justice, many prosecutors smugly overlook its importance. Even Edwin R. Meese, while serving as U.S. Attorney General, stated that "suspects who are innocent of a crime should [have the right to have lawyer present during police questioning]. But the thing is, you don't have many suspects who are innocent of a crime. That's contradictory. If a person is innocent of a crime, he is not a suspect" ("Attorney General Speaks," 1985, p. 67).

An examination of covert facilitation and the death penalty would not be complete without confronting the practice of deceptive interrogations and forced confessions. Many police interrogators are trained to talk suspects through the *Miranda* warning in ways that reduce that chance that they will request a lawyer, and once suspects waive their rights, courts permit interrogators to use tricks, deceptions, and lies to extract confessions. By contrast, other interrogators simply roar past the suspect's rights and continue the questioning. According to Peter Schoenburg, a defense lawyer, "When people assert the right to counsel, that's being dismissed by police in the field as, 'Well, O.K., you'll get a public defender down the road, but first answer my question' " (Hoffman, 1998, p. A-1). Law professor Charles D. Weisselberg added, "When detectives tell a suspect who has invoked his rights that they still want to question him, an ominous message is sent: 'We won't obey the law we just described to you, and the only way you're going to get out the door is to talk to us' " (Hoffman, 1998, p. 40).

The persistent attacks on *Miranda* rights have generated grave injustices. In *Miranda v. Arizona* (1966), Chief Justice Earl Warren warned that police interrogators, wearing a "badge of intimidation," could produce untrustworthy confessions even in capital cases. Following the brutal massacre of nine people, including six Buddhist monks, outside Phoenix, Arizona, in 1991, police subjected four suspects to grueling interrogations lasting as long as 20 continuous hours and threatened the suspects that they might wind up in the "gas chamber" or "in a lake with an anchor around their neck" (Whiting & Kelly, 1991, p. A1). The forcefulness of these interrogations became apparent: Each suspect eventually confessed to the killings. After spending 3 months in jail, the suspects were released when police captured the real murderers ("4 Cleared in Massacre," 1991).

Some suspects, especially the emotionally disturbed and the mentally retarded, are exceedingly vulnerable to covert facilitation in the form of unlawful interrogation tactics. Oklahoma City police, for instance, subjected Robert Lee Miller to an eight-and-a-half-hour interrogation in 1987, resulting in a bizarre confession in which he claimed to have had a dream vision about the rape and murder of two elderly women. Miller's confession was riddled with 112 inconsistencies; he had also told investigators that he was the Lone Ranger, that he was an Indian warrior, and that his family had visionary powers. Miller was convicted and placed on death row, but in 1995 DNA testing cleared him, and he was finally released from prison in 1998. Similarly, Rolando Cruz was convicted of the rape and murder of a 10-year-old Chicago girl, even though investigators could not produce any physical evidence linking Cruz to the crime and prosecutors could not establish a motive. Without much of a case against Cruz, prosecutors and the police claimed that during the interrogation, he had recounted a "dream" complete with specific details of the murder. Although the recorded interrogation did not include the so-called "dream" confession, Cruz was convicted and sentenced to death row. Eleven years later in 1996, Cruz was released when a new DNA test exonerated him; incidentally, the man who actually committed the murder had confessed to the crime 8 years earlier (Dieter, 1997; Kolarik, 1996).

Law enforcement officers know all too well the need to be protected against unlawful interrogations; indeed, when police themselves become suspects, they enjoy rights that far surpass the *Miranda* warnings. In New York City, for example, police officers who have been implicated in the death of a civilian are granted two business days to consult attorneys prior to a departmental investigation. Joseph McNamara, former police chief in Kansas City, Missouri, and San Jose, California, captures the essence of suspects' rights: "When it comes to police, then suddenly rights are precious because they know the danger of being innocently convicted. . . . This is the great irony of the police who resist Miranda" (Hoffman, 1998, p. 40).

In closing, the concept covert facilitation is useful in analyzing the complex ironies of capital punishment. From this perspective, we can look beyond *honest* mistakes occurring in capital cases and examine activities that are truly pernicious. In these cases, capital defendants not only face a flawed criminal justice process but also risk being falsely convicted by unethical prosecutors willing to frame suspects to advance their political aspirations. Again, minorities, the impoverished, and the mentally handicapped remain easy targets of covert facilitation.

Conclusion

Despite clear and compelling evidence that the system of capital punishment has glaring biases and errors, its popularity continues to rise. Approximately 80% of the U.S. population favors the death penalty for offenders convicted of first-degree murder (Moore, 1994), and this level of support is the highest since 1936 (Bohm, 1991).[4] Researchers have found, however, that Americans are greatly misinformed about capital punishment (Bohm, 1991, 1996; Bowers, 1993). Ironically, then, the enormous public support for the death penalty is based, not on a sophisticated understanding of the facts, but on beliefs rooted in popular myths of criminal justice.

In this chapter, we explored the machinery of death as it pertains to the ironies of social control, namely escalation, nonenforcement, and covert facilitation. To summarize, this chapter confronted significant contradictions apparent in American capital punishment. The United States is the only Western industrialized democracy to execute offenders, and this practice continues to violate contemporary standards of decency, especially the execution of juveniles and the mentally retarded. Contradictions also are found in the death penalty's failure to offer a deterrent effect, protect the community (including police; Bailey & Peterson, 1987), eliminate racial and socioeconomic biases, and ensure that innocent people are not falsely convicted or executed. In addition, the death penalty is confounded by several other problems that reveal deep structural contradictions in the social control apparatus, including financial costs, the alliance between the state and certain physicians and psychiatrists who facilitate the execution protocol, and the recent restriction of appeals, all of which paradoxically make errors more likely.

Modern executions depend enormously on the state's reliance on physicians to complete executions—signifying a crucial contradiction. Although the American Medical Association's standard of medical ethics prohibits physicians from participating in executions (AMA, 1992, "Physician Participation in Capital Punishment," Resolution 5, I-91), the state has little difficulty in recruiting medical personnel needed to carry out its executions (Davis, 1995; also see Bayer, 1984; Weiner, 1972). The participation of physicians in executions marks an ironic relationship between the state and a profession devoted to healing rather than harming; moreover, this relationship serves crucial technical and procedural objectives for the machinery of death. The state's case often rests on the expert testimony of a psychiatrist—commonly known as Dr. Death—to convict capital defendants (Rosenbaum, 1990). In Texas, Dr. James Grigson, dubbed "the hanging shrink," has offered 1,400 condemning testimonies that have resulted in 118 people convicted of murder being sentenced to death row. Dr. Grigson has presented compelling testimony even against defendants who are later exonerated: In his testimony against Randall Dale Adams, Grigson "guaranteed" that Adams "will kill again" (Rosenbaum, 1990, p. 142). As revealed previously, Adams was later released from prison when it became known that prosecutors relied on perjured testimony to convict him. Similarly, the state is required by law to have physicians at executions to supervise the injection of lethal doses of drugs and document the time of death—a procedure that, paradoxically, takes place in the prison's hospital unit (Trombley, 1992). Equally important, physicians and psychiatrists who participate in executions serve valuable social functions. Not only do physicians perpetuate the myth of *humane* executions, but in doing so, they contribute to the legitimacy of the state and its apparatus of social control (Johnson, 1990; Marquart, Ekland-Olson, & Sorensen, 1994).

The nation's enthusiasm for the death penalty has become a "fatal attraction" insofar as its contradictions and ironies lead to a self-defeating form of social control. In addition to producing a counterdeterrent effect (i.e., brutalization), a greater commitment to capital punishment creates more categories of violators (and victims), resulting in a higher volume of death sentences. A greater commitment to expediting capital cases by eliminating appeals also means more mistakes are likely to occur.[5] In the end, capital punishment policy is reckless and unjust—especially for people of color, the impoverished, and the mentally handicapped.

Notes

1. Frederick Taylor (1856-1915) promoted the "efficiency movement" in managing the industrial workforce, emphasizing the optimum use of time and motion.

2. A discussion of racism and the death penalty ought to include references to *racial hoaxes* in which black men are easily targeted as criminal suspects. Consider the cases of Charles Stuart, Susan V. Smith, and Jesse Anderson, all of whom committed premeditated murder and falsely reported to police that their crimes were the acts of a black man (Russell, 1998; Welch, 1996a).

3. Baldus et al. (1990) showed that disparities in the death penalty are more clearly understood by classifying murders into three types. The first category includes crimes of passion and killings in barroom brawls; these rarely draw the death penalty. The second category includes grisly murders such as mass and serial killings; these are typically sanctioned by capital punishment, regardless of race. However, racial disparities most commonly arise in the third category, known as "middle-ground" incidents in which homicide occurs during the commission of a felony (e.g., armed robbery); in this type of murder, the race of the victim is a crucial factor in determining the penalty. The killing of a white victim under these circumstances, especially when the perpetrator is black, has the highest chance of drawing capital punishment.

4. Researchers also conclude that the support for the death penalty may not be as deep as the polls suggest. When given the choice between favoring the death penalty and life imprisonment with absolutely no possibility of parole, support for the death penalty drops to less than half (Bohm, 1991, 1996; Bowers, 1993; Gallup & Newport, 1991; McGarrell & Sandys, 1996).

5. Opponents of the death penalty are alarmed and enraged over Congress's passing of the Anti-Terrorism and Effective Death Penalty Act of 1996, which sharply limits the prisoner's ability to file more than one habeas corpus petition. In 1996, Congress also voted to stop funding ($20 million) the Post-Conviction Defender Organizations that have played a vital role in representing death row inmates. In reaction to this move

and to Congress's curtailing of federal habeas corpus protections, the American Bar Association in 1997 called for the suspension of the death penalty until the system is changed to afford adequate due process ("A Lawyerly Cry of Conscience," 1997). Regarding the defender's program, the *New York Times* editorialized, "It deserves to live. A Congress committed to the death penalty cannot in good conscience deny competent legal counsel. Abolishing the Defender Organizations harms the causes of economy, speed, and justice" ("Shortchanging Inmates," 1995, p. A-32).

References

American Medical Association. (1992). *Code of medical ethics*. Chicago: Author.
Applebome, P. (1993, March 3). Alabama releases man held on death row for six years. *New York Times*, pp. A-1, B-11.
Attorney General speaks. (1985, October 14). *U.S. News and World Report*, p. 67.
Bailey, W. C. (1983). Disaggregation in deterrence and death penalty research: The case of murder in Chicago. *Journal of Criminal Law and Criminology, 74*, 827-859.
Bailey, W. C. (1998). Deterrence and brutalization, and the death penalty. *Criminology, 36*, 711-734.
Bailey, W. C., & Peterson, R. D. (1987). Police killings and capital punishment: The post-Furman period. *Criminology, 25*, 1-26.
Baldus, D. (in press). The death penalty in black and white: Who lives, who dies, who decides. *Cornell Law Review*.
Baldus, D., Pulaski, C., & Woodworth, G. (1983). Comparative review of death sentences: An empirical study of the Georgia experience. *Journal of Criminal Law and Criminology, 74*, 661-753.
Baldus, D., Woodworth, G., & Pulaski, C. (1990). *Equal justice and the death penalty: A legal and empirical analysis*. Boston: Northeastern University Press.
Bayer, R. (1984). Lethal injection and capital punishment. *Journal of Prison and Jail Health, 4*, 7-15.
Bedau, H. A., & Radelet, M. L. (1987). Miscarriages of justice in potentially capital cases. *Stanford Law Review, 40*, 21-179.
Bohm, R. (1991). American death penalty opinion, 1936-1986: A critical examination of the Gallup polls. In R. Bohm (Ed.), *The death penalty in America: Current research* (pp. 113-145). Cincinnati, OH: Anderson.
Bohm, R. (1996). Understanding and changing public support for capital punishment. *Corrections Now, 1*(1), 1-4.
Bowers, W. J. (1980). The pervasiveness of arbitrariness and discrimination under post-*Furman* statutes. *Journal of Criminal Law and Criminology, 74*, 1067-1100.
Bowers, W. J. (1984). *Legal homicide: Death as punishment in America, 1864-1982*. Boston: Northeastern University Press.
Bowers, W. J. (1988). The effect of execution is brutalization, not deterrence. In K. Hass & J. Inciardi (Eds.), *Challenging capital punishment: Legal and social science approaches* (pp. 49-90). Newbury Park, CA: Sage.
Bowers, W. J. (1993). Capital punishment and contemporary values: People's misgivings and the court's misperceptions. *Law and Society Review, 27*, 157-175.
Bowers, W. J., & Pierce, G. (1975). The illusion of deterrence in Isaac Ehrlich's research on capital punishment. *Yale Law Journal, 85*, 187-208.
Bowers, W. J., & Pierce, G. (1980a). Arbitrariness and discrimination under post-*Furman* capital statutes. *Crime and Delinquency, 74*, 1067-1100.

Bowers, W. J., & Pierce, G. (1980b). Deterrence or brutalization: What is the effect of executions. *Crime and Delinquency, 26*, 453-484.

Bragg, R. (1995, May 13). A killer racked by delusions dies in Alabama's electric chair. *New York Times*, p. 7.

Bright, S. B. (1994). Counsel for the poor: The death sentence not for the worst crime but for the worst lawyer. *Yale Law Review, 103*, 1835-1883.

Bright, S. B. (1997). Legalized lynching: Race, the death penalty and the United States courts. In W. Shabas (Ed.), *The international sourcebook on capital punishment* (pp. 3-29). Boston: Northeastern University Press.

Brundage, W. (1993). *Lynching in the New South: Georgia and Virginia, 1880-1930*. Champaign: University of Illinois Press.

Butterfield, F. (1998, June 7). New study adds to evidence of bias in death sentences. *New York Times*, p. 20.

Cochran, J. K., Chamlin, M., & Seth, M. (1994). Deterrence or brutalization? An impact assessment of Oklahoma's return to capital punishment. *Criminology, 32*, 107-134.

Coyle, M., Strasser, F., & Lavelle, M. (1990). Fatal trial and error in the nation's Death Belt. *National Law Journal, 12*(40), 30-44.

Davis, M. (1995). The state's Dr. Death: What's unethical about physicians helping at executions. *Social Theory and Practice, 21*(1), 31-60.

Decker, S., & Kohfeld, C. (1990). The deterrent effect of capital punishment in the five most active execution states: A time series analysis. *Criminal Justice Review, 15*, 173-191.

Dieter, R. (1997). *Innocence and the death penalty: The increasing danger of executing the innocent*. Washington, DC: Death Penalty Information Center.

Eckholm, E. (1995, February 25). Studies find death penalty tied to race of the victims. *New York Times*, pp. B-1, B-2.

Ehrlich, I. (1975). The deterrent effect of capital punishment: A question of life and death. *American Economic Review, 65*, 397-417.

Foley, L., & Powell, R. (1982. The discretion of prosecutors, judges, and jurists in capital cases. *Criminal Justice Review, 7*, 16-22.

Ford v. Wainwright, 477 U.S. 699 (1986).

Forst, B. (1983). Capital punishment and deterrence: Conflicting evidence? *Journal of Criminal Law and Criminology, 74*, 927-942.

4 cleared in massacre. (1991, November 23). *New York Newsday*, p. 8.

Gallup, A., & Newport, F. (1991, June). Death penalty support remains strong. *Gallup Monthly Report*, No. 321, pp. 3-5.

General Accounting Office. (1990). *Death penalty sentencing: Research indicates pattern of racial disparities*. Washington, DC: Government Printing Office.

Gregg v. Georgia, 428 U.S. 153 (1976).

Harlow, E., Matas, D., & Rocamora, J. (1995). *The machinery of death: A shocking indictment of capital punishment in the United States*. New York: Amnesty International.

Hentoff, N. (1995, February 21). Executing the retarded in our name. *Village Voice*, pp. 30-31.

Hoffman, J. (1998, March 29). Police tactics chipping away suspects' rights. *New York Times*, pp. A-1, A-40.

Huff, C. R., Rattner, A., & Sagarin, E. (1996). *Convicted but innocent: Wrongful conviction and public policy*. Thousand Oaks, CA: Sage.

Jackson, J. (1996). *Legal lynching: Racism, injustice, and the death penalty*. New York: Marlowe.

Johnson, R. (1990). *Deathwork: A study of the modern execution process*. Pacific Grove, CA: Brooks/Cole.

Keil, T., & Vito, G. (1989). Race, homicide severity, and application of the death penalty: A consideration of the Barnett Scale. *Criminology, 27*, 511-536.

King, D. (1978). The brutalization effect: Execution publicity and the incidence of homicide in South Carolina. *Social Forces, 57,* 683-687.

Klein, L., Forst, B., & Filatov, V. (1978). The deterrent effect of capital punishment: An assessment of the estimates. In A. Blumstein, J. Cohen, & D. Nagin (Eds.), *Deterrence and incapacitation: Estimating the effects of criminal sanctions on crime rates.* Washington, DC: National Academy of Sciences.

Kolarik, G. (1996, January). DNA, changed testimony, gain acquittal. *American Bar Association Journal,* pp. 34-35.

Kuntz, T. (1997, January 12). Banality, nausea, triple execution: Guards on inmates' final hours. *New York Times,* p. E-7.

A lawyerly cry of conscience. (1997, February 22). *New York Times,* p. 20.

Lee, H. (1960). *To kill a mockingbird.* New York: HarperCollins.

Lewis, P. (1978). Life on death row: A post-*Furman* profile of Florida's condemned. In P. W. Lewis & K. D. Peoples (Eds.), *The Supreme Court and the criminal process: Cases and comments.* Philadelphia: W. B. Saunders.

Lynch, M., & Groves, W. B. (1989). *A primer in radical criminology.* New York: Harrow & Heston.

Marquart, J., Ekland-Olson, S., & Sorensen, J. (1994). *The rope, the chair, and the needle: Capital punishment in Texas, 1923-1990.* Austin: University of Texas Press.

Marx, G. (1981). Ironies of social control: Authorities as contributors to deviance through escalation, nonenforcement, and covert facilitation. *Social Problems, 28,* 221-233.

McClesky v. Kemp, 41 CrL 4107 (1987).

McGarrell, E. F., & Sandys, M. (1996). Misperception of public opinion toward capital punishment: Examining the spuriousness explanation of death penalty support. *American Behavioral Scientist, 39,* 500-513.

Miller, K., & Radelet, M. (1993). *Executing the mentally ill: The criminal justice system and the case of Alvin Ford.* Newbury Park, CA: Sage.

Miranda v. Arizona, 384 U.S. 436 (1966).

Moore, D. W. (1994, September). Majority advocate death penalty for teenage killers. *Gallup Poll Monthly,* No. 321, pp. 2-5.

Myrdal, G. (1944). *An American dilemma.* New York: Harper Brothers.

Passell, P. (1975). The deterrent effect of the death penalty: A statistical test. *Stanford Law Review, 28,* 61-80.

Paternoster, R. (1983). Race of the victim and location of crime: The decision to seek the death penalty in South Carolina. *Journal of Criminal Law and Criminology, 74,* 754-785.

Paternoster, R. (1991). *Capital punishment in America.* New York: Lexington.

Penry v. Lynaugh, 57 U.S.L.W. 4958 (1989).

Peterson, R., & Bailey, W.. (1991). Felony murder and capital punishment: An examination of the deterrence question. *Criminology, 29,* 367-398.

Petrick, J. (1998, July 28). Case closed: Landano triumphs in cop-kill retrial. *Jersey Journal,* p. A-4.

Price, R. (1992). *Clockers.* New York: Avon.

Radelet, M., Bedau, H., & Putnam, C. (1992). *In spite of innocence: Erroneous convictions in capital cases.* Boston: Northeastern University Press.

Radelet, M., & Pierce, G. (1985). Race and prosecutorial discretion in homicide cases. *Law and Society Review, 19,* 587-621.

Reed, E. (1993). *The Penry penalty: Capital punishment and offenders with mental retardation.* Landam, MD: University Press of America.

Revived from overdose, inmate is executed. (1995, August 12). *New York Times,* p. 6.

Ridgeway, J. (1994, October 11). Slaughterhouse justice: Race, poverty, and politics: The essential ingredients for a death penalty conviction. *Village Voice,* pp. 23-24.

Riedel, M. (1976). Discrimination in the imposition of the death penalty: A comparison of the characteristics of offenders, sentenced pre-*Furman* and post-*Furman*. *Temple Law Quarterly, 49,* 261-283.

Rosenbaum, R. (1990, May). Travels with Dr. Death. *Vanity Fair,* pp. 141-166.

Russell, K. (1998). *The color of crime: Racial hoaxes, white fear, black protectionism, police aggression and other macroaggressions.* New York: New York University Press.

Shapiro, A. (1995, May 11). An insane execution. *New York Times,*, p. A-29.

Shapiro, A. (1997, April 7). Sleeping lawyer syndrome. *Nation,* pp. 27-29.

Shortchanging inmates on death row. (1995, October 13). *New York Times,* p. A-32.

Snell, T. (1997). *Capital punishment 1996.* Washington, DC: Bureau of Justice Statistics.

Stack, S. (1987). Publicized executions and homicide, 1950-1980. *American Sociological Review, 52,* 532-540.

Sullivan, J. (1995, February 8). Conviction thrown out, ex-inmate faces retrial. *New York Times,* p. B-5.

Terry, D. (1996, July 3). After 18 years in prison, 3 are cleared of murders. *New York Times,* p. A-14.

Terry, D. (1998, April 12). Jury to decide if condemned man comprehends his fate. *New York Times,* p. 22.

Tolnay, S., & Beck, E. (1992). Toward a threat model of Southern black lynchings. In A. E. Liska (Ed.), *Social threat and social control* (pp. 33-52). Albany: State University of New York Press.

Tolnay, S., & Beck, E. (1994). Lethal social control in the South: Lynchings and executions between 1880 and 1930. In G. Bridges & M. Myers (Eds.), *Inequality, crime, and social control* (pp. 176-194). Boulder, CO: Westview.

Trombley, S. (1992). *The execution protocol: Inside America's capital punishment industry.* New York: Crown.

van den Haag, E., & Conrad, J. (1983). *The death penalty: A debate.* New York: Plenum.

Verhovek, S. (1997). *Sense and nonsense about crime and drugs: A policy guide* (3rd ed.). Pacific Grove, CA: Brooks/Cole.

Verhovek, S. (1998a, April 26). Halt the execution? Are you crazy? *New York Times,* p. 4.

Verhovek, S. (1998b, April 18). Texas legislator proposes the death penalty for murderers as young as 11. *New York Times,* p. A-7.

Walker, S. (1994). *Sense and nonsense about crime and drugs: A policy guide* (3rd ed.) Belmont, CA: Wadsworth.

Welch, M. (1996a). *Corrections: A critical approach.* New York: McGraw-Hill.

Welch, M. (1996b). Critical criminology, social justice, and an alternative view of incarceration. *Critical Criminology: An International Journal, 7*(2), 43-58.

Weiner, D. B. (1972). The real Dr. Guillotine. *Journal of the American Medical Association, 220,* 85-89.

White man pleads guilty to killing a black man. (1998, May 31). *New York Times,* p. 22.

Whiting, B., & Kelly, C. (1991, September 28). Suspect: Monks resisted, slaughter began when 1 fought. *Arizona Republic,* p. A1.

Yunker, J. (1976). Is the death penalty a deterrent to homicide? Some time series evidence. *Journal of Behavioral Economics,5,* 1-32.

Zimring, F., Eigen, J., & O'Malley, S. (1976). Punishing homicides in Philadelphia: Perspectives on the death penalty. *University of Chicago Law Review, 43,* 227-252.

Zimring, F., & Hawkins, G. (1973). *Deterrence: The legal threat in crime control.* Chicago: University of Chicago Press.

CHAPTER
10

The Poverty of Interest in Human Rights Violations in U.S. Prisons

Human rights issues are well represented in this book, especially capital punishment, violence against prisoners, coercive contraception for female lawbreakers, inadequate medical treatment for prisoners with HIV/AIDS, and injustices against undocumented immigrants. Still, a separate chapter on human rights violations in American prisons is justified by the importance of the subject. In it, we shall explore in detail myriad human rights violations that persist partly because the public is not sufficiently apprised of such atrocities.

Drawing on the sociology of knowledge, particularly the social construction of reality, we begin this chapter with a brief conceptual overview explaining why human rights violations in prisons generally fail to generate public attention and concern. After discussing two tragic events in American history—the internment of Japanese Americans during World War II and the use of prisoners as human guinea pigs in medical experiments—we turn to several contemporary human rights violations in U.S. prisons: the revival of chain gangs, inhumane conditions of confinement in super-maximum-security penitentiaries, and political imprisonment.

Explaining the Poverty of Interest of Human Rights Violations in U.S. Prisons

Images of human rights atrocities and political imprisonment are commonly projected onto nations whose human rights records are deplorable, including China, Cuba, El Salvador, Kuwait, Northern Ireland, and Russia, to name just a few. But at home, Amnesty International (USA), Human Rights Watch, and numerous other human rights organizations frequently unveil human rights violations in U.S. prisons as well. Few American citizens, however, become fully aware of such abuses, and the "out of sight, out of mind" nature of the problem perpetuates the lack of interest on human rights. Because of the lack of public awareness concerning human rights violations, we first discuss the sociology of knowledge and the social construction of reality (Berger & Luckman, 1963; Mannheim, 1952). Ironically, the same sociological processes that generate a heightened public awareness of certain forms of harm (e.g., street crime) are also instrumental in perpetuating the neglect of other harms in society, including corporate violence, dangerous working conditions, and human rights violations in U.S. prisons.[1]

Street crime, for instance, is reified in a process of social constructionism that has three stages. First, crime is selected from among many social issues (e.g., poverty, unemployment, poor education, and lack of access to health care) and advanced to the status of a *problem* requiring serious policy consideration. Second, the crime *problem* is narrowed to include only street crime, thereby omitting other types of lawlessness and harm, including human rights violations in U.S. prisons. In the final stage, street crime is defined solely as a criminal justice *problem* (Michalowski, 1985), and it is this particular viewpoint of crime that typically dominates the public psyche (Kappeler, Blumberg, & Potter, 1996; Schoenfeld, Meier, & Griffin, 1979; Surette, 1992; Tunnell, 1992; Welch, Fenwick, & Roberts, 1997, 1998).

Drawing on the social construction of crime as a criminal justice problem, political leaders, criminal justice officials, and other state managers enjoy the privilege of filtering and feeding the media ideological definitions of harm (Hall, Critcher, Jefferson, Clarke, & Roberts, 1978; Kasinsky, 1994). Fishman (1978) reminded us that "all knowledge is knowledge from some point of view" (p. 531). The emphasis on street crime also tends to be *ideological* insofar as it represents the worldview of state managers who—benefiting from their elevated position within hierarchy of credibility—promote and legitimize their "law and order" crime control agenda (Becker, 1967, 1973; Ericson, Baranek, & Chan, 1987, 1989, 1991; Fishman, 1978; Hall et al., 1978; Humphries, 1981; Surette, 1992). In doing so, state managers alter the scope of lawlessness by concealing the abuses of authority (Ferrell, 1996; Marx, 1978; Reiman, 1998; Sahin, 1980; Welch & Bryan, in press). Critics charge that the prevailing construction of knowledge is reinforced by the media, which in effect function to produce propaganda for the state's ideology apparatus (Herman & Chomsky, 1988). As a result of their gatekeeping efforts, state managers and the media together determine what is *socially thinkable*. In the end, harm in the form of street crime is made socially thinkable, whereas harm in the form of human rights violations in U.S. prisons is not.

An analysis of the social construction of street crime—and the neglect of human rights violations—would not be complete without an exploration of the importance of propaganda as a mechanism that misrepresents the nature of social harm. Indeed, the elevation of street crime to the status of a social problem depends greatly upon the persuasiveness of propaganda, "a technique for influencing social action based on intentional distortions and manipulation of communications" (Kappeler et al., 1996, p. 24). Through numerous propaganda techniques, the media and the state together produce ideologically driven, distorted images of crime. These biased images of crime, however, are not the result of a conspiracy but rather the "unintended consequence of the process by which information is collected, processed, and prepared for dissemination by mass media, government, and interest groups" (Kappeler et al., 1996, pp. 22-23; also see Bohm, 1986; Marsh, 1991; Tunnell, 1992). Not all imagery related to street crime is the product of conscious attempts at propaganda; many distortions of lawlessness are generated by propaganda tactics deeply institutionalized and routinized in the media and the government (Hall et al., 1978; Kappeler et al., 1996; Kasinsky, 1994; Welch, Fenwick, & Roberts, 1997, 1998).

In sum, human rights violations in U.S. prisons have yet to penetrate the public consciousness partly because this form of harm has not been sufficiently channeled through the social construction process. Simply put, such human rights violations have not become reified to the degree necessary to become *socially thinkable*. Several obstacles further preclude this reification and conceptualization: In particular, disproportionate attention to street crime diverts scrutiny from the abuses of authorities. Relatedly, because correctional facilities are *closed* institutions, it is easy for authorities to conceal human rights abuses and limit the amount of scrutiny that might reveal horrific conditions and inhumane control tactics.

The Internment of Japanese Americans During World War II

The bombing of Pearl Harbor in 1941 dramatically altered the way the U.S. government treated people of Japanese ancestry, even those born and living as citizens in America. As a result of wartime hysteria and racism, 120,000 Japanese Americans (including children) were officially labeled enemies of the state and quickly rounded up to be detained in what amounted to concentration camps located predominately in America's western states. For decades to follow, this stain on American democracy would remain the government's "dirty little secret"—a subject of human rights rarely discussed in the public forum and certainly not taught in U.S. schools (Hansen, 1995; Nishimoto, 1995; Smith, 1995; Yoo, 1996; Yoshino, 1996).[2]

From 1942 to 1945, under the direction of the War Relocation Authority (WRA), Japanese Americans were *interned* to a system of 10 military-style barracks scattered across the nation in such remote areas as the Sierra Nevada mountains in California, Arizona, Arkansas, Mississippi, Montana, Oklahoma, and Utah. The camps were fortified by barbed wire fences and guard towers and were supervised by armed soldiers; at night, military search lights reminded the internees that they were prisoners of war, even in their own country. These men, women, and children were never accused or convicted of any crime. Their constitutional rights were trampled; their homes, property, businesses, and belongings were confiscated and never recovered. Two-thirds of the internees were U.S. citizens, and many of their sons (33,000 of them) served in the U.S. armed forces; when interned boys reached military age, they too were drafted into service (Wiener, 1995). Richard M. Sakakida, a young intelligence officer in the U.S. Army, was captured by the Japanese in the Philippines and subjected to months of torture; during his ordeal, he was determined to prove to the U.S. government that he was a loyal American citizen ("For Japanese-American Veterans," 1995).

Although the evacuation was reportedly organized around concerns of national security, critics insist that racism played a defining role in the detention of Americans of Japanese descent. Novelist John Steinbeck corresponded directly with President Roosevelt, reminding him that Japanese Americans were loyal citizens who had condemned the attack on Pearl Harbor

(Lewis, 1995). Oddly, the relocation program was confined to the contiguous states, not reaching Hawaii, where the concentration of those of Japanese ancestry was much higher (Kiyasu, 1991). Lieut. General John DeWitt, who oversaw the internment operation, publicly expressed racist sentiments: "A Jap is a Jap. . . . It makes no difference whether he's an American or not." In his military reports, DeWitt characterized people of Japanese descent as "subversive" members of an "enemy race" whose "racial strains are undiluted" (Raskin, 1991, p. 117). The U.S. Supreme Court supported DeWitt's evacuation plan under the umbrella of war powers. In *Korematsu v. United States* (1944), a case involving a Japanese American who defied the resettlement orders, the High Court insisted that Korematsu's constitutional rights were not violated. Conversely, critics claim that the Court erroneously validated racial discrimination (Raskin, 1991; Wiener, 1995).

The stigma imposed on the internees made their return to the larger society difficult. Moreover, the conditions of their release prohibited them to resettle on the West Coast. Many Japanese Americans migrated to the Midwest and East Coast, but even in those locales overt racism there blocked efforts to secure housing and jobs, marginalizing them for years. Racism occasionally escalated to physical and psychological victimization: Some Japanese Americans suffered beatings by whites, and some had their homes fire-bombed (Linehan, 1993; Okubo, 1946; see also the TV documentary *Starting Over, Fukami*, 1997). "It was the worst, most degrading, experience of my life" revealed Isaku Konoshima, a former internee, now a retired educator living in New York. "I couldn't understand how a democracy would permit something like that to happen" (Abrams, 1991, p. 57).

In 1988, Congress finally offered the internees a formal apology for this shameful violation of civil and human rights. Under the Civil Liberties Act, the federal government pledged restitution to 60,000 Americans of Japanese descent who had been incarcerated during the war. According to William Yoshimo, national director of the Japanese American Citizens League, "The $20,000 payment [per former internee] has more symbolic meaning than financial value: How do you put a price tag on years of confinement, denial of freedom and disgrace?" (quoted in Abrams, 1991, p. 57). The internment has left deep emotional scars on the psyche of Japanese Americans. It is both disturbing and ironic that this atrocity occurred in American democracy. As historian Jon Wiener (1995) warned, "It's especially depressing because a new anti-immigration movement is now on the rise. . . . The existing barracks are not just relics, they are a frightening reminder of what could come next" (p. 694). Wiener's concerns could not have been more timely. In the 1980s, the federal government reactivated one of its internment camps in Arizona so that the Immigration and Naturalization Service (INS) could detain hundreds of Central American refugees who had crossed the border to escape a war financed by the U.S. government (Deutsch & Susler, 1990; Kahn, 1996).

Prisoners as Human Guinea Pigs

Journalist Jessica Mitford rocked the corrections establishment in 1971 when she exposed controversial prison practices in her book *Kind and Usual Punishment: The Prison Business*. Among the targets of her attack on American corrections was the unethical use of prisoners as human guinea pigs in drug-testing experiments. Although the World Medical Association in 1961 had recommended that inmates not be used as subjects of experiments, the proposal was never formally adopted, in part because American physicians and commercial drug researchers opposed it. Indeed, a medical researcher defended the use of prisoners as human subjects, saying, "Criminals in our penitentiaries are fine experimental material—and much cheaper than chimpanzees" (Mitford, 1971, pp. 152-153).

Because the Food and Drug Administration (FDA) requires that all new drugs be tested on humans before being approved and marketed, pharmaceutical companies in the 1960s recruited readily available prisoners to participate in clinical trials. During that time, state and federal inmates nationwide accepted financial compensation (and in some cases, a reduction in their sentences) in return for their cooperation in drug experiments. Correctional institutions themselves also were generously compensated by drug companies for allowing them access to prisoners. In one such shameful experiment, inmates in Ohio and Illinois were injected with live cancer cells and blood from leukemia patients because researchers were interested in learning whether such diseases could be transmitted. Hundreds of inmates involved in various experiments during the 1960s were stricken with serious diseases, and an undetermined number of the victims died (Mitford, 1971). An inmate at Vacaville prison, California, discussed his participation in a drug-testing experiment in the following interview:

> Yeah, I was on research, but I couldn't keep my chow down. Like I lost about 35 pounds my first year in the joint, so I started getting scared. I hated to give it up because it was a good pay test. Hey man, I'm making $30 a month on the DMSO thing [chronic topical application of dimethylsulfoxide]. (Mitford, 1971, p. 158)

The use of inmates as human guinea pigs in drug experiments raises serious ethical issues and in many instances is a clear violation of human rights. Though some of the experiments were innocuous, others were extremely painful and potentially dangerous. During the late 1960s, efforts succeeded in curbing and eventually eliminating the use of prisoners in drug research. Although the controversy of using prisoners in drug experiments was believed to be a problem of the past, reports of a similar scandal broke recently in 1993, when the Department of Energy (DOE) declassified thousands of documents verifying the use of human guinea pigs in radiation experiments. From 1944 to 1973, the DOE conducted thousands of radiation tests on the elderly, terminally ill patients, mentally retarded children, and prisoners, as well as persons in good health ("Count of Subjects in Radiation," 1995; Hilts, 1994, 1995; "Nuclear Guinea Pigs," 1993). In 1963, the DOE continued its efforts to study the effects of radiation on 131 inmates at two prisons in Oregon and Washington State. Each volunteer was paid $200 and signed a consent form stating: "I hereby agree to submit to X-ray radiation of my scrotum and testes" ("America's Nuclear Secrets," 1993, p. 15). After the experiments, the prisoners were given vasectomies—"to avoid the possibility of contaminating the general population with irradiation-induced mutants," according to the chief researcher ("America's Nuclear Secrets," 1993, p. 15). That year, Robert White began serving a 15-year sentence at Walla Walla State Prison, Washington, where he was recruited as a subject into a federally financed research program. According to White,

> They said it would be like having a few chest X-rays, and if we cooperated, we might have our sentences reduced. . . . It turned out that it was more like 20,000 X-rays, focused on my testicles. . . . I've had problems there ever since. (D'Antonio, 1997, p. 41)

Like the other prison guinea pigs, White also had a vasectomy but was never informed that the X-rays could cause testicular cancer.

By refusing to comply with informed consent requirements to protect human subjects, U.S. government researchers violated the principles of the Nuremberg Code, established to prevent similar atrocities committed by Nazi scientists during the Second World War. In 1997, White continues to litigate against the state of Washington on claims of fraud, battery, and emotional distress. The former Navy serviceman reflects, "Once the lawsuit is over, I'm emigrating to South Africa. . . . People can say that I'm paranoid, but I don't trust America anymore" (D'Antonio, 1997, p. 41). It should be noted that Oregon prisoners filed a class action suit against the state in 1976. Subsequently, the state legislature granted medical attention to several inmates and awarded a lump sum of $2,215 to be divided among nine prisoners ("America's Nuclear Secrets," 1993; Ridgeway, 1994). Today, prisoners are no longer used as human guinea pigs. Still, past experiments illustrate how state and corporate officials targeted people deemed unpopular and expendable. The relative secrecy of these experiments kept abuses of authority conveniently hidden from public awareness (also see Gonnerman, 1998; Hornblum, 1998).

Chain Gangs and Nostalgia

In the middle of the last century, the inhumane practice of chaining prisoners together while they worked became customary in England and Australia. Fetters attached to the legs of prisoners that weighed from 6 to 7 or even 9 pounds compounded the pain and burden of hard labor. Iron chains were riveted by blacksmiths and inspected daily to prevent tampering, and they remained fastened to prisoners for the length of their sentences, between 6 months and 2 years (Ives, 1914/1970). From its inception, the rationale of chains typically expanded beyond the utilitarian notion of security; indeed, there is enormous symbolic value in chaining prisoners. Because chain gangs are spectacles of punishment, being chained, especially in public, is degrading and dehumanizing and reduces prisoners to beasts of burden (Adams, 1998).

Eventually, the practice of chain gangs reached America, where it took on additional symbolism, signifying racism and slavery. Following the Civil War, the Reconstruction required manual labor to rebuild the South's economy and infrastructure. While inmates in the North worked in prison factory shops, their Southern counterparts—disproportionately black—labored outside prison walls on the plantations and public works projects (Lichtenstein, 1993). Prisoners were chained together in crews of five to seven, and the grueling ordeal was heightened by nature's worst elements, most notably the debilitating heat (Barnes & Teeters, 1946).

During the Reconstruction period in particular, chain gangs represented a return to slavery. In this social context, the appeal of chain gangs was not limited to free labor; it also satisfied the racist sentiment that blacks should be shackled to the land. Stories of brutality and oppression often emanated from the Southern prison camps. It even was rumored that unlucky hitchhikers were arrested and railroaded to chain gangs, thus serving as a valuable source of free labor. Sadistic armed guards took delight in shooting at the feet of prisoners. Deploying the lash, "whipping bosses," like the slave drivers on antebellum plantations, routinely disciplined prisoners on chain gangs. According to a corrections officials of that era: "A Negro is punished to 'teach him respect for a white man,' or for 'inciting insurrection,' or because he 'tried to run away,' or because 'he is just a bad nigger' " (Barnes & Teeters, 1946, p. 631). Sick and injured convicts accused of malingering were typically whipped until they returned to work; at times, prisoners were beaten to death and clandestinely buried in quicklime (Ayers, 1984; Barnes & Teeters, 1946).

> The most brutal punishments imaginable are inflicted upon the hapless victims of the road camps of the South. Floggings are the rule. The *sweat-box*, a diabolical engine of torture, is a box just large enough for a man to stand erect when the door is closed. There is a breathing slot 1 X 4 inches, a little below the height of the average man, the only ventilation in the box. Often these boxes are placed in the broiling sun. Men are confined in them from a few hours to a few days. Swelling of the legs in extreme cases necessitates the victims being hospitalized for a week or more. It is not unusual for a convict to die of suffocation. (Barnes & Teeters, 1946, p. 628)

Larger sweat-boxes were designed to punish several prisoners collectively. In 1941, a grim report chronicled the appalling treatment of prisoners in Georgia who had been forced into a sweat box:

> A Negro convict had died of suffocation in a sweat-box $7\frac{1}{2}$ feet square, where he, together with 21 other prisoners, was incarcerated for 11 hours. There was only a six-inch opening in the roof of the box for the purposes of ventilation. (Barnes & Teeters, 1946, p. 628)

Eventually, the brutality of chain gangs was criticized publicly. In the 1930s, the story of Robert E. Burns shocked the common conscience: His book *I Am a Fugitive From a Georgia Chain Gang* (1932), and later the movie, brought attention to inhumane chain gangs in the South (also see John Spivak's *Georgia Nigger*, 1932). Burns's exposé was credited with playing a pivotal role in the campaign to abolish chain gangs. While a fugitive in New Jersey, Burns, armed with the courtroom tenacity of Clarence Darrow, successfully fought extradition to Georgia. Burns's hearing precipitated and amplified public outrage concerning chain gangs, prompting state officials across the South to discontinue the practice. Georgia, the last holdout, finally abolished its chain gangs in 1945 (Sifakis, 1992).

The prohibition of chain gangs would eventually give way to a "tough on crime" campaign that resurfaced in the 1990s. A particularly punitive feature of the recent "law and order" movement is the demand for retribution. As public outcry over crime has reached fever pitch, there has been renewed interest in returning to earlier penal practices, such as requiring prisoners to wear prison stripes and stripping them of amenities (e.g., television, weight-lifting, and cigarettes; Welch, 1996, 1997). The most anachronistic policy of the "tough on prisoners" strategy is the revival of chain gangs. The year 1995 became a watershed when state and county corrections departments in Alabama, Arizona, Florida, Indiana, Iowa, Maryland, Oklahoma, and Wisconsin reinstated chain gangs.

In Alabama, prisoners are shackled at the ankle in 3-pound leg irons, bound together by 8-foot lengths of chain, and forced to work the fields with shovels and swing blades for 12 hours a day (American Correctional Association, 1995). Other chain gangs spend their days breaking rocks into pea-sized pellets, a demeaning chore of pure punishment given that the state has no use for crushed rock ("Chain Gangs," 1996). Ron Jones, prison commissioner of Alabama, argued that chain gangs had been reinstated for purposes of "deterrence. . . . The sight of chains would leave a lasting impression on young people" (Bragg, 1995, p. 16). Jones even proposed that women inmates be shackled to chain gangs, though the measure was rejected by the governor ("Chain Gangs," 1996). Tough-talking Jones further boasted that guards armed with shotguns loaded with double-aught buckshot supervised the chain gangs and were obligated by law to shoot if a prisoner attempted to escape. Smugly, Jones remarked, "People say its not humane, but I don't get much flak in Alabama" (Bragg, 1995, p. 16). Civil libertarians and human rights advocates, however, take exception to Alabama's chain gangs: "People lose touch with humanity when you put them in chains. You are telling him he is an animal" (Alvin J. Bronstein, executive director of the National Prison Project of the American Civil Liberties Union, quoted in Bragg, 1995, p. 16). In 1995, the Southern Poverty Law Center filed suit in federal district court, arguing that chain gangs are barbaric and inhumane.

The issue of race is of major significance in the chain gang controversy in Alabama, in which observers point out that blacks are overrepresented in these gangs. "The only reason they're doing it is because an overwhelming majority of the prisoners are Black. If the majority were White, they wouldn't have the chain gang," stated Rep. Alvin Holmes (quoted in Jackson, 1995, p. 12). "I think it's a reminder of the way it used to be, putting the African-American male in chains," added Rep. John Hilliard (Jackson, 1995, p. 12). Serving 2 years for receiving stolen property, one inmate who spends his days on the chain gang breaking rocks said, "They're treating us like . . . slaves" (Jackson, 1995, p. 16).

In Queen Anne's County, Maryland, the antebellum notion of chain gangs has taken a futuristic twist. Corrections officials have proposed instituting "chainless" chain gangs by attaching stun belts to prisoners assigned outdoor work detail, leaving convicts writhing in the dirt if they attempt to escape or engage in violence. Supporters claim that stun belts reduce the costs of supervision and say that "there is no long-term physical damage to a prisoner who is stunned" (Kilborn, 1997, p. 11). Amnesty International has challenged the practice, arguing that stun belts are cruel, inhuman, and degrading and can be used to torture prisoners.

In reinstating chain gangs, corrections officials insist that they have the overwhelming support of citizens. However, many people question the logic, utility, and overall fairness of chain gangs. "If these guys are so dangerous, they shouldn't be out on those crews. And if they're not dangerous, why put them in chains?" asked Mary Chambers, a Maryland resident. Furthermore, Chambers noted, "You have people in there for drunk driving. Maybe they have a problem. But do you put them in chains?" (Kilborn, 1997, p. A-18).

As we shall see in our examination of super-maximum-security penitentiaries, the controversy over chaining extends beyond chain gangs to include inhumane restraining practices employed not as security measures but for disciplinary purposes. In Alabama, inmates filed a class action suit challenging the use of the "hitching post" at the Fountain Correctional Center, where those who refused to (or were late for) work were handcuffed to a triangular rail about $4\frac{1}{2}$ feet off the ground. Prisoners were hitched as long as 5 hours at a stretch, were exposed to the blazing sun, and often went for as long as 7 hours without water, food, and access to a toilet. This practice has been monitored by the American Civil Liberties Union Prison Project, which asserts that there are alternative, humane ways to discipline balky inmates (i.e., isolation cells and/or loss of privileges). Furthermore, there are claims of racism in that the hitching post appears to be reserved for black inmates ("Inmates Fight 'Work or Be Shackled' Policy," 1993). In 1997, a federal magistrate ruled that the Alabama corrections officials should not be allowed to hitch inmates to posts, commenting: "Short of death by electrocution, the hitching post may be the most painful and tortuous punishment administered by the Alabama prison system." State corrections officials have appealed the magistrate's opinion. But the Southern Poverty Law Center, which represents the inmates, promises to continue its legal battle against the hitching posts, calling the practice a form of torture (Nossiter, 1997; see *Austin v. Hopper,* 1998).

In her ruling, Magistrate McPherson fittingly likened the hitching post to the pillory of colonial times. And because we have already traced the history of the modern chain gang to slavery, it is apropos that we conclude this section with some thoughts on nostalgia and the "tough on crime" movement. The principal theme of this campaign is that prisons are not "tough" enough to fulfill their mission of imposing punishment, instilling discipline, and deterring lawbreakers from future offenses. Advocates of "get tough" campaigns insinuate that corrections coddles inmates and, by way of circular reasoning, imply that high rates of recidivism are the result of inadequately punitive institutional conditions. Though primarily motivated by retributionism, this movement also is inspired by *nostalgic* visions of criminal justice (Garland, 1990; Jameson, 1991; Simon, 1995; Stauth & Turner, 1988; Welch, Weber, & Edwards, 1998). "Get tough" proposals commonly include "three strikes" legislation and correctional boot camps as well as a return to hard labor and chain gangs. The nostalgic worldview developed as a reaction to the *modern* and so-called "liberal" U.S. prisons, where inmates are afforded certain constitutional protections, participate in institutional programs, and are permitted to keep personal belongings while incarcerated (e.g., cigarettes, civilian clothes, coffee, snack food, televisions).

Not only are the depictions of prisons as "country clubs" (or "three hots and a cot") exaggerated and often inaccurate, but this nostalgia marks a return to harsh images of prison life, similar to those projected in such classic movies as *Cool Hand Luke*. Governor Fife Symington invoked nostalgia with movie imagery in describing support for the "get tough" campaigns in Arizona (which include the sheriff's 400-member "executive posse" patrolling Phoenix): "I remember, going way back, watching Tom Mix and Gene Autry and Roy Rogers, . . . and I always remember the sheriff swearing in business people on a horse as posse men and saying, Go after the horse thieves" (Mydans, 1995, p. A-6; see Koppes & Black, 1987). Sounding the alarm of perceived lawlessness and social disorder, the nostalgic version of corrections expresses a supposed need to regain control of inmates and prisons, as well as a yearning for the return to a simpler society. Regarding the current use of chain gangs, Rep. Holmes remembers that as a child in Alabama he never saw a white man on a chain gang: "The only people you ever saw were Black. The whole purpose of having the chain gang is racist to the core. There are certain Whites in key positions who want things back the way they used to be" (Jackson, 1995, p. 14).

Incidentally, a common thread running through the campaigns of retribution is a disregard for basic human dignity. In turning back the clock to revive past forms of punishment, prison officials have trampled on fundamental human rights. Consider this final illustration of human rights violations in a Texas prison. Until recently, there had been little criticism of a long-standing practice of asking inmates to volunteer (but also rewarding them with "good time") for an exercise to train dogs to track escapees from the Texas Department of Corrections. The inmates would serve as prey in what was called by senior prison officials "the ultimate hunt." Texas is one of the few states that still uses prisoners known as "dog boys"; most other state correctional systems use professional dog trainers or civilian volunteers. Over the past several years, several inmates have been injured, two seriously. In 1983, the state prison system compensated two inmates $14,000 for injuries sustained during these exercises. One prisoner was bitten 120 times and another 56 times. Critics have called this a "slave sport," and a state representative said he would introduce legislation to abolish it (Belkin, 1990). Clearly, "the ultimate hunt" goes beyond a training exercise; it symbolizes a type of nostalgic recreation and contempt for basic human dignity.

Inhumane Conditions of Confinement as Human Rights Violations

Prisons are *institutions* in two senses of the word. First, they are physical institutions in the form of bricks and mortar, traditional gothic and monolithic symbols of state power. Second, they are also social institutions, reproducing patterns of behavior shaped by authority. Considering both of these of perspectives, we should acknowledge that the history of American prisons cannot be separated from its record of brutal conditions and harsh confinement (Rothman, 1971; Welch, 1996). Though American prisons were built on the notion of reform, the punitive assumptions governing penal policy make it easy for administrators to neglect the horrific conditions of their institutions. The contradiction is evident: American prisons are neither *civilized* nor *civilizing.* Simply put, inmates are subjected to a degrading prison environment, then returned to the community, not as better people, but probably as worse people due to their inhumane treatment behind bars (Clear, 1994; Johnson, 1996; Reiman, 1998; Richards, 1990; Robertson, 1997). Although physical violence against prisoners constitutes a major concern for human rights advocates, we must also attend to the brutality of inhumane conditions of confinement, which also deeply affect the lives of inmates. In this section, we explore federal and state prisons so terrible that their conditions of confinement have been condemned by international human rights organizations.

Though Amnesty International and Human Rights Watch are known for monitoring cases around the world, they also investigate allegations of human rights violations in American prisons. For years, Amnesty International has observed prisoner control techniques at the U.S. Penitentiary at Marion (IL), a super-maximum-security unit that has assumed the role of a modern Alcatraz. Marion holds 400 of the federal system's most incorrigible and high-risk inmates, and its most distinguishable feature is its practice of "lockdown." Under this form of institutional control, all prisoners are confined to their cells for 23 hours per day, granted 1 hour of exercise outside their cell, and allowed to shower 2 or 3 days a week. Handcuffs are fastened to inmates while they are transported within the facility, but it is the long-term chaining of prisoners to their beds that especially concerns Amnesty International. Though prison officials are permitted to restrain inmates only as long as necessary, numerous inmates have complained that they were routinely chained to their beds (mere concrete slabs) for periods lasting several days (see Dickey, 1990; Whitman, 1988). Amnesty International has criticized Marion officials for violating the United Nation's Minimum Rules for the Treatment of Prisoners.

In California, Pelican Bay Prison operates as the state's "Alcatraz," housing the system's most dangerous and disruptive prisoners. Approximately 1,200 inmates are incarcerated in this super-maximum-security unit, which was characterized by a former guard as the "toilet of the corrections system" (Hentoff, 1993b, p. 21). As in the case of Marion, corrections watchdog groups (ACLU Prison Project and the Pelican Bay Information Project) have repeatedly criticized the institution for its inhuman conditions. Inmates are confined to their cells (8- by 10-foot cells) $22\frac{1}{2}$ hours per day, where the temperature registers a constant 85 to 90 degrees. The unrelenting heat produces headaches, nausea, and dehydration and drains the inmates of their mental and bodily energy. One inmate reports: "The inside of your body always feels as though you have a fever and your skin is always moist with sweat, whether you move or not" (Hentoff, 1993b, p. 20; Haney, 1993).

At Pelican Bay, inmates are not permitted to work or study, and they are deprived of basic educational and vocational programs, including counseling and religious services. Revealingly, many inmates decline their 90 minutes of recreation in the exercise yard because they view it as just another form of isolation. "When they go up to the bare, concrete space—where there is no exercise equipment, not even a ball—they are still under the blinking eye of Big Brother. . . . They cannot see any of the surrounding landscape because of the solid concrete walls that extend up some 20 feet around them" (Hentoff, 1993b, p. 20).

A class action suit filed by Pelican Bay's prisoners contains more than 2,500 individual grievances of excessive force, inadequate medical treatment, and pervasive sensory deprivation maintained through isolation (Hentoff, 1993a, 1993c; also see Shakur, 1993). Human rights experts also criticize Pelican Bay officials for relying on cell extraction as a tool for controlling unruly prisoners. When an inmate confined to his cell refuses an order from an officer, the prisoner is forcibly removed from his cell by a team of specially trained guards sporting helmets and riot gear (including shields, batons, and guns that fire gas pellets or rubber or wooden bullets). Officers restrain and hog-tie the inmate, then carry him to an isolation cell. Though the guards are not suppose to harm the inmate, often prisoners are injured in the process of being tackled and restrained. There are also reports of serious errors committed in the use of cell extraction. The case of Lolofora Contreras, a deaf prisoner, draws attention to such problems. While an inmate count is conducted during the night, prisoners are required to "show skin" as they sleep. When a guard banged on the cell door and instructed Contreras to show skin, he kept sleeping because he couldn't hear the order. Rather than shining a flashlight on the deaf inmate to awaken him, the guard activated the prison's Special Operations Response Team to carry out a brutal cell extraction in which they beat Contreras, tied him up, and transferred him to an isolation cell. The incident happened not once to Contreras, but twice (Hentoff, 1993a, p. 20).

The harsh mistreatment of Contreras is indicative of how Pelican Bay staff abuse handicapped prisoners, especially those suffering from emotional and psychological problems. A case in point is Vaughn Dortch, a mentally ill inmate who bit an officer and smeared himself and his cell with feces. For these infractions, guards cuffed Dortch's hands behind his back and lowered him into a vat of 145-degree water. The nurse who witnessed the incident heard an officer say of Dortch, who is black, "It looks like were going to have a white boy before this is through; his skin is so dirty and rotten it's all fallen off" (Burkhalter, 1995, p. 17). Dortch's skin had peeled off and was hanging in clumps around his legs when brought to the emergency room by the prison medical staff.

The Dortch incident easily qualifies as an act of *torture*—the deliberate infliction of physical or mental pain for the purpose of coercion or punishment. In fact, the act violates key international standards ratified by the United Nations Convention Against Torture and Other Cruel, Inhuman or Degrading

Treatment or Punishment and the International Covenant on Civil and Political Rights, as well as the Eighth Amendment to the U.S. Constitution. Even though Dortch was awarded millions in damages in a settlement with the California Department of Corrections, his scars—physical and emotional— are likely to be permanent.

Contributing to the ongoing prison construction movement is the appeal of building additional super-maximum-security prisons and units (within existing prisons of all security levels). These prisons and units are exceedingly expensive, costing $75,000 per inmate annually, compared to $24,000 for a minimum-security cell (Welch, 1996). Aside from the exorbitant costs, another worrisome aspect of these units is that their high level of security conveniently conceals human rights violations from the free world. In some cases, however, human rights groups have penetrated the thick walls of super-maximum-security prisons in search of abuses against inmates. For instance, Human Rights Watch (1997) investigated human rights infractions in super-maximum-security units across the nation and concluded that units in 36 states violated some type of human rights. Resembling Marion and Pelican Bay, inmates in other super-maximum-security units are typically confined for 23 hours a day in poorly ventilated cells and are denied access to educational classes and outdoor exercise. Human Rights Watch also criticized these institutions for the procedures used to determine which inmates are remanded to the super-maximum-security units, charging that it is an unfair administrative decision that few inmates are allowed to appeal (also see the Correctional Association of New York, 1997).

In 1997, Human Rights Watch concluded that two Indiana super-maximum-security prisons inflict a degree of cruel and inhumane treatment on inmates that constitutes torture under international human rights law. A central complaint in their report concerns the punishment of emotionally disturbed inmates, who, for obvious reasons, have difficulty complying with rigid institutional rules. Rather than offering psychiatric treatment, mentally ill prisoners are disciplined for exhibiting bizarre and self-destructive behavior: "Prisoners rub feces on themselves, stick pencils in their penises, stuff their eyelids with toilet paper, bite chunks of flesh from their bodies, slash themselves, hallucinate, rant and rave, or stare fixedly at the walls" ("Rights Group Alleges 'Torture,'" 1997, pp. 1-2). Such psychotic symptoms are compounded by warehousing rather than treating prisoners and subjecting them to isolation and sensory deprivation (Human Rights Watch, 1997).

Human Rights Watch has also cited human rights violations in the super-maximum-security unit for women at the Broward Correctional Institution in

Miami, where inmates were routinely handcuffed while outside their cell as a means of punishment, regardless of the infraction. At the super-maximum-security wing of Oregon's maximum-security prison, the administration was ordered to stop the practice of stripping inmates and having them earn back their clothing through good behavior ("Study Finds Abuse in High Security Prisons," 1991). In 1992, investigators discovered physical and sexual assault in the Georgia women's prison at Hardwick. In what was described as "one of the worst episodes of its kind in the history of the nation's women's prisons," 14 former correctional employees (including a former deputy warden) were indicted for widespread physical and sexual abuse (Applebome, 1992, p. A-1). The indictments were based on statements of 119 female prisoners who reported incidents of rape, sodomy, and sexual assault. The staff was accused of coercing abortions as well as stripping and hog-tying a mentally disturbed woman and leaving her on a concrete floor (Applebome, 1992, p. A-1).

As noted previously, chaining practices in correctional and detention facilities continue to be criticized by human rights groups. The Boston-based Physicians for Human Rights has investigated numerous institutions and has concluded that the shackling of inmates is cruel and inhuman treatment, prohibited by international and medical standards, and in some cases constituting a form of torture. For instance, this group criticized the shackling practices at the Onondaga County Jail (NY) and recommended an investigation by the U.S. Attorney General. Specifically, Physicians for Human Rights condemned the use of four-point restraints involving the shackling of the wrists and ankles, thereby creating an unnatural body position in which the inmate's shoulders are suspended 5 to 6 inches off the bed. The group's report, which was corroborated by an investigation by the New York State Commission of Correction (a corrections watchdog group), also found that some inmates were denied food, water, and access to toilets while being shackled. Physicians confirm that lengthy periods of shackling lead to severe neck and back pain and in some cases nerve damage ("Jail's Use of Special Restraints Is Condemned by Rights Group," 1993).

Holly Burkhalter of Human Rights Watch pointed to an increased use of isolation in security housing as an alarming trend in U.S. imprisonment (Burkhalter, 1995). Using the U.S. penitentiary at Marion as a model, 36 states began to rely on super-maximum-security units and isolation as a means of punishing recalcitrant prisoners (including the denial of time outdoors, denial of reading material, and severe restriction of visits). Compounding matters, the use of isolation occurs outside the purview of the courts: Rarely are prisoners afforded due process. In fact, inmates committing even minor infractions have been subjected to isolation without appeal. For example, a prisoner in the Florida state prison at Starke was held in isolation for several years for spitting on a correctional officer (Burkhalter, 1995). Again, the prisoners most vulnerable to these draconian punishments are those who are mentally ill or retarded.

Given the volume of compelling medical evidence linking isolation to psychiatric symptoms, experts are astonished that corrections officials actually release prisoners to the community directly from isolation cells (see Haney, 1993; Korn, 1988). Vincent Schiraldi, executive director of the Center on Juvenile and Criminal Justice, cited the case of Robert Walker Scully as an example of this dangerous and reckless practice. Scully was released to the community after having served the final year of his sentence in the "hole" at Pelican Bay. Less than a week later, he murdered a police officer in California. According to Schiraldi (1995), "If restrictions against long-term isolation were strengthened by the Supreme Court instead of diminished, perhaps that officer would still be alive today" (p. A-16).

Political Prisoners

Political prisoners in the United States rarely appear on the radar of American consciousness, in large part because those behind bars are conveniently kept out of sight and out of mind. As a phenomenon, political prisoners rarely benefit from the reification process of social constructionism that otherwise would draw attention and concern to human rights violations. In this section, we shall explore several cases of political imprisonment, including cases of citizens targeted by government and law enforcement agencies for their political beliefs and activities. Likewise, we shall attend to cases involving protest in which demonstrations were reconstructed by authorities to appear more serious than they actually were.

A defining characteristic of most cases of political imprisonment is the harshness of their sentences, typically far surpassing penalties imposed for similar offenses of nonpolitical defendants. Our discussion of particular cases of political imprisonment is not intended to be exhaustive; although it is difficult to determine exact figures on political imprisonment, it has been estimated that there are currently 150 bona fide political prisoners in U.S. prisons (Ridgeway, 1990). To illustrate governmental tactics used in the incarceration of political prisoners, we begin this section with a glimpse at the former U.S. High Security Prison for Women at Lexington, Kentucky.

Sensory deprivation, psychological torture, and physical and sexual abuse by prison officials against political prisoners are allegations rarely documented in American prisons. Yet precisely these charges were launched against prison officials at the Federal Correctional Institution at Lexington, a facility for women prisoners featuring a super-maximum-security unit known as the Control Unit. In a documentary by Nina Rosenblum entitled *Through the Wire* (1990), the lives of several political prisoners were exposed in chilling detail. Inmates Alejandrina Torres, Susan Rosenberg, and Silvia Baraldini, all accused of being members of terrorist organizations, are serving excessive sentences for weapons possession and conspiracy (ranging from 35 to 58 years) and were interviewed about the conditions of the Control Unit. Their cells were situated underground, where bright lights and white walls deprived inmates of natural sensory activity, thereby creating a "living tomb." Inmates were also subjected to the indignity of frequent strip searches without cause (Harlow, 1991; Korn, 1988; Susler, 1991).

Following 2 years of operation, the Lexington Control Unit was closed in 1988, when the courts ruled that it "skirted elemental standards of human decency." However, since the Federal Court of Appeals decided in 1989 that political beliefs and associations are a legitimate basis for placing prisoners in special units, the Federal Bureau of Prisons has advanced plans to construct more control units similar to the one at Lexington (*Baraldini v. Meese,* 1998; Bader, 1989; *Baraldini v. Thornberg,* 1989).

POLITICAL ACTIVISTS, THE FBI, AND COINTELPRO

In 1972, Elmer (Geronimo, ji Jaga) Pratt was convicted of murder in a California court. In 1997, however, he was released when the volume of evidence proving his innocence and demonstrating government misconduct was too great for the judiciary to ignore. Pratt was a leader in the Black Panther Party, a militant African American organization striving for self-determination in the 1960s, when he and other black activists (e.g., Martin Luther King, Malcolm X) were monitored by the Federal Bureau of Investigation's Counter Intelligence Program (COINTELPRO).[3] Under the guise of national security, COINTELPRO's surveillance operation soon implemented a methodical arrest campaign, targeting thousands of Panthers and framing them for various crimes; in 1969 alone, 33 members of the Black Panther Party were shot and killed by police (Burnham, 1990).

Pratt serves as a reminder of the lengths to which the FBI and COINTELPRO would go to frame—"neutralize"—black activists. Not only was Pratt convicted of a murder that he did not commit, but the government had evidence in its possession proving his innocence. That is, the FBI withheld surveillance documents that established Pratt as being 350 miles from the scene of the crime at the time of the murder. During his trial, the victim's wife identified another man as the assailant but was coerced by the prosecution to accuse Pratt. Compounding matters, the prosecution relied on the testimony of witness Julius Butler, who, unbeknownst to the jury, was a paid FBI informant. Prosecutors knew that Butler was a police informant even though during the trial he testified that he was not. In overturning Pratt's conviction, Orange County Superior Court Judge Everett Dickey said that "jurors might have seen the case differently if the prosecution had not suppressed evidence bearing on Mr. Butler's credibility" ("Appeal in Ex-Panther's Case," 1998, p. 22; Kasindorf, 1997).

While serving time in more than five California prisons, Pratt was confined to solitary confinement for 8 years without reading material, a bed, or basic toilet facilities. He was denied parole 16 times: Fewer than 1% of convicted murderers in California serve as long as Pratt did (Kasindorf, 1997). After nearly 30 years behind bars, Pratt was released from prison when a judge reversed his conviction, noting that the prosecution had suppressed key evidence that would have probably exonerated him (Terry, 1997). Still, other Black Panthers remain in prison on convictions that legal experts seriously question, including Dhoruba al-Mujahid Bin Wahad, who was also targeted by COINTELPRO and is currently serving a term of 25 years to life. Bin Wahad and his supporters contend that he was falsely accused of attempted murder of a New York City policeman, and the FBI withheld crucial documents exposing witness tampering by government agents (Deutsch & Susler, 1990). Bin Wahad continues his fight to reopen his case.

In the 1960s and 1970s, the FBI and COINTELPRO expanded their investigative scope considerably, encompassing individuals and groups associated with the American Indian Movement (AIM). One of the most controversial prosecutions of American Indians is that of Leonard Peltier, who has been incarcerated for more than 20 years, convicted of killing FBI agents. Observers report that Peltier's trial was fraught with manufactured evidence and perjured FBI testimony. Furthermore, the FBI conceded that it could not prove who shot the agents, and Peltier's codefendant was acquitted on the basis of self-defense (Deutsch & Susler, 1990).

As the number of civil and Constitutional violations mounted, threatening the FBI's good-guy image, the agency announced that it would dismantle COINTELPRO. But still the FBI continued, and in some ways accelerated, *illegal* monitoring of U.S. citizens and domestic groups, especially those with leftist agendas. In the 1980s, the FBI deployed unauthorized wiretaps, physical surveillance, and informers to spy on hundreds of organizations opposed to President Reagan's policies in Central America, including the National Council of Churches, the Maryknoll Sisters, the Sanctuary Movement, and the Plowshare protestors (Barrenador, 1996; Bennett, 1996; Burnham, 1990; Kahn, 1996). The Reagan and Bush administrations also participated in other noteworthy cases, such as the deportation of Joe Doherty (an IRA soldier whose bona fide claim for political asylum was astonishingly rejected) and Brett Kimberlin, who was remanded to solitary confinement after he agreed to be interviewed by the media about his story that he sold marijuana to then vice presidential candidate Dan Quayle while Quayle was a law student ("Was This Prisoner Silenced," 1991; Welch, 1996).

Also during the 1980s, the U.S. Justice Department acquired several key tools to be used against political defendants, such as the Bail Reform Act of 1984 (contained within the Comprehensive Crime Control Act of 1984), which permits the government to detain suspects indefinitely without bail if officials determine them to be a danger to the community or a risk of flight. The Justice Department also reactivated a seldom-used criminal statute of seditious conspiracy against political dissenters and enjoyed the broad powers afforded by the newly created Racketeer Influenced Corrupt Organization Act (RICO). Although RICO was originally designed as a legal tactic in the battle against organized crime, U.S. attorneys quickly learned that it could also be used to prosecute political activists. Contributing to the growing arsenal of prosecutorial weapons are the expansive antiterrorist guidelines, granting law enforcement agents and prosecutors additional methods for investigation and law enforcement: anonymous petit jury, courtroom security, motions in limine, and ex parte submissions (Deutsch & Susler, 1990; also see Deutsch, 1984; Neier, 1995).

Conclusion

The conceptual framework of this chapter proposes that the poverty of interest in human rights violations is perpetuated by the prevailing social construction process, which remains focused largely on street crime. Images of street crime are influenced by those who have a vested interest in shaping popular notions of lawlessness, namely politicians, criminal justice officials, and other state managers. This particular social construction process also is facilitated by a reciprocal relationship existing between state managers and the media, who together generate a version of crime that lends itself to traditional strategies of criminal justice (Welch, Fenwick, & Roberts, 1997, 1998; also see Barak, 1994; Chermak, 1997; Ericson et al., 1987, 1989, 1991; Ferrell, 1996; Kasinsky, 1994; Surette, 1992; Welch & Bryan, in press).

In creating ideological and self-serving definitions of harm, state managers, along with the media, determine what is socially thinkable. Thus, human rights violations in U.S. prisons have yet to jar the public consciousness partly because state managers enjoy the privilege of cueing and sourcing the media about the relevance of certain social problems (i.e., street crime) to the exclusion of others (i.e., human rights violations). Considering this dimension of state power, it is unlikely that the criminal justice establishment would indict all—or even an aspect—of itself by directing attention to abuses of authority.

The impact of the mainstream media on the reification (and nonreification) of social problems should not be underestimated, especially in the realm of human rights violations and political imprisonment. As of 1999, Mumia Abu-Jamal faces the death penalty for being convicted of killing a Philadelphia police officer in 1982. Abu-Jamal, a vocal civil rights journalist and former Black Panther, claims that he was framed (Abu-Jamal, 1995). Along with his attorney Leonard Weinglass, Abu-Jamal charges the government with judicial and prosecutorial misconduct, intimidation of witnesses, coerced testimony, and suppression of evidence, and he demands a retrial. Among the obstacles keeping Abu-Jamal off balance, however, is the 1996 Anti-Terrorism and Effective Death Penalty Act (rushed into law following the Oklahoma City bombing), which guts longstanding habeas corpus protections. This law makes it " 'almost impossible' to get the federal courts, which had overturned 40 percent of state death penalties, to review such judgements" (Lindorff, 1997, p. 7). Weinglass stressed that it is crucial to generate public consciousness about Abu-Jamal's case, especially in light of evidence of judicial and prosecutorial misconduct. However, aside from scattered articles describing his ordeal in prison, Abu-Jamal has been silenced—literally—by National Public Radio, which abruptly canceled his scheduled commentaries on *All Things Considered* after caving in to pressure from heavyweight conservative politicians in 1994 (Abu-Jamal, 1995).

While addressing a 1997 People's Tribunal in Philadelphia (a major political and media event attracting more than 700 key supporters), Weinglass called for greater public pressure to influence the Pennsylvania Supreme Court in granting Abu-Jamal a new trial. To the dismay of Abu-Jamal supporters, two of the city's major newspapers, the *Philadelphia Inquirer* and the

Daily News, refused to cover the meeting (Lindorff, 1997). Again, we must not overlook the role of the media—and their relationship to the political and criminal justice establishment—in undermining the reification of human rights violations.

Not so coincidentally, one of Abu-Jamal's most visible and vocal supporters is Yuri Kochiyama of the National Committee for the Defense of Political Prisoners. Beginning in the 1960s, Kochiyama was one of the few Asian activists embraced by Malcolm X, the Black Panthers, and Puerto Rican nationalists. Recently, a long-time community organizer was asked whether Kochiyama was ever distanced by black activists, she responded: "No, Yuri has a track record. . . . In fact, she's part of the pattern" (Kochiyama, 1997). Here, "the pattern" refers to racism and discrimination perpetuated by the state. During the Second World War, Kochiyama was among the Japanese Americans interned by the U.S. government. In the 1940s, Kochiyama's father died shortly after being released from the U.S. Penitentiary at Terminal Island, California, where he was detained (without charges) when the FBI, albeit falsely, accused him of being a spy. Today, Kochiyama remains committed to raising public consciousness about human rights injustices, especially those motivated by racism (Kochiyama, 1997).

The low level of interest in human rights violations in U.S. prisons is further reproduced because legal remedies designed to protect prisoners are narrow and are becoming increasingly elusive. Although the U.S. Constitution offers prisoners some protections against cruel and unusual punishment, scholars remind us that as a legal document it suffers from serious limitations, especially in the realm of human rights. It should be noted that even though Congress banned the use of lease system for prisoners in 1934, it did not end the practice of chain gangs, and according to the American Correctional Association (1995), there is no case law pertaining to the legal nature of chain gangs. By international standards, the U.S. Constitution is "not only extremely limited but ignores some of the major premises of international human rights doctrine. . . . While it protects individual autonomy in the sphere of political and civil rights, it excludes rights to economic, social and cultural well-being" (Evenson, 1990, p. 15; Hinds, 1990; also see Burkhalter, 1995; Khan, 1998).

Yet another key structural obstacle continues to block the proper conceptualization and reification of human rights violations in American prisons. Despite ongoing, albeit anecdotal, data collection on human rights violations by key organizations (e.g., ACLU and NAACP), currently there is no comprehensive project systematically assembling such information (Ginger, 1990). Understandably, for human rights violations to become adequately recognized in the United States, precise definitions must be drafted along with mechanisms to enforce them; equally important, procedures must be installed for the collection and recording of such incidents. Such a system of data collection and accountability ought to be the responsibility of the federal government and monitored by nongovernment human rights experts.

To conclude, the purpose of this chapter was to shed light on the pervasive problem of human rights atrocities in U.S. prisons. By introducing the elements of social constructionism, we explained how the lack of reification thwarts efforts to draw public attention to human rights violations and, in the end, keeps awareness low. State managers have a vested interest in shaping popular images of lawlessness, thereby keeping the public focused squarely on street crime while diverting their attention from other harmful acts, including attacks on human rights (see Wilson, 1997).

Notes

1. Jeffrey Reiman (1998), among other scholars, verified that white-collar and corporate crime pose greater threats to public safety than street crime: We have a greater chance of being killed or disabled, for example, by an occupational injury or disease, by unnecessary surgery, or by shoddy medical emergency services than by aggravated assault or even homicide (p. 50). In widening the scope of social harm beyond street crime, it should be noted that more than 419,000 persons annually die from diseases caused by cigarettes in the United States; similarly, more than two-thirds of homicides and serious assaults involve alcohol (Johnson Foundation, 1993).

A principal aspect of the dominant ideology of crime is its insinuation that street offenses are the most costly, dangerous, and threatening form of crime (Welch, Fenwick, & Roberts, 1997, 1998). Financial assessments of the costs attached to different types of offenses, however, contradict the dominant ideology's image of crime. It is estimated that the cost of street crime hovers around $4 billion per year, whereas the expense of white-collar and corporate crime exceeds that figure 50 times, reaching $200 billion per year (Mokhiber & Wheat, 1995, p. 9; Albrecht, Wernz, & Williams, 1995). Further, approximately 24,000 homicides were committed in the United States in, for example, 1995. By contrast, during the same period, more than 56,000 workers died as a result of injuries or diseases caused by unsafe working conditions—more than 300 fatalities per day (since 1970, when the Occupational Safety and Health Agency began recording such fatalities) (Mokhiber & Wheat, 1995, p. 9; also see Reiman, 1998; Serrin, 1991, p. 80; Welch, 1996, pp. 21-24). In 1998, the *Journal of the American Medical Association* reported that more than 100,000 people a year die in American hospitals from adverse reactions to medication, which thus are one of the leading causes of death in the nation (Grady, 1998).

2. Recently, reports have surfaced that during World War II, 600,000 Italian and 11,000 German citizens living in the United States were also labeled enemies of the

state. They were interned for less than a year in Montana, and upon their release, they were placed on travel restrictions (Brooke, 1997).

3. In the 1960s and 1970s, the FBI and COINTELPRO, relying on tactics of questionable legality, implemented more than 285 counterintelligence actions against leftists campaigning for civil rights and for an end to the war in Vietnam. The purpose of COINTELPRO was to infiltrate, disrupt, and otherwise "neutralize" the entire leftist movement in the United States (Davis, 1997).

In 1998, following a 21-year court battle, the state of Mississippi unsealed more than 124,000 pages of secret files from a state agency that used "spy tactics, intimidation, false-imprisonment, jury tampering and other illegal methods" to disrupt the civil rights movement during the 1950s through the 1970s (Sack, 1998, p. A-1).

References

Abrams, A. (1991, June 19). It seemed so unfair. *New York Newsday,* Pt. II, pp. 49, 56-57.
Abu-Jamal, M. (1995). *Live from death row.* New York: Addison-Wesley.
Adams, R. (1998). *The abuses of punishment.* New York St. Martins.
Albrecht, S., Wernz, G. W., & Williams, T. L. (1995). *Fraud: Bringing light to the dark side of business.* Burr Ridge, IL: Irwin.
American Correctional Association. (1995). *Historical overview: Chain gangs in the United States, 1880s-1995.* Washington, DC: Author.
America's nuclear secrets. (1993, December 27). *Newsweek,* pp. 14-17.
Appeal in ex-Panther's case. (1998, February 1). *New York Times,* p. 22.
Applebome, P. (1992, November 14). 14 are charged with sex abuse in women's jail. *New York Times,* pp. A-1, A-7.
Austin v. Hopper, 95-T-637-N. (1998).
Ayers, E. (1984). *Vengeance and justice: Crime and punishment in the 19th century American South.* New York: Oxford University Press.
Bader, E. (1989, December 27). Prison control unit exposed in new documentary. *Guardian,* p. 19.
Barak, G. (1994). *Media, process, and the social construction of crime.* New York: Garland.
Baraldini v. Meese, 691 Fed. 7 432 (1988).
Baraldini v. Thornberg, 884 Fed. 7 615 (1989).
Barnes, H., & Teeters, N. (1946). *New horizons in criminology* (3rd ed.). New York: Prentice Hall.
Barrenador, G. (1996). On the political offense: Comment's on Bennett's "political trials." *Social Anarchism, 22,* 12-34.
Becker, H. S. (1967). Whose side are we on? *Social Problems, 14,* 239-247.
Becker, H. S. (1973). *Outsiders: Studies in the sociology of deviance.* New York: Free Press.
Belkin, L. (1990, August 16). Inmates are prey in "ultimate hunt." *New York Times,* p. B-10.
Bennett, J. R. (1996). Political trials and prisoners in the United States: A case for political defense. *Social Anarchism, 22,* 5-11.
Berger, P., & Luckman, T. (1963). *The social construction of reality.* New York: Doubleday.
Bohm, R. (1986). Crime, criminal, and crime control policy myths. *Justice Quarterly, 3,* 193-214.
Bragg, R. (1995, March 26). Chain gangs to return to roads of Alabama. *New York Times,* p. 16.
Brooke, J. (1997, August 11). After silence, Italians recall the internment: An official apology is sought from U.S. *New York Times,* p. A-10.
Burkhalter, H. (1995, July 3). Barbarism behind bars: Torture in U.S. prisons. *Nation,* p. 17.
Burnham, M. (1990). Human rights issue for the 90s in the United States. *International Review of Contemporary Law, 1,* 21-30.
Burns, R. (1932). *I am a fugitive from a Georgia chain gang.* New York: Vanguard.

Chain gangs for women cause furor. (1996, April 28). *New York Times*, p. 30.

Chermak, S. (1997). The presentation of drugs in the news media: News sources involved in the social construction of social problems. *Justice Quarterly, 14*, 687-718.

Clear, T. (1994). *Harm in American penology.* Albany: State University of New York Press.

Comprehensive Crime Control Act, 18 U.S.C. (1984).

Correctional Association of New York. (1997). *Special housing units (SHU'S) and Keeplock fact sheet.* New York: Author.

Count of subjects in radiation experiments is raised to 16,000. (1995, August 20). *New York Times*, p. 27.

D'Antonio, M. (1997, August 31). Atomic guinea pigs. *New York Times Magazine*, pp. 38-43.

Davis, J. K. (1997). *Assault on the left: The FBI and the sixties antiwar movement.* Westport, CT: Praeger.

Davis, M. (1995, February 20). Hell factories in the fields. *Nation*, pp. 116-120.

Deutsch, M. (1984, Winter). The improper use of the federal grand jury: An instrument for the internment of political activists. *Journal of Criminal Law and Criminology, 1,* 1159-1196.

Deutsch, M., & Susler, J. (1990). Political prisoners in the United States: The hidden reality. *International Review of Contemporary Law, 1,* 113-125.

Dickey, C. (1990, January 15). A new home for Noriega. *Newsweek*, pp. 66-69.

Ericson, R. V., Baranek, P. M., & Chan, J. B. L. (1987). *Visualizing deviance: A study of news organizations.* Toronto: University of Toronto Press.

Ericson, R. V., Baranek, P. M., & Chan, J. B. L. (1989). *Negotiating control: A study of news sources.* Toronto: University of Toronto Press.

Ericson, R. V., Baranek, P. M., & Chan, J. B. L. (1991). *Representing order: Crime, law, and justice in the news media.* Toronto: University of Toronto Press.

Evenson, D. (1990). Competing views of human rights: The U.S. Constitution from an international perspective. *International Review of Contemporary Law, 1,* 15-20.

Ferrell, J. (1996). *Crimes of style: Urban graffiti and the politics of criminality.* Boston: Northeastern University Press.

Fishman, M. (1978). Crime waves as ideology. *Social Problems, 25,* 531-543.

For Japanese-American veterans, a war at home. (1995, November 12). *New York Times*, p. 32.

Fukami, D. (Producer & Director). (1997, March 2). *Starting over: Japanese-Americans after the war.* New York: Public Broadcasting Service.

Garland, D. (1990). *Punishment and modern society: A study in social theory.* Chicago: University of Chicago Press.

Ginger, A. F. (1990). An international data base on human rights. *International Review of Contemporary Law, 1,* 136-144.

Grady, D. (1998, April 15). Study says thousands die from reaction to medicine. *New York Times*, p. 21.

Gonnerman, J. (1998, July 7). Lab rats. *Village Voice*, pp. 55-56.

Hall, S., Critcher, C., Jefferson, T., Clarke, J., & Roberts, B. (1978). *Policing the crisis: Mugging, the state and law and order.* New York: Holmes & Meiser.

Haney, C. (1993, Spring). Infamous punishment: The psychological consequences of isolation. *Journal of the National Prison Project, 410,* 1-4.

Hansen, A. A. (1995). Oral history and the Japanese American evacuation. *Journal of American History, 82,* 625-639.

Harlow, B. (1991). *Barred: Women, writing, and political detention.* Wesleyan University Press.

Hentoff, N. (1993a, July 6). The bloody art of prison cell extraction. *Village Voice*, pp. 20-21.

Hentoff, N. (1993b, June 22). Buried alive in Pelican Bay. *Village Voice*, pp. 20-21.

Hentoff, N. (1993c, June 15). Charles Dickens's report to Janet Reno. *Village Voice*, pp. 22-23.

Hentoff, N. (1995, April 4). Congress's brutal treatment of prisoners. *Village Voice*, pp. 18-19.

Herman, E. H., & Chomsky, N. (1988). *Manufacturing consent: The political economy of the mass media.* New York: Pantheon.
Hilts, P. (1994, October 22). Thousands of human experiments. *New York Times,* p. 10.
Hilts, P. (1995, January 19). Radiation tests used some healthy people. *New York Times,* p. B-10.
Hinds, L. (1990). Human rights violations in the United States: An introduction. *International Review of Contemporary Law, 1,* 5-14.
Hornblum, A. (1998). *Acres of skin: Human experiments at Holmesburg Prison, a true story of abuse and exploitation in the name of medical science.* New York: Routledge.
Human Rights Watch. (1997). *Cold storage: Super-maximum security confinement in Indiana.* New York: Author.
Humphries, D. (1981). Serious crime, news coverage, and ideology. *Crime and Delinquency, 27,* 191-205.
Inmates fight "work or be shackled" policy. (1993, September 5). *New York Times,* p. 43.
Ives, G. (1970). *A history of penal methods.* Montclair, NJ: Patterson Smith. (Original work published 1914)
Jackson, B. (1995, September 18). Is the Alabama prison system's return to the chain gang unfair to blacks? *Jet,* pp. 12-16.
Jail's use of special restraints is condemned by rights group. (1993, April 27). *New York Times,* pp. -4.
Jameson, F. (1991). *Postmodernism or the cultural logic of late capitalism.* Durham, NC: Duke University Press.
Johnson Foundation. (1993). *Substance abuse: The nation's no. 1 health problem.* Princeton, NJ: Author.
Johnson, R. (1996). *Hard time: Understanding and reforming the prison.* Monterey, CA: Brooks/Cole.
Kahn, R. (1996). *Other people's blood: U.S. immigration prisons in the Reagan decade.* Boulder, CO: Westview.
Kappeler, V. E., Blumberg, M., & Potter, G. W. (1996). *The mythology of crime and criminal justice* (2nd ed.). Prospect Heights, IL: Waveland.
Kasindorf, M. (1997, June 11). Black Panther Pratt free after 27 years. *USA Today,* pp. 1-A, 3-A.
Kasinsky, R. G. (1994). Patrolling the facts: Media, cops, and crime. In G. Barak (Ed.), *Media, process, and the social construction of crime* (pp. 203-236). In New York: Garland.
Khan, A. (1998). *Significant decisions regarding the Prison Litigation Reform Act.* Washington, DC: American Civil Liberties Union National Prison Project.
Kilborn, P. (1997, March 11). Revival of chain gangs takes a twist: Stun belts emerge as the latest tool to keep inmates in line. *New York Times,* p. A-18.
Kiyasu, J. (1991, July 21). Unfounded fears. *New York Newsday,* p. 31.
Kochiyama, Y. (1997, July 6). Yuri Kochiyama: Japanese-American activist. In P. Saunders & R. Tajiri (Coproducers & Codirectors), *Reel New York.* New York: Public Broadcasting Service.
Koppes, C., & Black, G. (1987). *Hollywood goes to war: How politics, profits, and propaganda shaped the World War II movies.* New York: Free Press.
Korematsu v. United States, 323 U.S. (1994).
Korn, R. (1988). The effects of confinement in HSU. *Social Justice, 15,* 8-19.
Lewis, C. (1995). John Steinbeck's alternative to internment camps: A policy for the president, December 15, 1941. *Journal of the West, 34,* 55-61.
Lichtenstein, A. (1993). Good roads and chain gangs in the Progressive South: The Negro convict is a slave. *Journal of Southern History, 59,* 85-110.
Lindorff, D. (1997, December 29). Blackout on Mumia. *Nation,* p. 7.
Linehan, T.M. (1993). Japanese American resettlement in Cleveland during and after World War II. *Journal of Urban History, 20,* 54-80.
Mannheim, K. (1952). *Essays on the sociology of knowledge.* New York: Oxford University Press.

Marsh, H. (1991). A comparative analysis of crime coverage in newspapers in the United States and other countries from 1960-1989: A review of the literature. *Journal of Criminal Justice, 19,* 67-79.

Marx, K. (1978). The German ideology. In R. D. Tucker (Ed.), *The Marx-Engels reader* (2nd ed., pp. 146-200). New York: Norton.

Michalowski, R. J. (1985). *Order, law, and crime: An introduction to criminology.* New York: Random House.

Mitford, J. (1971). *Kind and usual punishment: The prison business.* New York: Vintage.

Mokhiber, R., & Wheat, A. (1995, December). Shameless: 1995's 10 worst corporations. *Multinational Monitor, 16*(12), 9-16.

Mydans, S. (1995, March 4). Taking no prisoners, in a manner of speaking. *New York Times,* p. A-6.

Neier, A. (1995). Confining dissent: The political prison. In N. Morris & D. Rothman (Eds.), *Oxford history of the prison: The practice of punishment in Western society* (pp. 391-426). New York: Oxford University Press.

Nishimoto, R. (1995). *Inside an American concentration camp: Japanese-American resistance at Poston, Arizona.* Tuscon: University of Arizona Press.

Nossiter, A. (1997, January 31). Judge rules against Alabama's prison "hitching posts." *New York Times,* p. A-14.

Nuclear guinea pigs. (1993, January 5). *New York Times,* p. A-14.

Okubo, M. (1946) *Citizen 13660.* Seattle: University of Washington Press.

Raskin, J. (1991, February 4). Remember *Korematsu*: A precedent for Arab-Americans? *Nation,* pp. 117-118.

Racketeer Influenced and Corrupt Organization Act, 18 U.S.C. §§1961-1968 (1970).

Reiman, J. (1998). *The rich get richer and the poor get prison: Ideology, class and criminal justice* (5th ed.). Boston: Allyn & Bacon.

Richards, S. (1990). Sociological penetration of the American gulag. *Wisconsin Sociologist, 27*(4), 18-28.

Ridgeway, J. (1990, December 11). Hard time: Why the left goes to jail and the right goes home. *Village Voice,* pp. 19-20.

Ridgeway, J. (1994, January 11). This is not only a test. *Village Voice,* pp. 15-16.

Rights group alleges "torture" in Indiana super-max prisons. (1997). *Criminal Justice Newsletter, 28*(19), 1-3.

Robertson, J. E. (1997). Houses of the dead: Warehouse prisons, paradigm change, and the Supreme Court. *Houston Law Review, 34,* 1003-1063.

Rosenblum, N. (Producer & Director). (1991). *Through the wire* [Film]. Available from Daedalus Productions.

Rothman, D. (1971). *The discovery of the asylum: Social order and disorder in the new republic.* Boston: Little, Brown.

Sack, K. (1998, March 18). Mississippi reveals dark secrets of a racist time. *New York Times,* pp. A-1, A-16.

Sahin, H. (1980). The concept of ideology and mass communication. *Journal of Communication Inquiry, 61,* 3-12.

Schiraldi, V. (1995, June 27). Before prisoners get isolation treatment. *New York Times,* p. A-16.

Schoenfeld, A., Meier, R., & R. Griffin, R. (1979). Constructing a social problem: The press and the environment. *Social Problems, 27,* 38-61.

Serrin, W. (1991, January 28). The wages of work. *Nation,* pp. 80-82.

Shakur, S. (1993). *Monster.* New York: Smithmark.

Sifakis, C. (1992). *The encyclopedia of American crime.* New York: Smithmark.

Simon, J. (1995). They died with their boots on: The boot camp and the limits of modern penality. *Social Justice, 22*(2), 25-48.

Smith, P. (1995). *Democracy on trial: The Japanese American evacuation and relocation in World War II*. New York: Simon & Schuster.

Spivak, J. (1932). *Georgia nigger*. New York: Harcourt, Brace.

Stauth, G.,& Turner, B. (1988). Nostalgia, postmodernism, and the critique of mass culture. *Theory, Culture, and Society, 52/53*, 509-526.

Study finds abuse in high security prisons. (1991, November 15). *New York Times*, p. A-15.

Surette, R. (1992). *Media, crime and criminal justice: Images and realities*. Pacific Grove, CA: Brooks/Cole.

Susler, J. (1991). *Profiles of courage: The case of Puerto Rican women political prisoners/prisoners of war*. Chicago: People's Law Office.

Terry, D. (1997, July 20). Los Angeles confronts bitter racial legacy. *New York Times*, pp. A-1, A-14.

Tunnell, K. (1992). Film at eleven: Recent developments in the commodification of crime. *Sociological Spectrum, 12*, 293-313.

Was this prisoner silenced? (1991, November 13). *New York Times*, p. A-15.

Welch, M. (1996). *Corrections: A critical approach*. New York: McGraw-Hill.

Welch, M. (1997). Tougher prisons? An interview with Michael Welch. *Critical Criminologist, 8*(1), 7, 11.

Welch, M., & Bryan, J. (in press). Moral campaigns, authoritarian aesthetics, and amplification: Flag desecration in the post-*Eichman* era. *Critical Criminology: An International Journal*.

Welch, M., Fenwick, M., & Roberts, M. (1997). Primary definitions of crime and moral panic: A content analysis of experts' quotes in feature newspaper articles of crime. *Journal of Research in Crime and Delinquency, 34*, 474-494.

Welch, M., Fenwick, M., & Roberts, M. (1998). State managers, intellectuals, and the media: A content analysis of ideology in experts' quotes in featured newspaper articles on crime, *Justice Quarterly, 15*, 101-123.

Welch, M., Weber, L., & Edwards, W. (1998). *The state versus its dissenters: A content analysis of competing versions of corrections in the media*. Unpublished paper, Rutgers University.

Whitman, S. (1988, August 7). The Marion penitentiary: It should be opened up, not locked down. *Southern Illinoisan*, p. 25.

Wiener, J. (1995, March 15). Japanese-Americans remember: Hard times at Heart Mountain. *Nation*, p. 694.

Wilson, R. (1997). *Human rights, culture and context*. Chicago: Pluto.

Yoo, D. (1996). Captivating memories: Museology, concentration camps, and Japanese American history. *American Quarterly, 48*, 680-699.

Yoshino, R. (1996). Barbed wire and beyond: A sojourn through internment—a personal recollection. *Journal of the West, 35*, 34-43.

CHAPTER
11

Prisoners With HIV/AIDS

Discrimination, Fringe Punishments, and the Production of Suffering

The war on drugs has had a dual impact on the nation's correctional system. Quantitatively, more drug violators are being sentenced to prison now than at any other point in U.S. history. Qualitatively, the incarceration of intravenous (IV) drug users infected with acquired immunodeficiency syndrome (AIDS) and human immunodeficiency virus (HIV, the asymptomatic infection that leads to AIDS) is significantly transforming the role of corrections in social control. Prisons and jails continue to serve as human warehouses predominately reserved for society's impoverished, given that the vast majority of drug violators behind bars are economically marginalized. But due to the debilitating and lethal nature of HIV/AIDS, correctional facilities are increasingly—albeit reluctantly—assuming the traditional function of infirmaries: in effect, becoming repositories for infectious diseases.

By exploring HIV/AIDS at different levels of analysis, this chapter unveils related key concepts in the spheres of macro-, meso-, and microsociologies. Connections are drawn among the following: the production of deviance in the political economy, the process of stigmatizing problem populations, and the establishment of social control mechanisms designed to manage those marginalized. This examination further contextualizes HIV/AIDS ideologically by attending to adverse societal reactions that are dependent on metaphors and to the creation of distinct cultural meanings. For example, a prominent ideological theme in popular depictions of HIV/AIDS is a moralizing of the illness, insinuating that those infected are being judged and punished by a higher power for indulging in illicit drugs or homosexuality.

These ideological connotations also are prevalent in corrections, where prisoners with HIV/AIDS are stigmatized and often ostracized. As a result, their incarceration experience is marked by a greater degree of suffering, commonly traced to discrimination and various other fringe punishments. Whereas *fringe benefits* denotes extra rewards, *fringe punishments* refers to added forms of retribution. Throughout key periods in correctional history, prison reformers have struggled to improve the conditions of confinement; by making penal institutions more humane, they are better equipped to reform and rehabilitate their prisoners. Over the past few decades, however, the "penal harm movement" has emerged as the antithesis of prison reform. Currently, these campaigns lobby legislators to harshen prison conditions and to eliminate or scale down what they call amenities and luxuries: personal clothing, televisions, recreation, educational programs, and even medical care (Clear, 1994; Cullen, 1995; Flanagan, 1996; Johnson, Bennett, & Flanagan, 1997; Vaughn & Carroll, 1998; Welch, 1997). Proposals to abolish amenities are rooted in the perception that incarceration is not sufficiently harsh and that supplemental doses of retribution should be imposed in the form of fringe punishments to maximize suffering. In this chapter, it is argued that prisoners with HIV/AIDS are subjected to numerous fringe punishments, most notably victimization, discrimination, and the denial of adequate medical attention. Altogether, these fringe punishments produce a level of suffering for prisoners with HIV/AIDS that is rarely experienced by other inmates.

From an institutional perspective, correctional policies and practices have the potential to exacerbate or alleviate inmate suffering. Hence, one objective of this chapter is to enumerate the ways correctional management—intentionally or unintentionally—contributes to hardship for prisoners with HIV/AIDS. In doing this, we remain mindful of the mesosociological and organizational forces affecting the incarceration experience. Relatedly, our discussion also encompasses the microsociological elements of imprisonment, exploring phenomenology and the role that temporality plays in shaping the contours of suffering. Setting the stage for a multilayered and critical analysis of HIV/AIDS, we begin with a macrosociological examination of deviance production in capitalist society.

The Production of Problem Populations in Capitalist Society

A critical discussion of problem populations (such as prisoners with HIV/AIDS) should examine more generally the production of deviant classes in society, especially considering the dialectical nature of capitalism. Among the contradictions of capitalism is the production of deviance that excludes some people from economic activity (Spitzer, 1975). Unemployed workers are the most recognizable manifestations of the internal contradictions of capitalism, a system that ironically requires a certain level of unemployment to function properly (refer to Chapter 2 for a discussion of capitalism and its inherent contradictions). Still, unemployed workers (the surplus population) do not become a problem until they threaten the social relations of production; when that occurs, they are labeled a problem population by the state. More specifically, problem populations become eligible for social control when they disrupt or challenge the following components of a capitalist society:

1. The capitalist modes of appropriating the product of human labor (e.g., the poor who "steal" from the rich)
2. The social conditions under which capitalist production takes place (e.g., those who refuse or are unable to perform wage labor)
3. Patterns of distribution and consumption in capitalist society (e.g., those who use drugs for escape and transcendence rather than for sociability and adjustment)
4. The process of socialization for productive and nonproductive roles (e.g., youth who refuse to be schooled or those who deny the validity of "family life")
5. The ideology that supports the functioning of capitalist society (e.g., proponents of alternative forms of social organization) (Spitzer, 1975, p. 642)

As the problem population swells, it is in the interests of the state and capitalism to devise mechanisms of class (social) control in an effort to preserve the social order and status quo. In particular, two major groupings within the problem population are identified: social junk and social dynamite. From the perspective of the state, social junk are viewed as costly but as relatively harmless to the social order. "The discreditability of social junk resides in the failure, inability, or refusal of this group to participate in the roles supportive of the capitalist society" (Spitzer, 1975, p. 645). The category of social junk is made up of the elderly and the physically and mentally handicapped. Because social junk are deemed harmless, social control mechanisms in the form of therapeutic and welfare agencies serve to regulate rather than eliminate or suppress them. In contrast, the portion of the problem population labeled social dynamite is believed to pose a serious threat to the existing social and economic order. Due to their presumed volatility, social dynamite are processed through the coercive components of the social control apparatus, namely the criminal justice system.

Despite these seemingly discrete categories within the problem population, the social control apparatus operates equivocally in that members of the problem population, including the impoverished, drug users, and problem children, are processed as alternatively either social junk or social dynamite or are processed as both simultaneously. Gays and lesbians also are subjected to deviance processing because they represent a threat to the validity of the bourgeois family, essential to capitalism as a unit for consumption, socialization, and reproduction of the labor force (Frankford & Snitow, 1972; Plant, 1986, 1989; Secombe, 1973; Zaretsky, 1973a, 1973b). Indeed, gay and lesbian activists have been routinely funneled through the criminal justice machinery after being arrested at gay rights demonstrations.

It has been commonly observed that jails (even more so than prisons) fail to consistently distinguish between harmless social junk (or rabble, see Irwin, 1985) and menacing social dynamite; consequently, jails serve as unspecialized catch basins for both types of the problem population (Irwin, 1985; Shover & Einstadter, 1988; Welch, 1991a, 1994; see Chapter 6). Accounting for this lack of uniformity in processing deviance, Spitzer (1975) noted that social control is patterned by political, economic, and ideological priorities, which are continuously subject to change; likewise, Marx (1906) characterized capitalism as dynamic rather than static, a political economy in constant transformation. A key economic transformation in the United States during the past four decades has been the shift from industrial to corporate capitalism, resulting in the erosion of jobs formerly occupied by blue-collar workers in the inner city (many of them people of color) (refer to Chapter 2). In brief, this economic transformation has contributed to the growth of the surplus population, prompting the state to invest greater resources in coercive mechanisms of social control—the criminal justice and correctional systems. Indeed, containment has emerged as an increasingly expansive measure of social control, as currently evidenced by the largest incarceration rate in U.S. history and the world (Welch, 1996a; Welch Fenwick, & Roberts, 1997, 1998).

AIDS, Metaphors, and Morality

In her book *AIDS and Its Metaphors* (1989), Susan Sontag offered an interpretive narrative of AIDS, blending historical and literary references that parallel the sociologies of knowledge, medicine, and deviance. Much of her discussion underscored the processes and consequences of stigma and social control by illuminating the potency of metaphors: the tendency to give a thing a name that belongs to something else. Sociologically, the construction of metaphors is an initial process of labeling; this reification allows those who are perceived as different from so-called normal people to be stigmatized and marginalized (Becker, 1963; Goffman, 1963; Schur, 1971). Sontag, drawing on her previous work *Illness as Metaphor* (1980), reminded us of society's propensity to interpret diseases through the prism of morality and punishment. Still, AIDS is not confined solely to moral and punitive connotations but rather is subject to an array of metaphors.

> AIDS has a dual metaphoric genealogy. As a micro-process, it is described as cancer is: an invasion. When the focus is transmission of the disease, an older metaphor, reminiscent of syphilis, is invoked: pollution. (One gets it from the blood or sexual fluids of infected people or from contaminated blood products). (Sontag, 1989, p. 17)

In a sense, this metaphor moves in opposite directions: Inwardly, AIDS attacks the body of the infected, while outwardly it poses a threat to others. Not only is stigma imposed on those infected, but the outward threat (contagiousness) posed by AIDS spawns a different type of societal reaction: that is, moral panic—a turbulent and exaggerated response to a social problem (Cohen, 1973). AIDS is subject to demonization, evangelical condemnation, and judgments. In a nationally televised sermon, Jerry Falwell of the Moral Majority proclaimed that AIDS regarding homosexuals represented a "lethal judgment of God on America for endorsing this vulgar, perverted and reprobate lifestyle" (Bayer & Kirp, 1992, p. 34). Moreover, integrating moral metaphors with medical constructs produces another common reference to

AIDS: The disease is brought on by the lack of moral hygiene. This notion insinuates that homosexual sex is both immoral and unhealthy.

An understandable reaction to AIDS is fear; thus, we turn to the scientific community to help us understand the nature of the illness, not only in the hope of eventually developing a cure but also to learn how to protect ourselves from infection. Regrettably, not all members of the scientific community have acted responsibly: Some researchers have inaccurately characterized AIDS only to inflame fears and incite hysteria among the public. For example, the famous sex researchers Masters and Johnson published a popular book about AIDS in 1988. In *Crisis: Heterosexual Behavior in the Age of AIDS,* the authors made false statements about the nature of the transmission of AIDS, claims that ran counter to what was known about the disease at the time. They asserted that AIDS had "clearly broken out" among heterosexuals and that AIDS could be contracted from saliva and hard surfaces such as toilet seats. When confronted by the Presidential Commission of AIDS about such claims, Masters and Johnson conceded that they had no independent data to support their conclusions (Sirica, 1988). Critics charged that Masters and Johnson had knowingly disseminated false information about AIDS in an effort to capitalize commercially from book profits. As a result, Masters and Johnson fueled fear among the public and reinforced the myths and misconceptions about AIDS (see Thomas, 1985; Welch, 1989).

Originating from the traditional enforcement of conventional morality, stigma is a mark of social disgrace. In ancient Greece, unusual bodily markings were construed as signs of moral inferiority; similarly, lawbreakers were deliberately branded for the purpose of exposing their moral defects. During early Christian times, bodily signs in the form of eruptive blossoms on the skin were interpreted as being emblematic of holy grace, suggesting supernatural qualities. However, less aesthetic imperfections were believed to be indicative of physical and moral defects. Nathaniel Hawthorne's novel *The Scarlet Letter* (1850/1962) remains a compelling description of how colonial American communities publicly punished and humiliated women for moral—especially sexual—transgressions. Our contemporary understanding of stigma is largely indebted to the work of sociologist Erving Goffman, author of *Stigma: Notes on the Management of Spoiled Identity* (1963). Goffman delineated the processes and products of stigma, which devalues and disqualifies some people from full social acceptance. Stigma has numerous sources: physical (e.g., illnesses, injuries, disfigurements), documentary or character (e.g., mental illness, chronic unemployment, a prison record), and contextual (e.g., keeping "bad company"). Stigma that is ascribed or assigned to a person at birth is known as tribal (or class) stigma, in which all members of a particular race, ethnic group, or religion are tainted. Tribal stigma also connotes moral transgressions because it is inherited from the sins of one's parents.

The complex stigma attached to prisoners with HIV/AIDS is actually a configuration of several attributes—physical, documentary or character, contextual, and tribal—all of which are interpreted through the lens of morality. Physically, inmates with HIV/AIDS are devalued because they are afflicted with a lethal and contagious illness. Prisoners with HIV/AIDS typically became infected by injecting illicit drugs into their bodies with unclean needles or by having sexual contact with infected partners, either heterosexually or, even more stigmatizing, homosexually. As a result of the ways they contracted HIV/AIDS, these inmates are further discredited for lack of moral character and for keeping "bad company." The stigma of HIV/AIDS is potent, which explains why many of those infected refuse testing and treatment. Sheila Morris, an HIV-positive prisoner in Washington, D.C., reports: "You have a lot of people who know they're [HIV] positive who are in denial. I am surprised by people who are sick and won't admit it. They're more willing to admit they're drug addicts or murderers or pedophiles than admit they're sick and get care for it" (Purdy, 1997, p. 28).

Compounding their stigma, prisoners with HIV/AIDS are convicted felons and in many cases are ascribed a tribal (class) stigma: The vast majority are impoverished people of color from the inner city.[1] Given the proportion of inmates with HIV/AIDS who are nonwhite and urban, additional commentary about racism and HIV/AIDS is apropos. Throughout history, the interpretation of plagues and epidemics has been typically twofold. First, plagues have been depicted in moral terms, sent by a higher power as a punishment for society's sins; second, plagues have been depicted as coming from somewhere else. Sontag (1989) reminded us that the syphilis epidemic in Europe during the 15th century, the bubonic plague during the 18th century, and the outbreaks of cholera during the 19th century were all characterized as dreaded foreign diseases. Literally and figuratively, plagues are reified as pollution from alien and exotic lands. "AIDS is thought to have started in the 'dark continent,' then spread to Haiti, then to the United States and to Europe, then. . . . It is understood as a tropical disease: another manifestation from the so-called Third World" (Sontag, 1989, pp. 51-52). Popular beliefs on the origin of HIV/AIDS—commonly though inaccurately described as a plague—have fueled anti-African (black) prejudice in the Americas, Europe, and Asia.

The subliminal connection made to notions about a primitive past and the many hypotheses that have been fielded about possible transmission from animals (a disease of green monkeys? African swine fever?) cannot help but activate a familiar set of stereotypes about animality, sexual license, and blacks. (Sontag, 1989, p. 52; also see Huber & Schneider, 1992; Schneider, 1992)

Throughout history, urbanization also has been blamed for plagues, epidemics, and the spread of numerous diseases. Whereas rural communities have been long cherished as pure, simple, and wholesome, cities have represented the embodiment of crime, vice, and disease—aggravated by an influx of minorities and immigrants. Not surprisingly, HIV/AIDS is currently viewed by conservative extremists as another symptom of the immorality of urban life, specifically homosexuality and illicit drug use (see Shilts, 1987).

Prisoners With HIV/AIDS as a Problem Population in Corrections

Perhaps not so coincidentally, the term *problem population* is frequently used in the field of corrections to refer to prisoners who require special (in many cases medical) attention, including the infirm, the elderly, pregnant women, and inmates with various psychiatric needs. Among the most pressing issues in correctional management today is dealing with problem populations, especially prisoners with HIV/AIDS. The equivocal tendencies of social control are clearly evident in the harsh treatment of prisoners with HIV/AIDS, who not only are regarded as social junk, but, given the contagious and lethal nature of their illness, also are characterized as costly social dynamite (Welch, 1989; incidentally, many prisoners with HIV/AIDS fit also into Irwin's [1985] rabble category; see chap. 6). For instance, in 1995 the special officer for the Court of the District of Columbia released a document describing the abominable conditions concerning the delivery of medical care for inmates with HIV/AIDS. In particular, the report featured an account of the death of a male prisoner with AIDS who had remained neglected in his cell for 10 days: "The inmate died while being transported to the hospital strapped in a wheelchair and wrapped in a urine and feces stained sheet" (Perez, 1996, p. 8). Processed as social junk and social dynamite, prisoners with HIV/AIDS occupy the lowest stratum in the correctional caste system. As we shall discuss further, these inmates are likely to experience greater suffering than other prisoners, particularly discrimination and various fringe punishments.

The Scope of HIV/AIDS In Correctional Facilities

At year end 1995, 2.3% of all state and federal prisoners were reported to be infected with HIV. In state prisons, 23,404 inmates were HIV positive (2.4% of the total prison population) and in federal prisons, 822 (0.9%), marking a 14% increase since 1993 (Bureau of Justice Statistics, 1997; see Table 11.1). It is commonly believed that the actual number of HIV (and AIDS) cases is much higher in prisons than officially recorded due to the high concentration of IV drug users; moreover, many cases remain concealed by the lengthy incubation period of the disease, sometimes lasting several years (Hammett, Harrold, Gross, & Epstein, 1994; also compounding this health crisis behind bars are prisoners coinfected with HIV and tuberculosis; see Hammett & Harrold, 1994). Similar data are reported for jail inmates. The infection rate was highest in the largest jail jurisdictions, where nearly 3% of the inmates were reported to be HIV positive (Bureau of Justice Statistics, 1997; see Table 11.2).

Of all prisoners in U.S. prisons, 5,099 (0.5%) had confirmed AIDS, which was more than six times the rate in the U.S. population (0.08%), and 18,165 inmates were HIV positive without having confirmed AIDS. Of all HIV-positive prisoners, 21% were confirmed AIDS cases (21% of state inmates, 16% of federal). In 1994, 955 state inmates died of AIDS, and in 1995 this number increased to 1,010—an AIDS death rate of 100 state inmates per 100,000. Between 1991 and 1995, approximately one in three inmate deaths was attributable to AIDS-related causes; during the same period, the number of HIV-positive prisoners grew at about the same rate (38%) as the overall prison population (36%). New York held more than a third of all inmates (9,500) known to be HIV positive at year end 1995 (Table 11.1).

At year end 1995, 4.0% of all female state inmates were HIV positive, compared to 2.3% of male state inmates. From 1991 to 1995, the number of male state inmates infected with HIV increased 28% (from 16,150 to 20,690), while the number of females infected increased at a much faster rate—88% (from 1,159 to 2,182). The highest percentage of HIV-positive female inmates was in New York (22.7%) (Bureau of Justice Statistics, 1997; see Table 11.3); at Rikers Island jail, 26% of the women are HIV positive compared to 12% of the men (Purdy, 1997). Like their male counterparts, female inmates infected with HIV (and AIDS) are disproportionately minority and poor and have a history of IV drug use. (We shall return to the issue of gender and HIV in the conclusion.)

TABLE 11.1 Inmates in Custody of State or Federal Prison Authorities and Known to be Positive for the Human Immunodeficiency Virus, 1993-1995

Jurisdiction	Total known to be HIV positive			HIV/AIDS cases as a percentage of total custody population[a]		
	1993	1994	1995	1993	1994	1995
U.S. total[b]	21,475	22,717	24,226	2.4	2.4	2.3
Federal	959	964	822	1.2	1.1	.9
State	20,516	21,753	23,404	2.6	2.5	2.4
Northeast	10,690	11,001	12,262	7.5	7.4	7.8
Connecticut	886	940	755	6.6	6.6	5.1
Maine	8	8	4	.6	.5	.3
Massachusetts	394	388	409	3.9	3.4	3.9
New Hampshire	17	26	31	.9	1.3	1.5
New Jersey	881	770	847	4.4	3.6	3.7
New York	8,000	8,295	9,500	12.4	12.4	13.9
Pennsylvania	409	461	590	1.6	1.6	1.8
Rhode Island	89	113	126	3.4	3.8	4.4
Vermont	6	0	0	.5	0	0
Midwest	1,671	1,750	1,667	1.1	1.1	.9
Illinois	591	600	583	1.7	1.6	1.5
Indiana	—	—	—	—	—	—
Iowa	11	25	20	.2	.5	.3
Kansas	39	20	24	.7	.3	.3
Michigan	434	384	379	1.1	1.1	.9
Minnesota	30	35	46	.7	.8	1.0
Missouri	136	146	173	.8	.8	.9
Nebraska	17	16	19	.7	.6	.6
North Dakota	2	3	2	.3	.5	.3
Ohio	355	454	346	.9	1.1	.8
South Dakota	—	2	3	—	.1	.2
Wisconsin	56	65	72	.6	.6	.6
South	6,657	7,410	7,840	2.1	2.0	1.9
Alabama	194	210	222	1.1	1.1	1.1
Arkansas	80	81	83	1.0	1.0	1.0
Delaware	113	34	122	2.7	.8	2.5
District of Columbia	—	—	—	—	—	—
Florida	1,780	1,986	2,193	3.4	3.5	3.4
Georgia	745	854	828	2.7	2.6	2.4
Kentucky	42	44	41	.5	.5	.4
Louisiana	262	285	314	1.6	1.8	1.8
Maryland	769	774	724	3.8	3.7	3.4
Mississippi	118	119	138	1.4	11.2	1.4
North Carolina	485	521	526	2.2	2.2	1.9
Oklahoma	102	102	115	.8	.8	.8
South Carolina	452	434	380	2.7	2.5	2.0
Tennessee	88	89	120	.8	.7	.9

Jurisdiction	Total known to be HIV positive			HIV/AIDS cases as a percentage of total custody population[a]		
	1993	1994	1995	1993	1994	1995
Texas	1,212	1,584	1,890	1.7	1.6	1.5
Virginia	207	285	134	1.1	1.4	.6
West Virginia	8	8	10	.4	.4	.4
West	1,498	1,592	1,635	.8	.8	.8
Alaska	—	—	5	—	—	.2
Arizona	89	143	140	.5	.7	.7
California	1,048	1,055	1,042	.9	.8	.8
Colorado	74	79	93	.8	.9	1.0
Hawaii	21	14	12	.7	.5	.4
Idaho	26	20	11	1.0	.8	.4
Montana	5	7	4	.3	.4	.2
Nevada	100	122	147	1.6	1.8	1.9
New Mexico	11	19	24	.3	.5	.6
Oregon	29	24	29	.4	.3	.4
Utah	26	48	31	.9	1.5	.8
Washington	63	55	92	.6	.5	.8
Wyoming	6	6	5	.5	.6	.4

SOURCE: Bureau of Justice Statistics. 1997. *HIV in Prisons and Jails, 1995* (page 2). Washington, D.C.: U.S. Department of Justice.
— = Not reported.
a. The custody population includes only those inmates housed in a jurisdiction's facilities.
b. Totals exclude those inmates in jurisdictions that did not report data on HIV/AIDS.

Discrimination and Fringe Punishments

HIV and AIDS generate special medical and psychological needs, and the degree of suffering from these illnesses is generally determined by how adequately such needs are met. In prison, medical and psychological needs are complicated by the very nature of incarceration, including the adverse conditions of confinement (Welch, 1991b). Though being infected with HIV/AIDS is physically and emotionally debilitating in and of itself, imprisonment merely adds to the suffering by exacerbating depression, helplessness, worthlessness, and grief. Even worse, at the later stages of AIDS, neurological deficits develop along with encephalopathy, dementia, psychomotor retardation, disorientation, and seizures (McArthur, 1987). Understandably, prisoners with HIV/AIDS direct their anger not only at the disease but also at the institution for rejection, discrimination, and the denial of adequate medical care (Gostin & Lazzarini, 1997; Lawrence & Zwisohn, 1991; Potler, 1988).

TABLE 11.2 Local Jail Inmates Ever Tested for HIV and Results, by Selected Characteristics, 1995-1996

	1995-96 Survey of Local Jail Inmates		
		Tested inmates who reported results	
Characteristics	Percentage of all inmates who were ever tested	Number	Percentage who were HIV positive
All inmates	61.5	289,991	2.2
Sex			
Male	62.1	258,019	2.1
Female	68.6	31,972	2.4
Race/Hispanic origin			
White non-Hispanic	62.4	110,023	1.4
Male	62.0	98,745	1.3
Female	65.7	11,278	2.1
Black non-Hispanic	67.2	125,259	2.6
Male	66.3	110,453	2.5
Female	74.5	14,806	3.2
Hispanic	55.1	45,759	3.2
Male	53.9	40,985	3.5
Female	67.6	4,774	1.3
Other	55.3	8,950	0
Age			
24 or younger	57.6	81,228	.7
25-34	66.9	116,532	2.1
35-44	64.4	70,776	3.8
45 or older	57.8	21,455	3.0
Marital status			
Married	62.3	45,890	1.4
Widowed/divorced	61.4	48,695	3.0
Separated	64.7	25,929	2.1
Never married	62.9	169,270	2.1
Education			
Less than high school	57.8	121,589	2.3
GED	68.8	45,431	1.3
High school graduate or more	66.5	122,597	2.3

SOURCE: Bureau of Justice Statistics. 1997. *HIV in Prisons and Jails, 1995* (page 8). Washington, D.C.: U.S. Department of Justice.

As previously noted, many prisoners with HIV/AIDS are stigmatized by the society according to a larger constellation of disreputable attributes: Typically, they are lawbreakers who are impoverished, urban, minority, IV drug users (and in some cases gay), and infected with a terminal and contagious illness. Within the prison world, inmates with HIV/AIDS are devalued

TABLE 11.3 State Prison Inmates Known to be Positive for the Human Immunodeficiency Virus, by Sex, Yearend 1995

Jurisdiction	Male HIV cases		Female HIV cases	
	Number	Percentage of population	Number	Percentage of population
Total	20,690	2.3	2,182	4.0
Northeast	11,080	7.5	1,182	14.7
Connecticut	627	4.6	128	13.4
Maine	4	.3	0	0
Massachusetts	340	3.5	69	10.5
New Hampshire	17	.9	14	11.4
New Jersey	748	3.4	99	9.8
New York	8,678	13.4	822	22.7
Pennsylvania	561	1.8	29	2.0
Rhode Island	105	3.9	21	14.5
Vermont	0	0	0	0
Midwest	1,553	.9	114	1.2
Illinois	528	1.5	55	2.5
Indiana	—	—	—	—
Iowa	18	.3	2	.5
Kansas	24	.4	0	0
Michigan	364	.9	15	.8
Minnesota	41	.9	5	2.5
Missouri	164	.9	9	.8
Nebraska	19	.7	0	0
North Dakota	1	.2	1	2.7
Ohio	324	.8	22	.8
South Dakota	3	.2	0	0
Wisconsin	67	.6	5	1.0
South	6,598	1.8	740	3.2
Alabama	209	1.1	13	1.0
Arkansas	79	1.0	4	.7
Delaware	—	—	—	—
District of Columbia	—	—	—	—
Florida	1,971	3.3	222	6.1
Georgia	747	2.3	81	4.0
Kentucky	40	.4	1	.2
Louisiana	299	1.8	15	2.4
Maryland	665	3.3	59	5.5
Mississippi	136	1.4	2	.3
North Carolina	437	1.7	89	5.3
Oklahoma	105	.8	10	.8
South Carolina	—	—	—	—
Tennessee	118	.9	2	.5
Texas	1,648	1.4	242	3.0

(continued)

TABLE 11.3 Continued

Jurisdiction	Male HIV cases		Female HIV cases	
	Number	Percentage of population	Number	Percentage of population
Virginia	134	.6	0	0
West Virginia	10	.4	0	0
West	1,459	.7	146	1.0
Alaska	5	.2	0	0
Arizona	128	.6	12	.8
California	957	.8	85	.9
Colorado	87	1.0	6	.8
Hawaii	12	.5	0	0
Idaho	11	.4	0	0
Montana	4	.3	0	0
Nevada	93	1.3	24	4.6
New Mexico	23	.6	1	.3
Oregon	25	.3	4	.9
Utah	29	.8	2	.9
Washington	81	.7	11	1.4
Wyoming	4	.3	1	1.1

SOURCE: Bureau of Justice Statistics. 1997. *HIV in Prisons and Jails, 1995* (page 6). Washington, D.C.: U.S. Department of Justice.
NOTE: The sex of inmates was not reported for 502 HIV cases. Totals exclude inmates in jurisdictions that did not report data on HIV/AIDS or sex of inmates.
— = Not reported.

by both staff and other inmates to the extent that they become institutional outcasts, subjected to a level of suffering rarely found among their free-world counterparts. Even though persons with HIV/AIDS in the free world also are subjected to prejudice and discrimination, the degree of fear and hostility often is magnified in prison and jail due to the nature of captivity.

> Additional factors, unique to the incarcerated, aggravate that stress. Segregation and isolation, witnessing the deteriorating health and eventual death of fellow inmates, and the fear—heightened in the total institution of the prison—that health care is inadequate cause additional anxiety. (Juvelis, 1995, p. 6)

Under such adverse conditions, myths and misconceptions about HIV/AIDS take on a life of their own, manifesting in prison fiction that is used to justify mistreating unpopular inmates. Ostracizing—and worse, victimizing—prisoners with HIV/AIDS serves the function of informally controlling the pariahs of the prison society, thus reinforcing the hierarchy and status boundaries among different classes of inmates (see Akerstrom, 1986). Consider the following passage:

> You are a marked prisoner when you are housed on the AIDS ward. When you go down for x-rays, you see other inmates and they would say to you, "I heard you were dying." And their hand would go out as though they were about to shake hands with you and then they would hesitate and put it down. Some stand on the bench in the x-ray area so that they don't have to go near you. It really hurts. You can't wait to get out and get the "sign" off—the one around your neck that says "he's got AIDS." (Potler, 1988, p. 8)

As discussed in Chapter 8, victimization often conforms to patterns of nonenforcement and covert facilitation when abuse is permitted and encouraged by prison staff. Victimization occurs in the form of harassment and physical attacks against inmates with HIV/AIDS, and in some incidents, their prison cells are flooded with water or set afire (Potler, 1988; Welch, 1989, 1991a, 1991b).

Institutional policies and practices have the potential to either alleviate or exacerbate the suffering of prisoners with HIV/AIDS. Therefore, policies and practices that contribute directly or indirectly, intentionally or unintentionally, to pain and suffering of prisoners with HIV/AIDS shall be referred to as fringe punishments, including victimization, lack of adequate medical care, and various other forms of discrimination. We will next examine significant aspects of prison and jail management while attending to policies and practices that result in fringe punishments for prisoners with HIV/AIDS.

MYTHS, MISCONCEPTIONS, AND CORRECTIONAL POLICY ON HIV/AIDS

After more than 15 years of medical and scientific research demonstrating that HIV/AIDS cannot be transmitted through casual contact, many criminal justice and security personnel still behave on the basis of myths and misconceptions. For example, in 1995, 50 gay and lesbian officials were invited to the White House, where four security guards wore plastic gloves while conducting routine security checks on briefcases and other personal belongings (Kappeler, Blumberg, & Potter, 1996). In corrections, many staff also stray from medical and scientific knowledge and rely more on exaggerated fears in shaping their views of HIV/AIDS; contributing to these misconceptions are deep-seated anxieties and prejudices against the impoverished, urban minorities, IV drug users, and homosexuals. A common fear among correctional officers is contracting HIV while carrying out their duties, even though the Centers for Disease Control and Prevention (CDC) have not documented a single case of occupational transmission among correctional officers (or police officers) (Hammett et al., 1994; also see Flavin, 1998). Nevertheless, some offenders with HIV have been sentenced harshly by the courts for engaging in assaultive behaviors that pose relatively little danger to others; appellate courts in Georgia, Indiana, New Jersey, and Texas have upheld attempted homicide charges against seropositive offenders who bit or spit on correctional staff. In addition to spitting and biting, two other types of assaults by HIV-positive offenders have recently become subjects of controversy in corrections: injuries sustained in altercations and stabbings with an infected hypodermic needle (Kappeler et al., 1996).

In scenarios involving spitting, laboratory tests reveal that HIV is present in saliva but only in a very few infected persons (Ho et al., 1985) and that the quantity of HIV in saliva is minute, making transmission extremely unlikely (CDC, 1988). In Texas, a HIV-positive prisoner was convicted of attempted murder for spitting in the face of a correctional officer and was sentenced to life imprisonment (*Weeks v. Texas,* 1992). Curtis Weeks testified at trial that he was provoked to spit at the guard after being denied bathroom facilities while being transported between two prisons. An expert witness for the prisoner testified it is impossible to transmit HIV by spitting and reported that there had never been a documented case of such transmission, but to no avail.

Contracting HIV through biting is also remote. Researchers Richman and Richman (1993) have concluded that "the transmission of HIV through human bites is biologically possible but remains unlikely, epidemiologically insignificant, and as yet, not well documented" (p. 402). But in New Jersey, an HIV-positive prisoner was convicted of attempted murder for biting a correctional officer and was sentenced to 25 years (*New Jersey v. Smith,* 1993). The Appellate Division was not concerned whether HIV can be transmitted by biting as long as the inmate believed that it could. During the scuffle in which the officer was bitten, the inmate was reported to have shouted, "Now die, you pig! Die from what I have" (Sullivan, 1993, p. B-7). The trial judge instructed the jury: "Impossibility is not a defense to the charge of attempted murder. That is because our law, our criminal statutes, punish conduct based on state of mind" (Sullivan, 1993, p. B-7). The prosecution maintained that whether the biting could transmit HIV was legally irrelevant, but the appellants argued that Smith "was as likely to have caused the death of [corrections officers] by biting them as he was to have caused their deaths by sticking pins in dolls bearing their likenesses" ("NJ Inmate Argues for Reversal," 1992, p. 1).

Attorneys for the inmate insisted that the guilty verdict and 25-year sentence were not founded on current medical evidence or sound legal reasoning but rather driven by public hysteria regarding HIV/AIDS.

Regarding altercations with seropositive persons, transmission of HIV through open wounds has been documented in the medical literature (O'Farrell, Tovey, & Morgan-Capner, 1992). Though such cases are rare and have not involved criminal justice personnel, public safety workers are advised to follow CDC (1989) guidelines: keeping all open wounds bandaged and wearing gloves when anticipating contact with blood (or body fluids containing visible blood). Being wounded by HIV-contaminated needles also remains a concern of those working in criminal justice because such injuries do present a risk—albeit a relatively low one—of HIV transmission; experts recommend that safety procedures be followed to reduce the likelihood of these incidents (Richman & Richman, 1993).

Another popular myth suggests that HIV/AIDS is spreading rapidly within the correctional population. This myth is driven by the fear of homosexual rape and IV drug use among inmates, as well as by a general misunderstanding of how HIV is transmitted. As noted in Chapter 8, the prevalence of homosexual rape in correctional facilities is greatly exaggerated. Even though transmission does occur during incarceration, it is a relatively infrequent event, and at this time there is no evidence to support the claim that there is widespread transmission of HIV/AIDS among inmates (Hammett et al., 1994; Hammett & Moini, 1990; Vlahov et al., 1991; also see Blumberg, 1990a, 1990b; Blumberg & Langston, 1995).

Confronting myths about HIV/AIDS is important because misinformation can inflame fear and hysteria, resulting in discriminatory management practices. For instance, in 1992, Louise K. Nolley was awarded $155,000 for what a judge called humiliating and improper treatment at the Erie County Jail, where she was held on charges of forgery and passing a check without sufficient funds. Staff placed Nolley in a forensic unit usually reserved for suicidal and mentally disturbed inmates, required that she wear plastic gloves when she used the typewriter in the jail library, and denied her regular attendance at Roman Catholic services. Jailers also attached red stickers on all her belongings indicating that she had AIDS, a violation of New York State law, which prohibits the disclosure that a person has tested positive for HIV. Judge John T. Curtain concluded: "There is no question that the red sticker policy was developed, not in response to contagious diseases in general, but specifically in response to the hysteria over HIV and AIDS" (Sullivan, 1992, p. B-4). Judge Curtain also cited the Erie County Jail for violating regulations adopted by the New York State Department of Correction Services in 1987, under which inmates who test positive for HIV cannot be isolated from the general prison population. The basis of the ruling and award rested on compensatory and punitive damages for AIDS discrimination (*Nolley v. County of Erie,* 1991). Norman Siegel, executive director of the New York American Civil Liberties Union (ACLU), added: "We applaud Judge Curtin for his courageous and legally correct decision. It sends a strong message that such stigmatization will not be tolerated by the courts and that once and for all we must end this kind of hysteria" (Sullivan, 1992, p. B-4).

The red sticker alert controversy in *Nolley* is reminiscent of other correctional practices that blatantly stigmatize and humiliate unpopular prisoners. For more than 15 years, homosexual inmates held at the Polk County Jail in Florida were segregated and required to wear pink bracelets symbolizing their sexual preference. In 1989, jail officials, facing legal action, discontinued the practice of tagging and segregating homosexuals. Six lesbians complained to the ACLU that being "pink-tagged" had limited their privileges and brought harsh treatment from jailers. According to ACLU attorney Jim West, "It reflects homophobia. . . . Labeling people's clothing based on a sexual preference seems an extreme response that doesn't warrant it" ("Pink Bracelets for Homosexuals," 1989, p. 35; "Red Tags for Gays," 1990). (Incidentally, in 1987, a federal court ruled against segregation of homosexuals in Indiana correctional facilities.) Red-tagging homosexual prisoners also should be understood in a larger social and historical context. During the Third Reich of the 1930s and 1940s, German Nazis held between 10,000 and 15,000 homosexuals in concentration camps for violating Paragraph 175 of the German criminal code, which called for the imprisonment of any "male who commits lewd and lascivious acts with another male." Under Nazi rule, homosexuality was referred to as sinfully deviant and sexually subversive. While in the camps, homosexuals wore uniforms bearing pink triangles. Many were tortured and castrated; 60% of the incarcerated homosexuals died in the camps (Dunlop, 1995; Heger, 1972; Plant, 1986, 1989).

Mass Screening and Prisoner Stratification

Among the most controversial management issues in dealing with HIV/AIDS in corrections is mass screening, "the mandatory testing of all inmates, or all releases, in the absence of clinical indicators" (Hammett & Moini, 1990, p. 4). Proponents of mass screening often rely on exaggerated views or myths about HIV/AIDS to support their views. For instance, proponents assume that the rates of transmission are higher in correctional institutions than in the larger society and that screening is therefore necessary to identify infected inmates. Opponents of mass screening point out that there is no evidence of higher transmission rates in prisons and jails. More importantly, educational programs can be offered to all inmates without identifying infected prisoners. Hammett (1989) further emphasized that mass screening can lead to unnecessarily and falsely stratifying the inmate population into a stigmatized class and a "safe" class. (This limitation of mass screening is particularly evident in light of the lengthy incubation period during which infected persons do not test positive.)

Mass screening also raises issues of confidentiality and reliability. Opponents assert that the confidentiality of test results is difficult to protect and that patient information (or rumors) can lead to victimization during incarceration and to discrimination upon release (e.g., in obtaining health insurance, housing, and employment). The reliability of testing has been questioned, and the cost of repeat tests to confirm cases is prohibitive, especially in large institutions (Carroll, 1992).

Legal issues related to mass screening also must be addressed. Opponents point out that mass screening (which involves involuntary testing) can be challenged on the basis of existing laws that require the person's informed consent. Because of these issues, voluntary (or on-request) testing for early detection (or if clinical symptoms are present) and therapeutic intervention have become the trend; arrangements for voluntary testing are made with local public health departments or other agencies. In addition, voluntary testing is available to inmates and staff in response to possible transmission incidents. Mass screening creates additional funding difficulties for corrections and in the end often creates more problems than it solves (Hammett et al., 1994; Hammett & Moini, 1990).

Currently, each state, the District of Columbia, and the Federal Bureau of Prisons test their inmates for HIV on the basis of certain criteria (Table 11.4). Most jurisdictions (45 out of 52) test inmates if they have HIV-related symptoms or if the inmates request a test. Twenty-four states test inmates after they are involved in an incident, and 15 states test inmates who belong to specific "high-risk groups." Sixteen states test all inmates who enter their facilities. Three of these states (Alabama, Missouri, and Nevada) and the Federal Bureau of Prisons test inmates upon their release. Rhode Island, Utah, and Wyoming test all inmates currently in custody. Massachusetts, New York, and the Federal Bureau of Prisons test inmates selected at random (Bureau of Justice Statistics, 1997).

TABLE 11.4 Prison System Testing Policies for the Antibody to the Human Immunodeficiency Virus, by Jurisdiction, 1995

	All Inmates								
Jurisdiction	Entering	Custody	Upon release	High-risk group	Inmate request	Clinical indication	Involvement in incident	Random sample	Other
Federal					■	■		■	
Northeast									
Connecticut						■			
Maine								■	
Massachusetts	■			■	■				
New Hampshire					■ ■	■	■		
New Jersey									■
New York				■	■ ■	■	■	■	
Pennsylvania					■ ■	■ ■	■ ■		
Rhode Island	■	■			■	■	■		
Vermont									
Midwest									
Illinois	■			■ ■	■ ■	■ ■	■ ■		
Indiana				■	■	■			
Iowa									
Kansas					■	■	■		
Michigan	■			■ ■	■ ■	■ ■	■ ■		
Minnesota	■		■	■ ■	■ ■	■ ■	■ ■		
Missouri	■				■	■	■		
Nebraska	■				■	■	■		
North Dakota									
Ohio				■	■	■	■		
South Dakota					■ ■	■			■
Wisconsin					■				■

South
Alabama
Arkansas
Delaware
District of Columbia
Florida
Georgia
Kentucky
Louisiana
Maryland
Mississippi
North Carolina
Oklahoma
South Carolina
Tennessee
Texas
Virginia
West Virginia

West
Alaska
Arizona
California
Colorado
Hawaii
Idaho
Montana
Nevada
New Mexico
Oregon
Utah
Washington
Wyoming

SOURCE: Bureau of Justice Statistics. 1997. *HIV in Prisons and Jails, 1995* (page 7). Washington, D.C.: US Department of Justice.

DENIAL OF ADEQUATE MEDICAL CARE

The denial of adequate medical care to prisoners with HIV/AIDS constitutes a fringe punishment because it exacerbates both physical and emotional suffering among this population. Partially as a result of the "penal harm movement," proposals to allocate health care dollars to corrections have become increasingly unpopular, especially when those who require the expensive medications and services are infected with illnesses brought on by IV drug use and homosexual sex. Efforts to generate greater public concern for treating prisoners with HIV/AIDS often are hampered by lack of awareness, apathy, and in some instances, hostility. According to Ronald Bogard, a former general counsel of the New York City Health Department, there has been little effort to determine the extent of the problem: "Not only do we not know, we don't really care, because of the people that are involved and the money that is involved" (Purdy, 1997, p. 28).

A particularly expensive feature of HIV/AIDS intervention is the distribution of azidothymidine (AZT), a medication that is believed to retard the progression of the disease in some patients. Due to its cost, however, correctional systems may not properly distribute AZT in ways required for effectiveness: For example, dosages may be improperly rationed. Hammett and Moini (1990) found that nearly one-fourth of the prisons and jails do not dispense AZT to all prisoners who meet the eligibility requirements, even though physicians acknowledge that such behavior is unethical (see Purdy, 1997). A similar treatment gaining interest in and outside of prison is the so-called HIV cocktail, a combination of medications designed to prevent the reproduction of the virus. However, financial barriers abound. In New Jersey, the annual expense for treating one prisoner with the HIV cocktail costs $10,000 to $15,000, and the cost jumps to $70,000 for prisoners with full-blown AIDS. These and other medical costs have prompted New Jersey's Correctional Health Services—a private contractor—to renegotiate part of its contract. Currently, the medical plan covers annual expenses to the tune of $2,900 per inmate; in 1997, Correctional Health Services requested an additional $5 million to meet HIV-related expenses (Sforza, 1998b).

Overall, correctional health care is woefully inadequate, and even under the best circumstances it is marred by inconsistent care; indeed, the quality of medical services varies from state to state and prison to prison. Whereas it is tempting to compromise medical care for inmates because of budgetary constraints, many administrators deal with these problems by lobbying state officials for additional funding. In some cases, litigation geared toward increasing spending for medical services in corrections has obtained support from the courts. Attorneys representing prisoners with HIV/AIDS, often in class action suits, insist that the denial of adequate care constitutes cruel and unusual punishment, which is unconstitutional under the Eighth Amendment of the U.S. Constitution. "A sick person on the street can go to an emergency room. But these people can't because they're under lock and key, so that puts a big responsibility on the person holding the key" says Maddie LaMarre, clinical services coordinator for the Georgia prison system (Purdy, 1997, p. 28). Despite some important legal victories, financial obstacles combined with larger social forces (e.g., political apathy) and organizational forces (e.g., lack of equipment, supplies, and staff) continue to strain medical attention for inmates with HIV/AIDS (see Blumberg, 1990a, 1990b; Blumberg & Mahaffey-Sapp, 1997; Bolonsky et al., 1994; Koehler, 1994; Thomas & Moerings, 1994). Michael Wiseman of the Prisoners Rights Project of the Legal Aid Society of New York comments: "Prisons were never designed to deliver medical treatment, they were designed to keep people locked up. Before HIV prisons never gave good care. But with HIV, its turned a lot of them into death camps" (quoted in Gross, 1993, p. A-12).

For several years, many prisoners with HIV/AIDS have formally complained to the courts that they have been denied adequate medical care. As a result of litigation, some medical services have improved. Nevertheless, disparities in treatment for HIV/AIDS persist because prisoners do not have a constitutional right to "every potential beneficial medical procedure" (Friedman, 1992, pp. 933-934; also see *Adams v. Poag,* 1995; Vaughn & Carroll, 1998). In *Harris v. Thigpen* (1991), the district court ruled that inmates are not entitled to state-of-the-art medical care and that reasonable care (determined by community standards) is constitutionally sufficient. Questions persist as to whether many prisoners with HIV/AIDS are receiving even basic medical attention: "Prisoners with AIDS live about half as long following diagnosis as persons in the community" (Committee on the Judiciary, 1991, p. 86; U.S. General Accounting Office, 1994; Vaughn & Carroll, 1998). Admittedly, the accelerated death rate among inmates also may be related to the poor health of inmates before entering prison (Marquart, Merianos, Cuvelier, & Carroll, 1996). Still, it is commonly argued that denial of medical care is the result of deliberate indifference to the prisoners' medical needs or a form of retaliation against prisoners for exercising their right to contest the charges against them *(Proctor v. Alameda County,* 1992). Adhering to U.S. Public Health Guidelines, the New Jersey Department of Corrections promised to provide HIV-positive prisoners with comprehensive medical care and education *(Roe et al. v. Fauver et al.,* 1992; also see *Fitzhugh v. Wyoming*

Board of Charities and Reform, 1991). Remember, the quality of medical care for prisoners is uneven and varies from state to state as well as facility to facility; relatedly, prisoners with HIV/AIDs at some institutions have been denied participation in programs and activities that present no risk of viral transmission, constituting a clear examples of exclusion, rejection, and discrimination (Cauchon, 1995; also see Jacobs, 1995, and Middleton & Lee, 1997, for other legal issues pertaining to prisoners with HIV/AIDS).

RELATED FORMS OF DISCRIMINATION

Many issues germane to prisoners with HIV/AIDS addressed thus far—stigma, victimization, segregation, and denial of adequate health care—involve a common complaint: namely, discrimination. Indeed, discrimination toward prisoners with HIV/AIDS not only reinforces stigma and related manifestations of inequality but also constitutes another fringe punishment. Whether intentional or unintentional, discrimination against prisoners with HIV/AIDS produces an added degree of suffering. Many discrimination lawsuits filed by prisoners with HIV/AIDS have reached the judiciary, resulting in complex and conflicting rulings. In addition to demanding adequate medical care, other chief areas of litigation are challenges to mandatory testing, confidentiality, segregation, and access to programs.

In resolving a complaint against Nevada's mandatory HIV-testing policy, the court reversed a district court's summary judgment holding that the state did not offer evidence that its policy was reasonably related to legitimate penological interests (*Walker v. Sumner,* 1990; also see *Turner v. Safley,* 1987). Conversely, the Tenth Circuit in 1989 rejected appellants' claims that they had been unconstitutionally tested for HIV and segregated from the general prison population (*Dunn v. White,* 1989). Recognizing inmate confidentiality and privacy interests, a federal district court limited disclosure of medical records to those involved in litigation who needed access to them (*Doe v. Meachum,* 1989; also see *Doe v. City of Cleveland,* 1991).

Segregation in correctional housing, viewed as discrimination by prisoners with HIV/AIDS, remains an ongoing issue in litigation. As noted previously in *Nolley,* the court ruled against the segregation of a female prisoner with AIDS; however, in *Harris,* the Federal Appeals Court for the Eleventh Circuit upheld the regulation of the Alabama Corrections Department (DOC) requiring the HIV antibody testing and segregation of those determined to be HIV positive. The district court insisted that segregation was not a form of discrimination; rather, it was a necessary measure to protect all inmates from victimization. But the HIV-positive inmates claimed that their blanket exclusion from prison education, employment, and community placement programs violated section 504 of the Rehabilitation Act of 1973. Supporting DOC's policies, the district court determined that even after reasonable accommodations, a significant risk of HIV transmission would exist (see Dalrymple-Blackburn, 1995). Conversely, a consent decree in New Jersey (*Roe et al. v. Fauver et al.*, 1992) terminated the practice of segregating inmates with AIDS from the general population and initiated the development of treatment and education programs.

In *Farmer v. Moritsugu* (1990), a federal court ruled that the Federal Bureau of Prisons did not violate equal protection rights by prohibiting HIV-positive inmates from working in prison hospitals and food services; the institution claims that such a policy is necessary to maintain order and security. However, a district court in Arizona determined that the state department of correction's prohibition against assignment of prisoners with HIV to food service jobs violated Section 504 of the Rehabilitation Act. The court permitted the department of corrections to institute individual determinations that would bar certain HIV-positive inmates from such employment (by demonstrating a significant risk) but ruled that the department could not enforce a blanket policy (*Casey v. Lewis,* 1991). In 1994, a federal appeals court overturned a federal judge's ruling allowing HIV-positive prisoners to serve food to the general prison population at the Vacaville penitentiary in California, citing the authorities' fears of a prison riot: "Other inmates will perceive a threat regardless of the scientific research or medical pronouncements," and this practice may result in "violent actions against the inmates who have the virus, inmates they perceive have the virus, or the staff that permits the perceived risk," said the U.S. Court of Appeals for the Ninth Circuit (*Gates v. Rowland,* 1994). ACLU attorney Matthew Coles said the ruling was "a serious setback for the rights of disabled prisoners" ("Limits Are Put on Prisoners," 1994, p. 40) that would reinforce irrational fears and prejudice, resulting in employment discrimination (see Lazzo & McElgunn, 1986).

Finally, the ongoing controversy over the distribution of condoms has become an ideological battleground in corrections. Many criminal justice officials oppose condom distribution, often citing reasons of morality. "It's ludicrous. If we issue condoms, then it would send a message that the Sheriff's Department would be responsible for illegal or immoral behavior," said Jack Quigley, Bergen County, New Jersey, undersheriff. Revealing his belief that homosexuality is wrong and that gays should be converted to straight, Quigley continued, "The most basic concept of rehabilitation is to accept responsibility for one's behavior" (quoted in Sforza, 1998a, p. A-12). Many public health experts, however, favor condom distribution, including the New Jersey Governor's Advisory Council and the HIV Prevention Community Planning Group (PCPG), which offers recommendations to the state's health department. Gisele Pemberton of the HIV PCPG argued, "This is one of the populations already marginalized and discriminated against. They of all people should have access to condoms" (Sforza, 1998a, p. A-12). Currently, only five correctional systems make condoms available to inmates; administrators defend this practice by arguing that they are not condoning the behavior but recognizing that sexual contact does occur in institutions (Hammett et al., 1994).

The Phenomenology of Imprisonment and Suffering

When imprisonment eventually replaced public spectacle and corporal punishment as the prevailing method of punishment, retribution was concealed behind prison walls, where its aim shifted from the body to the mind; consequently, a qualitatively different form of suffering was produced (Foucault, 1979). Since then, inflicting emotional pain on lawbreakers has remained a significant rationale for incarceration; such anguish is achieved by the deprivation of liberty, goods and services, heterosexual relationships, autonomy, and security (Sykes, 1958; also see Johnson & Toch, 1982; Welch, 1996b). Suffering inherent to the prison experience also is compounded by the length of time a convict spends incarcerated; indeed, a prominent feature of contemporary sentencing is its quantification, measuring prison terms by years, months, and days. This construction of punishment, which Foucault (1979) termed the penal calculus, is to a great extent based on the temporal component of imprisonment, thus invoking lessons of phenomenology.

As a framework for studying the diversity of consciousness and experience, phenomenology has benefited from the richly layered works of philosophers and sociologists, especially concerning time. Husserl (1962) theorized that temporality significantly shapes the way people apprehend the world around them, and Heidegger (1949) offered an existentially informed interpretation of the temporal field, noting that perceptions of time direct the course of future actions. Drawing on both of these insights, Sartre (1966) reasoned that futureness—the projected plans of action—creates meaning for the present. The role of time remains an integral part of the life-worlds that extend beyond personal to social experience; in this context, the construction of time becomes a shared reality, offering a unity of meaning (Schutz & Luckmann, 1973). Meisenhelder (1985) summarized these ideas, contending that "all human activity, as seen phenomenologically, is then temporally structured through and as a casting of oneself toward the future" (p. 42). The perspective is reminiscent of the old adage that life is what one does while planning the future.

The prison world is structured to be distinct and separate from the free world, deliberately adopting the model of institutionalization in routinizing, scheduling, and controlling the lives of inmates (Goffman, 1961; Rothman, 1971; Sykes, 1958). "Prisoners are effects, rather than causes: That is, they perceive themselves as being nearly wholly determined by the institution" (Meisenhelder, 1985, p. 43). Foucault (1979) similarly concluded that modern imprisonment transforms prisoners from subjects to objects. The unique shift of the temporal field further contributes to the nature of the prison world in that time is experienced as a burden rather than a resource. Looking toward the future gives meaning to one's life: "Without a definite sense of attainable future, time is likely to be experienced as meaningless, empty, and boring" (Meisenhelder, 1985, p. 45). Farber (1944) also advanced our understanding of the phenomenology of the prison world, proposing that suffering is exacerbated by making prisoners feel that their future is uncertain. With this in mind, the phenomenology of suffering has particular relevance to prisoners with HIV/AIDS, especially given the gravity of the temporal field and its significance to futureness.

In directing our attention to the suffering of prisoners with HIV/AIDS, we have explored the physical and psychological dimensions of the illness along with their sociological implications: adverse societal reaction, stigma, discrimination, and various fringe punishments, including the denial of adequate health care. As mentioned throughout, prisoners with HIV/AIDS are presumably subjected not only to qualitatively different pains of imprisonment, but to quantitatively greater suffering than that of other inmates. To decipher these differences in suffering, it is crucial to return to phenomenology, the temporal component of incarceration, and the basic human tendency to look toward the future in creating meaning for life and personal existence. Because prisoners perceive time as a burden rather than a resource, their suffering is compounded by the sense that their lives are wasting away. For this reason, many inmates feel that their personal existence has little meaning; when asked rhetorically what they do while imprisoned, convicts flatly reply, "Time." Similarly, the official views of the state and the sentiments popular among citizens are that prisoners should serve time.

A sense of futurelessness for most inmates is temporary because they resume their meaningful lives upon returning to the free world, but for prisoners dying of AIDS it is not: They must cope with a permanent sense of futurelessness. The nature of their suffering is compounded by the physical and psychological aspects of AIDS, including anxiety, confusion, depression, and disorientation. In the context of the prison world, these sources of stress are exacerbated by feelings of isolation brought on by victimization and discrimination (Welch, 1991a). While imprisoned, inmates alter their sense of self as a result of developing a heightened self-consciousness due to continuous and intense introspection (Meisenhelder, 1985). Such reflection, however, can lead them to an alarming awareness of their own physical deterioration, especially if they are afflicted with terminal illnesses such as AIDS.

Given the burden of a shifting temporal field in the prison world, many inmates engage in consuming activities (e.g., education, employment) for the purpose of making time pass quickly, thus partially alleviating their suffering. But this coping mechanism may not be useful for prisoners dying from AIDS, presumably owing to their reluctance to accelerate death. Arguably, for prisoners dying of AIDS, experiencing time slowly merely prolongs their suffering and deepens their sense of futurelessness. Therefore, prisoners dying of AIDS are subjected to greater degrees of suffering intensified by the harsh conditions of confinement and the temporal component of imprisonment (Welch, 1991a).

Depending on the circumstances of the illness, suffering can be portrayed as honorable or dishonorable. Sontag (1989) reminded us that etymologically, *patient* means "sufferer" and that "it is not suffering as such that is most deeply feared but suffering that degrades" (p. 37). Rarely are those dying of AIDS behind bars depicted as patients, an identity that might connote dignity and honor; rather they die as prisoners, an identity spoiled by degradation and dishonor.

Conclusion

This chapter set out to explore the subject of prisoners with HIV/AIDS by integrating concepts drawn from macro-, meso-, and microsociologies. From a macro perspective, we attended to the production of deviance in capitalist society and its mechanisms to socially control those marginalized. The correctional system as a whole serves a macrosociological function in the social control apparatus, but penal institutions are governed more by mesosociological and organizational forces that directly and indirectly shape the prison experience, a microsociological phenomenon. These levels of analysis contributed to our examination of prisoners with HIV/AIDS and punishment, with particular relevance to the processing of deviance, stigmatization, and the production of suffering. It was proposed that retribution against prisoners with HIV/AIDS is driven largely by punitive conceptions of the illness, perpetuating the belief that they are being judged and punished by a higher power for having indulged in illegal drugs or homosexuality. As Sontag (1989) noted, AIDS is "a theodicy as well as a demonology, it not only stipulates something emblematic of evil but makes this the bearer of a rough, terrible justice" (p. 57). Indeed, the stigma attached to prisoners with HIV/AIDS is also amplified by their status as lawbreakers. As a result, they are subjected to fringe punishments during their incarceration, including victimization and various forms of discrimination—most notably, the denial of adequate medical care. Altogether, these fringe punishments intensify and heighten the suffering of prisoners with HIV/AIDS.

As mentioned repeatedly, the war on drugs continues to transform significantly the size and scope of corrections. Not only are prison and jail populations growing at unprecedented rates, but the influx of IV drug users infected with HIV/AIDS is straining the traditional function of penal institutions because greater consideration is now being given to medical and health care. These transformations can be understood in terms of importation and deprivation in the prison world. The harsh character of prison society is shaped by the attributes of inmates imported from the street. Still, the suffering inherent in life behind bars is produced by the deprivations inherent in incarceration. Both perspectives apply to our analysis: The war on drugs imports offenders infected with HIV/AIDS into correctional facilities, where they are deprived of, among other things, adequate medical attention.

The importation and deprivation models also have gender implications, especially in the case of women drug offenders caught in the machinery of the coercive drug control. Since 1986, the volume of women sentenced to state prisons for drug violations has nearly tripled (Bureau of Justice Statistics, 1994). More to the point, many of these women also are infected with HIV or have been diagnosed with AIDS. As previously noted, the percentage of HIV-positive female inmates (4.0%) is substantially higher than that of male inmates (2.3%), and between 1991 and 1995, the number of HIV-infected female prisoners increased 88% (Bureau of Justice Statistics, 1997). Like their male counterparts, HIV-infected women prisoners are typically minorities with low socioeconomic status; moreover, nearly 64% of female inmates are mothers, and 56% have children under the age of 18 (Bureau of Justice

Statistics, 1994). Undoubtedly, the pain of separation—another deprivation of incarceration—for these mothers (and their children) is immense, and in cases in which the mother also is inflicted with HIV/AIDS, their suffering is compounded exponentially. (The emotional toll for these mothers is even higher in situations where their children also are infected with HIV; see Clark & Boudin, 1990; Hammett et al., 1994; Luxemberg & Guild, 1993; Mahan, 1996; Schneider, 1992; Viadro & Earp, 1991; refer to Chapter 5). In view of a heightened form of suffering among prisoners with AIDS, some government officials have begun to support legislation known as "compassionate release" or "medical parole" that leads to the early release of prisoners who are dying of AIDS and other terminal diseases (except those convicted of violent offenses; see Clines, 1993; New York State Commission of Correction, 1987).[2]

Ironically, the problem of HIV/AIDS in corrections is exacerbated rather than resolved by larger social (macro) and criminal justice (meso) policies, namely the criminalization of drugs and the reluctance (or inability) of institutions to administer adequate health care. This form of discrimination is fueled by a lack of general awareness on the one hand and apathy (or even hostility) against prisoners with HIV/AIDS on the other. According to John Miles, a special assistant for corrections and substance abuse at the CDC, "This is not just a hidden population. This is an invisible population. The public doesn't like to spend the money" (Purdy, 1997, p. 28). Due to the multiple and diverse problems caused by the war on drugs, correctional institutions are increasingly forced to function also as infirmaries for prisoners with HIV/AIDS; but without sufficient funding for medical care, they merely contain and aggravate the suffering of illness instead of relieving it.

Notes

1. In the United States, the HIV/AIDS epidemic was concentrated among urban gay men in the early 1980s; however, in the late 1990s, the proportion of those with the disease has become increasingly black. "African-Americans make up 13% of the U.S. population. But they account for about 57% of all new infections with HIV, according to CDC" (Stolberg, 1998, p. A-1). For people aged 13 to 24 with AIDS, the proportion of blacks is even higher, 63%. Currently, AIDS is the leading cause of death among black people aged 25 to 44 (Ireland, 1998; Stolberg, 1998).

2. Additional policy recommendations have been made by the National Commission on HIV/AIDS advancing efforts to medicalize, not criminalize, problems associated with drugs and HIV/AIDS—among them that (a) the federal government should devise a single plan for the nation to combat HIV/AIDS; (b) treatment for drug abuse should be made available to all who need it; (c) laws and regulations preventing drug users

from getting clean needles and bleach for cleaning them should be abolished; and (d) medical coverage should be provided for all citizens, and the cost of prescription drugs should be covered. These suggestions have the potential to improve the effectiveness of the criminal justice system by relieving it of unnecessary responsibilities and inappropriate demands, such as those related to drug control.

References

Adams v. Poag 61 F.3d 1537 (11th Cir 1995).
Akerstrom, M. (1986). Outcasts in prison: The cases of informers and sex offenders. *Deviant Behavior, 7,* 1-12.
Bayer, R., & Kirp, D. (1992). The United States at the center of the storm. (pp. 7-47). In D. Kirp & R. Bayer (Eds.), *AIDS in the industrialized democracies: Passions, politics, and policies.* New Brunswick, NJ: Rutgers University Press.
Becker, H. (1963). *Outsiders: Studies in the sociology of deviance.* New York: Free Press.
Blumberg, M. (1990a). *AIDS: The impact on the criminal justice system.* Columbus, OH: Merrill.
Blumberg, M. (1990b). The transmission of HIV: Exploring some misconceptions related to criminal justice. *Criminal Justice Policy Review, 4,* 288-305.
Blumberg, M., & Langston, D. (1995). The impact of HIV/AIDS and tuberculosis on corrections. In K. Haas & G. Alpert (Eds.), *The dilemmas of corrections: Contemporary readings* (pp. 572-584). Prospect Heights, IL: Waveland.
Blumberg, M., & Mahaffey-Sapp, C. (1997). Health care issues in correctional institutions. In M. Schwartz & L. Travis (Eds.), *Corrections: An issues approach* (4th ed., pp. 333-344). Cincinnati, OH: Anderson.
Bolonsky, S., Kerr, S., Harris, B., Gaiter, J., Fichtner, R., & Kennedy, M. (1994). HIV prevention in prisons and jails: Obstacles and opportunities. *Public Health Reports, 109,* 615-625.
Bureau of Justice Statistics. (1994). *Women in prison.* Washington, DC: U.S. Department of Justice.
Bureau of Justice Statistics. (1997). *HIV in prisons and jails, 1995.* Washington, DC: U.S. Department of Justice.
Carroll, L. (1992). AIDS and human rights in the prison: A comment on the ethics of screening and segregation. In C. A. Hartjen & E. E. Rhine (Eds.), *Correctional theory and practice.* Chicago: Nelson-Hall.
Casey v. Lewis 773 F.Supp. 1365 (D. Ariz. 1991).
Cauchon, D. (1995, March 31). AIDS in prison: Locked up and locked out. *USA Today,* p. 6-A.
Centers for Disease Control and Prevention. (1988, June 24). Update: Universal precautions for prevention of transmission of human immunodeficiency virus, hepatitis B virus, and other bloodborne pathogens in health-care settings. *Morbidity and Mortality Weekly Report, 37,* 2.
Centers for Disease Control and Prevention. (1989). Guidelines for prevention of transmission of HIV and hepatitis B virus to health-care and public safety workers. *Morbidity and Mortality Weekly Report, 38,* S-6.
Clark, J., & Boudin, K. (1990). Community of women organize themselves to cope with the AIDS crisis: A case study from Bedford Hills Correctional Facility. *Social Justice, 17*(2), 90-109.
Clear, T. (1994). *Harm in American penology: Offenders, victims, and their communities.* Albany: State University of New York Press.
Clines, F. (1993, January 5). Freeing inmates with AIDS in time to die. *New York Times,* pp. A1, B-4.
Cohen, S. (1973). *Folk devils and moral panics.* Herts, UK: Paladin.

Committee on the Judiciary, House of Representatives. (1991). *Medical care for the prison population*. Washington, DC: Government Printing Office.

Cullen, F. (1995). Assessing the penal harm movement. *Journal of Research in Crime and Delinquency, 32*, 338-358.

Dalrymple-Blackburn, D. (1995). AIDS, prisoners, and the Americans with Disabilities Act. *Utah Law Review, 717*, 839-885.

Doe v. City of Cleveland, 788 F.Supp. 979 (N.D. Ohio 1991).

Doe v. Meachum, 126 F.D.R. 444 (D. Conn. 1989).

Dunlop, D. (1995, June 26). Personalizing Nazis' homosexual victims. *New York Times*, pp. A-1, B-4.

Dunn v. White, 800 F.2d 1188 (10th Cir. 1989).

Farber, M. (1944). Suffering and time perspective in the prisoner. In K. Lewin (Ed.), *Authority and frustration* (pp. 155-213). Iowa City: Iowa University Press.

Farmer v. Moritsugu, 742 F.Supp. 525 (W.D. Wisc. 1990).

Fitzhugh v. Wyoming Board of Charities and Reform, No. 91-CV-0106-B, DC Wyoming (1991).

Flanagan, T. (1996). Reform or punish: Americans' views of the correctional system. In T. Flanagan & D. Longmire (Eds.), *Americans view crime and justice* (pp. 75-92). Thousand Oaks, CA: Sage.

Flavin, J. (1998). Fear and policing in the age of HIV/AIDS. *Critical Criminologist, 8*(3), 12-15.

Foucault, M. (1979). *Discipline and punish: The birth of the prison*. New York: Vintage.

Frankford, E., & Snitow, A. (1972, July/August). The trap of domesticity: Notes on the family. *Socialist Revolution, 9*, 83-94.

Friedman, M. (1992). Cruel and unusual punishment in the provision of prison medical care: Challenging the deliberate indifference standard. *Vanderbilt Law Review, 45*, 921-949.

Gates v. Rowland. 39 F 3d 1439 (9th Cir. 1994).

Goffman, E. (1961). *Asylums: Essays on the social situation of mental patients and other inmates*. Garden City, NY: Anchor.

Goffman, E. (1963). *Stigma: Notes on the management of spoiled identity*. Englewood Cliffs, NJ: Prentice Hall.

Gostin, L., & Lazzarini, Z. (1997). *Human rights and public health in the AIDS pandemic*. New York: Oxford University Press.

Gross, J. (1993, January 25). California inmates win better prison AIDS care. *New York Times*,, p. A-12.

Hammett, T. M. (1989). *1988 update: AIDS in correctional facilities*. Washington, DC: National Institute of Justice.

Hammett, T., & Harrold, L. (1994). *Tuberculosis in correctional facilities*. Washington, DC: National Institute of Justice.

Hammett, T., Harrold, L., Gross, M., & Epstein, J. (1994). *1992 update: HIV/AIDS in correctional facilities*. Washington, DC: National Institute of Justice.

Hammett, T., & Moini, S. (1990). *Update on AIDS in prisons and jails*. Washington, DC: National Institute of Justice.

Harris v. Thigpen, 941 F.2d 1495 (11th Cir. 1991).

Hawthorne, N. (1962). *The scarlet letter*. Columbus: Ohio State University Press. (Original work published 1850)

Heger, H. (1972). *The men with the pink triangle*. New York: Alyson.

Heidegger, M. (1949). *Existence and being*. Chicago: Henry Regnery.

Ho, D., Byington, R., Schooley, R., Flynn, T., Rota, T., & Hirsch, M. (1985). Infrequency and isolation of HTLV-111 virus from saliva in AIDS. *New England Journal of Medicine, 313*, 1606-1616.

Huber, J., & Schneider, B. (1992). *The social contexts of AIDS*. Thousand Oaks, CA: Sage.

Husserl, E. (1962). *Ideas*. New York: Collier.

Ireland, D. (1998, April 20). Silence kills blacks. *Nation,*, pp. 6-7.
Irwin, J. (1985). *The jail: Managing the underclass in American society.* Berkeley: University of California Press.
Jacobs, S. (1995). AIDS in correctional facilities: Current status of legal issues critical to policy development. *Journal of Criminal Justice, 23,* 209-221.
Johnson, R., & Toch, H. (1982). *The pains of imprisonment.* Prospect Heights, IL: Waveland.
Johnson, W., Bennett, K., & Flanagan, T. (1997). Getting tough on prisoners: Results from the National Corrections Executive Survey, 1995. *Crime and Delinquency, 43*(1), 24-41.
Juvelis, J. (1995, April/May). The stress factor for HIV+ prisoners. *AIDS and Society, 6,* 6, 10.
Kappeler, V., Blumberg, M., & Potter, G. (1996). *The mythology of crime and criminal justice* (2nd ed.). Prospect Heights, IL: Waveland.
Koehler, R. (1994). HIV infection, TB, and the health crisis in corrections. *Public Administration Review, 54,* 31-35.
Lawrence, J., & Zwisohn, V. (1991). AIDS in jail. In J. A. Thompson & G. L. Mays (Eds.), *American jails: Public policy issues* (pp. 116-129). Chicago: Nelson-Hall.
Lazzo, M., & McElgunn, C. (1986). Recent developments: Public health and employment issues generated by the AIDS crisis. *Washburn Law Review, 25,* 505-535.
Limits are put on prisoners with H.I.V. (1994, November 6). *New York Times,* p. 40.
Luxemberg, J., & Guild, T. E. (1993). Women, AIDS, and the criminal justice system. In R. Muraskin & T. Alleman (Eds.), *It's a crime: Women and justice* (pp. 77-160). Englewood Cliffs, NJ: Regents/Prentice Hall.
Mahan, S. (1996). *Crack cocaine, crime and women: Legal, social and treatment issues.* Thousand Oaks, CA: Sage.
Marquart, J., Merianos, E., Cuvelier, S., & Carroll, L. (1996). Thinking about the relationship between health dynamics in the free community and the prison. *Crime and Delinquency, 42,* 331-360.
Marx, K. (1906). *Capital* (Vol. 1; S. Moore & E. Aveling, Trans.; F. Engels, Ed.). New York: International Publishers.
Masters, W., & Johnson, V. (1988). *Crisis: Heterosexual behavior in the age of AIDS.* New York: Grove.
McArthur, J. C. (1987). Neurological manifestations of AIDS. *Medicine, 66,* 407-437.
Meisenhelder, T. (1985). An essay on time and the phenomenology of imprisonment. *Deviant Behavior, 6,* 39-56.
Middleton, J., & Lee, D. (1997). *1997 AIDS docket.* New York: American Civil Liberties Union AIDS Project.
National Commission on Acquired Immune Deficiency Syndrome. (1991). *Report: HIV disease in correctional facilities.* Washington, DC: Author.
New Jersey v. Smith, NJ Super.Ct., App. Div., No. A-636389-T4 (1993).
New York State Commission of Correction. (1987). *Acquired immune deficiency syndrome: A demographic profile of New York State inmate mortalities, 1981-1986.* Albany, NY: Author.
NJ inmate argues for reversal of 25-year AIDS bite jail sentence. (1992, December 22). *AIDS Litigation Reporter,* , p. 1.
Nolley v. County of Erie, 776 F.Supp. 715 W.D. N.Y. (1991).
O'Farrell, N., Tovey, S., & Morgan-Capner, P. (1992). Transmission of HIV-1 infection after a fight. *Lancet, 339,* 246-252.
Perez, H. (1996, Summer). Incarcerated populations: Have they been forgotten? *Active Voice,* pp. 7-8.
Pink bracelets for homosexuals in Florida jail are challenged. (1989, December 3). *New York Times,* p. 35.
Plant, R. (1986). *The pink triangle: The Nazi war on homosexuals.* New York: Henry Holt.
Plant, R. (1989, November 7). Nazis' forgotten victims: Gays. *New York Times,* p. A-23.

Potler, C. (1988). *AIDS in prison: A crisis in New York State corrections.* New York: Correctional Association of New York.
Proctor v. Alameda County, Calif. Super.Ct., Alameda Cnty., No. 693983-8 (1992).
Purdy, M. (1997, May 26). As AIDS increases behind bars, costs dim promise of new drugs. *New York Times,* pp. 1, 28.
Red tags for gays scrapped. (1990, Spring). *Civil Liberties,* No. 369, p. 7.
Rehabilitation Act, 29 U.S.C. 794 (1973).
Richman, K., & Richman, L. (1993). The potential for transmission of human immunodeficiency virus through human bites. *Journal of Acquired Immune Deficiency Syndromes, 6,* 402-406.
Roe et al. v. Fauver et al., D.NJ No.88-1225-AET (1992).
Rothman, D. (1971). *The discovery of the asylum: Social order and disorder in the new republic.* Boston: Little, Brown.
Sartre, J. P. (1966). *Being and nothingness.* New York: Washington Square.
Schneider, B. (1992). AIDS and class, gender, and race relations. In J. Huber & B. Schneider (Eds.), *The social contexts of AIDS* (pp. 19-43). Thousand Oaks, CA: Sage.
Schur, E. (1971). *Labeling deviant behavior: Its sociological implications.* New York: Harper & Row.
Schutz, A., & Luckmann, T. (1973). *The structures of the lifeworld.* Evanston, IL: Northwestern University Press.
Secombe, W. (1973, January/February). The housewife and her labour under capitalism. *New Left Review, 82,*, 3-24.
Sforza, D. (1998a, June 2). Jails prefer education, not condoms, to curtail HIV. *Record [Bergen County, NJ],* p. A-12.
Sforza, D. (1998b, June 2). Terms of treatment: Prisons tested by costs, burdens of HIV. *Record [Bergen County, NJ],* pp. A-1, A-12.
Shilts, R. (1987). *And the band played on: Politics, people and the AIDS epidemic.* New York: St. Martin's.
Shover, N., & Einstadter, W. (1988). *Analyzing American corrections.* Belmont, CA: Wadsworth.
Sirica, J. (1988, May 19). Testimony on AIDS. *New York Newsday,* p. 14.
Sontag, S. (1980). *Illness as metaphor.* New York: Doubleday.
Sontag, S. (1989). *AIDS and its metaphors.* New York: Farrar Straus Giroux.
Spitzer, S. (1975). Toward a Marxian theory of deviance. *Social Problems, 22,* 638-651.
Stolberg, S. (1998, June 29). Eyes shut, black America is being ravaged by AIDS. *New York Times,* pp. A-1, A-12.
Sullivan, J. (1993, February 18). Inmate with HIV who bit guard loses appeal. *New York Times,* pp. B-7.
Sullivan, R. (1992, August 26). Ex-inmate wins award in bias case. *New York Times,* p. 4.
Sykes, G. (1958). *The society of captives.* Princeton, NJ: Princeton University Press.
Thomas, E. (1985, September 23). The new untouchables: Anxiety over AIDS is verging on hysteria in some parts of the country. *Time,* pp. 24-26.
Thomas, P., & Moerings, M. (1994). *AIDS in prison.* Aldershot, VT: Dartmouth.
Turner v. Safley, 428 U.S. 78, 107 S.Ct. 2254 (1987).
U.S. General Accounting Office. (1994). *Bureau of Prisons health care.* Washington, DC: Government Printing Office.
Vaughn, M., & Carroll, L. (1998). Separate and unequal: Prison versus free-world medical care. *Justice Quarterly, 15,* 3-40.
Viadro, C. I., & Earp, J. A. (1991). AIDS education and incarcerated women: A neglected opportunity. *Women and Society, 17,* 105-117.
Vlahov, D., Brewer, T., Castro, K., Narkunus, J., Salive, M., Ullrich, J., & Munoz, A. (1991). Prevalence of antibody to HIV-1 among entrants to U.S. correctional facilities. *Journal of the American Medical Association, 265,* 1129-1132.

Walker v. Sumner, 917 F.2d 382 (9th Cir. (1990).
Weeks v. Texas, Texas Ct.Crim.App., No.92-1154 (1992).
Welch, M. (1989). Social junk, social dynamite and the rabble: Persons with AIDS in jail. *American Journal of Criminal Justice, 14,* 135-147.
Welch, M. (1991a). Persons with AIDS in prison: A critical and phenomenological approach to suffering. *Dialectical Anthropology, 16,* 51-61.
Welch, M. (1991b). Social class, special populations and other unpopular issues: Setting the jail agenda for the 90s. In G. L. Mays (Ed.), *Setting the jail research agenda for the 1990s: Proceedings from a special meeting* (pp. 17-23). Washington, DC: U.S. Department of Justice, National Institute of Corrections.
Welch, M. (1994). Jail overcrowding: Social sanitation and the warehousing of the urban underclass. In A. R. Roberts (Ed.), *Critical issues in crime and justice* (pp. 251-276). Newbury Park, CA: Sage.
Welch, M. (1996a). *Corrections: A critical approach.* New York: McGraw-Hill.
Welch, M. (1996b). Prisonization. In M. D. McShane & F. P. Williams (Eds.), *Encyclopedia of American prisons* (pp. 357-363). New York: Garland.
Welch, M. (1997). Tougher prisons? *Critical Criminologist, 8*(1), 7-11.
Welch, M., Fenwick, M., & Roberts, M. (1997). Primary definitions of crime and moral panic: A content analysis of experts' quotes in feature newspaper articles of crime. *Journal of Research in Crime and Delinquency, 34,* 474-494
Welch, M., Fenwick, M., & Roberts, M. (1998). State managers, intellectuals, and the media: A content analysis of ideology in experts' quotes in featured newspaper articles on crime. *Justice Quarterly, 15,* 101-123.
Zaretsky, E. (1973a, January/April). Capitalism, the family and personal life: Part 1. *Socialist Revolution, 10,* 69-126.
Zaretsky, E. (1973b, May/June). Capitalism, the family and personal life: Part 2. *Socialist Revolution, 10,* 19-70.

CHAPTER 12

The Immigration Crisis

Detention as an Emerging Mechanism of Social Control

As a result of worldwide political and economic shifts, immigration has emerged as an international problem affecting most Western nations. Indeed, immigration in the United States has increasingly become politicized at the national and local levels of government. Making matters worse, political leaders have yet to define and adequately implement a singular national immigration policy. Consequently, government officials tentatively initiate one set of policies, only to abruptly reverse their position in favor of more repressive measures.

Historically, immigration has always met formidable resistance from mainstream citizens. Similarly, in recent times immigration has become a lightning rod for anger, and this outrage has taken many forms. Immigration has

AUTHOR'S NOTE: I gratefully acknowledge Carrissa Griffing, Marie Mark, Judy Rabinovitz of the ACLU Immigrants' Rights Project, Stephanie Marks of the Lawyers Committee for Human Rights, and Mark Dow for their valuable assistance in preparing this chapter, which is reprinted with permission from *Social Justice, 23*(3).

contributed to a renewed sense of nativism, nationalism, and political isolationism, as well as to institutionalized racism. This antagonism is largely fueled by economic tensions, insofar as immigrants and undocumented immigrants ("illegal aliens") serve as convenient scapegoats—viewed as threats to scarce employment opportunities and blamed for draining public resources and social services.

Problems concerning immigration are as numerous as they are complex. Indeed, the complexity of the problems affects all aspects of immigration control, including immigration law, asylum hearings, border patrol, and parole. This chapter, however, concentrates on one particular mechanism in the control of immigration—the *detention* of undocumented immigrants. Although most illegal immigration takes place at the Mexican border (the Border Patrol reports apprehending and returning 1,000 aliens to Mexico each day; "62 New Guards," 1995), more than 6,000 undocumented immigrants are currently being detained by the Immigration and Naturalization Service (INS) (American Civil Liberties Union [ACLU], 1993). Even a cursory examination of INS operations indicates that detention policy is often as ambiguous and contradictory as current immigration policy itself.

Recent investigations of INS policy have revealed major problems in the detention of undocumented immigrants. For instance, the ACLU Immigrants' Rights Project (ACLU, 1993) inspected INS detention centers in New York City and documented numerous institutional problems, as well as allegations of human rights violations. Moreover, similar institutional problems and human rights violations have been reported at several other INS detention centers (Welch, 1991, 1993, 1994a, 1994b, 1998). The objective of this chapter is to explore institutional problems facing INS detention centers. INS detention policy also is discussed in the context of the new penology (Feeley & Simon, 1992), thereby conceptualizing detention as an emerging mechanism of social control.

INS Detention as an Emerging Mechanism of Social Control

Detaining large numbers of undocumented immigrants marks a relatively recent development in INS policy. "For twenty-five years prior to the 1980s, the INS maintained a policy of detaining only those individuals deemed likely to abscond or who posed a security risk" (Marks & Levy, 1994, p. 2). Policy shifts during the early Reagan administration marked a significant change in immigration and detention. With the arrival of the Mariel Cubans and the Haitian boat people, widespread detention was used as a deterrent to illegal immigration. Under this policy, all "excludable" aliens were detained for further inquiry. In July 1982, this policy was further formalized as an interim rule in the *Federal Register*, later codified in 3 C.F.R. §212.5 and §235.3. "Under these rules, which are still in effect, all aliens arriving without proper travel documents are detained pending a determination of their status, unless they are considered eligible for parole for 'emergent reasons' or reason 'strictly in the public interest' " (Marks & Levy, 1994, p. 2; see 8 C.F.R. §212.5 (a) [1993]).

As a result of the shift in immigration policy, the use of detention by the INS grew significantly during the 1980s. According to the ACLU Immigrants' Rights Project, "In 1981, the average stay in an INS detention facility was less than four days. By 1990, it had grown to 23 days, with many individuals detained for more than a year" (ACLU, 1993, p. 1; see U.S. General Accounting Office, 1992). The General Accounting Office (1992) reported that during the 1980s, the INS detention budget grew from $15.7 million to more than $149 million, thereby expanding the detention capacity to hold more than 6,000 persons. The estimated daily cost to taxpayers is approximately $50 per detainee.

Since the 1980s, more than 26 INS detention centers have opened; currently, more than 6,000 undocumented persons are detained, most of whom are people of color. Indeed, allegations of Eurocentrism and racism in U.S. immigration policy have multiplied. Critics argue that whites seeking asylum in the United States have encountered much less resistance and generally are not detained for indefinite periods of time. However, persons of color are typically detained while they apply for residency. Among those persons most commonly detained are Cubans, Haitians, Central Americans, and Nigerians. Many of these refugees seek political asylum in the United States because they fear persecution in their homelands (Arp, Dantico, & Zatz, 1990; Marks & Levy, 1994; Welch, 1991, 1997, 1998; see also Cook, 1993). Although the INS claims that it does not keep records on the nationality of detainees, immigration and human rights lawyers who visit detention centers report that the vast majority of detainees are people of color (S. Marks, personal communication, Lawyers Committee for Human Rights, March 1, 1995).

In 1986, Congress passed the Immigration Reform and Control Act (IRCA, also known as the Simpson-Rodino law), requiring all employees to document their citizenship. A major consequence of IRCA has been the emergence of repressive measures against undocumented immigrants. For example, before 1980, INS detention was the exception. During the 1990s, however, "INS policy changed significantly. As a result, many individuals previously eligible for release are now subject to mandatory detention" (ACLU, 1993, p. 3). Other detainees, though not subject to mandatory detention, also are held because they cannot meet the excessively high bonds demanded for their release.

The ACLU Immigrants' Rights Project and the Varick Street Investigation, New York City, 1993

As a result of the increased use of detention, institutional problems plaguing INS detention centers have become significantly compounded, including poor staffing, obstructed access to counsel and the courts, inhumane living conditions, and inadequate medical care. Allegations of human rights violations, such as physical and sexual assault by staff, also are reported.

One reason why the institutional problems evident in INS detention centers have remained concealed is the lack of systematic inspections and routine monitoring. However, one of the few comprehensive investigations of an INS detention facility was coordinated by Judy Rabinovitz, staff counsel of the ACLU Immigrants' Rights Project. This project engages in litigation, public education, and advocacy and professional training to protect immigrants against discrimination and to enforce the fundamental safeguards of due process and equal protection (ACLU, 1993).

In its report *Justice Detained,* the ACLU Immigrants' Rights Project summarized a 2-year investigation of the INS's Varick Street detention facility in New York City (ACLU, 1993: see also Sontag, 1993a, 1993b). In addition to documenting the substandard conditions at Varick Street, the investigation exposed egregious errors by the INS. For example, U.S. citizens have occasionally been mistakenly detained by INS. In fact, during the ACLU study, researchers assisted the release of a detainee who had been held for 14 months, long beyond the statutory release period. In this case, the detainee was being held despite uncontroverted evidence of U.S. citizenship. Also during the investigation, two other detainees were in the process of verifying their U.S. citizenship.

The report confirmed that many detainees at Varick Street are legal permanent residents with long-standing ties to this country, with family members who are U.S. citizens, and with bona fide legal claims to remain in this country. Moreover, the report revealed that INS detention policies and practices subject detainees to lengthy periods of confinement in a facility that was designed solely for short-term detention. At Varick Street, detention averages 6 months and sometimes lasts as long as 3 years.

According to Lucas Guttentag, director of the ACLU Immigrants' Rights Project, "Immigrants awaiting administrative hearings are being detained in conditions that would be unacceptable at prisons for criminal offenders" (Sontag, 1993a). In addition to the lengthy periods of confinement, the report revealed that the Varick Street facility is characterized by inhumane living conditions, including overcrowding, staffing problems, substandard sanitation leading to poor hygiene among detainees, lack of fresh air and sunlight, inadequate food, medical, and legal services, arbitrary and punitive use of segregation, and lack of grievance mechanisms. Even when detainees are ruled deportable, often they are held for several more months or years because the INS fails to promptly arrange travel and execute their departures (ACLU, 1993).

Complaints over conditions at INS facilities in New York are not new. During the 1980s, the INS was sued twice. In fact, the facility at Varick Street was opened in the wake of one of the previous lawsuits—yet more problems followed. In 1986, the U.S. General Accounting Office (1986) issued a report that also criticized the Varick Street facility for, among other things, the lack of outdoor exercise facilities and poor-quality staffing.

The investigation of the conditions at the Varick Street facility further disclosed an important characteristic of the detainee population: "Virtually all of the detainees we spoke with had close family members who were either U.S. citizens or legal permanent residents" (ACLU, 1993, p. 10):

- Mr. D had lived in the United States for 27 years, 25 as a legal permanent resident. Almost all of his relatives reside in the United States.
- Mr. C had lived in the United States almost 10 years after fleeing from Bangladesh as a political refugee. His wife is a legal permanent resident of the United States, and his three children are U.S. citizens.
- Ms. A had lived in the United States for 22 years, 17 as a legal permanent resident. Her two children are U.S. citizens.
- Ms. M had been a legal permanent resident for 18 years, immigrating from Haiti with her family at the age of 7. All of her immediate family members live in the United States, including her 9-month-old U.S. citizen daughter.

In light of these cases, serious questions remain concerning the usefulness and fairness of current INS detention policy. Clearly, these detainees do not meet the most basic justification for mandatory detention because they do not pose a security risk. Moreover, their risk of absconding is minimal because they have family and relatives in the United States. Because detention interferes with the ability of detainees to pursue their legal claims, it is recommended that current INS detention policy be reexamined. Beyond the inhumane conditions at the detention centers, INS detention practices are costly, unnecessary, and unjust for most undocumented immigrants.

Problems Affecting Other INS Detention Centers, Queens, New York

The problems at the Varick Street facility are generally representative of several other INS detention centers. In fact, similar problems are associated with INS detention practices nearby in Queens, New York. At Kennedy Airport, INS officials confront numerous travelers without visas (TWOVs); however, the detention practice employed points up a double standard.

> INS has forced airlines to act as jailers for the TWOVs, even though the agency lets most political asylum applicants enter the country without much fuss. Applicants are simply told to show up months later when their case is called. But the INS has decided any TWOV who requests asylum should get different treatment. All TWOVs must be detained by the air carrier that ferried them into the country—at the airline's expense. ("Motel Kafka," 1993, p. 3)

The INS detention policy costs the airline industry $8 million per year, including the expense of detaining TWOVs in neighboring motels—nicknamed "Motel Kafkas." Indeed, such detention is quite Kafkaesque. Private guards are hired by the airlines to serve as detention officers, but these officers do not answer to the government. Moreover, while being held in a motel room for months, detainees are deprived of fresh air and access to a telephone and in some cases are shackled and sexually abused. The following cases further illuminate problems with current INS detention policy:

> In August [1993], three teenagers—two boys and a girl—from Sri Lanka arrived at Kennedy Airport on a Northwest Airlines flight and requested asylum. Northwest detained them for about two months, footing the motel and security guard bills until the airline persuaded the city to arrange for foster care. During those two months, the teenagers' lawyer never knew where they were being held. And the young people weren't allowed to call him. They told him that they were only

fed twice a day because the guard said there wasn't enough money for three meals. ("Motel Kafka," 1993, p. 3)

In May 1992, Delta Airlines found itself with 13 TWOV passengers from China who requested asylum. Two escaped, a pregnant woman was paroled, and Delta ended up housing, feeding, and guarding the remaining 10 until August, when INS arranged for them to get an asylum hearing. Delta shelled out $181,000, which included $9,800 in medical bills for a woman who broke her arm when she leapt from her hotel room in an attempt to escape. ("Motel Kafka," 1993, p. 3; see also Hartocollis, 1990)

However, recent court decisions have significantly affected INS detention policy, especially as it relates to owners of ships and airplanes carrying stowaways. In June 1994, the Federal Court of Appeals for the Third Circuit in Philadelphia overturned an INS policy that required the owners of ships and airplanes to pay the cost of detaining stowaways while awaiting asylum proceedings. The court ruled that the INS had violated federal guidelines in establishing its detention policy. The decision marks the "first blow against rules that human rights advocates have long attacked for forcing owners of ships and airplanes into the expensive and unwarranted role of jailing stowaways" (Levy, 1994, p. B-1).

The case referred to an incident in which 20 Rumanian stowaways arrived in Boston by hiding in huge metal cargo containers loaded on a freighter in France. The INS required that the shipping company, Sea Land Service, detain the stowaways. Consequently, the Rumanians were detained in hotels in Newark, New Jersey, shackled together by leg irons. Later, the detainees were transferred to a county jail in Pennsylvania, but the INS still required Sea Land Service to pay for the use of jail space (Levy, 1994).

As a result of the ruling, shipping companies could sue the federal government for the costs of detaining stowaways for the last 6 years—the statute of limitations. Companies in other states are expected to file similar lawsuits. "I am quite pleased by the decision," said Stephanie Marks, coordinator of the asylum program for the Lawyers Committee for Human Rights. "I would hope now that the INS would see the error of this policy of requiring shipping companies to act as jailers" (Levy, 1994, p. B-8).

Krome Detention Center, Miami

Major problems at INS detention centers are not confined to New York. During the past several years, the Krome Detention Center in Miami has been plagued with numerous institutional problems, including complaints of sexual harassment and physical abuse. Moreover, the controversy surrounding Krome heightened in 1990 when three educational contract employees working at the detention center were dismissed. Each of them was a whistleblower who had complained of the mistreatment of the detainees (mostly Haitian). INS officials concede that there are institutional problems at Krome but point to understaffing as a major source of their difficulties (LeMoyne, 1990).

At Krome, detainees "wear orange uniforms, and the guards on the grounds are armed, and the intimidating sound of a gunfire can echo through the camp from a nearby target range where INS officers practice" (Rohter, 1992, p. E-18). When Richard Smith, the immigration service regional director, was asked why Krome looks so much like a jail, he replied, "That's because it is a jail, albeit a minimum security jail. The sign outside may say that it's a processing center, but that's just semantics" (Rohter, 1992, p. E-18).

Though Krome was designed for short-term detention, many detainees spend more than 90 days there. Another point of controversy concerns the detention of minors, who by INS regulations are not to be held in the same facility with adults. According to Joan Freidland, an immigration lawyer at Krome, "The basic problem is that there are no rules. . . . Everything is discretionary" (Rohter, 1992, p. E-18).

INS officials at Krome deny allegations of violence and human rights abuses. Constance K. Weiss, an INS administrator at Krome, argued, "Why would we want to run a place where we beat the hell out of people?" To this, refugee advocates reply with a two-part answer: "To discourage other potential refugees and because it is easy to get away with. Detained immigrants are a powerless group . . . without recourse to normal political or legal channels" (Rohter 1992, p. E-18; see also DePalma, 1992).

A key decision by the Clinton administration, announced August 19, 1994, has greatly affected the INS detention center at Krome, as well as other detention centers such as Port Isabel, Texas. As outlined in an INS memorandum from the Office of the Deputy Commissioner (1994) to district directors, the new directive marks a reversal from a previous position allowing nearly all Cuban immigrants to be granted political asylum: "Due to the situation confronting the Service in August 1994 relative to a massive flow of Cuban migrants to the United States, the Attorney General decided that all excludable Cubans arriving in the United States should be detained." (The memorandum also specifies that unaccompanied children and other persons presenting compelling humanitarian concerns must be paroled.)

Between August 5 and September 13, 1994, the Coast Guard picked up 32,051 Cuban refugees. At Guantanamo Bay, the U.S. has detained 28,266 Cubans and 14,181 Haitians. An additional 2,851 Cubans were held on Coast Guard and Navy ships; 607 Cubans were detained at Krome detention center; 1,102 Cubans were detained in Panama and Texas (Silver, 1994).

The INS detention policy pertaining to Cubans parallels recent initiatives to control immigration in California. On September 18, 1994, Attorney General Janet Reno announced that the new immigration directive targeting Mexicans would "shut the door on illegal immigration" ("Reno Initiative," 1994, p. 40). The new initiative, referred to as "Operation Gatekeeper" by the Justice Department, brings more federal personnel and money to California. The political atmosphere in California, Florida, and Texas ought not be overlooked, for the immigration issue profoundly shapes state and local politics.

Forced Tranquilizing, Deportation, and Human Rights Violations: The Case of Tony Ekpen Ebibillo (1993)

INS detention practices recently drew additional controversy when a detainee was forcibly tranquilized and deported. On three occasions, the INS tried and failed to deport Tony Ekpen Ebibillo, an asylum seeker from Nigeria. Ebibillo resisted his deportation and allegedly fought and bit INS officers. On the third attempt, INS staff forcibly drugged Ebibillo at Krome detention center, placed him in a straightjacket and leg weights, and transported him to the airport. "Gagged, groaning, and surrounded by four officers, one with a syringe, the Nigerian had been drugged at the direction of immigration authorities" (Booth, 1993, p. A-1). Yet the airline captain would not allow the INS to board Ebibillo while in such condition. Finally, the INS quietly chartered another airplane and deported Ebibillo and 77 other Nigerian deportees on December 15, 1993 (Viglucci, 1994, p. 2B).

Amnesty International (AI) intervened, but its efforts came too late. The INS deported Ebibillo before AI representatives could negotiate for a fair asylum hearing. "Had I known his deportation was in the works, we would have asked them not to do this," said Nick Rizzo, refugee coordinator for the U.S. section of AI in San Francisco. "I think he probably had a case for asylum. He seemed credible. And the facts hung together" (Viglucci, 1994, p. 2B).

Indeed, supporters of Ebibillo suspect that the INS quietly deported him because they were aware that AI was looking into the case. Public interest lawyer Cheryl Little, who advocated for Ebibillo's asylum, concluded that "Tony was deprived of his day in court" (p. 2B). INS officials deny doing anything improper in deporting Ebibillo, noting that a judge had ordered him expelled from the country 2 years earlier. Ebibillo had requested political asylum after entering the country illegally, claiming that he was a prodemocracy activist fleeing persecution by Nigeria's military. He had no criminal convictions.

Ebibillo had been detained by the INS since December 18, 1990. To ensure his deportation, INS staff at the clinic at Krome placed him in restraints for 48 hours while Public Health Service physicians drugged him with Thorazine (a powerful antipsychotic medication). INS officials defended the forced drugging by arguing that Ebibillo was passive-aggressive (a personality disorder). Though medical records show that Ebibillo had not been diagnosed as psychotic, he was medicated "apparently to control him during deportation" (Booth, 1993, p. A-1; see also Ezem, 1991). Government policy allows the use of drugs for detainees who are mentally ill or dangerous, but it bars the use of drugs for the purpose of deporting people who offer physical resistance. Ebibillo was apparently never diagnosed as having a mental illness. But government doctors said the use of drugs was justified because Ebibillo was acting aggressively and posed a threat to himself and others (Viglucci, 1994, p. 2B).

Questions persist as to the extent to which the deportees are involuntarily drugged for the purposes of facilitating their departure. "I am aware that it was a practice for very difficult deportees," said a former INS official at Krome who asked not to be named. "It wasn't the practice in every case, but they did use drugs for the purpose of getting somebody quietly on a plane" (Booth, 1993, p. A-20).

According to Gregg Bloch, a psychiatrist and associate professor at Georgetown University Law Center and specialist in medical ethics, "It sounds as if they are transparently using the medication for police purposes, and that is a violation of medical ethics and tort law" (Booth, 1993,p. A20). Bloch elaborated:

> It is not even a gray area. It is not ethical or legal to take difficult-to-handle people, even violent criminals, and drug them to make them less violent. It would be like a doctor riding around with the police and injecting violent offenders (quoted in Booth, 1993, p. A20)

Arthur Helton, director of the Refugee Project for the Lawyers Committee for Human Rights in New York, added, "This sounds like an extraordinary procedure, and it seems there must be some kind of review process so the use of drugs is not abused by local enforcement personnel" (quoted in Booth, 1993, p. A20).

For nearly a year, supporters of Ebibillo continued their efforts to locate him with the help of human rights groups (i.e., Human Rights Watch/Africa) in Lagos, Nigeria. Upon his arrival in Lagos, he was reportedly arrested (along with other deportees facing drug charges) by the Security Service. In December 1994, a year after being forcibly deported, Cheryl Little received a letter from Ebibillo. In the letter, Ebibillo reports being in satisfactory physical condition; however, he faces criminal charges in Nigeria. (It is unknown what he is charged with, although it is suspected that he is being detained for his prodemocracy activism against the military regime.) Ebibillo alleges additional human rights violations by the INS, including physical abuse and psychological manipulation. For instance, Ebibillo claims being told that he was being transported to a court hearing when in fact he was being driven to the airport for deportation (Dow, 1994).

Undocumented Immigrant Children

Another aspect of INS policy that remains controversial is the detention of undocumented immigrant children. Whereas some undocumented adults are eligible for release to await their hearings, undocumented children are detained if they lack a close relative or legal guardian in the United States. In 1993, the United States Supreme Court (*Reno* v. *Flores,* 1993) upheld this INS detention policy. However, an earlier decision by the U.S. Court of Appeals for the Ninth Circuit in San Francisco held that the policy had violated the children's constitutional right to due process. The appeals court ruled that children are entitled to a hearing, including an inquiry into whether an unrelated adult is available to care for the child during the deportation hearing.

Each year, thousands of children are arrested on suspicion of being deportable aliens. Of the 8,500 arrested in 1990, 70% were not accompanied by adults. Most of these youths are teenage boys from Mexico and Central America. Currently, the INS holds more than 2,000 undocumented youth. The INS reports that it has neither the resources nor the expertise to conduct thousands of hearings to approve suitable caretakers.

Justice Stevens, in a dissenting opinion of the 1993 decision, argued that the Constitution requires that the INS demonstrate in each case why detention was better than being released to an unrelated adult. The conditions of confinement also have been challenged in several lawsuits concerning the detention of undocumented children. In 1987, a consent decree ordered the INS to improve such conditions (Greenhouse, 1993; Johnson, 1992).

Detention, Social Control, and the New Penology

The prevailing response to the immigration crisis has encouraged government officials to resort to detention. In this case, detention has emerged as a mechanism of social control for unpopular and powerless persons, namely undocumented immigrants of color. Since the 1980s, detention has become a practice widely used to control and deter undocumented immigrants. Currently, such policies persist despite the recommendations of immigration experts who argue that the existing detention policy is costly, unnecessary, and unjust for most undocumented immigrants (ACLU, 1993; Marks & Levy, 1994).

In light of these developments, the popularity of detaining undocumented immigrants mirrors the practice of incarcerating increasing numbers of offenders in the criminal justice system. Incarceration continues to enjoy considerable ideological popularity among political leaders and mainstream citizens—in 1994, the prison population in the United States surpassed the 1 million mark. In explaining the prevailing trend in incarceration, Feeley and Simon (1992) presented an alternative view of correctional policy that they called the *new penology*. They contended that a new set of terms, concepts, and strategies has begun to replace those of traditional penology. Whereas traditional penology stems from criminal law and criminology, with their emphasis on punishing and correcting individual offenders, the new penology adopts an actuarial approach in which *specialists* assess the risks of specific criminal subpopulations (e.g., drug offenders) and recommend strategies that attempt to control these *aggregates*. The main objective of the new penology is to improve social control measures for high-risk and dangerous groups, thereby establishing a greater reliance on imprisonment—that is, correctional "warehousing" (Welch, 1996).

Because the new penology represents a strikingly different course for the future direction of correctional policy, there are several areas of concern. For instance, the new penology does not set out to intervene or respond to either the individual offender or adverse societal conditions that serve as the root causes of many forms of street crime. "It does not speak of impaired persons in need of treatment or of morally irresponsible persons who need to be held accountable for their actions" (Feeley & Simon, 1992, p. 452). Rather, the new penology concentrates on maximizing social control, using prediction tables and population projections to streamline the criminal justice system.

Because the new penology takes an actuarial approach, it emphasizes efficiency, management, and control instead of individualized justice and reform attempts. Simply put, the criminal justice system recycles human beings from one form of custodial management to another without attempting to impose justice or reintegrate offenders into society (Feeley & Simon, 1992; see also Gordon, 1991; Platt, 1994).

Perhaps the most distressing contradiction of the new penology is that its actuarial approach strives to improve public safety without attempting to reduce crime. According to Feeley and Simon (1992),

> The new penology is neither about punishing nor about rehabilitating individuals. It is about identifying and managing unruly groups. It is concerned with the rationality not of individual behavior or even community organization, but of managerial process. Its goal is not to eliminate crime, but to make it more tolerable through systemic coordination. (p. 455)

The new penology also has implications for poverty and the underclass—a segment of society, typically African American and Hispanic, that is permanently marginalized economically and otherwise removed from America's mainstream. Because members of the underclass as a whole are unemployed and uneducated and possess few or no work skills, they are generally characterized as posing a threat to society and are depicted as constituting a dangerous class. According to the new penology, this so-called dangerous and high-risk group must be controlled and managed by the criminal justice system. For decades, a clear trend of incarcerating impoverished and minority offenders has been emerging. Mauer and Huling (1995) documented this trend by noting that approximately one in three African American males between the ages of 20 and 29 is either in prison, in jail, or on probation or parole.

As the imprisonment trend continues, the actuarial impetus of the new penology becomes evident—that is, social management and social sanitation override individualized justice (Welch, 1994b; see also Adler, 1994; Irwin, 1985; Spitzer, 1975; Welch, 1996). Unfortunately, the prospects for the future remain bleak because both poverty and imprisonment continue to escalate. Feeley and Simon (1992) concluded, "This, in turn, can push corrections even further toward a self-understanding based on the imperative of herding a specific population that cannot be disaggregated and transformed, but only maintained—a kind of waste management function" (pp. 469-470).

Comparing the new penology to prevailing INS detention policy further illuminates the form of social control emerging from the immigration crisis. Indeed, the practice of INS detention mirrors the new penology. Instead of reviewing individualized cases of asylum and applications for citizenship, the INS tends to resort to the processing of large aggregates—groups of specific nationalities, namely Cubans, Haitians, Central Americans, and Nigerians. The recent executive order that instructs the INS to detain all excludable Cubans arriving in the United States as of September 14, 1994, is in keeping with this larger policy (Sale, 1994). Moreover, during the 1980s the U.S. Attorney General targeted Salvadorans by granting the INS the authority to make arrests without warrants, leading to the detention of hundreds of Salvadorans (see *Orantes-Hernandez v. Thornburgh*, 1990, and *Orantes-Hernandez v. Meese*, 1988).

The actuarial approach further complements a detention policy that emphasizes efficiency, management, and control. Regarding INS detention, the actuarial strategy manifests according to bureaucratic and rational-legal procedures. The INS relies on specialists, experts, and technicians to *classify* aliens (i.e., excludable and deportable aliens) as well as to *predict* and *forecast* immigration trends. In doing so, immigration specialists apply actuarial methods to determine the costs of immigration (e.g., establishing financial estimates related to health care, education, and other social services). From the perspective of the new penology, INS specialists are given the task of managing aggregates—insofar as groups, not individuals, are the unit of analysis. The emphasis here is on management of categories rather than on accommodation, equity, and significant social transformation.

Similarly, the current INS detention policy does not endeavor to reintegrate undocumented immigrants into the community. In fact, it often resists and opposes such reintegration. A case in point is the controversy surrounding the Asylum Pre-Screening Officer (APSO) Program, which was designed to use detention space more judiciously and to expand the use of the Pilot Parole Project.[1] Though the Pilot Parole Project has been found to create a more rational and economic detention policy and is supported by officials from the United Nations High Commissioner for Refugees, the Department of Justice, Amnesty International, and the Lawyers Committee for Human Rights, there are reports of noncompliance in certain districts. Marks and Levy (1994) found that "the district directors in Harlingen and New York have rejected a significant number of positive parole recommendations" (p. 10).

Marks and Levy (1994) also found "the New York district director's action in this regard particularly troubling in light of evidence that aliens are denied parole in New York solely because of national origin" and expressed particular concern about "reports that Nigerian asylum seekers face a presumption against parole solely because they are Nigerian" (p. 11). In response to these findings, the allegation of discrimination and institutionalized racism in the New York district has been brought to the attention of the New York City Commission on Human Rights, which issued a letter of concern to the INS district director.

Finally, whereas the new penology addresses the social control of the impoverished people of color in the nation, INS detention policy also targets unpopular immigrants of color.

Conclusion

The purpose of this chapter was to identify and describe the problems surrounding INS detention policy, as well as to acknowledge the poor institutional conditions and services that exist at many of the INS detention centers. In sum, immigration lawyers emphasize that INS detention practices are costly, unnecessary, and unjust for most undocumented immigrants (ACLU, 1993; Marks & Levy, 1994). An important thrust of this chapter was to present INS detention policy in a broader social context and in particular to demonstrate how detention policy has emerged as a more repressive mechanism of social control. The immigration crisis has fueled a renewed sense of nativism, nationalism, political isolationism, and institutional racism. Due to the political forces resisting immigration, INS detention is used as a form of deterrence and social control against select racial and ethnic groups.

The new penology (Feeley & Simon, 1992) is applicable to INS detention policy for several reasons. First, the new penology is based on an actuarial model to control large aggregates by emphasizing efficiency and management. The actuarial approach facilitates INS detention policy in that it rests on bureaucratic and rational-legal procedures. Second, both the new penology and INS detention policy resist efforts to reintegrate certain groups into the community, especially impoverished people of color and undocumented immigrants of color. Finally, critiques of the new penology point out that imprisonment, as a mechanism of social control, is likely to escalate, paralleling a similar trend among undocumented immigrants.

Note

1. The Pilot Parole Project was initiated in 1990 by the INS commissioner in an effort to create a more rational and economic detention policy. According to the project, INS district directors were instructed to take into account a number of criteria (e.g., certainty of true identity and strength of the asylum claim) in making parole decisions. A final assessment of the Pilot Parole Project, which concluded in October 1991, demonstrated the desirability of a durable release authority (see Marks & Levy, 1994, pp. 5-6).

References

Adler, J. S. (1994). The dynamite, wreckage, and scum in our cities: The social construction of deviance in industrial America. *Justice Quarterly, 11,* 7-32.

American Civil Liberties Union, Immigrants' Rights Project. (1993). *Justice detained: Conditions at the Varick Street Immigration Detention Center, a report by the ACLU Immigrants' Rights Project.* New York: Author.

Arp, W., Dantico, M. K., & Zatz, M. S. (1990). The Immigration Reform and Control Act of 1986: Differential impacts on women? *Social Justice: A Journal of Crime, Conflict and World Order, 17*(2), 23-39.

Booth, W. (1993, October 7). U.S. accused of sedating deportees: Tranquilizers given to those who resist. *Washington Post,* pp. A-1, A-20.

Cook, D. (1993). Racism, citizenship, and exclusion. In D. Cook & B. Hudson (Eds.), *Racism and criminology* (pp. 136-157). Newbury Park, CA: Sage.

DePalma, A. (1992, September 21). Winds free 40 aliens, stirring second storm. *New York Times,* p. A-10.

Dow, M. (1994, December 20). A letter of correspondence regarding Tony Ebibillo. United States of America vs. Tony Ebibillo. August 1993.

Ezem, N. (1991, December 19). Nigerian arrested after 10 years in Miami, accuses INS of mistreatment. *Miami Times,* pp. 1-A, 2-A.

Feeley, M. M., & Simon, J. (1992). The new penology: Notes on the emerging strategy of corrections and its implications. *Criminology, 30,* 449-474.

Gordon, D. R. (1991). *The justice juggernaut: Fighting street crime, controlling citizens.* New Brunswick, NJ: Rutgers University Press.

Greenhouse, L. (1993, March 24). Detention upheld on alien children: Justices affirm a U.S. policy on deportation hearings. *New York Times,* p. A-19.

Hartocollis, A. (1990, July 25). A woman without a country. *New York Newsday,* Pt. II, pp. 8-9.

Immigration Reform and Control Act, Public Law 99-603 (1986).

Irwin, J. (1985). *The jail: Managing the underclass in American society.* Berkeley: University of California Press.

Johnson, D. (1992, November 30). Choice of young illegal aliens: Long detentions or deportation. *New York Times,* pp. A-1, A-12.

LeMoyne, J. (1990, May 16). Florida center holding aliens is under inquiry: Additional complaints made of abuse. *New York Times,* p. A-16.

Levy, C. J. (1994, June 30). Court upsets law on costs of stowaways: Companies had to pay expenses for detention. *New York Times,* pp. B-1, B-8.

Marks, S., & Levy, J. (1994, September). *Detention of refugees: Problems in implementation of the asylum pre-screening officer program. A briefing paper issued by the Lawyers Committee for Human Rights.* New York: Lawyers Committee for Human Rights.

Mauer, M. & Huling, J. (1995). *Young black Americans and the criminal justice system: Five years later.* Washington, DC: Sentencing Project.

Motel Kafka [Editorial]. (1993, October 24). *New York Newsday,* pp. 2-3.

Office of the Deputy Commissioner, Immigration and Naturalization Service. (1994, September 14). Memorandum to district directors.

Orantes-Hernandez v. Meese, 685 F. Supp. 1488 (C.D. Cal. (1988).

Orantes-Hernandez v. Thornburgh, 919 F. 2d 549 (9th Cir. (1990).

Platt, A. M. (1994). Rethinking and unthinking "social control." In G. S. Bridges & M. A. Myers (Eds.), *Inequality, crime and social control* (pp. 72-79). Boulder, CO: Westview.

Reno initiative aims to control immigration. (1994, September 18). *New York Times,* p. 40.

Reno v. Flores, 507 U.S. 292 (1993).

Rohter, L. (1992, June 21). "Processing" for Haitians is time in a rural prison. *New York Times,* p. E-18.

Sale, C. (1994, September 14). INS memorandum from Office of the Deputy Commissioner to district directors, subject: Parole authorization.

Silver, V. (1994, September 14). Some Cubans are released from detention in Florida. *New York Times,* p. A-6.

62 new guards will reinforce Arizona border. (1994, February 6). *New York Times,* p. A-12.

Sontag, D. (1993a, September 21). New York City rights chief investigating U.S. immigration center. *New York Times,* p. B3.

Sontag, D. (1993b, August 12). Report cites mistreatment of immigrants: A.C.L.U. says aliens are detained too long. *New York Times,* pp. B1, B8.

Spitzer, S. (1975). Toward a Marxian theory of deviance. *Social Problems, 22,* 638-651.

U.S. General Accounting Office. (1986). *Criminal aliens: INS detention and deportation activities in the New York area.* Washington, DC: Government Printing Office.

U.S. General Accounting Office. (1992). *Immigration control: Immigration policies affect INS detention efforts.* Washington, DC: Government Printing Office.

Viglucci, A. (1994, January 12). INS deports Nigerian without telling lawyers. *Miami Herald,* p. 2-B.

Welch, M. (1991). Social class, special populations, and other unpopular issues: Setting the jail research agenda for the 1990s. In G. L. Mays (Ed.), *Setting the jail research agenda for the 1990s: Proceedings from a special meeting* (pp. 17-23). Washington, DC.: U.S. Department of Justice, National Institute of Corrections.

Welch, M. (1993). *A summary report on INS detention practices.* Submitted to the ACLU Immigrants' Rights Project, New York.

Welch, M. (1994a). *Detention practices in Immigration and Naturalization Service (INS) facilities: Policies, procedures, and allegations of human rights violations.* Paper presented at the annual meeting of the Academy of Criminal Justice Sciences, Chicago.

Welch, M. (1994b). Jail overcrowding: Social sanitation and warehousing of the urban underclass. In A. R. Roberts (Ed.), *Critical issues in crime and justice* (pp. 251-276). Thousand Oaks, CA: Sage.

Welch, M. (1996). *Corrections: A critical approach.* New York: McGraw-Hill.

Welch, M. (1997). Questioning the utility and fairness of INS detention. *Journal of Contemporary Criminal Justice, 13,* 41-54.

Welch, M. (1998). Problems facing Immigration and Naturalization Service (INS) detention centers: Policies, procedures and allegations of human rights violations. In R. L. Gido & T. Alleman (Eds.), *Turnstile justice* (pp. 192-204). Englewood Cliffs, NJ: Prentice Hall.

CHAPTER
13

The Corrections Industry

Economic Forces and the Prison Enterprise

The term *enterprise* has two basic definitions: "project" and "business organization." In corrections, both definitions of enterprise are fast becoming appropriate: Not only is the continued effort to expand prison construction a massive project, but it has become a major growth industry. Approaching punishment as an enterprise reinforces the perspective that economic and market forces have an enormous impact on imprisonment rates—even more so than what is uncritically accepted to be the cause, namely crime. In his aptly titled book *Punishment, Crime and Market Forces* (1991), Leslie Wilkins explored the role of economics in the formation of criminal justice policy and practice. At first glance, some conventional thinkers might suspect that the concepts listed in the book's title are slightly out of sequence and that perhaps the cover should read *Crime, Punishment, and Market Forces*. Wilkins, however, situates punishment befire crime to punctuate a main point: that the rates of incarceration vary independently from those of crime.

Contrary to popular and political belief that the use of prisons deters crime, numerous investigations dispel this deeply entrenched myth. For instance, Lynch (1998) pointed out that the correlation between imprisonment and deterrence is clouded in "mathematical mysticism"; relatedly, Walker (1994) characterized deterrence as a crime control "theology" in that it rests on faith more so than facts. In testing empirically the age-old notion that a greater reliance of imprisonment reduces crime, Lynch (1998) concluded that "over the long run, imprisonment has no suppression effect on the rate of criminal offending. . . . These data, in short, seem to indicate what drives the rate of criminal offending is external to the crime-punishment nexus" (pp. 10-11) (also see Butterfield, 1997, 1998a; Christie, 1994; Currie, 1985; Cushman, 1998; Irwin & Austin, 1994; Melossi, 1985; Rusche & Kirchheimer, 1939/1968; Sullivan, 1997; Welch, 1996a; Wilkins, 1991).

In search of better predictors of imprisonment, scholars turn to economic indicators, especially the impact that unemployment has on incarceration (Box & Hale, 1982; Chiricos & Bales, 1991; Greenberg, 1977; Jankovic, 1982; Lynch & Groves, 1989; Wilkins, 1991; Yeager, 1979; Zimring & Hawkins, 1991; refer to Chapter 2). Wilkins (1991) reported that "both between and within countries, unemployment rates tend to be strongly associated with the proportion of the population serving terms of imprisonment" (p. 96) and noted that a similar relationship does not exist between unemployment and crime (see Welch, 1996b). Moreover, additional economic measures, particularly the polarity between extreme wealth and poverty, improve the prediction of incarceration rates even further (Wilkins, 1991; also see Arvanites & Asher, 1995). Still, other economic factors such as market forces also are linked to the expansion of corrections; as we shall see, prisons have become a lucrative industry, paying financial as well as ideological dividends (Christie, 1994; Foucault, 1979; Lynch, 1998; Reiman, 1998).

In brief, the economic-punishment nexus comprises two significant forces: the tendency in a capitalist system to reduce labor and the commercial features of the political economy. Together, these economic forces drive the corrections industry. Under the normal conditions of capitalism, the surplus population swells as opportunities for labor are diminished, resulting in unemployment and marginalization. Subsequently, some members of the surplus population inevitably become trapped in the ever-widening net of the criminal justice apparatus, where they serve as raw materials for the corrections industry—an enterprise responding to the forces of a free-market economy. These mutually reinforcing developments contribute additionally to the economic-punishment nexus, thus reproducing coercive mechanisms of social control.

Especially given the lack of a strong relationship between the rates of incarceration and crime, the expansion of social control in the form of building more prisons promises to have chilling effects on democracy and social equality. According to Nils Christie (1994), "The major dangers of crime in modern societies are not the crimes, but that the fight against them may lead societies towards totalitarian developments" (p. 16). The purpose of this chapter is to examine the corrections industry in a larger theoretical and conceptual framework featuring the political economy. In doing so, it explores the role of market forces in the escalating criminal justice system along with the social and individual harms they create. Indeed, the ever-expanding corrections machinery is an ironic and self-defeating mechanism of social— and crime—control, generating profound and negative effects for society as well as its citizens. Setting the stage for this inquiry is an overview of the production of prisoners in a capitalist society, followed by an in-depth analysis of the corrections industry and its consequences.

The Production of Prisoners in Capitalist Society

As previously discussed in Chapters 2 and 11, among the contradictions of capitalism is the economic marginalization of a large segment of society, thus creating a surplus population from which deviance and crime is produced. Because those marginalized are significant in both sheer numbers and their perceived threat to the social order, the state invests heavily in mechanisms of social control (Barnett & Cavanaugh, 1994; Spitzer, 1975). Law enforcement and corrections constitute some of the more coercive measures of social control designed to deal with the portion of the surplus population considered to be a problem. Within the political economy, the criminal justice system functions traditionally as a social control apparatus by protecting capitalist relations of production. Given the emergence of the corrections enterprise, however, it is clear that such operations of social control themselves are engaged in the accumulation of capital. Before identifying the structure and composition of the corrections industry, it is fitting that we acknowledge key dimensions of the political economy that contribute to lawlessness, an activity that produces raw materials necessary for the corrections industry, namely prisoners.

Because large-scale economic marginalization restricts opportunities for legitimate financial survival in a market economy, illegitimate—or unlawful—economic enterprises emerge. Perhaps the most widespread underground economy is the illicit drug industry, a form of financial survival (and mood-altering escape from the harsh conditions of poverty) created by the structural inequality of capitalism. However, the selling and consumption of illegal drugs has become increasingly criminalized to the extent that vast resources of the state are allocated to control these behaviors (refer to Chapter 4). It is crucial to emphasize that additional strategies to prohibit the drug industry (i.e., harsher penalties and mandatory minimum sentences) create an ironic effect due to the prevailing market forces. Even though the drug trade is an outlaw industry, its underground economy conforms to free-world, free-market, capitalist principles insofar as prices attached to illegal drugs are contingent upon demand and scarcity. Therefore, reducing the supply merely drives up the price of the drug, which makes trafficking more profitable, hence attracting more individuals and groups willing to venture such risks. As noted in Chapter 4, Wilkins (1994) pointed out that the cost of illegal drugs reflects the risk, not the type or quality of the product: Drug peddlers are not so much selling drugs as they are, like insurance companies, trading in risk (also see Welch, Bryan, & Wolff, 1999; Welch, Wolff, & Bryan, 1998).

In sum, the criminalization of drugs paradoxically escalates the drug trade: Higher penalties increase the risk of selling drugs, making the activity more lucrative and, in the end, recruiting an endless supply of peddlers who already have been marginalized economically. As drug peddlers are apprehended, convicted, and incarcerated, they serve as raw materials for the corrections industry, an economic enterprise considered by many proponents of a free market as legitimate.

As noted in Chapter 11, the criminal justice machinery has long exhibited equivocal tendencies insofar as relatively harmless lawbreakers (i.e., social junk) are treated like menacing and predatory offenders (i.e., social dynamite) (Spitzer, 1975; also see Adamson, 1984). However, the equivocal nature of the criminal justice system is accentuated by the economic needs of the corrections industry, which demand a greater supply of prisoners to remain profitable, even if those offenders are nonviolent and convicted of low-level crimes. The phenomenon of net widening is well documented empirically. In their research, Irwin and Austin (1994) found that 80% of those in prison are not serious or violent criminals: 65% of inmates were convicted of property, drug, and public disorder crimes, and another 15% were returned for violations of the conditions of their parole, such as curfew violations, failure to participate in a program, or evidence of substance abuse. Similarly, in 1997, New York Governor George Pataki argued that an additional 7,000 prison beds (priced at $635 million) were needed to handle what he claimed to be a growing number of violent offenders. Pataki's rhetoric is contradicted by the fact that New York's crime rates are dropping and the fact that in 1996, 60% of those sentenced to prison were convicted of nonviolent offenses. Pataki is accused of grandstanding on the crime issue and placating upstate legislators who see corrections as economic development engines for their districts ("New York's Prison Building Fever," 1997). Manufacturing false claims and manipulating fear are common strategies that politicians rely on to rip off taxpayers. This type of deception represents what Steven Donziger of the National Center on Institutions and Alternatives and the National Criminal Justice Commission called the political "bait and switch."

> A policy that pretends to fight violence by locking up mostly nonviolent offenders is an inefficient use of taxpayer resources. The scam works like the classic "bait and switch" marketing ploy, in which customers are "baited" into a store by an advertisement for an item at an extremely low price. Once in the store, the salesperson "switches" the customer to a higher-priced product than the scheme was designed to promote. In the criminal justice field, the "bait" is citizen fear of violent crime. The "switch" occurs when public officials fight crime by building more prisons *but then fill the new cells with nonviolent offenders.* This scheme profits those who wish to appear "tough" on crime but in reality are failing to make America safe. One consequence of this policy is that the criminal justice system spends tens of billions of dollars on prisons and then underfunds effective drug treatment, educational programs, and violence prevention programs by asserting that there is not enough money. (Donziger, 1996b, p. 18)

Undoubtedly, the "bait and switch" tactic works: Between 1990 and 1995, corrections officials built 213 state and federal prisons ("In '90s, Prison Building," 1997). Politicians know intuitively the campaign boost they receive by playing the crime card and capitalizing on the public's fear. John O. Bennett, state senator and sponsor of New Jersey's "tough on crime" legislation, expressed this: "I many times say that it is too bad that not every year is an election year" (quoted in Peterson, 1997, p. NJ-6). The "bait and switch" scam also benefits other individuals and organizations linked financially to the corrections industry. As mentioned previously, a crucial function of the war on drugs (and other "tough on crime" initiatives resulting from moral panic over perceived "crime waves") is its production of massive quantities of prisoners—raw materials—for the corrections industry. This economic-punishment nexus also is undergirded by lengthy sentences (especially mandatory minimums), which ensure profitability because long-term occupancy in prison translates into a handsome financial per diem. In a trade publication geared toward investors, the *Cabot Market Letter* compared a private corrections facility (Corrections Corporation of America, CCA) to "a hotel that's always 100% occupancy . . . and booked to the end of the century" (Bates, 1998a, p. 13).

The Corrections Industry in a Market Economy

As summarized in Chapter 2, imprisonment has become big business, and the bitter "not-in-my-backyard" attacks on prisons have been replaced with warm welcomes, such as the sign in Canon City, Colorado, reading "Corrections Capital of the World." The mayor of Canon City boasts, "We have a nice, nonpolluting, recession-proof industry here" (Brooke, 1997, p. 20). In Leavenworth, Kansas, a community that recently added a private prison to an already extensive corrections system that features a federal penitentiary, a state prison, and a military stockade, a billboard reads "How about doin' some TIME in Leavenworth?" Bud Parmer, site acquisition administrator for Florida Department of Corrections conceded, "There's a new attitude. . . . Small counties want a shot in the arm economically. A prison is a quick way to do it" (Glamser, 1996, p. 3A). Economically strapped towns induce jail and prison construction by offering land, cash incentives, and cut-rate deals on utilities; in return for these accommodations, locals receive jobs and spur other businesses such as department stores, fast-food chains, and motels, all of which contribute to the tax base (see Hallinan, 1995; Hernandez, 1996; Thomas, 1994b; Walsh, 1994; Williams, 1997).

Not only are prisons courted assiduously on Main Street, but on Wall Street the larger corrections industry has created a bull market—further evidence that crime does indeed pay. Tremendous growth in the prison population, coupled with astonishing increases in expenditures, has generated a lucrative market economy with seemingly unlimited opportunities for an array of financial players: entrepreneurs, lenders, investors, contractors, vendors, and service providers. In 1995, the American Jail Association promoted its conference with advertisements reeking of crass commercialism: "Tap Into the

Sixty-Five Billion Dollar Local Jails Market" (Donziger, 1996a). The World Research Group organized a 1996 convention in Dallas entitled "Private Correctional Facilities: Private Prisons, Maximize Investment Returns in This Exploding Industry." Without much hesitation, corporate America has caught the scent of new public money. The Dallas meeting included representatives from AT&T, Merrill Lynch, Price Waterhouse, and other golden logo companies (Teepen, 1996). The prison industry also has attracted other capitalist heavyweights, including the investment houses of Goldman Sachs and Co. and Smith Barney Shearson, Inc., who compete to underwrite corrections construction with tax-exempt bonds that do not require voter approval. Defense industry titans Westinghouse Electric, Alliant Techsystems, Inc., and GDE Systems, Inc. (a division of the old General Dynamics) also have entered the financial sphere of criminal justice, not to mention manufacturers of name-brand products currently cashing in on the spending frenzy in corrections. While attending the American Correctional Association's annual meeting, Rod Ryan, representing Dial Corporation, delightedly announced, "I already sell $100,000 a year of Dial soap to the New York City jails. Just think what a state like Texas would be worth" (Elvin, 1994-1995, p. 4).

Privatization in Corrections: From Walnut Street to Wall Street

The operative word for describing corrections in a free-market economy is *privatization*. Although private financial interests have shaped the course of criminal justice throughout modern history (Spitzer & Scull, 1977a, 1977b), the recent wave of commercialization and profiteering is traced to the Reagan revolution of the early 1980s. At that time, the prevailing political and economic philosophies encouraged government officials to turn to the private sector to administer public services, such as sanitation, health care, security, fire protection, and education. It was believed that the application of free-market principles to public services would enable private corporations to compete against each other to provide the best service at the lowest cost. In this context, the privatization of prisons was introduced as a new and novel approach to some old correctional problems (i.e., overcrowding and mounting costs).

The privatization of punishment and corrections has a rich and lengthy history that cannot be fully appreciated without addressing political and economic forces. The transportation of prisoners to penal colonies where they worked as indentured servants was administered by independent businessmen contracted by government; likewise, the construction of early correctional institutions was underwritten by the private sector (Barnes, 1927/1968; Barnes & Teeters, 1946; Powers, 1966). In 1666, a Maryland entrepreneur agreed to build a prison for the colony in exchange for a thousand pounds of tobacco and a lifetime appointment as its superintendent (Semmes, 1938). During the colonial and Jacksonian periods, correctional institutions such as the Walnut Street Jail in Philadelphia and New York penitentiaries at Newgate, Auburn, and Sing Sing were associated intimately with the private sector. The mutually beneficial relationship between government and the private sector was based largely on manufacturing and sales. Contracts with independent businessmen permitted them to use prisoners to produce goods to be sold on the open market, and a portion of the profits was returned to the prison to offset the expenses of institutional operation. Similar financial arrangements were customary in the Southern plantation prisons under the lease system, which emerged as a new form of slavery (Barnes & Teeters, 1946). In sum, economic forces were powerful determinants in shaping prisons into economically self-sufficient institutions that would not have to depend on heavy tax expenditures.

Eventually the presence of the private sector in corrections was challenged by organized labor and competing businesses. Labor officials protested against the unfair practice of using cheap inmate labor to manufacture goods, resulting in the loss of jobs among law-abiding citizens. Similarly, fellow businessmen challenged privatization on the grounds that the bidding system was rigged and engendered unfair competition. As early as the 1840s in New York, legislation was passed that curbed privately operated prison industries. Prison shops were managed by state officials, and the products were sold in a closed market of state agencies (Durham, 1989, 1994; Lewis, 1965).

Whereas private interests were evident as early as Walnut Street, modern-day privatization has brought profits onto Wall Street. Beginning in the early 1980s, the privatization movement spread swiftly nationwide: By 1984, 80% of the states had contracted the services of private correctional companies, and more than 9,000 beds in adult correctional facilities were in private institutions in 1990 (Camp & Camp, 1984; Logan, 1990, 1993). In juvenile corrections and halfway houses, privatization has an even greater presence. Privatization has also encompassed maximum-, medium-, and minimum-security units; local and county jails; women's institutions; and Immigration and Naturalization Service (INS) detention centers.

Today, the scope of privatization is quite large, reaching beyond institutions that are owned and operated by private companies. In fact, most correctional institutions use some form of privatization in such areas as medical and mental health services, substance abuse counseling, educational programs, food services, and the management of prison industries. However, private ownership and management of correctional institutions themselves generates the most controversy. "Although the correctional system has long contracted for various private services with good results, contracting for facility ownership and management is a significant departure from traditional reliance on private support services" (Durham, 1994, p. 264; James, Bottomley, Liebling, & Clare, 1997).

The Corrections-Industrial Complex

The most significant development emerging from the current wave of privatization is the *corrections-industrial complex,* a term reminiscent of the *military-industrial complex* popularized by sociologist C. W. Mills and President Dwight D. Eisenhower. In his critically acclaimed work *The Power Elite* (1956), Mills presented evidence of an integrated collective of politicians, business leaders (i.e., defense contractors), and military officials who together determine the course of state policy. Eisenhower (1985) went further in his 1961 farewell address, commenting that government "must guard against the acquisition of unwarranted influence" by the military-industrial complex (p. 748). Nowadays, scholars are applying similar concepts to the growing corrections industry, insisting that a corrections-industrial (or corrections-commercial) establishment has emerged that includes politicians, business leaders, and criminal justice officials (Adams, 1996; Christie, 1994; Donziger, 1996b; Ethridge & Marquart, 1993; Irwin & Austin, 1994; Nuzum, 1998). More specifically, the corrections-industrial complex is an incarnation of the "iron triangle" of criminal justice where subgovernment control is established (Thomas, 1994a). Operating well below the radar of public visibility, key players in the corrections subgovernment influence the course of policy and spending. They include (a) private corporations eager to profit from incarceration (e.g., Corrections Corporation of America, Correctional Services Corporation, Wackenhut Corrections), (b) government agencies anxious to secure their continued existence (e.g., Bureau of Justice Assistance, National Institute of Justice), and (c) professional organizations (e.g., the American Bar Association, the American Correctional Association) (Lilly & Deflem, 1996; Lilly & Knepper, 1993). The "iron triangle" of criminal justice draws on power from each of these sectors in a formidable alliance and, according to critics, is a source of powerful influence over government (see Adams, 1996; Christie, 1994; Donziger, 1996b; Irwin, 1996; Irwin & Austin, 1994; Nuzum, 1998).

According to the research by Lilly and Knepper (1993), the corrections-industrial complex conforms to the subgovernmental model in four key aspects:

1. "Each of the participants in the corrections subgovernment shares a close working relationship supported by the flow of information, influence, and money" (p. 157).
2. "There is a distinct overlap between the interests of for-profit companies and professional organizations and the interests of the federal agencies maintained by the flow of influence and personnel" (p. 158).
3. "The corrections-commercial complex operates without public scrutiny and exercises enormous influence over corrections policy" (p.160).
4. "The corrections-commercial complex shows signs of becoming a fixture within national policy area of punishing lawbreakers as the participants define their activities in the public interest" (p. 161).

It should be emphasized that the vast majority of economic activity in the corrections-industrial complex is restricted to purchasing of goods and services (Lilly & Deflem, 1996). Only a relatively small percentage of prisoners are confined to privately owned and operated correctional facilities: Of the more than 1.8 million prisoners in the United States, about 77,500 are confined in private facilities (Bates, 1998a). "States pretty much have a monopoly in the prison industry. . . . Although private companies, backed by venture capital firms, have been trying to cash in on the prison boom, so far they have only made progress through niche marketing" (Adams, 1996, pp. 462-463). Still, there is considerable speculation that state (and federal) officials will eventually transfer a proportion of their inmates to private corrections.

The corrections industry operates according to a somewhat unique set of economic dynamics in that the supply-demand principle functions in reverse. "More supply brings increased demand. Industry insiders know that there are more than enough inmates to go around" (Adams, 1996, p. 463). This point is particularly significant considering the ongoing production of prisoners in

American capitalist society, fueled by the war on drugs and other "tough on crime" initiatives. Thus, investors are betting that the corrections industry will continue to proliferate because its raw materials—prisoners—are relatively cheap and in constant supply. Taking into account an investor's view of the corrections industry and its future in the market economy, the next section demonstrates how private correctional companies present themselves financially to the stock market. Growth expectations of privatized corrections already have materialized on Wall Street, where correctional corporations, investors, and shareholders are enjoying healthy returns, compounding capital for an expanding industry of social control.

An Investor's View of the Corrections Industry

In an effort to survey the economic scene and assess the sometimes unpredictable trends of the stock market, we contacted a financial analyst, Patricia Cavuoto, for assistance.[1] Our objective was to approach the corrections industry from the perspective of an investor, and Cavuoto agreed to serve as both tour guide and consultant. Like any prospective investor attracted to the corrections market, we were interested in evaluating the portfolio performance of leading private corrections companies. Cavuoto's analysis focused on financial highlights of the three largest developers of private prisons: Corrections Corporation of America, Wackenhut Corrections Corporation, and Correctional Services Corporation. All information and data included in Cavuoto's assessment were drawn from the annual reports released by each of these companies, which are available on their Web site via Microsoft Investor and the *Wall Street Journal*'s research Web site.

CORRECTIONS CORPORATION OF AMERICA

Based in Nashville, Tennessee, Corrections Corporation of America (CCA) is the world's leading private sector corrections company: It has more than 52% of the market share and owns approximately 43,000 beds in nearly 60 prisons in the United States, the United Kingdom, and Australia (Table 13.1). CCA promotes, builds, and operates for-profit prisons, marketing their products and services as a solution to overcrowding and skyrocketing costs of public sector institutions. CCA owns about half of the prisons it operates and leases the others. CCA International is a subsidiary of CCA offering management services abroad, and another subsidiary, TransCor America, provides prison transportation, marketing its services to government entities. The

TABLE 13.1 Financial Figures of the Three Leading Corrections Companies

	Corrections Corporation of America	Wackenhut Corrections	Correctional Services Corporation
Earnings Growth Rate (5 yrs)	43.50%	39.30%	31.70%
EPS	0.61	0.52	0.37
ROE	16.4	12.3	7.2
Revenues (mil)	462.2	210.4	59.9
Net Income (mil)	54	11.9	3
Beta	1.7	1.5	0.7
Market Capitalization (mil)	3311.8	645.9	103.8
Market Share	52%	25%	2.77%
Payout Ratio	0	0	0
P/E Ratio	56.6	51.7	39.5
Book Value/Share	$3.64	$4.25	$5.45
Current Ratio	2.9	4	2.9
Quick Ratio	2.7	3.5	2.7
Debt Equity Ratio	0.24	0	0.13

SOURCE: Prepared by Patricia Cavuoto.

company also established CCA Prison Realty Trust, a real estate investment trust formed to take over the ownership of several correctional facilities developed by CCA, which leases them back.

CCA was founded with the backing from the investors behind Kentucky Fried Chicken in 1983. At the time, CCA was operating three correctional facilities and went public 2 years later; currently, its stock is traded on the New York Stock Exchange. In 1991, CCA paid a $2 million, one-time interest payment resulting in a loss, but the company rebounded by securing larger and more lucrative contracts and was profitable once again in 1992. Whereas Wackenhut Corrections' market capitalization is estimated at 645.9 million, CCA greatly overshadows the competition, boasting 3,311.8 million. This means that if an individual or group were interested in purchasing CCA, it would cost over $3 billion.[2] CCA's earning growth rate over the next 5 years is 43.5% (only a little higher than Wackenhut Corrections' 40.0%), and its EPS has increased considerably, from –0.5 in 1991 to .61 in 1997, confirming a steady stream of growth (Figure 13.1).[3] The company's P/E ratio was 56.6 in 1997, which was slightly lower than the industry's P/E ratio of 62 but much higher than the S&P's P/E of 26 (Table 13.1).[4] These financial figures indicate that CCA is a growth stock and probably a strong long-term investment; investors are willing to pay a great deal for its stock because it is viewed as having a great deal of potential. By 1998, CCA's performance was in the top 20% of the stock market returns over the past 10 years (Bates, 1998a).

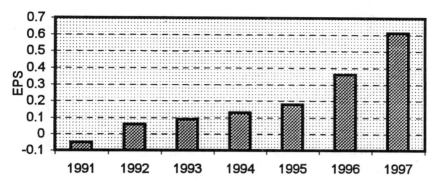

Figure 13.1. CCA's Earnings Per Share, Annually (1991-1997)
SOURCE: Prepared by Patricia Cavuoto.

In addition, CCA appears to be standing clear of cash flow problems: Its 1997 current ratio was 2.9, and its quick ratio was 2.7.[5] The company's ROE was 16.4% in 1997, which, although lower than the S&P's 17.1%, was much higher than the industry's 9.3% (all corporations in the same business).[6] At $3.64, CCA's book value/share in 1997 was considered low, indicating that it has not had a high return on its assets;[7] still, its sales for that period were $462 million with a net income of $54 million, considered by industry analysts to be quite impressive (Figure 13.2). In light of these financial figures, CCA is viewed as a sound investment, but brokers advise stockholders to invest for a minimum of 3 years for any significant return.

WACKENHUT CORRECTIONS CORPORATION

Wackenhut Corrections Corporation was established in 1984 as a division of Wackenhut Corporation and become a wholly owned corporate subsidiary in 1988. Wackenhut Corporation is a supplier of security guards that owns 55% of Wackenhut Corrections. Wackenhut Corrections is the second largest developer and operator of private prisons in the United States (following Corrections Corporation of America). Wackenhut Corrections manages private correctional and detention facilities in the United States, the United Kingdom, and Australia and is the leader in the offshore market. Wackenhut has contracts to manage more than 40 facilities within federal, state, and local jurisdictions, and its services include prison design, construction, consulting, and rehabilitative and educational programs. In 1994, Wackenhut Corrections became a publicly traded company, currently traded on the New York Stock

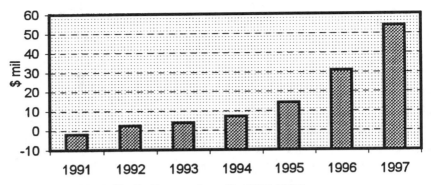

Figure 13.2. CCA's Net Per Income, Annually (1991-1997)
SOURCE: Prepared by Patricia Cavuoto.

Exchange (as WHC) and constituting approximately 25% of the market share. Wackenhut Corrections was among *Forbes* magazine's "200 Best Small Companies," with 10 years of at least 10% growth. On the basis of its annual reports, investors view Wackenhut Corrections as a solid corporation and a sound investment for long-term growth: Its earnings in the next 5 years are expected to reach 40%, which is much higher than the industry's expected earnings growth rate of 26% or the S&P 500's (whole market) expected earnings growth of 7.10%. Figure 13.3 shows that Wackenhut Corrections' earnings per share (EPS) have increased handsomely from 1993 (.06) to 1997 (5.2), suggesting that it will continue to meet investor's high growth expectations. Likewise, Wackenhut Corrections' high growth expectation is supported by the P/E (price/earnings) ratio, which has remained above .50 over the past several years (Table 13.1), as well as by its book value per share of 4.25 for the 1997.

In looking for stability and short-term solvency, investors rely on the current ratio of a company; Wackenhut Corrections's current ratio has reached 4, which is much higher than the industry's 1.7 and the S&P's 1.3, indicating that this company has a lot of assets and probably will not experience cash flow problems in the near future. Along similar lines, the quick ratio for Wackenhut Corrections is 3.5, which is comforting for an investor to know because it means that this company can cover its liabilities in the event of a financial crisis. Investors set out to beat the market or at least do as well; hence, they commonly look to the ROE (return on equity), which measures the return on stockholders' investment. Wackenhut Corrections' ROE is 12.3%, which is less than the current market ROE (which is over 17%); however, it is higher

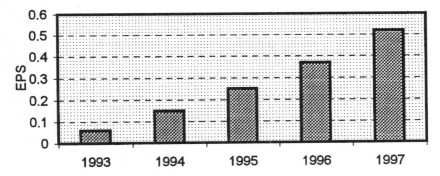

Figure 13.3. Wackenhut Corrections' Earnings Per Share (EPS), Annually (1993-1997)
SOURCE: Prepared by Patricia Cavuoto.

than the industry's ROE of 9.3%. In sum, Cavuoto concludes that an investment in Wackenhut Corrections would be wise financially insofar as its revenues ($210.4 million in 1997) and net income ($11.9 million in 1997) have steadily increased over the years (see Figures 13.4 and 13.5).

CORRECTIONAL SERVICES CORPORATION

Formerly known as ESMOR Correctional Services, Inc., Correctional Services Corporation (CSC) was incorporated in 1993. Currently, CSC operates and manages secure and nonsecure corrections and detention facilities for federal, state, and local agencies. CSC became a publicly traded company in 1994 (listed under the NASDQ exchange as CSCQ), and in 1997 it had a market share of 2.77%, which is typical for other private corrections companies that reside in the corporate shadows of CCA (52%) and Wackenhut Corrections (25%). CSC's EPS has been unsteady, as Figure 13.6 reveals: It was $-0.19 and $-0.32 in 1995 and 1996, respectively. It is speculated that this drop in CSC's EPS was caused by a 1995 riot at an INS facility that CSC operated in Elizabeth, New Jersey, while the company was known as ESMOR (see Chapter 8 for a description of the riot). Despite the riot and the subsequent loss of its contract with INS, CSC's EPS (0.37) and P/E ratio (39.5) rebounded considerably by 1997. Compared to the S&P 500's of 25.9, CSC's investors are willing to pay much more than the earnings of the company, a strong sign for the company in view of the entire market (though not as successful as the rest of industry's P/E ratio of 62.3). Other recent financial indicators for CSC

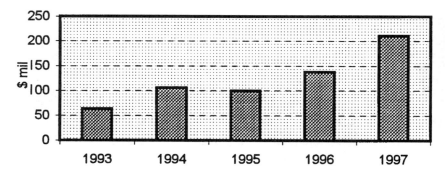

Figure 13.4. Wackenhut Corrections' Revenues, Annually (1993-1997)
SOURCE: Prepared by Patricia Cavuoto.

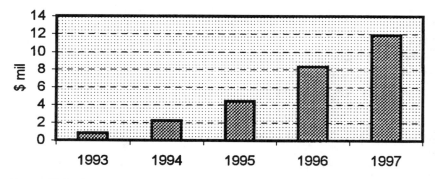

Figure 13.5. Wackenhut Corrections' Net Income, Annually (1993-1997)
SOURCE: Prepared by Patricia Cavuoto.

have been positive: In 1997, its current ratio was 2.9, and its quick ratio was 2.7, which were comparable to those of CCA. Whereas its book value/share was a solid $5.46, Cavuoto's calculations of CSC's ROE and return on assets find a negative return. This is common for smaller corporations, especially those that have been established for only a few years; still, industry analysts expect growth for such companies. Of interest, CSC's beta was 0.6 in 1997, meaning that its stock was less risky than that of CCA (1.7) and Wackenhut Corrections (1.5).[8]

In sum, the financial figures of the three largest corrections companies indicate that there is considerable speculation that privatization will flourish, thus fulfilling its enormous growth potential and generating significant capital and dividends. Simply put, participants in the corrections industry optimisti-

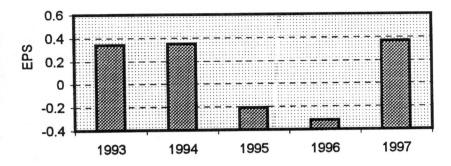

Figure 13.6. CSC's Earnings Per Share, Annually (1993-1997)
SOURCE: Prepared by Patricia Cavuoto.

cally are expecting more prisoners to be incarcerated for longer periods of time; as a result, investors, chief executive officers (CEOs), and other financial players anticipate profiting immensely from this enterprise. Over the next 5 years, industry analysts project the private share of the prison market to more than double (Bates, 1998a). Evidence of current—and future—financial gain in private corrections is another blunt reminder of the economic forces shaping the course of incarceration and social control. Whereas many individuals and groups benefit from the privatization of corrections, there exists a downside with adverse and tragic effects. As we shall see, the casualties of the corrections industry and privatization extend beyond prisoners who serve as raw materials; communities and society at large also are harmed by the prevailing economic-punishment nexus.

Issues and Harms in Privatized Corrections

Financial players in private corrections claim emphatically that their motives are forthright and benevolent and insist that their investments serve not only the private sector but the common good as well. Private businessman Ted Nissen of Behavior Systems Southwest stated that the prison system was a disaster and that he simply wanted to improve it while earning a profit (Nissen, 1985, p. 194). CCA founder Tom Beasely intoned: "There are rare times when you get involved in something that is productive and profitable and humanistic. We're on the verge of a brand new industry" (Egerton, 1984, p. 19; see Lilly & Knepper, 1993). Proponents of privatization point out correctly that government has generally failed at establishing a correctional system that meets even its most basic objectives. As we speak, correctional facilities continue to be plagued by overcrowding and inadequate programs and services. The strategy of private corrections corporations has remained unchanged for two decades: Persuade state officials that privatization can save tax dollars because their companies can build and operate prisons more cheaply than government. To their advantage, businesses, unlike their government counterparts, do not have to deal with red tape, such as open bidding on contracts and job security for state employees. Advocates say that because privatization has shown promise in other spheres of public services (e.g., health care, sanitation), a similar approach can succeed in corrections. Invoking their own sense of legitimacy, defenders of privatization proclaim: "Law and tradition both make quite clear that privatization has been, and continues to be, an acceptable alternative to conventional governmental discharge of public responsibilities" (Durham, 1994, p. 274).

Supporters of private corrections also believe many of the attacks on privatization are driven by ideologies biased against profit motives. To these charges, critics insist that profiting from corrections is different fundamentally from other forms of privatization because it reduces the administration of justice to the accumulation of capital at the expense of programmatic and humanitarian ideals; relatedly, they argue that the right and power to punish are reserved for and limited to the state. The American Civil Liberties Union challenges privatization on the grounds that the government should not retreat from its responsibility of safely securing the incarceration of those sentenced to prison or jail. Abdicating this authority to the lowest bidder runs counter to the fundamental principles of the administration of justice because criminal punishment is a public, not a private matter (see Shicor, 1995). In surveying the privatization of corrections, several other issues and criticisms persist: legal liability and accountability, questionable claims of cost savings, encouragement of excessive use of incarceration, abuse of inmates and security lapses, and the reproduction of inequality (see Durham, 1994). In examining each of these issues, we present evidence of the harmful effects of private corrections on people, communities, and society.

LEGAL LIABILITY AND ACCOUNTABILITY

For years, concerns have been raised about liability and accountability in private corrections, heightening fears that a legal limbo might exist where neither the state nor the private sector would be held answerable for infringements of the constitutional rights of its prisoners. This problem has been particularly evident in cases in which private corrections managers have failed to comply with safety codes, or, even more dramatic, when the death or serious injury of prisoners has resulted. In 1984, the terrain of legal liability was clarified when a court found both the government and the private company liable for damages in the death of one inmate and the serious injury of another (*Medina v. O'Neill,* 1984). Even more significantly, the U.S. Supreme Court, in *Richardson v. McKnight* (1997), ruled that employees of private correctional firms under contract with a state or local government are not entitled to the immunity from prisoner lawsuits that protects prison guards who are on the public payroll. In this case, an inmate in a CCA facility sued two guards for injuries caused by keeping him in unduly tight physical restraints. In his dissenting opinion, however, Justice Antonin Scalia echoed the chorus of privatization, claiming that the decision would make private corrections more expensive for taxpayers. Revealing cynicism and contempt for those behind bars, Scalia added that this case would also lead to windfalls for prisoners who bring suits and lawyers who represent them (see Greenhouse, 1997; Verhovek, 1997).

A lack of clear lines of accountability can create surreal scenarios, such as the one in Texas where 240 sex offenders from Oregon were transferred to a private correctional facility owned and operated by CCA (which earned more than $14,000 per day). Two of these inmates (with histories of sexual violence) escaped, assaulted a guard, and stole an automobile. When CCA managers notified Houston law enforcement officials of the escape, police wanted to know why they had not been apprised of the shipment of sex offenders to their jurisdiction. CCA responded they had no legal obligation to notify city or county officials. Susan Hart, a CCA spokeswoman, answered defensively: "We designed and built the institution. It is ours" (Bates, 1998a, p. 11). But the plot thickens. CCA expected Texas law enforcement officials to hunt down and apprehend the escaped convicts; Hart told reporters, "It's not our function to capture them" (Bates, 1998a, p. 11). The plot thickens even more. Although Texas officials had the legal authority to arrest the escapees for assault and car theft, they could not charge them with escape because in Texas it was not yet a crime to flee a private corporation. Lawmakers quickly remedied the problem by passing the appropriate legislation. (Other states lag behind: For instance, in New York, an escapee from a private prison cannot be charged with escape; Williams, 1997). Still, this scenario raises concerns about not only the legality of privatization but also the potential to jeopardize public safety and impose unnecessary burdens on other sectors of the criminal justice system (i.e., law enforcement). This problem is especially disconcerting given that private corrections companies have dubious records of hiring poorly trained security staff. Many of these poorly trained corrections officers work at low wages, contributing to high turnover and a work environment lacking professionalism. (In Chapter 8, a description of the riot at the ESMOR facility in Elizabeth, New Jersey, illustrates each of these points.)

QUESTIONABLE CLAIMS OF COST SAVINGS

Though the claim of cost savings is the main justification of the privatization movement, there remains little evidence of significant cost-effectiveness. Even the most optimistic assessments of cost savings are cautious at best. Some observers believe this is because modern privatization is only beginning and an accurate measure of cost-effectiveness is still years away (Durham, 1994; Logan, 1990, 1993). It should be mentioned that one of the keys to lowering costs is promoting competition whereby private companies will try to outbid each other by keeping their costs to a minimum. However, if there are fewer private companies in the correctional marketplace, as is the case today, it is less likely that costs will be controlled. As noted previously, CCA holds 52% of the market, Wackenhut Corrections has 25%, and other competitors struggle to attain even 3% (e.g., CSC at 2.77%). What is good news for the leading private correctional companies in terms of a greater share of the market and increased profits is bad news for government in terms of less choice among competitors and increased costs. In 1996, the General Accounting Office concluded that private corrections did not fulfill the claim that their services would generate a substantial savings; moreover, there is evidence that privatization of corrections invites political corruption, leads to poor-quality services, and exacerbates the conditions that lead to abuse and violence. Whereas the financial figures of CCA and Wackenhut Corrections confirm high dividends, these windfalls remain in the private sector without passing a savings to taxpayers, even though the raw materials (i.e., prisoners) belong legally to the public sector (as wards of the state). Upon closer scrutiny, we see that privatizing corrections has less to do with saving tax dollars and more to do with shifting funds from the public to the private sector.

ENCOURAGEMENT OF EXCESSIVE USE OF INCARCERATION

As mentioned earlier, the profit motive in the privatization movement raises concerns that excessive use of incarceration may be encouraged merely because it is good for business. The scheme comes quickly into focus: If correctional companies intend to keep costs down for purposes of bidding competitively, then presumably they will set out to earn profits by generating volume. Simply put, an increase in volume means a continuous expansion of the correctional population because the formula for accumulating capital requires a steady influx of commodities. A Corrections Corp. cofounder said of the move to privatize corrections, "You just sell it like you were selling cars or real estate, or hamburgers" (Bates, 1998a, p. 12). This perspective reveals the extent to which prisoners are commodified in a free market, and the likelihood of long-term growth explains why many privatization enthusiasts are attracted to the corrections industry in the first place. According to one CCA warden, "I don't think we have to worry about running out of product" (Bates, p. 1998a, p. 18).

Not surprisingly, self-serving interests driving privatization now operate inside correctional institutions as well as outside. Staff in CCA facilities have the option to buy their company's stock, so corrections officers are placed in a privileged position where they can manipulate the lengths of sentences. As stockholders, guards have a vested interest in maintaining high occupancy for protracted periods of time; consequently, they may be inclined to ensure that inmates maximize their stay behind bars. Disciplining prisoners for rule infractions can result in the loss of "good time," extending the duration of time served and thus increasing profits. The New Mexico Corrections Department found that inmates at the CCA facility lost "good time" eight times more frequently than prisoners in a state institution. With the financial incentive to revoke "good time," not only are prisoners unjustly treated by private corrections companies, but so are taxpayers who foot the bill for extra time served. In Tennessee, CCA guards say privately that they are encouraged to send balky inmates to administrative segregation; by placing prisoners in the "hole," the company earns an extra $1,000 because 30 days are added to the sentence (Bates, 1998a).

Given the influence of capital over politics, critics also fear the emergence of a private "prison lobby" in which a full-fledged corporate public relations campaign sets out to whip up crime hysteria in order to generate profits. "Sentencing guidelines, parole rules, corrections budgets, and new criminal legislation are areas in which private prison operators have a vested interest and could influence policy decisions" (Smith, 1993, p. 6). The "prison lobby" could not only pressure lawmakers to rely more heavily on incarceration but manipulate public fear of crime through the media (see Mathews, 1994; Tunnell, 1992; Welch, Fenwick, & Roberts, 1997, 1998).

In the public sector, corrections officers unions already have stormed the political arena to lobby for their financial interests. For instance, the California Correctional Peace Officers Association (CCPOA) has emerged as a fierce and effective lobby, spending hefty amounts of its $8-million annual membership dues to defeat political candidates it deems soft on crime and to persuade lawmakers to pass prison-friendly legislation (e.g., "three strikes" laws). Of the last 44 CCPOA-sponsored bills, 38 became law. Over the past decade, California's spending on corrections has increased from 3.9% to 9.8%; the average salary and benefits for guards exceeds $55,000—the highest in the country (far surpassing of salaries of California public school teachers, who earn $43,000, as well as salaries of tenured associate professors at most state universities; Macallair, 1997, p. 22). Similar corrections union activity has surfaced in other states, most notably New York (Sullivan, 1998; also see Davey, 1998).

The National Institute of Justice (NIJ, the research division of the U.S. Department of Justice) also has contributed to the rise of a "prison lobby." In 1987, NIJ submitted a press release (cited in Lilly & Knepper, 1993, p. 160) to the Associate Press and United Press International (the nation's largest conduits for print media) about a study claiming that society spends an average of $25,000 a year to incarcerate an offender, whereas it costs $430,000 for that person to remain free to commit crime. Criminologists challenged vehemently the accuracy of these figures, but the report's momentum already was affecting policy. California Governor George Deukmejian cited the study in his 1989 address justifying the state's $1.5-billion corrections budget. Assistant Attorney General Richard Abell referred to the report in a letter mass-mailed to policymakers throughout the nation. Correspondingly, while director of NIJ, James K. Stewart had publicized previously his support for private corrections in a 1985 *New York Times* op-ed piece entitled "Breaking up Government's Monopoly on Prison Cells" (Stewart, 1985; also see Lilly & Knepper, 1993, and the section "The Corrections-Industrial Complex" earlier in this chapter). Interestingly, the Texas legislature, in 1987, passed a bill that would add another 2,000 beds to its correctional system: "A legislative aide commented that salesmen wearing strange polyester suits and funky perfume descended on the state capital to hawk corrections products such as electronic wristbands that monitor released inmates" (Vogel, 1987, p. 33; Lilly & Knepper, 1993).

Finally, opponents of privatization also raise the issue of governmental dependency as a worst-case scenario and state that an overreliance on the private sector in corrections may result in disaster. Suppose an entire state correctional system became privatized and managed by a single company and then the company went bankrupt. Who would take over? If the government had already dismantled its correctional apparatus, who would it turn to, and at what cost? Given these possibilities, governmental dependency could lead to placing a correctional system in a terrifyingly vulnerable situation (Durham, 1994).

ABUSE OF INMATES AND SECURITY LAPSES

Opponents of privatization contend that the safety of inmates hangs in the balance when private correctional companies assume custody. Although it is difficult to determine whether inmates are abused more by staff in private facilities than in governmental institutions (see Chapters 8, 10), there is evidence that improperly screened and inadequately trained corrections officers in private facilities lack skills necessary to deal with frustrated and potentially aggressive inmates. Poorly trained staff have been known to instigate and escalate prison tension, resulting in disturbances and riots; in fact, an investigation team concluded that the riot at the INS facility in New Jersey was partially caused by guards harassing and abusing inmates. Adding to the list of human rights violations (including sexual and physical assault) in privately operated INS facilities around the country, detainees are typically confined to warehouselike dormitories for 23 hours a day, where they are denied fresh air and natural light. Detainee access to visitors, counsel, and the courts also is routinely obstructed by arbitrary rules of the staff and corporation. Idleness due to the lack of institutional programs contributes further to inmate stress, thus enhancing the risk of disorder and violence (see Chapter 8).

In 1997, at a private corrections facility in Texas, guards were videotaped assaulting prisoners with stun guns; the officers were hired despite records showing that they had abused prisoners while working in state institutions. CCA currently employs at least two wardens in Texas who were disciplined for beating inmates while working for the state department of corrections. Even company president David Myers supervised an assault on inmates who took a guard hostage while Myers was serving as warden of a Texas prison in 1984; in that incident, 14 guards were found to have used excessive force, beating subdued and handcuffed prisoners with riot batons. In a CCA facility for juveniles in South Carolina, child advocates were horrified to learn that children were abused by staff, including instances in which some boys were hogtied and shackled together (Bates, 1998a). Allegations of rape and assault at a privately run juvenile facility in Colorado prompted state officials to concede that the safety of children at private jails is not guaranteed (Robbins, 1997).

In Tullulah, Louisiana, an economically depressed town of 10,000, James R. Brown set out to build a private corrections facility for juveniles, a venture that, by 1994, became the community's largest employer and taxpayer. Brown, a local businessman with no experience in corrections, is the son of an influential former state senator. Not surprisingly, he secured a no-bid contract for his company (Trans-American), which he formed with two close friends of Governor Edwin W. Edwards. In 1997, Brown and his associates were pulling in $24,448 for each of the company's 620 boys and young men aged 11 to 20; however, this operation had become "so rife with brutality, cronyism and neglect that many legal experts say it is the worst in the nation" (Butterfield, 1998c, p. A-1). Abuse ran rampantly through this crowded institution, which held the state's poorest and most vulnerable minority youths: 82% were black, and many were mentally retarded or emotionally disturbed. Injuries such as black eyes, broken noses or jaws, and perforated eardrums stand from fights between the detainees as well as beatings by the inadequately trained, poorly paid guards (who were earning $5.77 an hour): In 1997, the staff turnover reached 100%. Staff also used pepper spray on the boys and occasionally pitted inmates against each other for sport. Amid the stifling heat and poor ventilation, many youths deliberately violated rules to be sent to solitary confinement where the cells were air-conditioned. Meals were meager and clothes were in short supply, precipitating scuffles over shirts and shoes. Until recently, there were no books. Nearly all the teachers were uncertified, and instruction was limited to an hour a day. Medical and psychiatric services were commonly inaccessible and inadequate; the infirmary was often closed because there were not enough staff for supervision.

The appalling conditions at Tullulah are symptomatic of larger contradictions produced by shifting resources from social services to criminal justice and then again to privatized corrections. The incarceration of adolescents (including the retarded or mentally ill) is escalated by politicians who rush to build new prisons while neglecting education and psychiatric services; as in the case of Tullulah, the problem is compounded by the states' handing over the responsibility for juvenile offenders to private interests (Butterfield, 1998c; Wideman, 1995).[9]

Under privatization there are also fiscal incentives to cut corners on security features of an institution, resulting in noncompliance with safety standards. In fact, private corrections companies are cutting corners by introducing "innovations." A corrections official in Virginia who oversees the operations of private prisons in the state recently inspected a medium-security institution being constructed by CCA that did not have guard towers: an "innovation" that saved the corporation $2.5 million (Bates, 1998a). One can imagine that in the public sector, prison officials who eliminated guard towers in a prison would probably lose their jobs, but in the private sector, the focus of attention is on profit, not custodial security.

Hiring fewer guards is another sure way to reduce operating and labor costs, thereby guaranteeing greater profits for private corrections corporations. For security purposes, however, this personnel strategy runs counter to conventional wisdom of maintaining an appropriate ratio of guards to inmates. CCA claims that the use of "pods," whereby one guard in a control room can supervise 250 prisoners, does not jeopardize security. Astonishingly, when CCA opens its facility in Lawrenceville, Virginia, in 1999, it will employ only five guards to supervise 750 inmates during the day shift and two at night. Corrections and security experts argue that prisons of that size require many more staff to ensure safety (Bates, 1998a).

Allegations of inadequate medical services for prisoners continue to surface, especially in light of the escalating costs of health care (refer to Chapter 11). A shift supervisor in a CCA facility testified that an inmate who died from an undiagnosed complication during pregnancy suffered in agony for more than 12 hours before CCA officials permitted her to be transported to a hospital (Bates, 1998a). It has been reported that private corrections companies ensure profits by "picking jackets"—selecting only the healthiest inmates from the state prison population to minimize medical expenditures. Once prisoners become ill, private corrections officials ship them back to state facilities, where taxpayers underwrite the inmates' health care (Bates, 1998b). (It should be noted that the increased incarceration of nonviolent offenders is welcomed by private corrections companies interested in "picking jackets" for docile inmates.)

Attending to basic economic principles necessary for securing assets, private corrections companies are aware that it is easy to cut corners and pocket money that, in state institutions, would be spent on personnel, training, medical services, and even food. In Texas, "Vita-Pro," an inexpensive, soybean-based meat extender, has been added to prison meals, curtailing the cost of food. An unanticipated benefit quickly followed. "The taste of food became so offensive that inmates refused to eat, and guards were no longer tempted to pilfer from the prison pantry. Food costs plummeted" (Adams, 1996, p. 465). Realizing the market potential for "Vita-Pro," Texas maneuvered to become the exclusive distributor of this food substitute, enabling them to enjoy savory profits.

THE REPRODUCTION OF INEQUALITY

As noted throughout this chapter, the rising correctional population has generated financial opportunities for investors in privatized corrections, reinforcing a vicious circle of incarceration and dividends. Moreover, prisoners function as commodities for a corrections industry operating on expectations of growth, thereby widening the net of coercive social control. These developments have direct implications for the reproduction of inequality. Those individuals most vulnerable to becoming commodified by social control are the poor and people of color, given their overrepresentation in the criminal justice system (see Buck, 1994; Tonry, 1998). Indeed, the prevailing trend in imprisonment portends grave consequences for racial minorities in the United States. At its current pace, the nation's prison population will exceed 10 million, which means that 6 out of 10 African Americans will be incarcerated (Donziger, 1998). A key irony is that the impoverished and racial minorities who have been marginalized and devalued in the mainstream economy have considerable value in the corrections industry, ranging from $25,000 to $74,000 per year.

Marc Mauer of the Sentencing Project reminded us that another danger of privatization is that it threatens to erode any humanistic approaches to crime. "Apparently, we need no longer worry about either harm suffered by victims of crime or the dismal state of our prison system as long as investors are getting good returns. This may prove to be the most lasting impact of the movement to translate societal problems into profit-making opportunities" (Mauer, 1998, p. 2; also see Clear, 1994). Relatedly, debts accrued in building a corrections empire are paid at the expense of vital social services: education, health care, and housing. California, Connecticut, New York, Ohio, Pennsylvania, and other states have cut millions from their public education and social service budgets while increasing their spending on corrections (Butterfield, 1995; Cass, 1996). In Idaho, where crime is low, the government "locks up people for crimes that most states do not even consider felonies [e.g., simple drug possession, writing a bad check, drunken driving, and driving without a valid license]. Among the states, its rate of incarceration is growing swifter than all but two. Its prisons are filling so quickly that Idaho has to fly people out of state to find cells for them" (Egan, 1998, p. A-1). Idaho is one of the poorest states in the union: It is near the bottom in spending for children and at the

The Corrections Industry

top in reported child abuse (Egan, 1998). These developments serve as a reminder that social services have functioned traditionally as noncoercive measures of crime control.

These regressive social policies are made possible by not only the pull of private capital but also the push of political rhetoric that panders to fears about crime. By playing on citizens' fear of crime, politicians not only weaken the bonds of communities, producing alienation, but fail to protect people because imprisonment does not deter lawlessness (also refer to the previous discussion on "bait and switch" tactics). One observer noted a broader paradox: "The tremendous profits accruing to the prison-industrial complex demonstrate that the free market works best when people aren't free" (Pranis, 1998, p. 3). In a similar vein, penologist John Irwin (1996) characterized the escalation of the correctional apparatus as a "march of folly" because it represents another tragic move down the path of disaster, causing irreparable damage to democracy and efforts to promote social equality and justice. Lilly and Deflem (1996) concurred: "As the economic system intrudes further into matters of law, justice, and punishment, the picture that may emerge may be one of the 'business of law and order' being run by 'merchants in justice and punishment' whose only interest lie in the law of the free market (profit)" (p. 14).

Conclusion

While critics question the tortured logic of increasing expenditures in criminal justice, the corrections industry continues to generate ideological and financial windfalls for politicians, corporations, and a growing cast of opportunists. Through various channels of communication and propaganda, political and economic elites reinforce their hegemony, insisting that the escalation of the prison apparatus serves positive functions for private and public sectors (Tunnell, 1992; Welch, Fenwick, & Roberts, 1997, 1998). Their version of the corrections enterprise is additional evidence that history is written by the winners. Still, keeping privatization in a favorable light requires the reproduction of several interlocking myths.

The first myth is that street crime is rising; however, the painful reality for the governmental-business alliance fueling a fortress economy is that over the past 20 years, crime has remained constant or dropped. Second, the belief that our government is "soft on crime" is easily dispelled. In no uncertain terms, the United States deals more harshly with crime than any comparable industrial nation, especially in the realm of coercive drug control and its mandatory minimum sentences. Myth number three claims that most people in prison are violent, but on the contrary, out of every 100 arrests, 86 are for nonviolent offenses (of the 14 arrests for violent offenses, 8 are for assault that do not result in injury). The fact remains there are more prison cells than violent offenders to fill them. Conveniently, nonviolent offenders are incarcerated (rather than supervised in the community) for the purpose of occupying expensive correctional space—particularly drug addicts, who are among the real casualties of the war on drugs. Finally, the myth persists that prisons save money. Certainly, it is a wise investment to incapacitate violate offenders, but to impose lengthy sentences on individuals for marijuana possession, as has been done to 192 people under California's "three strikes" law, strains the legitimacy of incarceration (Donziger, 1996a, 1996b; also see Clear, 1994; Lichenstein & Kroll, 1990; Welch, 1996a). (In reference to serious drug addictions, see Chapter 4 for the cost-benefits of treatment over imprisonment.) Donziger (1996a) pointed to the broader error of mythologizing the relationship between imprisonment and crime: "If more prisons paid off in less crime, the results would be obvious by now" (p. 24).

This chapter contributes to a sociology of punishment by turning attention from the uncritically accepted notion of a crime-punishment nexus to market forces shaping the contours of social control. To reiterate, the relationship of economics and punishment rests on two related phenomena. First, under its normal operations, capitalism tends to reduce labor, thereby enlarging the surplus population, a proportion of which is subject to the state's mechanisms of coercive control. Second, the commercial features of the market economy enable private interests to commodify prisoners as raw materials for a corrections industry, creating a high-volume, profit-driven system of punishment.[10]

As elaborated throughout this chapter, the economic-punishment nexus produces ironies and harms realized at the individual and societal levels. Numerous accounts confirm that a prison enterprise geared toward accumulating capital does so by slashing operating costs, most notably labor (i.e., professional, well-trained staff) and much needed programs and services (e.g., education, medical care, substance abuse treatment); the end results are neglect, abuse, and violence. At the societal level, the prevailing reliance on incarceration, for purposes of social control, generating profits, or both, threatens democracy by shifting even greater power to the state and the corporate class. In its wake, citizens, especially the impoverished and racial minorities, are left vulnerable to an overzealous, overfinanced criminal justice machine. The enormous corrections enterprise is referred to as the regressive socialism of the conservative right: It is the only expanding public housing and the only growing public sector employment ("The Prison Boom," 1995). Tom Hayden, California state senator, characterized the prison-building binge as "another Vietnam moral quagmire in the making, only worse. . . . In Vietnam, at least you could withdraw" (Butterfield, 1995, p. A-21).

Notes

1. Patricia Cavuoto served as my research assistant at Rutgers University in 1998; currently, she is employed as a researcher at the Federal Reserve Bank of New York.

2. Market capitalization is the current price of the stock multiplied by the number of shares outstanding, measuring the relative size of the company.

3. Earnings per share (EPS) are calculated by dividing the number of shares into the profit. If earnings increase each year, this is evidence that the company is growing.

4. Price/earnings ratio (P/E ratio), also known as the "multiple," is the latest closing price divided by the EPS. This figure can give an indication of how expensive the security is. A high P/E indicates that investors are expecting a high earnings growth for these stocks. Fast-growing companies usually have higher P/E ratios. S&P (Standard and Poor's) 500 incorporates a broad base of 500 stocks. It is widely considered the benchmark for large stock investors. The index of the S&P 500 is usually used as a measure of how the market is doing. Investors typically base their personal portfolio on the S&P index to compare their own returns to market returns.

5. Current ratio is the total current assets divided by the total current liabilities. This measures how liquid a stock is. One would want to invest in a company that had a current ratio that was at least greater than 1 because it would mean that the company was able to cover its liabilities in case of a crisis. Quick ratio is the sum of cash and receivables divided by current liabilities: hence, it serves as another measure of how liquid a stock is.

6. Return on equity (ROE) is the ratio of net income to common equity, also known as the rate of return on the stockholder's investment.

7. Book value per share is the most recent quarter common stock equity divided by the latest shares outstanding. It offers an indication of how investors regard the company. Companies with relatively high rates of return on assets sell at higher multiples of the book value than those with low returns.

8. Beta measures the volatility of a stock's return relative to the market (S&P 500). A beta of 1 means that the market and the stock move up and down together, at the same rate.

9. During a wave of negative publicity over the private juvenile facility in Tullulah, the state of Louisiana took over temporary management when the warden resigned following a lawsuit, critical reports by federal investigators, and several disturbances by inmates (Butterfield, 1998b).

10. Another aspect of the economic-punishment nexus is the current misuse of prison labor in the United States (see Burton-Rose, 1998; Parenti, 1996).

References

Adams, K. (1996). The bull market in corrections. *Prison Journal, 76,* 461-467.

Adamson, C. (1984). Toward a Marxian theory of penology: Captive criminal populations as economic threats and resources. *Social Problems, 31,* 435-458.

Arvanites, T., & Asher, M. (1995). The direct and indirect effects of socio-economic variables on state imprisonment rates. *Criminal Justice Policy Review, 7*(1), 27-53.

Barnes, H. (1968). *The evolution of penology in Pennsylvania.* Montclair, NJ: Patterson Smith. (Original work published 1927)

Barnes, H., & Teeters, N. (1946). *New horizons in criminology* (3rd ed.). New York: Prentice Hall.

Barnett, R., & Cavanaugh, J. (1994). *Global dreams: Imperial corporations and the new world order.* New York: Touchstone.

Bates, E. (1998a, January 5). Private prisons. *Nation,* pp. 11-18.

Bates, E. (1998b, May 4). Private prisons, cont. *Nation,* p. 5.

Box, S., & Hale, C. (1982). Economic crisis and the rising prisoner population in England and Wales. *Crime and Social Justice, 17,* 20-35.

Brooke, J. (1997, November 2). Prisons: A growth industry. *New York Times,* p. 20.

Buck, P. D. (1994). "Arbeit macht frei": Racism and bound, concentrated labor in U.S. prisons. *Urban Anthropology and Studies of Cultural Systems and World Economics, 23,* 331-344.

Burton-Rose, D. (1998). *The celling of America: An inside look at the U.S. prison industry.* Boston: Common Courage.

Butterfield, F. (1995, April 12). New prisons cast shadow over higher education. *New York Times,* p. A-21.

Butterfield, F. (1997, September 28). Crime keeps on falling, but prisons keep on filling. *New York Times,* pp. 4-1, 4-4.

Butterfield, F. (1998a, January 19). "Defying gravity," inmate population climbs. *New York Times,* p. A-10.

Butterfield, F. (1998b, July 24). Jail for youths is taken over by Louisiana. *New York Times,* p. A-16.

Butterfield, F. (1998c, July 15). Profits at a juvenile prison come with a chilling cost. *New York Times,* pp. A-1, A-14.

Camp, C., & Camp, G. (1984). *Private sector involvement in prison services and operations.* Washington, DC: U.S. Department of Justice.

Cass, J. (1996, May 20). As public fears swell, so do Pa. prisons: Other budget items face cuts to fund cells. *Philadelphia Inquirer,* pp. A-1, A-8.

Chiricos, T. G., & Bales, W. (1991). Unemployment and punishment: An empirical assessment. *Criminology, 29,* 701-724.

Christie, N. (1994). *Crime control as industry.* Oslo: Universite-flag.

Clear, T. R. (1994). *Harm in American penology: Offenders, victims, and their communities.* Albany: State University of New York Press.

Currie, E. (1985). *Confronting crime: An American challenge.* New York: Pantheon.

Cushman, J. (1998, May 18). Serious crime in U.S. fell in 1997 for a 6th year. *New York Times,* p. A-15.

Davey, J. D. (1998). *The politics of prison expansion: Winning elections by waging war on crime.* Westport, CT: Greenwood.

Donziger, S. (1996a, March 17). The prison-industrial complex: What's really driving the rush to lock 'em up. *Washington Post,* p. 24.

Donziger, S. (1996b). *The real war on crime: The report of the National Criminal Justice Commission.* New York: HarperPerennial.

Donziger, S. (1998, March 16). Profits from prisons. *Nation,* pp. 2, 24.

Durham, A. (1989). Origins of interest in the privatization of punishment: The nineteenth century American experience. *Criminology, 27*, 1.

Durham, A. (1994). *Crisis and reform: Current issues in American punishment.* Boston: Little, Brown.

Egan, T. (1998, April 16). As Idaho booms, prisons fill and spending on poor lags. *New York Times,* pp. A-1, A-16.

Egerton, J. (1984, September). The Tennessee walls. *Progressive,* p. 19.

Eisenhower, D. D. (1985). Farewell radio and television address to the American people. In A. Mason & G. Baker (Eds.), *Free government in the making* (pp. 747-749). New York: Oxford University Press.

Elvin, J. (1994/1995). "Corrections-industrial complex" expands in U.S. *National Prison Project Journal, 10,* 1-4.

Ethridge, P., & Marquart, J. (1993). Private prisons in Texas: The new penology for profit. *Justice Quarterly, 10,* 29-48.

Foucault, M. (1979). *Discipline and punish: The birth of the prison.* New York: Vintage.

General Accounting Office. (1996). *Private prisons and cost savings.* Washington, DC: Government Printing Office.

Glamser, D. (1996, March 13). Towns now welcoming prisons. *USA Today,* p. 3-A.

Greenberg, D. (1977). The dynamics of oscillatory punishment process. *Journal of Criminal Law and Criminology, 68,* 643-651.

Greenhouse, L. (1997, June 24). Immunity from suits is withheld for guards in privately run jails. *New York Times,* p. B-10.

Hallinan, J. (1995, March 19). Growth of U.S. prisons ensured: Local economies reaping benefits. *Times-Picayune,* p. 18.

Hernandez, R. (1996, February 26). Give them the maximum: Small towns clamor for the boon a big prison could bring. *New York Times,* pp. B-1, B-4.

In '90s, prison building by states and U.S. government surged. (1997, August 8). *New York Times,* p. A-14.

Irwin, J. (1996). The march of folly. *Prison Journal, 76,* 489-494.

Irwin, J., & Austin, J. (1994). *It's about time: America's imprisonment binge.* Belmont, CA: Wadsworth.

James, A., Bottomley, A., Liebling, A., & Clare, E. (1997). *Private prisons: Rhetoric and reality.* Thousand Oaks, CA: Sage.

Jankovic, I. (1982). Labor market and imprisonment. In A. Platt & P. Takagi (Eds.), *Punishment and penal discipline* (pp. 93-104). San Francisco: Crime and Justice Associates.

Lewis, D. (1965). *From Newgate to Dannemora: The rise of the penitentiary in New York, 1797-1848.* Ithaca, NY: Cornell University Press.

Lichenstein, A., & Kroll, M. (1990). *The fortress economy: The economic role in the U.S. prison system.* Philadelphia: American Friends Service Committee.

Lilly, J. R., & Deflem, M. (1996). Profit and penality: An analysis of the corrections-commercial complex. *Crime and Delinquency, 42*(1), 3-20.

Lilly, J. R., & Knepper, P. (1993). The corrections-commercial complex. *Crime and Delinquency, 39,* 150-166.

Logan, C. (1990). *Private prisons: Cons and pros.* New York: Oxford University Press.

Logan, C. (1993, February). Well-kept: Comparing quality of confinement on private and public prisons. *Journal of Criminal Law and Criminology, 83,* 15-24.

Lynch, M. (1998). *Beating a dead horse: Is there any basic empirical evidence for the deterrent effect of imprisonment?* Unpublished manuscript, University of South Florida, Tampa.

Lynch, M., & Groves, W. B. (1989). *A primer in radical criminology* (2nd ed.). New York: Harrow & Heston.

Macallair, D. (1997, December 21). Lock 'em up legislation means prisons gain clout: In California, guards form a potent lobby to protect their interests. *Christian Science Monitor,* p. 22.

Mathews, J. (1994, November 22). Ads that go bump in the night: Marketers, taking a cue from political attack ads, push anti-crime products. *Washington Post,* pp. C-1, C-9.

Mauer, M. (1998, March 16). Letter to the editor. *Nation,* p. 2.

Medina v. O'Neill, 589 F. Supp. 1028 (1984).

Melossi, D. (1985). Punishment and social action: Changing vocabulary of punitive motive within a political business cycle. *Current Perspectives in Social Theory, 6,* 169-197.

Mills, C. W. (1956). *The power elite.* New York: Oxford University Press.

New York's prison building fever. (1997, July 24). *New York Times,* p. A-20.

Nissen, T. (1985, September 14). Free-market prisons. *Nation,* p. 194.

Nuzum, M. (1998, Summer). The commercialization of justice: Public good or private greed? *Critical Criminologist, 1,* 5-8.

Parenti, C. (1996, January 29). Making prisons pay: Business finds the cheapest labor of all. *Nation,* pp. 11-14.

Peterson, M. (1997, August 10). Before an election, prisons are good. The bills come later. *New York Times,* p. NJ-6.

Powers, E. (1966). *Crime and punishment in early Massachusetts.* Boston: Beacon.

Pranis, K. (1998, March 16). Letter to the editor. *Nation,* pp. 2-3.

The prison boom. (1995, February 20). *Nation,* pp. 223-224.

Reiman, J. (1998). *The rich get richer and the poor get prison: Ideology, class, and criminal justice* (5th ed.). Boston: Allyn & Bacon.

Richardson v. McKnight, 96-318 (1997).

Robbins, I. (1997, January 5). The problems with prisons for profit. *Washington Post,* p. 27.

Rusche, G., & Kirchheimer, O. (1968) *Punishment and social structure.* New York: Russell & Russell. (Original work published 1939)

Semmes, R. (1938). *Crime and punishment in early Maryland.* Baltimore: Johns Hopkins University Press.

Shicor, D. (1995). *Punishment for profit: Private prisons/public concerns.* Thousand Oaks, CA: Sage.

Smith, P. (1993, Fall). Private prisons: Profits of crime. *Covert Action Quarterly,* pp. 1-6.

Spitzer, S. (1975). Toward a Marxian theory of deviance. *Social Problems, 22,* 638-651.

Spitzer, S., & Scull, A. (1977a). Privatization and capital development: The case of privatization. *Social Problems, 25,* 18-29.

Spitzer, S., & Scull, A. (1977b). Social control in historical perspective: From private to public responses to crime. In D. Greenberg (Ed.), *Corrections and punishment* (pp. 265-286). Beverly Hills, CA: Sage.

Stewart, J. (1985, March 3). Breaking up government's monopoly on prison cells. *New York Times,* p. E-22.

Sullivan, D. (1998). Editor's welcome to this forum. *Contemporary Justice Review, 1,* 1-5.

Sullivan, J. (1997, March 2). Felonies drop, but jail wait is increasing. *New York Times,* pp. 29, 32.

Teepen, T. (1996, December 10). Locking in the profits. *Atlanta Constitution,* p. 21.

Thomas, P. (1994a, May 12). Making crime pay: Triangle of interests creates infrastructure to fight lawlessness: Cities see jobs, politicians sense a popular issue—and business cashes in. *Wall Street Journal,* p. A-1.

Thomas, P. (1994b, July 11). Rural regions look to prisons for prosperity. *Wall Street Journal,* pp. B-1, B-8.

Tonry, M. (1998). Racial disproportion in U.S. prisons. In T. Flanagan, J. Marquart, & K. Adams (Eds.), *Incarcerating criminals* (pp. 287-301). New York: Oxford University Press.

Tunnell, K. (1992). Film at eleven: Recent developments in the commodification of crime. *Sociological Spectrum, 12,* 293-313.

Verhovek, S. H. (1997, June 24). Operators are not worried by ruling. *New York Times,* p. B-10.

Vogel, T. (1987, April 20). Jails could be Texas' next ten-gallon business. *Business Week,* p. 33.

Walker, S. (1994). *Sense and nonsense about crime and drugs: A policy guide* (3rd ed.). Belmont, CA: Wadsworth.

Walsh, E. (1994, December 24). Strapped small towns try to lock up prisons: Building boom is seen as economic salvation. *Washington Post,* p. A-3.

Welch, M. (1996a). *Corrections: A critical approach.* New York: McGraw-Hill.

Welch, M. (1996b). A review of Leslie T. Wilkins' *Punishment, crime, and market forces. Social Pathology: A Journal of Reviews, 2*(1), 67-69.

Welch, M., Bryan, N., & Wolff, R. (1999). Just war theory and drug control policy: Militarization, morality, and the war on drugs. *Contemporary Justice Review, 2*(1), 49-76.

Welch, M., Fenwick, M., & Roberts, M. (1997). Primary definitions of crime and moral panic: A content analysis of experts' quotes in feature newspaper articles of crime. *Journal of Research in Crime and Delinquency, 34,* 474-494.

Welch, M., Fenwick, M., & Roberts, M. (1998). State managers, intellectuals, and the media: A content analysis of ideology in experts' quotes in featured newspaper articles on crime. *Justice Quarterly, 15,* 101-123.

Welch, M., Wolff, R., & Bryan, N. (1998). Decontextualizing the war on drugs: A content analysis of NIJ publications and their neglect of race and class. *Justice Quarterly, 15,* 601-624.

Wideman, J. (1995). Doing time, marking race. *Nation, 261,* 503-506.

Wilkins, L. T. (1991). *Punishment, crime and market forces.* Brookfield, VT: Dartmouth.

Wilkins, L. T. (1994). Don't alter your mind—it's the world that's out of joint. *Social Justice, 21,* 148-153.

Williams, M. (1997, March 24). Down-and-out town sees survival in a private prison. *New York Times,* pp. B-1, B-4.

Yeager, M. (1979). Unemployment and imprisonment. *Journal of Criminal Law and Criminology, 70,* 586-588.

Zimring, F., & Hawkins, G. (1991). *The scale of imprisonment.* Chicago: University of Chicago Press.

Author Index

Abbott, J., 142, 146, 153
Abell, R., 292
Abrams, A., 191, 211
Abu-Jamal, M., 208, 209, 211
Adams, K., 279, 280, 295, 300
Adams, R., 131, 153, 194, 211
Adams, R. D., 178, 181
Adamson, C., 8, 9, 10, 11, 12, 31, 32, 274, 300
Adler, J., 265, 268
Ager, J., 79, 80, 85
Ainlay, J., 29, 32
Akers, R., 29, 32
Akerstrom, M., 139, 153, 231, 247
Albiston, C., 81, 83, 85
Albrecht, S., 210n, 211
Alexander, R., 77, 85
Anderson, G., 79, 85
Anderson, J., 76
Anderson, Jesse, 182n
Annas, G., 78, 87
Applebome, P., 175, 183, 203, 211
Aronowitz, S., 26, 32, 58, 65, 119, 124
Arp, W., 255, 268
Arthur, S., 81, 85
Arvanites, T., 272, 300
Asher, M., 272, 300
Austin, J., 52, 53, 65, 120, 126, 272, 274, 279, 280, 301
Autry, G., 198
Ayers, E., 195, 211
Aziz, D., 111, 125

Backstand, J., 99, 105
Bader, E., 205, 211
Bailey, W. C., 163, 181, 183, 185
Baldus, D., 171, 172, 182n, 183
Bales, W., 26, 27, 32, 44, 116, 125, 272, 300
Barak, G., 25, 32, 207, 211
Baraldini, S., 205
Baranek, P., 189, 212
Barbanel, J., 91, 105
Barlow, D., 116, 124
Barlow, M. H., 116, 124
Barnes, H., 71, 85, 114, 116, 119, 120, 124, 194, 195, 211, 278, 300
Barnett, R., 273, 300
Barrenador, G., 207, 211
Bartone, P., 110, 126

305

Bartrum, T., 82, 85
Bates, E., 276, 280, 282, 287, 289, 291, 293, 295, 300
Bayer, R., 181, 183, 221, 247
Beccaria, C. 108, 125
Beck, E., 171, 186
Becker, H., 129, 136, 154, 189, 211, 221, 247
Bedeau, H., 174, 183, 185
Beasely, T., 287
Belkin, L., 199, 211
Benn, J., 176
Bennett, J. O., 274
Bennett, J. R., 207, 211
Bennett, K., 216, 249
Bennett, W., 76
Berenson, A., 79, 85
Berg, E. H., 77, 87
Berger, P., 188, 211
Bernard, T., 29, 32, 34
Bernstein, J., 119, 127
Berrien, J., 80, 85
Bin Wahad, D., 206
Bishop, D., 46, 47
Black, G., 198, 213
Blackman, H., 159
Blank, R., 82, 85
Bloch, G., 262
Blumberg, M., 188, 213, 231, 233, 239, 247, 249
Blumer, H., 129, 154
Blumstein, A., 43, 47
Bogard, R., 238
Bohm, R., 18, 21, 22, 32, 180, 182n, 183, 189, 211
Bolonsky, S., 239, 247
Bonger, W., 17, 32
Booth, W., 261, 262, 263, 268
Bottomley, A., 279, 301
Boudin, K., 246, 247
Bourque, B. B., 109, 125
Bowers, W. J., 162, 163, 171, 172, 180, 182n, 183, 184
Bowker, L, 140, 145, 154
Box, S., 27, 32, 44, 116, 125, 272, 300
Bragg, R., 167, 184, 196, 211
Brame, R., 108, 126
Brandl, S., 39, 47
Brecheen, R., 169
Brewer, T., 250
Bridges, G., 42, 47

Bright, S., 177, 184
Broadman, H., 81
Brockway, Z., 110, 116
Bronstein, A., 169, 196
Brooke, J., 210n, 211, 276, 300
Brown, D., 39
Brown, J., 294
Browning, S., 39, 47
Brownstein, H., 55, 65
Brundage, W., 171, 184
Bryan, J., 140, 158, 189, 208, 215
Bryan, N., 43, 46, 49, 53, 67, 274, 303
Buck, P., 296, 300
Buckley, W. F., 53
Buckner, J. C., 112, 125
Burford, E., 70, 85
Burkhalter, H., 201, 203, 204, 209, 211
Burks, C., 176
Burnham, M., 205, 207, 211
Burns, R., 195, 211
Burton-Rose, D., 299, 300
Bustamante, C., 166
Butler, J., 206
Butterfield, F., 171, 184, 272, 294, 296, 299, 300
Byington, R., 248

Camp, C., 278, 300
Camp, G., 278, 300
Campbell, C. S., 114, 126
Campbell, D., 77, 87
Campbell, J. C., 79, 80, 85
Cao, L., 39, 47
Carlin, G., 117
Carroll, L., 44, 47, 218, 235, 239, 247, 249, 250
Cass, J., 296, 300
Castellano, T., 111, 125
Castro, K., 250
Cauchon, D., 240, 247
Cavanaugh, J., 273, 300
Cavender, G., 112, 125
Cavuoto, P., 281, 299n
Cederblom, J., 42, 49
Ceparano, L., 173
Chambers, M., 197
Chambliss, W., 55, 56, 57, 59, 65, 121, 125
Chamlin, M., 163, 184
Champion, D., 103, 105

Author Index

Chan, J., 189, 212
Chavkin, W., 78, 86
Chermak, S., 208, 211
Chesney, K., 102, 105
Chesney-Lind, M., 112, 125
Chiricos, T., 26, 27, 32, 44, 45, 47, 116, 125, 272, 300
Chomsky, N., 189, 212
Chonco, N., 145, 154
Christianson, S., 43, 47
Christie, N., 59, 65, 272, 273, 279, 280, 300
Clare, E., 279, 301
Clark, C. L., 111, 115, 125
Clark, J., 246, 247
Clarke, J., 188, 212
Clear, T., 30, 32, 64, 65, 92, 105, 122, 125, 153, 154, 199, 211, 218, 247, 296, 298, 300
Clines, F., 246, 247
Clinton, B., 168
Close, B., 46, 49
Cloward, R., 7, 12, 98, 106
Clutchette, J., 151
Coale, D., 82, 86
Cochran, J., 163, 184
Cockburn, A., 81, 86
Cohen, F., 148, 149, 154
Cohen, S., 153, 154, 221, 247
Cole, G. F., 92, 105, 110, 125
Coles, C. D., 77, 86
Coles, M., 241
Collins, P., 45, 47
Colvin, M., 129, 133, 142, 154
Conrad, J., 173, 186
Contreras, L., 201
Cook, D., 255, 268
Coupez, T., 139, 154
Cowles, E. L., 111, 115, 125
Coyle, M., 177, 184
Cray, J., 110
Critcher, C., 188, 212
Cronin, R., 108, 125
Crouch, B., 143, 144, 154, 156
Crutchfield, R., 42, 47
Cruz, R., 179, 180
Culbertson, R., 114, 125
Cullen, F., 28, 33, 39, 47, 115, 125, 218, 248
Cullen, J.B., 115, 125
Cunningham, D., 133, 154

Currie, E., 22, 32, 33, 58, 64, 65, 105, 119, 125, 300
Curtain, J., 233, 234
Cushman, J., 272, 300
Cuvelier, S., 239, 249

Dabiri, G., 77, 88
Dalrymple-Blackburn, D., 241, 248
Dammer, H., 115, 125
Dannefer, D., 46, 47
Danner, M., 18, 33
Dantico, M., 255, 268
D'Antonio, M., 193, 212
Dao, J., 124, 125
Darrow, C., 195
Davey, J., 292, 300
Davis, A., 45, 47
Davis, J. K., 211n, 212
Davis, M., 181, 184
Dawson, J., 24, 33
Day, N. L., 77, 86, 87
de Beaumont, G., 4, 12
Decker, S., 163, 184
Deflem, M., 280, 297, 301
del Carmen, R., 148, 155
del Olmo, R., 55, 65
DeLone, M., 43, 49, 59, 66, 116, 125
DePalma, A., 260, 268
de Tocqueville, A., 4, 12
Deukmejian, G., 292
Deutsch, M., 133, 154, 192, 206, 207, 211
DeWitt, J., 191
Dickey, C., 200, 212
Dickey, E., 206
Dieter, R., 174, 175, 180, 184
DiFazio, W., 26, 32, 58, 65, 119, 124
DiIulio, J., 144, 154
Dobash, R., 70, 86
Dobash, R. E., 70, 86
Doherty, J., 207
Dolente, A., 63, 66
Donziger, S., 119, 120, 124, 125, 275, 277, 279, 280, 296, 298, 300
Dortch, V., 201, 202
Dow, M., 263, 268
Dreyfus, H., 10, 12
Drumgo, F., 151
Duke, D., 82
Dunlop, D., 234, 248

Durham, A., 8, 9, 10, 12, 278, 279, 288, 290, 293, 301
Duster, T., 43, 47
Dwight, L., 6, 12

Earp, J., 246, 250
Ebibillo, T., 261, 262, 263
Eckholm, E., 172, 184
Edalman, M., 122, 125
Edelman, M., 55, 65
Edwards, E., 294
Edwards, W., 198, 215
Egan, T., 296, 297, 301
Egerton, J., 287, 301
Egler, D., 24, 33
Eigen, J., 172, 186
Eigenberg, H., 145, 154
Einstadter, W., 250
Eisenberg, S., 79, 86
Eisenhart, R. W., 110, 117, 125
Eisenhower, D., 279, 301
Ekland-Olson, S., 143, 156, 182, 185
Ellis, D., 135, 140, 154
Ellis, H., 73
Elvin, J., 147, 154, 301
Embert, P., 103, 105
Engel, K., 143, 154
Epstein, J., 225, 248
Ericson, R., 189, 208, 212
Erlich, I., 162, 184
Ethridge, P., 279 301
Evenson, D., 209, 212
Ezem, N., 262, 268

Faith, K. 70, 71, 72, 73, 74, 75, 86
Falwell, J., 221
Farber, M., 243, 248
Faris, J., 110, 125
Farmer, D., 144
Farnworth, M., 42, 47
Farr, K. A., 77, 78, 86
Feeley, M., 39, 47, 113, 122, 125, 254, 264, 265, 267, 268
Fenwick, M., xvii, xix, 188, 189, 207, 210n, 215, 221, 251, 291, 297, 303
Ferrell, J., 129, 140, 154, 189, 208, 212
Ferrero, W., 71, 87
Fichtner, R., 247

Filatov, V., 163, 185
Finckenauer, J., 112, 125
Fink, E., 133 154
Fishman, M., 188, 189, 212
Flanagan, T., 218, 248, 249
Flavin, J., 232, 248
Fleisher, M., 130, 154
Flynn, T., 248
Fogerty, T., 41, 48
Foley, L., 172, 184
Ford, A., 169
Ford, T. E., 62, 63, 67, 114, 128
Forer, L., 52, 65
Forst, B., 162, 163, 184, 185
Fortune, E., 114, 125
Foucault, M., 9, 10, 12, 31, 107, 113, 114, 115, 122, 125, 153,154, 242, 243, 248, 272, 301
Fowles, R., 113, 116, 126
Fox, J., 114, 126
Frank, J., 39, 47
Frankford, E., 218, 248
Frazier, C., 46, 47
Freedman, E., 71, 72, 86
Friday, P., 46, 49
Friedman, M., 239, 248
Friedman, Milton, 53
Friedrichs, D., 18, 23, 31, 34
Fry, E., 70, 71
Fukami, D., 191, 212

Gaiter, J., 247
Gallup, A., 182n, 184
Gans, H., 113, 119, 126
Garfinkel, H., 136, 154
Garland, D., 10, 11, 12, 29, 113, 115, 120, 126, 198, 212
Gendreau, P., 115, 126
Gentry, C., 63, 65
Gibbons, 99, 105
Gibbs, J., 98, 105
Giddens, A., 10, 12
Gieringer, D., 76, 86
Gil, D., 154
Gilman, B., 140, 154
Ginger, A., 209, 212
Glamser, D., 276, 301
Glantz, L., 78, 87
Glaser, D., 92, 105

Author Index

Glyn, A., 19, 20, 33
Goffman, E., 99, 105, 108, 126, 136, 154, 221, 222, 243, 248
Goldenson, R. M., 74, 86
Goldfarb, R., 92, 105
Gonnerman, J., 194, 212
Goode, E., 58, 65, 76, 77, 86
Gordon, D., 55, 65, 121, 122, 126, 268
Gostin, L., 227, 248
Gowdy, V., 111, 126
Grady, D., 210n, 212
Gransky, L., 111, 125
Grapendaal, M., 56, 65
Grasmick, H., 140, 154
Greenberg, D., 21, 26, 28, 33, 44, 47, 116, 126, 272, 301
Greene, J., 77, 87
Greenhouse, L., 264, 268, 289, 301
Griffin, R., 188, 214
Grigsson, J., 181
Gross, B., 28, 33
Gross, J., 225, 239, 248
Groves, B., 21, 25, 26, 27, 28, 31, 32, 33, 159, 185, 272, 302
Guild, T., 246, 249
Gunther, D., 149, 158
Gustavsson, N., 76, 86
Guttentag, L., 257
Gutteridge, S., 70, 86

Habermas, J., 113, 126
Hacker, A., 46, 48
Hagan, J., 41, 48
Hale, C., 27, 32, 44, 116, 126, 125, 126, 272, 300
Hall, B., 6, 12
Hall, S., 188, 189, 212
Hallinan, J., 276, 301
Hamel, S. C., 77, 87
Hamm, M., 139, 154
Hammett, T., 225, 232, 233, 234, 235, 242, 246, 248
Han, M., 109, 125
Haney, C., 139, 154, 200, 204, 212
Hansen, A., 190, 212
Harold, L., 225, 248
Harlow, B., 205, 212
Harlow, E., 159, 167, 184
Harris, B., 247

Hart, C. B., 114, 126
Hartocollis, A., 259, 268
Hassel, J., 135, 154
Hawkins, G., 26, 34, 44, 49, 53, 55, 56, 57, 67, 162, 186, 272, 303
Hawkins, J., 129, 155
Hawthorne, N., 222, 248
Hayden, T., 299
Hayes, L., 148, 155
Heger, H., 234, 248
Heidegger, M., 242, 248
Heller, S., 82, 87
Helton, A., 80, 86
Helton, Arthur, 263
Henderson, J., 130, 155
Hentoff, N., 168, 184, 200, 201, 212
Hepburn, J., 39, 48, 121, 126
Herman, E. B., 189, 213
Herman, E. S., 55, 65
Hernandez, R., 276, 301
Hilberman, E., 79, 86
Hill, S. M., 109, 125
Hilliard, J., 196
Hilts, P., 191, 212
Hinds, L., 209, 213
Hirsch, A., 4, 11, 12
Hirsch, M., 248
Hirschi, T., 129, 155
Hirst, P., 29, 33
Ho, D., 232, 248
Hoffman, J., 179, 180, 184
Holmes, A., 196
Holmes, S., 25, 33
Holmes, S. A., 135, 155
Hornblum, A., 194, 213
Hoy, D., 10, 12
Hoze, F., 139, 154
Huber, J., 224, 248
Hudson, K., 147
Huff, C. R., 174, 184
Huling, T., 43, 48, 52, 59, 66, 265, 269
Humphrey, J., 41, 48, 78, 86
Humphries, D., 189, 213
Husserl, E., 242, 248
Hyams, J., 148, 156

Ignatieff, M., 9, 10, 12, 31, 116, 126
Inciardi, J., 58, 63, 65, 66, 76, 86
Ingraham, L., 110, 126

Ireland, D., 246n, 248
Irwin, J., 25, 33, 39, 40, 52, 53, 65, 92, 98, 99, 100, 101, 102, 105, 120, 126, 143, 155, 220, 249, 265, 268, 272, 274, 279, 297, 301
Ives, G., 213

Jackson, A., 3
Jackson, B., 196, 197, 198, 213
Jackson, Bruce, 133, 136, 137, 155
Jackson, G., 150, 151, 155
Jackson, J., 171, 184
Jackson, P., 45, 47
Jacobs, J. B., 114, 121, 126, 143, 155
Jacobs, S., 240, 249
James, A., 279, 301
Jameson, F., 198, 213
Jankovic, I., 27, 33, 44, 45, 48, 272, 301
Jefferson, T., 188, 212
Jimerson, V., 175, 176
John, E., 79, 86
Johns, C., 55, 65
Johnson, D., 264, 268
Johnsen, D. E., 80, 86
Johnson, Darlene, 81
Johnson, G. P., 173
Johnson, R., 46, 48, 169, 182, 184, 199, 213, 218, 249
Johnson, V., 222, 249
Johnson, W., 249
Johnson, W. W., 116, 124
Jones, C., 60, 61, 66
Jones, J. F. 99, 105
Jones, M. B., 39, 48
Jones, R., 145, 155
Jones, Ron, 196
Juvelis, J., 230, 249

Kahn, R., 192, 207, 213
Kalinich, D., 92, 106, 141, 155
Kalven, H., 48
Kane, T., 145, 156
Kappeler, V., 148, 155, 188, 189, 213, 231, 232, 249
Kasindorf, M., 206, 213
Kasinsky, R., 188, 189, 208, 213
Katz, J., 140, 155
Kearns, W., 63, 66
Keil, T., 171, 185

Kelly, C., 179, 186
Kelly, H., 168, 169
Kendall, K., 73, 75, 86
Kennedy, J. F., 12, 51
Kennedy, M., 247
Kerle, K., 93, 105
Kerr, S., 247
Keys, C., 103, 106
Khan, A., 209, 213
Kilborn, P., 197, 213
Kimball, P. A., 132, 133, 157
Kimberlin, B., 207
King, D., 163, 185
King, M. L., 205
Kinkade, P., 92, 106, 115, 128
Kirchheimer, O., 11, 13, 25, 31, 34, 116, 119, 120, 127, 272, 302
Kirp, D., 221, 247
Kitsuse, J., 129, 155
Kiyasu, J., 191, 213
Klein, P., 6, 12
Klein, L., 163, 185
Klein, S., 41, 48
Klepper, D., 42, 48
Klockars, C., 29, 33
Klofas, J., 53, 59, 66, 92, 98, 100, 102, 105, 106
Knepper, P., 280, 287, 292, 301
Kochiyama, Y., 209, 213
Koehler, R., 239, 249
Kohfeld, C., 163, 184
Kolarik, G., 180, 185
Konoshima, I., 191
Kopache, R., 39, 47
Koppes, C., 198, 213
Korn, R., 204, 205, 213
Kramer, J., 42, 43, 48
Kroll, M., 298, 301
Kuntz, T., 160, 185
Kwan, K., 176

LaMarre, M., 239
Landano, V. J., 178
Langston, D., 233, 247
Lauder, R., 91
Lavelle, M., 177, 184
Lawrence, J., 227, 249
Lazzarini, Z., 227, 248
Lazzo, M., 241, 249
Lee, D., 240, 249

Author Index

Lee, H., 174, 185
Lee, S., 172
Leighton, L., 46, 48, 122, 126
Lemert, E., 129, 155
LeMoyne, J., 260, 268
Leonard, E., 71, 86
Leone, M., 92, 106, 115, 128
Lesieur, H., 64, 66, 75, 84, 86
Leuw, E., 56, 65
Levy, C., 254, 255, 259, 264, 268, 266, 267, 268n, 269
Lewin, T., 82, 84, 86
Lewis, C., 191, 213
Lewis, D., 278, 301
Lewis, P., 172, 185
Lichtenstein, A., 194, 213, 298, 301
Liebling, A., 279, 301
Lilly, J., 280, 287, 292, 297, 301
Lindorf, D., 208, 213
Linehan, T., 191, 213
Little, C., 262, 263
Lockwood, D., 76, 86, 145, 155
Logan, C., 278, 290, 301
Logli, P., 77, 87
Lombroso, C., 71, 87
Lowman, J., 130 155
Luckasson, R., 167, 168
Luckman, T., 188, 211, 243, 250
Lusane, C. 43, 48, 53, 59, 66
Luxemberg, J., 246, 249
Lynch, M., 18, 21, 25, 26, 27, 28, 31, 32, 33, 36, 40, 41, 49, 59, 66, 130, 156, 159, 185, 272, 301, 302

Mabli, M., 62, 63, 67, 114, 128
Macallair, D., 292, 302
MacKenzie, D. L., 108, 109, 111, 114, 124, 125, 126
MacLean, B., 130, 155
Maguire, B., 19, 21, 22, 23, 24, 33
Maguire, K., 115, 116, 118, 122, 126
Mahaffey-Sapp, C., 239, 247
Mahan, S., 132, 133, 155, 246, 249
Maher, L., 78, 84, 85, 87
Mann, C. R., 37, 45, 48
Mannheim, K., 188, 214
Mantsios, G., 45
Mariner, W., 78, 87
Marks, S., 254, 255, 259, 264, 266, 267, 268n, 269

Marlowe, D., 110, 126
Marongiu, P., 130, 155, 156
Marquart, J., 143, 144, 148, 154, 156, 182, 185, 239, 249, 279, 301
Marquez, M., 168
Marsh, H., 189, 214
Martin, J. A., 110, 126
Martin, P., 61
Martin, S. J., 143, 156
Marton, J., 140, 156
Marx, G., xvii, xix, 129, 130, 131, 136, 140, 141, 147, 150, 152, 153, 156, 162, 163, 170, 173, 185
Marx, K., 16, 17, 189, 214, 220, 249
Masters, W., 222, 249
Matas, D., 159, 184
Mathews, J., 291, 302
Mauer, M., 43, 48, 52, 59, 66, 104, 106, 265, 269, 296, 302
May, R., 63, 66
Mayfield, M., 150, 156
Mazur, R., 168
McArthur, J., 227, 249
McCarthy, B. R., 102, 106, 141, 156
McCorkle, R., 111, 127
McDowall, D., 108, 126
McElgunn, C., 241, 249
McFarland, G., 176, 177
McFarlane, J., 80, 87
McGarrell, E., 182n, 185
McGauhey, P., 77, 86
McKelvey, B., 110, 127
McMillian, W., 174, 175
McNamara, J., 180
McNulty, M., 80, 87
Mead, G., 7
Meese, E., 178
Megill, A., 10, 12
Meier, R., 188, 214
Meisenhelder, T., 108, 127, 243, 244, 249
Melamed, S., 176
Melossi, D., 11, 12, 116, 127, 272, 302
Merianos, E., 239, 249
Merlo, A., 78, 79, 87
Mertus, J., 82, 87
Merva, M., 113, 116, 126
Michalowski, R., 18, 22, 32, 33, 188, 214
Micklow, P., 79, 86
Middleton, J., 240, 249
Miles, J., 246
Miller, J., 43, 46, 48

Miller, K., 167, 169, 185
Miller, R. L., 179
Miller, Z., 112
Mills, C. W., 279, 302
Mishel, L., 119, 127
Misseck, R., 135, 154, 156
Mitford, J., 192, 214
Mix, T., 198
Moerings, M., 239, 250
Moini, S., 233, 234, 235, 248
Mokhiber, R., 210n, 214
Moore, D. W., 180, 185
Morash, M., 109, 110, 112, 117, 122, 127
Morgan, J., 38
Morgan-Capner, P., 233, 249
Morris, A., 75, 87
Morris, E., 178
Morris, R., 133, 138, 139, 156
Morrison, R., 174
Moynahan, J. M., 92, 106
Mullen, N., 178
Mulvaney, J., 38, 48
Munoz, A., 250
Munson, K., 79, 86
Murphy, L. 60
Murrin, M., 63, 66
Murton, T., 148, 156
Musto, D., 58, 66
Mydans, S., 198, 214
Myers, D., 293
Myers, M., 42, 48
Myers, R., 174, 175
Myrdal, G., 172, 185

Nacci, P., 145, 156
Nadelmann, E., 58, 66
Nagin, D., 42, 48
Nagourney, A., xv, xix
Narcunus, J., 250
Neier, A., 214
Nelen, H., 56, 65
Nelson, J. F., 42, 48
Neuspiel, D. R., 77, 87
Newman, G., 114, 127, 130, 155, 156
Newport, F., 182n, 184
Nieves, E., 152, 156
Nishimoto, R., 190, 214
Nissen, T., 287, 302
Nolley, L., 233

Norris, R., 6, 12
Nossiter, A., 109, 112, 127, 197, 214
Nuzum, M., 279, 280, 302

Okubo, M., 191, 214
O'Farrell, N., 233, 249
O'Malley, J., 175
O'Malley, S., 172, 186
O'Maolchatha, A., 18, 29, 34
Osborne, J. A., 74, 87
Osler, M., 112, 127
Oswald, R., 156

Packer, H., 140, 156
Parenti, C., 299, 302
Parker, R. J., 161
Parmer, B., 276
Pataki, G., xv, 275
Pallone, N., 64, 66
Passell, P., 162, 185
Pastore, A., 115, 116, 118, 122, 126
Paternoster, R., 43, 48, 167, 169, 171, 185
Pavarini, M., 11, 12, 116, 127
Peat, B. J., 114, 127
Peet, J., 134, 156
Peltier, L., 178, 206
Peretz, P., 78, 79, 80, 88
Perez, H., 224, 249
Persels, J., 82, 87
Peters, R., 63, 66
Patterson, E., 36, 40, 41, 49, 59, 66
Penn, W., 4
Perrin, J., 138, 139, 146
Petersilia, J., 30, 33, 41, 44, 48, 49
Peterson, D., 46, 49
Peterson, M., 275, 302
Peterson, R. D., 163, 181, 183, 185
Petrick, J., 178, 185
Phillips, K., 27, 33, 119, 127
Pierce, G., 163, 172, 183, 184, 185
Piquero, A., 109, 126
Pitts, J., 166
Piven, F., 7, 12, 98, 106
Plant, R., 234, 249
Platt, T., 28, 33, 269
Poland, M. L., 79, 80, 85
Poland, R., 24, 33
Pollak, O., 71, 87

Author Index

Pollitt, K., 80, 87
Pollock-Byrne, J., 78, 79, 87, 114, 127
Pontell, H., 92, 106, 115, 128
Porporino, F., 130, 135, 140, 156
Potler, C., 147, 156, 227, 231, 250
Potter, G., 188, 213, 231, 249
Pottieger, A., 63, 66 76, 86
Powell, R., 172, 184
Powers, E., 278, 302
Powers, G., 6, 12
Pranis, K., 297, 302
Pratt, G., 178, 205, 206
Press, A., 142, 156
Price, R., 172, 185
Pulaski, C., 171, 172, 183
Purdy, M., 223, 238, 239, 246, 250
Putnam, C., 174, 185

Quayle, D., 207
Quigley, J., 241
Quinney, R., 21, 33

Rabinovitz, J., 256
Rabinow, P., 10, 12
Radelet, M., 167, 169, 172, 174, 183, 185
Rainge, W., 175
Raskin, J., 191, 214
Rattner, A., 174, 184
Raupp, E., 110, 127
Reagan, N., 55
Rector, R., 168
Reed, E., 167, 186
Reed, S. O., 78, 87
Reed, W., 46, 49
Reiman, J., 28, 33, 129, 156, 189, 199, 210n, 214, 272, 302
Reiss, A., 129, 156
Reno, J., 261
Richards, S., 199, 214
Richardson, G. A., 77, 86, 87
Richman, K., 232, 233, 250
Richman, L., 232, 233, 250
Ridgeway, J., 168, 177, 186, 194, 204, 214
Riedel, M., 172, 186
Rittenhouse, A., 73, 74, 87
Rizzo, N., 261
Robbins, I., 294, 302
Roberts, B., 188, 212

Roberts, D. E., 78, 87
Roberts, M., xvii, xix, 188, 189, 207, 210n, 215, 221, 251, 291, 297, 303
Robertson, J. E., 138, 142, 145, 146, 148, 149, 153, 156, 157, 199, 214
Robinson, J. W., 114, 126
Robinson, R., 79, 87
Rocamora, J., 159, 184
Rohter, L., 260, 269
Rolland, M., 133, 139, 157
Roosevelt, F., 190
Rosenbaum, J. L., 46, 49
Rosenbaum, M., 59, 66
Rosenbaum, R., 181, 186
Rosenberg, S., 205
Rosenblum, E. R., 81, 87
Rosenblum, N., 205, 214
Rosenthal, A. M., 76
Ross, E., 7
Ross, J., 9, 13
Rota, T., 248
Rothman, C., 81
Rothman, D., xvi, xix, 1, 2, 3, 4, 5, 6, 7, 8, 9, 10, 11, 12, 114, 115, 116, 119, 127, 199, 214, 243, 250
Rothman, S., 143, 154
Rowan, J., 148, 155
Rozenweig, J., 170
Rucker, L., 109, 110, 112, 117, 122, 127
Rusche, G., 11, 13, 25, 31, 34, 116, 119, 120, 127, 302
Russell, K., 182n, 185
Ryan, R., 277

Sack, K., 211n, 214
Saenz, A., 133, 157
Sagarin, E., 174, 184
Sagatun, I., 78, 87
Sahin, H., 189, 214
Sakakida, R., 190
Sale, C., 269
Salive, M., 250
Sampson, R., 31, 33
Sandler, D., 79, 86
Sandys, M., 182n, 185
Sartre, J., 252, 250
Savitz, D., 79, 86
Scarpitti, F., 63, 66
Scheff, T., 129, 157

Schiraldi, V., 204, 214
Schmid, T., 145, 155
Schneider, B., 224, 246, 250
Schneider, L., 129, 153, 157
Schneider, R. J., 110, 126
Schoenburg, P., 179
Schoenfeld, A., 188, 214
Schooley, R., 248
Schroedel, J., 78, 79, 80, 88
Schulman, S., 70, 85
Schultz, G., 53
Schur, E., 221, 250
Schutt, R., 46, 47
Schutz, A., 243, 250
Schwab, D., 134, 156
Schwartz, M., 18, 31, 34
Scull, A., 277, 302
Scully, R., 204
Sechrest, D., 122, 127
Secombe, W., 220, 250
Segal, S., 84
Semmes, R., 278, 302
Serrin, W., 210n, 214
Seth, M., 163, 184
Sforza, D., 238, 242, 250
Shakur, S., 201, 214
Shapiro, A., 167, 168, 176, 177, 186
Shaw, J., 109, 111, 126
Shicor, D., 288, 302
Shilts, R., 224, 250
Shover, N., 220, 250
Siegel, N., 234
Sifakis, C., 195, 214
Silberman, M., 130, 157
Silver, V., 261, 269
Simon, D., 130, 155
Simon, J., 109, 113, 118, 122, 127, 198, 214, 254, 264, 265, 267, 268
Simpson, E., 42, 47
Simpson, S., 45, 49
Singleton, C., 170
Sirica, J., 222, 250
Smart, C., 84, 88
Smith, B. A., 116, 127
Smith, G. B., 77, 88
Smith, P., 190, 215, 291, 302
Smith, R., 260
Smith, S. V., 182n
Smolowe, J., 52, 66
Smothers, R., 60, 61, 66, 135, 136, 157
Snell, T., 160, 164, 166, 186

Snitow, A., 218, 248
Snodgress, F., 80, 86
Sontag, D., 257, 269
Sontag, S., 147, 157, 221, 223, 224, 244, 245, 250
Sorensen, J., 182, 185
Souryal, C., 108, 126
Sparks, R., 29, 31, 34
Spitzer, S., xvii, xix, 59, 66, 102, 106, 121, 127, 219, 220, 250, 256, 269, 273, 274, 277, 302
Spivak, J., 195, 215
Spohn, C., 42, 43, 49, 59, 66
Stack, S., 163, 186
Staples, W., 4, 11, 13, 153, 157
Stark, R., 131, 157
Stauth, G., 198, 215
Steffensmeier, D., 42, 43, 48, 49
Steinbeck, J., 190
Stevenson, T., 39, 47
Stewart, J., 292, 302
Stewart, J. B., 119, 127
Stewart, E. K., 92, 106
Stichman, A., 39, 47
Stiehm, J., 110, 127
Stiglich, N., 79, 85
Stojkovic, S., 92, 106, 141, 155
Stolberg, S., 246n, 250
Stone, L., 10, 13
Stone, W. G., 133, 139, 157
Stoppard, J., 73, 75, 88
Strasser, F., 177, 184
Stretesky, P., 36
Stuart, C., 38, 182n
Sullivan, D., 129, 157, 292, 302
Sullivan, J., 135, 157, 178, 186, 232, 233, 234, 250, 272, 302
Surette, R., 188, 189, 208, 215
Susler, J., 192, 205, 206, 212
Sykes, G., 31, 34, 108, 127, 142, 157, 242, 243, 250
Symington, F., 198

Takagi, P., 23, 34
Talarico, S., 42, 48
Taylor, F., 160, 182n
Teepen, P., 277, 302
Teeters, N., 71, 85, 114, 116, 119, 120, 124, 194, 195, 211, 278, 300
Terry, D., 168, 175, 176, 186, 206, 215

Author Index

Teske, R., 42, 47
Tewksbury, R., 145, 157
Thomas, E., 222, 250
Thomas, J., 18, 29, 34
Thomas, P., 250, 276, 279, 302
Thurman, G., 42, 47
Tiedeman, G., 129, 155
Tierney, L., 42, 48
Toby, J., 29, 34
Toch, H., 138, 140, 157, 242, 249
Tollet, T., 46, 49
Tolnay, S., 171, 186
Tonry, M., 43, 49, 59, 66, 296, 303
Torres, A., 205
Tovey, S., 233, 249
Trombley, S., 181, 186
Tunnell, K., 188, 189, 215, 291, 297, 303
Turk, A., 29, 34
Turner, B., 198, 215
Turner, S., 41, 48

Ullrich, J., 250
Ulmer, J., 42, 49
Useem, B., 132, 133, 157

Vaitkus, M., 110, 126
van den Haag, E., 173, 186
Vaughn, M., 144, 145, 155, 157, 218, 239, 250
Verhovek, S., 160, 166, 170, 186, 289, 303
Viadro, C., 246 250
Viglucci, A., 261, 269
Vito, G. F., 112, 128, 171, 185
Vlahov, D., 233, 250
Vliet, H., 56, 66
Vogel, T., 292, 303

Waldo, S., 45, 47
Walker, S., 43, 49, 53, 59, 66, 162, 186, 272, 303
Waller, J., 79, 80, 85
Walsh, A., 41, 49
Walsh, E., 276, 303
Warren, E., 179
Weber, L., 198, 215
Weeks, C., 232
Weeks, V., 167

Weiner, D. B., 181, 186
Weinglass, L., 208
Weinstein, C., 139, 154
Weisheit, R., 98, 100, 106
Weisselberg, C., 179
Weiss, C., 260
Weiss, R. P., 132, 157
Welch, M., xvii, xix, 2, 4, 9, 25, 26, 38, 39, 40, 43, 46, 49, 53, 60, 62, 63, 64, 65, 67, 71, 75, 84, 86, 88, 92, 98, 104, 106, 108, 113, 114, 115, 115, 116, 120, 122, 128, 130, 132, 135, 140, 142, 147, 149, 157, 158, 159, 182n, 186, 188, 189, 196, 198, 199, 202, 207, 210n, 215, 218, 221, 222, 224, 227, 242, 244, 251, 254, 255, 264, 265, 269, 272, 274, 291, 297, 298, 303
Welsh, W., 92, 106, 115, 128
Werner, R. E., 103, 106
Wernz, G., 210n, 211
Wheat, A., 210n, 214
White, R., 193
Whiting, B., 179, 186
Whitman, S., 200, 215
Wicker, T., 132, 158
Wideman, J., 294, 303
Wiener, J., 189, 191, 215
Wijngaart, G., 56, 67
Wilbanks, W., 41, 44, 49
Wilkins, L., 29, 34, 54, 67, 116, 128, 129, 141, 158, 271, 272, 272, 274, 303
Wilkinson, G., 79, 85
Williams, D., 175, 176
Williams, K., 175
Williams, M., 276, 289, 303
Williams, T. L., 210n, 211
Wilson, D. G., 112, 128
Wilson, P., 166
Wilson, R., 210, 215
Wilson, W. J., 46, 49, 58, 67, 98, 106, 113, 119, 128
Winfree, L. T., 114, 127, 148, 158
Wiseman, M., 239
Wolff, R., 43, 46, 49, 53, 67, 274, 303
Woodworth, D., 171, 172, 183
Wooldredge, J., 148, 158
Wozniak, J., 28, 33, 115, 125

X, Malcolm, 205, 209

Yablonsky, I., 114, 128
Yeager, M., 27, 34, 44, 49, 272, 303
Yoo, D., 190, 215
Yoshimo, W., 191
Yoshino, R., 190, 215
Young, J., 129, 158
Young, T., 21, 34
Yunker, J., 162, 186

Zaretsky, E., 220, 251
Zatz, M., 42, 49, 255, 268
Zedner, L., 73, 88
Zeisel, H., 48
Zimmer, L., 55, 67, 122, 128
Zimring, F., 26, 34, 44, 49, 53, 55, 56, 57, 67, 162, 172, 186, 272, 303
Zupan, L., 142, 158
Zwisohn, V., 227, 249

Subject Index

AIDS. See HIV/AIDS
Androcentric positivism, 70-75, 84
Asylum pre-screening officer program, 266-267
Attica prison riot, 131-133, 136-137

Bait and switch tactic, 275-276, 297
Brutalization, 162-163
Building tenders, 142-144

COINTELPRO, 205-207
Correctional Services Corporation, 285-287
Corrections Corporation of America, 281-283
Corrections-industrial complex, 279-281
Covert facilitation, 150-152, 173-180
Crack babies, 76-79
Crime-punishment nexus, 272-273

Deliberate indifference, 144-146
Deterrence, 162-163
Disciplinary technologies, 113-118
Dog boys, 199

Drugs:
    decriminalization, 56-58
    prevention and education, 55-56
    supply reduction, 54
    treatment, 54-44, 61-64, 123-124

Economic-punishment nexus, 272-273
Escalation, 131-141, 162-170
ESMOR prison riot, 133-135, 285
Executions:
    Dr. Death, 181-182
    juveniles, 166
    mentally handicapped offenders, 167-170
    the innocent, 173-180

Forced tranquilizing, 261-263

Hitching post, 197-198
HIV/AIDS:
    denial of adequate medical care, 238-240
    discrimination, 240-242
    mass screening, 234-237
    myths and misconceptions, 231-234

317

Immigration Reform and Control Act, 255-256

Jail experience, 90, 98-102
Job Corps, 118-120

Lexington prison for women, 204-205
Lynchings, 170-173

Makework devices, 120
Marion penitentiary, 200
Masculinity, 110, 117-118
Miranda warning, 178-180
Motel Kafka, 258-259

Net widening, 163-165, 274-275
New Mexico state prison riot, 133, 137-139
New penology, 264-268
Nonenforcement, 141-150, 170-173

Pelican Bay prison, 200-202
Penal calculus, 107-108
Phenomenology, 242-244
Picking jackets, 295
Police sweeps, 37-40
Principle of less eligibility, 120-121
Privatized corrections:
    abuse of inmates and security lapses, 293-296
    encouragement of excessive use of incarceration, 290-293
    legal liability and accountability, 288-290
    questionable claims of cost savings, 290
    reproduction of inequality, 296-297

Rabble, 98-99
RICO, 207

Scared straight, 112
Self-fulfilling prophecies, 136-139
Secondary gains, 140-141
Social constructionism, 188-190, 207-208
Social dynamite, 220
Social junk, 220
Social sanitation, 92, 102
Soledad prison, 150-150
Suicide, 148-150
Sweat box, 195

Unquestioned obedience, 110

Vita-Pro, 295-296

Wackenhut Corrections Corporation, 283-285

About the Author

Michael Welch received a PhD in sociology from the University of North Texas, Denton, and is Associate Professor in the Administration of Justice Program at Rutgers University, New Brunswick, New Jersey. He has correctional experience at the federal, state, and local levels. His research interests include corrections and social control, and he has published dozens of book chapters and articles that have appeared in such journals as *Justice Quarterly, Journal of Research in Crime and Delinquency, Crime, Law and Social Change, Social Justice, Critical Criminology: An International Journal, American Journal of Criminal Justice, Journal of Contemporary Criminal Justice, Women and Criminal Justice, Journal of Sport and Social Issues, Criminal Justice Policy Review, Journal of Crime and Justice, Addictive Behaviors: An International Journal, Dialectical Anthropology, Journal of Offender Counseling, Services, and Rehabilitation, Social Pathology, Crisis Intervention and Time-Limited Treatment, Federal Probation: Journal of Correctional Philosophy and Practice,* and *The Justice Professional.* He is also author of *Corrections: A Critical Approach.* Currently, he is writing books on the flag-burning controversy and the detention of undocumented immigrants. He serves as Coeditor for *Social Pathology: A Journal of Reviews.*